To the Ends of the Earth

D1589997

To the Ends of the Earth

Pentecostalism and the Transformation of World Christianity

ALLAN HEATON ANDERSON

OXFORD
UNIVERSITY PRESS

OXFORD
UNIVERSITY PRESS

Oxford University Press is a department of the University of Oxford.
It furthers the University's objective of excellence in research, scholarship,
and education by publishing worldwide.

Oxford   New York
Auckland   Cape Town   Dar es Salaam   Hong Kong   Karachi
Kuala Lumpur   Madrid   Melbourne   Mexico City   Nairobi
New Delhi   Shanghai   Taipei   Toronto

With offices in
Argentina   Austria   Brazil   Chile   Czech Republic   France   Greece
Guatemala   Hungary   Italy   Japan   Poland   Portugal   Singapore
South Korea   Switzerland   Thailand   Turkey   Ukraine   Vietnam

Oxford is a registered trademark of Oxford University Press
in the UK and certain other countries.

Published in the United States of America by
Oxford University Press
198 Madison Avenue, New York, NY 10016

CIP data is on file at the Library of Congress

ISBN: 978-0-19-538642-4 (Pbk)
ISBN: 978-0-19-538643-1 (Hbk)

1 3 5 7 9 8 6 4 2
Printed in the United States of America
on acid-free paper

Contents

Preface

But you will receive power when the Holy Spirit comes on you,
and you will be my witnesses in Jerusalem, and in all Judea
and Samaria, and TO THE ENDS OF THE EARTH.
(Acts 1:8, New International Version)

AS IS TRUE of any author, I have my own agenda in writing this book. In particular, my view has been influenced by more than two decades of activism in Southern African Pentecostalism and my reading of such groundbreaking texts as those of Walter J. Hollenweger, the doyen of pentecostal studies, and Lamin Sanneh's more recent work on world Christianity. For more than forty years I have been in pentecostal and Charismatic churches, indoctrinated in a particular form of pentecostal theology, and for twenty-three years was a full-time pentecostal minister. This insider perspective sometimes affects my objectivity but enables me to understand what happens in pentecostal practice with relative ease. I am not apologetic or uncritical, being painfully aware of the darker, hypocritical, seamier side of Pentecostalism. Yet being critical does not prevent me from sharing a worldview and admitting that this influences my analysis. This also means that I will sometimes lay aside skepticism and refer to accounts of healing and miracles at face value. My personal experiences may occasionally blur the boundaries between truth and confession, but a researcher must take the experiences recounted by others as they are and offer an interpretation of them. Pentecostals, like many other Christians, claim that their experiences are as the result of an encounter with God. It is neither my task to question these assertions nor to try to reduce them to facile explanations. There will always be religious or "mystical" reasons for people joining and continuing to adhere to religious movements, and these factors should not be underestimated in scientific research. The integrity of research is violated by excluding the possibility of a reality that is not physical, or what pentecostals believe is the presence and power of the Holy Spirit in their experience.

So, I do not apologize for the ideological perspectives in this book that will be apparent to the careful reader. There is much more to be said on the particular themes I have chosen as representative of the whole. There will be other themes, events, and personalities I have overlooked in trying to cover a vast subject in a limited space. Some of my arguments are intentionally provocative. But I will consider this book to have succeeded if after reading it through and considering its arguments, the reader is provoked enough to become more culturally and theologically sensitive, more politically and socially sensitized, and more globally oriented. I hope that this book and the conversations that follow its reading will help us together understand more adequately this movement of the Spirit "to the ends of the earth."

Acknowledgments

I OWE AN enormous debt of gratitude to many people. Friends have read and commented on an early draft: Mark Cartledge, William Kay, Connie Au, Mel Robeck, and Amos Yong. University of Birmingham theology graduate Heather Williams discovered resources for some of the chapters during her scholarship in summer 2011. The inimitable and provocative Yale historian of world Christianity, Lamin Sanneh, graciously invited me to write in his series. Through the infinite patience of the senior editor at Oxford University Press in New York, Theo Calderara, I received deadline extensions and silence when I did not meet them. His meticulous work on the manuscript to make it more readable and his incisive comments were invaluable. I am also grateful for space provided and freedom to work steadily at the project during summer 2011, relieving burdens of administrative duties and personal challenges.

To many pentecostal friends all over the world, I apologize if I may have sometimes misrepresented you, but of course, the views expressed here are my own and I have tried to avoid generalizations. Thank you for your gracious welcome when among you and for allowing me to observe your strengths and weaknesses. I have been personally enriched by these experiences, through attending international conferences, and by interaction with many scholars of Pentecostalism—especially postgraduates at my university, but also others in more than a dozen countries in Africa, Asia, and South America.

I dedicate this book to two people who have inspired me more than most on this journey: Walter J. Hollenweger, my Birmingham predecessor, and Marthinus (Inus) L. Daneel, supervisor of my two research degrees more than twenty years ago. Your considerable influence on my academic development endures.

My greatly loved "children," Matt and Tami, you have walked with me through difficult times and you continue to give me pride and hope for the future.

Birmingham
April 2012

Abbreviations

Advocate	*The (Pentecostal Holiness) Advocate*
AF	*The Apostolic Faith* (Los Angeles)
AFM	Apostolic Faith Mission of South Africa
AG	Assemblies of God
AJPS	*Asia Journal of Pentecostal Studies*
ANC	African National Congress
AV	Bible, Authorised (King James) Version
BM	*The Bridegroom's Messenger*
CCR	Catholic Charismatic Renewal
CE	*The Christian Evangel*
CEM	Congo Evangelistic Mission
CfAN	Christ for All Nations
CG	Church of God (Cleveland, Tennessee)
CIM	China Inland Mission
CMA	Christian and Missionary Alliance
CMS	Church Missionary Society
Conf	*Confidence: A Pentecostal Paper for Great Britain*
COP	Church of Pentecost
FF	*Flames of Fire*
FGBMFI	Full Gospel Business Men's Fellowship International
IMC	International Missionary Council
IRM	*International Review of Mission*
IVP	InterVarsity Press
JEPTA	*Journal of the European Pentecostal Theological Association*
JPM	Jesus People movement
JPT	*Journal of Pentecostal Theology*
LMS	London Missionary Society
LRE	*The Latter Rain Evangel*

NAE	National Association of Evangelicals
NIDPCM	Burgess, *New International Dictionary of the Pentecostal and Charismatic Movements*
NIV	Bible, New International Version
PE	*The Pentecostal Evangel*
Pent	*The Pentecost*
PFN	Pentecostal Fellowship of Nigeria
PMU	Pentecostal Missionary Union for Great Britain and Ireland
Pneuma	*Pneuma: Journal of the Society for Pentecostal Studies*
RCCG	Redeemed Christian Church of God
SCM	Student Christian Movement
SGS	Spiritual Gifts Society
SPS	Society for Pentecostal Studies
TF	*Triumphs of Faith*
TJC	True Jesus Church
WCC	World Council of Churches
WE	*The Weekly Evangel*
WW	*Word and Work*
WWit	*Word and Witness*
UR	*The Upper Room*
YFGC	Yoido Full Gospel Church
YMCA	Young Men's Christian Association
YWCA	Young Women's Christian Association
ZCC	Zion Christian Church

Introducing the Oxford Series

Lamin Sanneh

AMONG THE MANY breathtaking developments in the post–World War II and the subsequent post-colonial eras, few are more striking than the worldwide Christian resurgence. With unflagging momentum, Christianity has become, or is fast becoming, the principal religion of the peoples of the world. Primal societies that once stood well outside the main orbit of the faith have become major centers of Christian impact, while Europe and North America, once considered the religion's heartlands, are in noticeable recession. We seem to be in the middle of massive cultural shifts and realignments whose implications are only now beginning to become clear. Aware that Europe's energies at the time were absorbed in war, Archbishop William Temple presciently observed in 1944 that this global feature of the religion was "the new fact of our time." An impressive picture now meets our eyes: the growing numbers and the geographical scope of that growth, the cross-cultural patterns of encounter, the variety and diversity of cultures affected, the structural and anti-structural nature of the changes involved, the kaleidoscope of cultures often manifested in familiar and unfamiliar variations on the canon, the wide spectrum of theological views and ecclesiastical traditions represented, the ideas of authority and styles of leadership that have been developed, the process of acute indigenization that fosters liturgical renewal, the production of new religious art, music, hymns, songs, and prayers—all these are part of Christianity's stunningly diverse profile.

These unprecedented developments cast a revealing light on the serial nature of Christian origins, expansion, and subsequent attrition. They fit into the cycles of retreat and advance, of contraction and expansion, and of waning and awakening that have characterized the religion since its birth, though they are now revealed to us with particular force. The pattern of contrasting development is occurring simultaneously in various societies across the world. The religion is now in the twilight of its Western phase and at the beginning of its formative non-Western impact. Christianity has not ceased to be a Western religion, but its future as a world religion is now being formed and shaped at the hands and in the minds of its non-Western adherents. Rather than a cause for unsettling gloom, for Christians this new situation is a reason for guarded hope.

Today students of the subject can stand in the middle of the recession of Christianity in its accustomed heartland while witnessing its resurgence in areas long considered receding missionary lands, but that is the situation today. In 1950, some 80 percent of the world's Christians lived in the northern hemisphere in Europe and North America. By 2005 the vast majority of Christians lived in the southern hemisphere in Asia, Africa, and Latin America. In 1900 at the outset of colonial rule there were just under 9 million Christians in Africa, of whom the vast majority were Ethiopian Orthodox or Coptic. In 1960 at the end of the colonial period the number of Christians had increased to about 60 million, with Catholics and Protestants making up 50 million, and the other 10 million divided between the Ethiopian Orthodox and Coptic Churches. By 2005, the African Christian population had increased to roughly 393 million, which is just below 50 percent of Africa's population.

It is estimated that there are slightly more than 2 billion Christians worldwide, making Christianity among the world's fastest growing religions. In terms of the languages and ethnic groups affected, as well as the variety of churches and movements involved, Christianity is also the most diverse and pluralist religion in the world. More people pray and worship in more languages and with more differences in styles of worship in Christianity than in any other religion. Well over 2000 of the world's languages are embraced by Christianity through Bible translation, prayer, liturgy, hymns, and literature. Over 90 percent of the languages have a grammar and a dictionary only because the Western missionary movement provided them, thus pioneering the largest, most diverse, and most vigorous movement of cultural renewal in history. At the same time, the post-Western Christian resurgence is occurring in societies already set in currents of indigenous religious pluralism. In addition to firsthand familiarity with at least one other religion, most new Christians speak at the minimum two languages. It is not the way a Christian in the secular West has been used to looking at the religion, but it is now the only way.

Increasingly and in growing numbers, Third World churches are appearing in the towns and cities of the West, while Third World missionaries are also arriving to serve in churches in Europe and North America. This suggests the commencement of the re-evangelization of a secularized West by orthodox Christians of former missionized countries. It is sobering to reflect on the implications and political impact of such a sharp cultural encounter. The empty churches of the West are being filled with mounting numbers of non-Western Christians whose orthodox religious views will pose a radical challenge to the secular liberal status quo, while institutions of liberal theological education are busy redefining themselves to preempt a cultural collision with the post-Western Christian resurgence. Orthodox Christian groups in the West are meanwhile positioning themselves to effect a complex strategic alliance with the new resurgence.

Mainline denominations have already felt the force of this shift. In the Roman Catholic Church the structural adjustment of Vatican II has allowed the new wind of change to sweep through the church (if at times it has been impeded), producing movements in several different directions and across the world. The New Catholic Catechism reflects the change in language, mood, and style, and the rapid creation of bishops and cardinals in the non-Western church, accompanied by a steady stream of papal encyclicals, testifies to the fresh momentum of post-Western Christianity. The papacy has been not only an observer of the change but also an active promoter of it, and, in the particular case of Pius XII, the source of a well-tempered preparation for it. Similarly, churches and denominations encompassed in the Protestant ecumenical movement have felt jostled in unexpected, uncomfortable ways by the sudden entrance into their ranks of new Third World churches. The worldwide Anglican Communion has been reeling under pressure from the organized and concerted Third World reaction to the consecration and installation of a practicing gay bishop by the Episcopal Church USA. The other Protestant Churches with sizable Third World memberships have paused to reflect on the implications for them of such a culture clash. Not since the Reformation has there been such a shake-up of authority in the Western church, with unrehearsed implications for the West's cultural preeminence.

In the meantime, the number of mainline Protestant missionaries is decreasing, while evangelical missionary numbers are increasing steadily, complemented by a rising tide of African, Asian, and other Third World missionaries, including more than 10,000 from South

Korea alone. In 1950, Christians in South Korea numbered barely half a million; today they number some 13 million and are among the most prosperous and mobile of people anywhere. It is likely that churches in South Korea rather than churches in the West will play a key role on the new Christian frontier about to open in China, which might well become a dominant axis of the religion, with hard-to-imagine implications for the rest of the world.

These facts and developments afford a unique opportunity and challenge for cross-cultural study of the asymmetry of the turnover and serial impact of Christianity, where a dip here is followed by a bounce there. The intersection of the path of decline in the West with the upward swing of momentum of post-Western Christianity makes the subject a compelling and deeply rewarding one for comparative study and critical reflection.

The new reality brought about by the shift in the center of gravity of Christianity from the northern to the southern hemisphere provides the context for the volumes in this series, which are designed to bring the fruits of new research and reflection to the attention of the educated, non-specialist reader. The first volume offers a panoramic survey of the field, exploring the sources to uncover the nature and scope of Christianity's worldwide multicultural impact. The agents, methods, and means of expansion are investigated closely in order to clarify the pattern and forms as well as issues of appropriation and inculturation. The cultural anticipations that allowed the religion to take root in diverse settings under vastly different historical and political circumstances are assessed for how they shaped the reception of Christianity. Similarly, Christianity's intercontinental range as well as its encounter with other religions, including Islam, elicited challenges for the religion in the course of its worldwide expansion. These challenges are examined.

This volume and subsequent volumes will be devoted to specific themes and regions within the general subject of Christianity's development as a world religion. While each volume is conceived and written individually, together the volumes are united in their focus on post-Western developments in Christianity and in the elaborations, variations, continuities, and divergences with the originating Western forms of the religion.

To the Ends of the Earth

Introduction

Making Sense of Global Plurality

Pentecostalism has experienced amazing growth from its humble beginnings with a handful of people at the beginning of the twentieth century to some half billion adherents at the end of the century. There are many reasons, but perhaps the most important is that it is fundamentally an "ends of the earth," missionary, polycentric, transnational religion. The experience of the Spirit and belief in world evangelization are hallmarks of Pentecostalism, and pentecostals believe that they are called to be witnesses for Jesus Christ to the farthest reaches of the globe in obedience to Christ's commission. And they have been remarkably successful. They have contributed enormously to the southward shift of Christianity's center of gravity and provided a powerful argument against the inevitability of secularization. During the second half of the twentieth century the most significant changes in the global demography of Christianity have occurred through the growth of Pentecostalism, which has its origins in a series of revival movements at the beginning of the century. Pentecostalism has been arguably the fastest growing religious movement in the contemporary world. Ironically, most of the growth of Pentecostal and Charismatic Christianity, both inside and outside the older Protestant and Roman Catholic churches, has occurred in the very period when secularization was at its height in Europe. The unanticipated global expansion of Pentecostalism in the last quarter of the twentieth century and the expansion of other religions like Islam indicate that religion continues to play an important role in the contemporary world. The enormous growth of Pentecostalism is a fact accepted by all informed observers, though there is some debate over the extent of that growth and its impact on older churches. This book takes the fact of Pentecostalism's growth as its starting point and attempts to give an explanation for it.[1]

Pentecostalism is above all else a missionary movement—this premise enables us to understand the primary motivation for its global expansion throughout the twentieth century. Global Pentecostalism began as a restorationist or revitalization movement among radical evangelicals who were expecting a worldwide, Holy Spirit revival before the imminent coming of Christ. The words of an early twentieth-century revivalist gospel song and a favorite of an earlier generation of English-speaking pentecostals includes the lines: "Lord, send the old-time power, the pentecostal power...That sinners be converted and thy name glorified." These words express why "old-time power" is so emphasized by pentecostals worldwide. It is not just a mystical experience of God through the Holy Spirit; the fundamental conviction of pentecostals is that the power they receive through the Spirit is to evangelize all nations and so glorify Jesus Christ. It is estimated that Pentecostalism had reached fifty different nations within the first decade of its existence. Although growth was at first modest, as the world of the twentieth century lurched through two devastating world wars and colonial empires crumbled, Pentecostalism expanded and adapted to the changing world. By the end of the century it had become predominantly a non-Western phenomenon, with thousands of mutations from large urban mega-churches with high-tech equipment and sophisticated organizations to remote village house churches in which handfuls of believers meet in secret. The largest pentecostal churches in the world are now found in sub-Saharan Africa, Latin America, and on the eastern rim of Asia from Indonesia to Korea. One debatable estimate gave Pentecostalism some 614 million adherents in 2010, a quarter of the world's Christian population. Even if these figures are inaccurate or inflated, no observer of Christianity can deny the significance of Pentecostalism in today's religious landscape.[2]

Lamin Sanneh asserts that "Charismatic Christianity...is largely responsible for the dramatic shift in the religion's center of gravity." Philip Jenkins has given us a comprehensive account of the shifting locus of world Christianity in the twentieth century, an epochal shift in demography that has been discussed by scholars at least since the 1970s. Jenkins speculates that pentecostal and independent churches will soon "represent a far larger segment of global Christianity, and just conceivably a majority," resulting in Pentecostalism being "perhaps the most successful social movement of the past century." Considering that this movement had a tiny number of adherents at the beginning of the twentieth century, this is a remarkable achievement. The many varieties of Pentecostalism have contributed to the reshaping of the nature of global religion itself, with enormous implications. For example, its adherents are often on the cutting edge of the encounter with people of other faiths, sometimes confrontationally so. The future of global religion is affected by this seismic change in the character of the Christian faith. It is no coincidence that the southward shift in Christianity's center of gravity over the twentieth century has coincided with the emergence and expansion of Pentecostalism.[3]

The thrust of this book is to focus on the innovations, challenges, and achievements of Pentecostalism in the majority world, where over three quarters of its adherents live. Making sense of the bewildering varieties of Pentecostalism found throughout the world today is not an easy task. This is not a homogeneous movement, for there are literally thousands of different pentecostal denominations, many independent of those forms founded in North America and Europe at the start of the twentieth century. Notwithstanding these very significant differences, however, these varieties can all be described as "pentecostal" in character, theology, and ethos, with certain features and beliefs held in common throughout its many manifestations, most of which emerged in the early twentieth century. This book attempts to comprehensively survey these pentecostal characteristics, tracing the complex historical and theological developments that led to the emergence of the various global movements that make up contemporary pentecostal and Charismatic Christianity. It discusses what it is in Pentecostalism's religious makeup that makes its message attractive and distinctive. It traces and analyzes the various impulses that have led to the proliferation and diversification of its various global forms. The sheer impossibility of doing justice to the many different kinds of Pentecostalism means that this analysis will be selective and give representative case studies. Certain figures in pentecostal history will be given prominence, especially those in the majority world. The analysis will also make reference to primary texts written by adherents of the movement itself in its formative years, focusing on the ideas and impulses that motivated its vigorous expansion throughout the twentieth century. The book explores the theological history of global Pentecostalism, examines current issues in the light of the past, and seeks patterns facilitating its rapid globalization.

Types and Definitions

Although the term "Pentecostalism" is now widely used by scholars of religion (especially by social scientists) and most of these scholars seem to know what it means, "Pentecostalism" has been used to embrace large movements as widely diverse as the celibacy-practicing Pentecostal Mission in India, the Saturday-Sabbath keeping and "Oneness" True Jesus Church in China, the uniform-wearing, highly ritualistic Zion Christian Church in Southern Africa, and Brazil's equally enormous, prosperity-oriented Universal Church of the Kingdom of God. These are lumped together with the Assemblies of God, the various Churches of God, the Roman Catholic Charismatic movement, "Neocharismatic" independent churches with prosperity and "Word of Faith" theologies, the "Third Wave" evangelical movement with their use of spiritual gifts framed within a non-subsequence theology, and many other forms of Charismatic Christianity as diverse as Christianity itself. Clearly, such a widely inclusive definition is difficult to maintain. Classical pentecostal scholars tend to imply that statistics establish the numerical strength of their particular form of Pentecostalism. These scholars begin at Los Angeles (or Topeka, Kansas) and state rather triumphally that Pentecostalism has grown to a half billion members without analyzing either what are included in these figures or what are the very different historical trajectories that brought about such diversity.[4]

Some statisticians claim that there were 614,010,000 "Pentecostals, Charismatics, Neocharismatics" in the world in 2010 (a figure projected to rise to 797 million by 2025). Although not expressly defined, presumably "Pentecostal" here means "classical pentecostal" as defined later in the chapter; "Charismatic" means those who practice spiritual gifts in the older Catholic and Protestant denominations (with Catholics forming the great majority); and "Neocharismatic" includes all others, especially the vast number of independent churches—perhaps two thirds of the total. There are thousands of possible permutations. Social scientists and others place all these movements under the generic title "Pentecostalism," based on phenomenological evidence but with little regard to theological and historical differences. This book is an attempt to unravel these complexities, even though any definition will fall short of precision. Scholars should no longer assume that there are some 600 million pentecostals in the world without further qualification, as only a minority of these are classical pentecostals with direct or indirect connections to North

American revivals. One hundred fifty million classical pentecostals after only a century, however, is still impressive. But if we are to do justice to this global movement of the Spirit, we must include its more recent and more numerous expressions in the Charismatic and Neocharismatic movements.[5]

So, what exactly do we mean when we talk of "Pentecostalism"? There is no exact way to answer this question—and debates will rage on. Defining anything is a hazardous exercise. Douglas Jacobsen has pointed out that from its earliest times Pentecostalism has defied precise definition. It is "clear to everyone with regard to its general meaning but impossible to define in detail in a way that will satisfy everyone." The nearest Jacobsen gets to a definition is this: "In a general sense, being pentecostal means that one is committed to a Spirit-centered, miracle-affirming, praise-oriented version of the Christian faith," but he concludes that "there is no meta-model of Pentecostalism—no essence of Pentecostalism or normative archetype." Any attempt to define the term is bound to have detractors. Although it is probably more correct to speak of "Pentecostalisms" in the contemporary global context, the singular form will be used here to describe these movements as a whole.[6]

The Western reader familiar with so-called classical Pentecostalism must beware of confusing this specific section of Pentecostalism with other forms that are more common. It is inaccurate to refer to Pentecostalism as a Christian "tradition," although this word is emerging with increasing frequency in the literature. Global Pentecostalism is more diverse than any other Christian expression precisely because its different forms are rooted in local contexts. This has consciously influenced the presentation of this book. Pentecostalism's localness makes any attempt to understand the dynamics of its globalization a hazardous exercise. My desire to do justice to the forms of Pentecostalism found outside the Western world and to be inclusive in my definition of "Pentecostalism" is a perspective that sometimes solicits controversy. Pentecostalism has mutated from its diverse beginnings into several different forms today, each with its own family resemblances. A classification of these forms with broad strokes includes the following, each with its own subtypes:

1. *Classical pentecostals* are those whose faith can be shown to have originated in the evangelical revival and missionary movements of the early twentieth century, particularly in the Western world. Considering theological differences, these can be further divided into (a) *Holiness pentecostals,*

whose roots are in the nineteenth-century holiness movement with a belief in a second work of grace called "sanctification" and a third stage called "baptism in the Spirit"; (b) *"Finished Work" pentecostals*, who differ in their approach to sanctification, seeing it as a consequence of conversion to be followed by Spirit baptism as a second work of grace; and from the latter stem (c) *Oneness pentecostals*, who reject the doctrine of the Trinity and posit a Unitarianism that includes the deity of Christ; and (d) *Apostolic pentecostals*, both Oneness and Trinitarian, who emphasize the authority of present-day "apostles" and "prophets" and are especially strong in West Africa. These four categories apply mostly to those denominations emanating from Western Pentecostalism, such as the significant number of Apostolic pentecostals in Nigeria and Ghana influenced by the Apostolic Church in Britain. All of these groups have a theology of a subsequent experience of Spirit baptism usually accompanied by speaking in tongues.

2. *Older Church Charismatics*, including *Catholic, Anglican, Orthodox,* and various *Protestant Charismatics*. These movements are widespread and sometimes approach the subject of Spirit baptism and spiritual gifts from a sacramental perspective. These Charismatics differ from each other in the same ways that their denominations differ in theology but because they do not leave their churches and create schism, they also constitute a powerful force for ecumenical contact. In some countries like Nigeria and the Philippines, they constitute a large percentage of the Christian population.

3. *Older Independent Churches*, especially the Chinese "Old Three-Self Churches" that did not join the government-recognized Three Self Patriotic Movement, and contemporary house churches in China of a "pentecostal" nature, the Indian pentecostal churches emanating from the (Ceylon) Pentecostal Mission and the Indian Pentecostal Church, and the multitudes of "Spirit churches" in sub-Saharan Africa. These churches differ considerably from each other; they sometimes (but often do not) have links with classical Pentecostalism, they do not always have a clearly defined theology nor necessarily see themselves as "pentecostal," but their practices of healing, prayer, and spiritual gifts are decidedly so.

4. *Neopentecostal or Neocharismatic Churches*, often regarded as "Charismatic" independent churches, including mega-churches, and consisting of many, often overlapping kinds: (a) *"Word of Faith" churches* and similar churches where the emphasis is on physical health and material prosperity by faith; (b) *"Third Wave" churches*, which usually conflate

Spirit baptism with conversion and see spiritual gifts as available to every Christian believer without there being a necessary "crisis" experience; (c) *new Apostolic churches*, which have reintroduced an apostolic leadership to their governance not unlike that of the earlier Apostolic pentecostals; and (d) probably the largest group, consisting of all other *different independent churches* that overlap and vary considerably in their theology between "Third Wave," "Word of Faith" and "classical pentecostal," and are therefore difficult to categorize. Some of the churches in the "new church" category are among the largest pentecostal churches in the world, among them the Universal Church of the Kingdom of God (from Brazil) and the Redeemed Christian Church of God (from Nigeria). These various churches are constantly mutating and proliferating, creating new forms of independent churches literally every week.

The developments that brought about these various strands of Pentecostalism will be outlined in this study. These different forms are in constant interaction with each other, affecting each other fundamentally. The first and fourth strands are the two groups that most identify themselves as "pentecostal" or "Charismatic" and have the characteristics and family likenesses that are most common in the literature. Some classical pentecostals see a distinction between themselves and "Charismatics," and they sometimes make charges of "syncretism" against those actually close to them in theology and history such as the African independent Spirit churches. However "syncretism," although loaded with pejorative connotations in evangelical circles, is not always a negative word. In fact, Pentecostalism in all its different forms is permeated with syncretism of all kinds, from a mixture of American capitalism and the "success" ethos of the Western world, to the shamanist and spiritistic cultures of the East and South.

There are indeed fundamental and substantial differences between classical pentecostals and Charismatics on the one hand, and between Pentecostalism in the global South and that in the North on the other. Basic to this book's presentation is an emphasis on variety and heterogeneity. I argue that even within classical Pentecostalism (sometimes within the same pentecostal denomination) there are fundamental differences that mirror those between classical pentecostals and Charismatics. This book poses the question, for example, whether the eschatological emphasis of early pentecostals is still a prominent feature of Western classical Pentecostalism. And was the "prosperity theology" that arose in the 1970s really a stranger or newcomer to classical Pentecostalism's theological history? It may have mutated, but its themes go back at least to early healing evangelists and are implicit in much of its "holistic" approach to Christian life. But there are far more commonalities between these different groups than there are differences, essential emphases common to all that distinguish them from the rest of Christianity, and these theological and historical commonalities justify such an inclusive definition. There are admittedly dangers inherent in such an approach, which will be discussed.

I have adapted the definition of the social historian Robert Mapes Anderson, whose American-focused study admittedly cannot be applied to the rest of global Pentecostalism without qualification. In this book, "Pentecostalism" includes all those movements and churches where the emphasis is on an ecstatic *experience of the Spirit* and a tangible *practice of spiritual gifts*. The experience of the Spirit may or may not include speaking in tongues as "initial evidence" of baptism in the Spirit, which for many classical pentecostals is an essential characteristic. However, different forms of Pentecostalism will always include an emphasis on a spiritual experience (especially in communal worship and in Spirit baptism) and the practice of spiritual gifts as found in Paul's first Corinthian letter. In particular, distinctive spiritual gifts include those that are more unusual in the Christian church: prophecy, healing, exorcism, speaking in tongues, and revelations through dreams and visions. This, for me, is what Pentecostalism is all about. Using a narrower theological definition (as some classical pentecostals do) like "initial evidence," "speaking in tongues," or even "baptism in the Spirit" is fraught with difficulties because there are numerous exceptions worldwide. This is even the case with those who can partially and indirectly trace their origins to the United States, such as most forms of European classical Pentecostalism. Establishing the criteria for our definitions is essential, for it is often easier to criticize the "inclusive" definitions of others without providing a clear alternative. I do not pretend or assume that "pentecostal," "Charismatic," and "Neopentecostal" (or "Neocharismatic") are identical or interchangeable terms, but they do often overlap.[7]

Nobody can adequately treat the subject of classical Pentecostalism in contemporary Christianity without noting its constant interplay with and influence on the Charismatic and Neocharismatic movements. Examples of this will be recounted in the chapters that follow. Some of the best-known leaders described here were either classical pentecostals themselves or were influenced by classical Pentecostalism, and they played catalytic roles in the emergence of the Charismatic and Neocharismatic movements. Similarly, the liturgies of classical Pentecostalism, particularly styles of worship and song, have been fundamentally affected and changed by the Charismatic movement. The independent churches in Africa, China, and elsewhere have been indelibly influenced by their own encounters with classical Pentecostalism. The new churches in Africa have been fundamentally shaped by older independent African churches. It would be simplistic to deny these associations, for we live in a globalized world where religious acculturation is a fact of life. The present needs to be understood in the light of the past, and this is the starting point this book adopts in its attempt to make sense of the contemporary proliferation of global Pentecostalism.

This study will make use of primary sources, especially those from the early stages in Pentecostalism. It will also focus on global Pentecostalism and provide an explanation for its diversity and proliferation. The first two decades of Pentecostalism was the period in which precedents were set down for posterity and the contours of the contemporary diffusion first drawn. The theological configuration of global Pentecostalism today was almost entirely determined in this period, although I do not think that pentecostal theology stopped changing afterward. But for this reason I draw more extensively on the early writings than on later ones. In particular, the pentecostal periodicals, with their international circulation, were the most effective media for spreading the message throughout the world before the advent of electronic media. The media have always played an important part in the propagation of Pentecostalism. I will also give some prominence to the transnational representatives of Pentecostalism during this period, for the missionaries were often catalysts in the expanding transmission of pentecostal ideas.

The chapters that follow are arranged thematically to discuss what I consider to be significant defining features of global Pentecostalism and how these developed into the varieties that exist today. I will show how these themes are directly linked to the reasons for the growth and expansion of Pentecostalism, and this is why I have chosen these specific themes in the construction of the book. Although a historical methodology is used, many of the themes treated are also theological ones, for Pentecostalism needs to be understood from its religious heart. Throughout the book these themes are highlighted and form an integrating whole for what is often a most bewildering and elusive phenomenon.

The emphasis on the Spirit, the "born-again" experience, incessant evangelism, healing and deliverance, cultural flexibility, a place-to-feel-at-home, religious continuity, an egalitarian community, meeting "felt needs"; all these features combine to provide an overarching explanation for the appeal of Pentecostalism and the transformation of Christianity in the majority world.

I

Revivalist Precedents

Pentecostalism and Revivalism

Pentecostalism did not arise in a vacuum, but was deeply molded by several factors in nineteenth-century Evangelicalism. Revivalism, with its focus on an emotional encounter with God through the Spirit, was part of the very fabric of Evangelicalism. Revival took place in the Scottish Presbyterian church in 1830–31 through the preaching of controversial minister Edward Irving (1792–1834) in London, who had arrived there in 1822 and came to believe in premillennialism—that the Lord's coming was imminent and that charismatic gifts including prophecy, healing, and speaking in tongues, and the fivefold offices of apostles, prophets, evangelists, pastors, and teachers were being restored to the church. Glossolalia—speaking in tongues—occurred in Glasgow in 1830, in Irving's congregation in Regent's Square, London, in 1831, and in several other places. Irving himself was censured for allowing women and unordained men to speak during his services, and he was tried for what were considered his heretical views overemphasizing the human nature of Christ. He was dismissed from the London congregation in 1832, after which he led 800 of his members to form the Catholic Apostolic Church. But because he had not received any spiritual gifts himself, his place as leader of the new church was taken by "apostles," including the wealthy banker Henry Drummond. Irving was sent to Glasgow in 1834 where he became ill and died. Spiritual gifts were practiced and recorded in the Catholic Apostolic Church until about 1879. The New Apostolic Church, which seceded from this church in Germany in 1863, continued the charismatic tradition longer. Although the Irvingite movement separated from Evangelicalism and has been regarded as a "sect," it is an important precedent for John Alexander Dowie's Zion movement and for Pentecostalism.[1]

The pentecostal mission historian Gary McGee writes about radical Evangelicalism and its expectation of a worldwide outpouring of the Spirit with accompanying miracles during the late nineteenth and early twentieth centuries. Unlike most histories of Pentecostalism, McGee spends a considerable amount of space describing the background to the rise of Pentecostalism in Christian history. He emphasizes continuity rather than the discontinuity often assumed in pentecostal historiography, particularly through the influence of "latter rain" teaching, which referred to the "former" and "latter rain," terms used by Hebrew prophets as pointing to two separate outpourings of the Spirit. This suggested a historical gap between the first and twentieth centuries, when "signs and wonders" were restored to a prodigal church. However, signs and wonders, including healing, miracles, and glossolalia, were always part of the expectations that would accompany mission work in Catholic, Orthodox, and radical evangelical circles; and these manifestations did not begin in the late nineteenth century. Of course, Pentecostalism was to bring them more into focus, but there are historical precedents for everything the pentecostals did. Miracles were referred to by Western and Eastern Church Fathers and during medieval Catholic missions, and it was only Lutheran and Reformed Europe that introduced the denial of the possibility of contemporary miracles. The nineteenth-century British Catholic historian Thomas Marshall refers to miracles as essential for mission work, and he charges Protestants with practicing a form of deism where, in effect, God had withdrawn to become an absent and inactive Deity. Yet many nineteenth-century Protestant missionaries were aware of the enormous gap between what they read in the New Testament and their own mission practices—and how much more effective they would be if they could have the same power that marked the ministry of the first apostles. Their efforts had been met with few converts and the most significant achievements were the medical and philanthropic activities they had engaged in.[2]

Against this backdrop McGee traces the expectations on the margins of Evangelicalism as far back as the eighteenth century, in writers like Jonathan Edwards and later William Carey, the famous English Baptist missionary to India. Among these and especially among late nineteenth-century premillennialists (the "radical evangelicals") there was a conviction that a great, worldwide outpouring of the Spirit would result in the restoration of miraculous power to the church's mission, so that the nations could be reached for Christ before the impending end of the ages. The nineteenth century saw a series of evangelical revivals resulting in an unprecedented missionary movement, the birth of new evangelical denominations, and the holiness and healing movements. Many of these movements defined what we mean by "Evangelicalism" today and had a profound influence on the emergence of Pentecostalism and its globalization in the twentieth century. Evangelicalism, especially of the Methodist variety, was the dominant subculture in the United States in the nineteenth century. The revivals introduced a new method of evangelism characterized by emotion, large and long nightly services indoors or outdoors, often led by laypeople, that brought evangelical faith and often profound moral change to communities. But revivals and the intensity of religious activity that they bring can only last for a limited time. Not all revival converts remain committed churchgoers. A new outbreak of revival took place from 1857 to 1860 in the northeastern United States and in Ulster, Wales, and Scotland, eventually reaching as far as Liberia and India. Reports of revivals in various parts of the world began to filter back to the West, as there was an increasing belief in these circles of a second work of grace to be brought about by the infilling of the Spirit. Indigenous revivals in which prophecies and tongues broke out occurred in places like China, Uganda, and especially South India and often met with opposition from Western missionaries and resistance to the more emotional manifestations. Faith missions (independent of ecclesiastical organizations) arose in which missionaries were expected to exercise faith in God alone for daily provision; the healing movement added momentum to these expectations, and missionaries began to write about healing and exorcising demons. Expectant faith in the miracle power of God with the restoration of spiritual gifts began to increase.[3]

This was taken a step further when radical evangelicals, including some in A. B. Simpson's Christian and Missionary Alliance, began to expect the restoration of the gift of tongues for the speedy and effective preaching of the gospel to the nations. The stage was set for this doctrine to become the hallmark of early American Pentecostalism via Frank Sandford and Charles F. Parham. Parham's linking tongues with Spirit baptism was the radically new idea that caught fire in the early twentieth century. But the pentecostals believed that they alone had the "apostolic mission" that would return the power of the Spirit lost since the "Dark Ages." This seamless web of evangelical expectations in history means that instead of a sudden new start in 1901 or 1906, there is a continuation and growth of ideas that have their origins much earlier.[4]

Pentecostalism was a movement that took on characteristics of those revival movements that preceded it. William Kay observes that "Pentecostalism is revivalistic. Patterns of revival behaviour became part of pentecostal worship. There was lay leadership and emotion and unpredictability." One of the fundamental characteristics of Pentecostalism and its common denominator amid so many varieties is the practice of spiritual gifts, or "gifts of the Spirit" as outlined in Paul's letters to the Corinthians. In particular are those gifts that pentecostals believed were "restored" after years of neglect: healing, prophecy, miracles, casting out demons, and speaking in tongues. It was the latter in particular that was to cause the most controversy and initially set pentecostals apart from other forms of Christianity. Pentecostals of all shades proclaim that these "charismata" are to be exercised in the world as a means to evangelism and a demonstration of the power of the Spirit. Whenever "revivals" have been reported in the history of Christianity there have been manifestations of such gifts. A "revival," as defined by the historian of "evangelical awakenings" J. Edwin Orr, is "a revival of New Testament Christianity in the Church of Christ and in its related community." This is brought about, he writes, by the "outpouring of the Spirit" whereby the "revived Church...is moved to engage in evangelism, in teaching, and in social action." The "major marks" of such a revival "are always some repetition of the phenomena of the Acts of the Apostles."[5]

The independent American Methodist missionary Minnie Abrams, in the midst of the Mukti revival in India, wrote in 1906 that "the Holy Spirit has been poured out on many Indian churches, as on us as at the beginning." She went on:

> He [God] is teaching the Indian Christians to know and understand spiritual things. Many are being anointed with the spirit of intercessory prayer, spending hours, lost to time and surroundings, pleading for the unsaved. Young men and women are receiving the GIFTS of the Spirit, speaking with tongues, interpreting tongues previously unknown to them; the sick are being healed and unclean spirits cast out in answer to prayer....
>
> There are many indications that the coming of the Lord draweth nigh and that the time for the outpouring of the Holy Spirit spoken of in Acts 2:17 has fully come. Let Christians in all parts of the world seek earnestly this Pentecostal outpouring for themselves and fellow believers, and pray mightily for an outpouring of the Spirit

upon the unconverted and the heathen. The promise is "I will pour forth of My Spirit upon all flesh."[6]

So it was that Pentecostalism in these circles was seen as a fulfill-ment of prophecy, an end-time, worldwide, cataclysmic event that would result in ordinary people in every culture understanding and experienc-ing "spiritual things," in particular, the gifts and manifestations of the power of the Holy Spirit. Pentecostalism is a revivalist movement with roots in Pietism, Methodism, and the nineteenth century evangelical and revivalist holiness and healing movements. German Pietism—with its emphasis on personal experience or "new birth" by the Holy Spirit and exemplified through Nicolaus von Zinzendorf's Moravians—spread to Methodism through John Wesley and his theologian associate John Fletcher. The personal, "born-again" conversion experience that became the hallmark of Evangelicalism stressed individual decision and was therefore in synch with the individualism that characterized modernity in contrast to the monolithic ecclesiastical systems that dominated pre-modern Europe. The early Methodist doctrine of "entire sanctification," by which a Christian could claim "perfection" through a crisis experience claimed by faith, and the possibility of personal spiritual experiences sub-sequent to conversion, undoubtedly constituted the sparks that ignited the holiness movement and its direct offspring Pentecostalism. The holiness movement radicalized the ideas of Wesley and Fletcher and focused on a personal encounter, a crisis experience of "holiness" that became known as "baptism with the Spirit." Phoebe Palmer, Charles Finney, William and Catherine Booth, and William Taylor were among its best-known advocates. The holiness movement was a reaction to liberalism and for-malism in established Protestant churches as a whole, and not just in the Methodist church. Its main principles were a biblical literalism, the need for a personal, emotional, and individual experience of conversion, and the moral perfection or "holiness" of the Christian individual. The Keswick Conventions that began in the English Lake District in 1875 were another expression of the holiness movement (although more Reformed in orientation), where the emphasis shifted from Spirit baptism as "holi-ness" or "sanctification" to Spirit baptism as "the higher Christian life" and the bestowing of power for witness to the world and mission. This was the theology of Spirit baptism continued by the pentecostals but to which they added the practice of spiritual gifts—in particular, speaking in tongues.

Later in the nineteenth century the healing movement arose in western Europe and North America mostly within radical and pietistic Protestant circles. Its chief proponents were J. C. Blumhardt, Dorothea Trudel, Charles Cullis, John A. Dowie, Carrie Judd Montgomery, and A. B. Simpson. The healing movement was one of the most important influences on early Pentecostalism and another expression of the popular beliefs on the fringes of Evangelicalism. Former Methodist preacher turned healing evangelist Charles Parham, who is credited with formulating the doctrinal link between tongues-speaking and Spirit baptism, came from these circles. For unknown reasons, Parham never sent out missionaries—despite his doctrine of missionary tongues. This would not happen until the Azusa Street revival in 1906, marking American Pentecostalism's outreach into a newly globalized world. Like the earlier advocates of divine healing, even though they suffered from severe illnesses and many of their missionaries died from tropical diseases, pentecostals remained unshaken in their conviction that divine healing had been restored to the church in the worldwide revival of the last days. Healing and "signs and wonders" were both an indispensable ingredient of their message and the means by which the nations would be brought to faith in Christ. The presence of healing gifts sometimes broke down barriers of gender and race discrimination. One of the earliest healing ministries in North America was that of African American Elizabeth Mix; she prayed for Carrie Judd Montgomery (1858–1946), an Episcopalian and later Salvation Army member, Christian and Missionary Alliance leader, and finally pentecostal, that Montgomery would be healed of an incurable disease. Mix had a formative influence on Montgomery's extensive healing ministry. Montgomery's long ministry was extremely significant and bridged the holiness, healing, and pentecostal movements.[7]

The first pentecostals tended to come from one or other of these radical evangelical groups. All held a conviction that the second coming of Christ was imminent and that a worldwide revival would usher it in. They were conditioned by a movement reacting to rationalism and secularism, a response to modernity that focused on personal spirituality, emotional release, and divine intervention in human affairs—even if it used modernity's rational tools to formulate and justify this reaction. By the end of the nineteenth century, the idea grew that there would be a great outpouring of the Spirit throughout the world before the second coming of Christ— and it was hoped, at the beginning of the twentieth century. Those upon whom the Spirit had fallen were to prepare for this by offering themselves for missionary service. Mission was thereby given a new pneumatological and eschatological dimension that was to become the preoccupation of early pentecostals. Pentecostalism was missionary by nature; its central experience of the power of the Spirit which all pentecostal believers affirmed was inextricably linked to going out and being witnesses to all nations. This, together with rapid improvements in transportation and communications, and colonial hegemony, facilitated their rapid spread into many parts of the world in the early twentieth century. Add to this the fact that outside the Western world there were hundreds of voluntary mission societies creating a Christian plurality in places like India, China, and British Africa. The entrance of independent lay pentecostal missionaries and native revivalists was neither unexpected nor unusual in these regions, which were those where Pentecostalism has proliferated most.[8]

David Martin writes of the voluntarism and pluralism born in British and American nineteenth-century denominational splits that "rapidly indigenizes in the developing world, partly on account of its astonishing combination of motifs from both black and white revivalism." Pentecostals, like the radical evangelicals they descended from, were firm believers in the privatization of religion: for them, because the only "real" Christians were the "born again" ones, the vast majority (whether they attended church or not) were simply not Christians. This is why proselytizing was engaged in without compunction and comity agreements on the mission fields were largely ignored. Unencumbered by ecclesiastical organizations and "doctrinal purity," pentecostals relied on their own instincts and a raw interpretation of the Bible. Led by the Spirit, they could do whatever they felt was God's direction at the time, and they created structures according to this subjective guidance. Similarly, and also because of their ostracism from other churches, pentecostals remained isolated and within a few years had corralled themselves into new denominations.[9]

Although the Azusa Street revival was the most significant North American center of early Pentecostalism, it was neither the only one nor the earliest. Various revivals occurred in different parts of the world during the late nineteenth and first decade of the twentieth century within a few years of each other. These revivals had decidedly pentecostal characteristics, with gifts of the Spirit like healings, tongues, prophecy, and other "miraculous" signs. They were conscious and deliberate attempts by ordinary people to adapt revivalist Christianity to their own local contexts, thereby giving expression to their desire for a more satisfying and relevant religious life. Furthermore, there were precedents laid down by

earlier revivalists that were to mold the expectations of the first pentecostals. Many of these expectations were nurtured in the holiness and
healing movements, the soil out of which Pentecostalism grew and without which it would not have survived. There were examples in eastern
Europe, such as a revival that began in Russia and Armenia in 1855 with
people speaking in tongues, and resulting in a group in the Black Sea
area called "Pentecostal Christians," who formed congregations there
that predated pentecostal denominations in origin by fifty years. Keswick
leader F. B. Meyer visited Estonian Baptist congregations in 1902 and
reported approvingly that "marvellous manifestations" of the Spirit were
frequent occurrences, and "the gift of tongues is heard quite often in
the meetings," accompanied by interpretations about the soon coming
of Christ.[10]

There were other precedents in the nineteenth and early twentieth centuries that illustrate that the soil preparing the way for the emergence of
Pentecostalism was not only found in the Western world. Here we begin
in India and examine some of the revivals that ultimately influenced the
emergence of Pentecostalism. These revival movements were in many
respects revolutionary, paving the way for momentous change within
the church, society, and nations, and in particular, creating a heightened
awareness of personal dignity and identity. These revolutionary forces
were affected by political energies geared toward independence from
colonialism that characterized the early twentieth century. The numerous
independent churches and movements that emerged in Pentecostalism
were preceded by the revival events that not only served to further "spiritual" concerns, but also possessed far-reaching implications for political
action, patriotic fervor, and social activism.

John Christian Arulappan (1810–67) and the Christian Pettah Revival

Although the Irvingite revival occurred in the 1830s, one of the earli-
est pentecostal revivals in the nineteenth century of which we have any
knowledge was that associated with the Tamil evangelist John Christian
Arulappan in Tamilnadu in 1860–65, when many charismatic gifts
were reported. There is a little information on Arulappan in the Church
Missionary Society (CMS) archives, and the unstructured account by the
Brethren writer G. H. Lang published in 1939 is the only source of detail.
This contains long quotations from Arulappan's diary and letters, as

well as commentaries by missionaries who witnessed the effects of his revival movement. This is particularly interesting because the Brethren movement has largely been opposed to pentecostal manifestations such as those described in Lang's book, and Lang himself was no supporter of Pentecostalism. His account is limited in that it is based on a single source, with all the dangers of selective information and misinterpretation that this brings. Nevertheless, the most significant parts of this account have bearing on the general principle of precedents that this chapter illustrates.[11]

Arulappan was born into a Christian family in Tirunelveli in 1810. His family sent him at the age of fifteen to study at the CMS seminary led by the famous German missionary C. T. E. Rhenius (1790–1837). On one occasion Arulappan reportedly ran away from the seminary with other students, but on his return he was reinstated and began to make progress. At the end of 1826 Rhenius wrote of Arulappan, "This good young man lately gave way to the tempter, whereby he greatly injured his Christian character. . . . He feels it now and is greatly humbled. Has maintained his former good character. Sometimes negligent & sleeping." He also reported that Arulappan was "good" in Tamil and Geography, and "average" in English and Hebrew. In 1833 Arulappan came into contact with Anthony Norris Groves (1795–1853), a British Brethren missionary and prominent leader in that movement, and he agreed to travel with Groves to the Nilgiri hills, preaching en route. This was the beginning of Arulappan's extensive itinerant ministry. He would work with Groves for the next four years. After a taunt from a bystander, Arulappan refused to receive any remuneration from Groves and thereafter lived "by faith," relying on support from locals. He soon returned to Tirunelveli and may have joined Rhenius after his resignation from the CMS, partly supported by gifts received from the people in Tirunelveli.[12]

Groves himself made the following observation (emphasis in original):

Dear Aroolappen has declined any *form* of salary, because the people, he says, would not cease to tell him that he preached because he was hired. . . . Those who know the natives will, I am sure, feel with me, that this plan of missions, whereby the native himself is thrown *on God,* is calculated to develop that *individuality of character,* the absence of which has been so deeply deplored, and the remedy for which has so seldom been sought.[13]

Fifteen years later, Groves's son Henry described Arulappan: "independent of every individual, or body of individuals, he has endeavoured to preach the gospel...looking to the Lord for the supply of his temporal wants and of those who...have been helpers with him." In practicing an individualistic and anti-establishment form of Christianity that denied the traditions of the time, Arulappan followed the radical Evangelicalism of Pentecostalism's forebears. He also challenged the prevailing idea that church leadership and the right to minister the sacraments were the exclusive preserves of ordained clergy, another precedent for Pentecostalism. When Arulappan and his colleague Andrew, the leaders of the mission in Pilney Hills, presided over Holy Communion and baptisms, it caused, in the words of Groves, "more stir and enquiry than you can imagine." Arulappan's radical Evangelicalism emphasized the empowerment of the Spirit for all followers of Christ regardless of race or caste, the priesthood of all believers, and faith missions that did not rely on a stipend from a church headquarters. He also practiced open worship services after the pattern of the Brethren movement, which included the breaking of bread and a simple biblical exposition based on the pattern of the early, "apostolic" church, and a communitarian lifestyle. Following the example of Rhenius and Groves, in 1842 Arulappan began a self-supporting agricultural village for Christians that included a boarding school, printing press, itinerant preaching base, a church, and periodic Bible training and conventions. The settlement was named Christian Pettah ("Christian village"), although some of those receiving its benefits were not Christians. Arulappan and his colleagues were also responsible for establishing churches and schools in the area. By 1858 there were thirty villages with 673 people attending these churches. The following year there were thirty-three villages and around 800 converts.[14]

These and later churches followed local mores and were independent of foreign mission authorities. They represented the first independent churches in India in modern times, long before the "three-self" formula made famous by Henry Venn and Rufus Anderson. The revival that began under Arulappan's ministry significantly extended the reach and vitality of this indigenous movement and confirmed its contextual relevance. Arulappan had been reading in the *Missionary Reporter* of the revival that had occurred in America and Britain over the previous three years. Orr suggests that the most significant result of this revival was the "outbreak of revivals among indigenous Christians, and the folk movements of Indian communities to Christianity that resulted therefrom."

The American Presbyterian mission in Ludhiana, Punjab, issued a call for Christians to set aside the second week of January 1860 for prayer for such a worldwide revival.[15]

When Arulappan read of this development he became very enthusiastic for a similar revival. He gave himself to earnest prayer and mobilized others to do the same. By March 1860 the manifestations of these revivals were beginning, in Arulappan's words:

> I am thankful to the Lord, who is pleased to pour His Spirit upon poor sinners without distinction of white or black, and rich or poor.... The next Sunday [March 4th]...I exhorted them.... In the night when we broke the bread, I exhorted the church on three subjects....
>
> The next day morning two of the females went to the next village and spoke about Christ and they read and searched the Scriptures with one of my sons-in-law. The next morning after prayer was over, they came into the house and wanted me to pray for them, and cried with groans and tears, and told me that they were sinners, and that they should pray for the Holy Spirit.... I could not stop their crying until I had prayed thrice with them, and shewed them several passages.... Some of my daughters attended their meeting. When they came to me in the middle of the day they were still trembling and crying but I comforted them.... They were much pleased but their trembling did not leave them at once. [16]

The main characteristics of this revival movement were confessions of sin and an emphasis on holiness, features of the revivals at the beginning of the twentieth century in India and Wales. There was also the remarkable use of women in leadership—most unusual in nineteenth-century India, but a portent of even greater things to come. Lang commented that in Arulappan's study of the Bible, he did not find "that rigid, inflexible prohibition of public ministry of women that Christendom in general seems to think it sees there." This was even more remarkable, he observed, in that "India is a place beyond most of the suppression of woman."[17]

This revival also had more "pentecostal" characteristics. Arulappan described the events from May to August 1860 in some detail:

> From the 4th May to the 7th instant [August] the Holy Ghost was poured out openly and wonderfully. Some prophesied and rebuked

the people: some beat themselves on their breasts severely, and trembled and fell down through the shaking of their bodies and souls. They wept bitterly, and confessed their sins. I was obliged to pray without ceasing for the consolation of everyone. I thought it was strange to see them without their senses. They saw some signs in the air. They were much pleased to praise God. Some ignorant [uninstructed] people gave out some songs and hymns which we never heard before. Some of those who were not baptized had no peace until we baptized them; so about twenty souls were baptized after they received the Holy Ghost. [Ac 10. 44–48]…

In the month of June some of our people praised the Lord by unknown tongues, with their interpretations. In the month of July the Spirit was poured out upon our congregation at Oleikollamm and above 25 persons were baptised by one of my sons-in-law and two other brothers who labour among them. They are steadfast in prayers.

Then my son and a daughter and three others went in to visit their own relations, in three villages, who are under the Church Missionary Society, they also received the Holy Ghost. Some prophesy, some speak by unknown tongues with their interpretations. Some Missionaries admit the truth of the gifts of the Holy Ghost. The Lord meets everywhere one after another, though some tried to quench the Spirit.…We hold three meetings at every day.…We understand that the Holy Ghost dwells and abides among us, and leads us by His blessed words.[18]

Arulappan goes on to describe preaching and distributing tracts printed by his own press to thousands, and building a prayer room in Christian Pettah for 500 people. This "outpouring of the Spirit" and his use of Acts passages is expressed in language that would characterize the pentecostal revival of the twentieth century and, like the latter, it resulted in aggressive evangelism. The ecstatic gifts of the Spirit like prophecy and tongues are not mentioned again in the edited versions of Arulappan's and Groves's accounts, but they may have been more frequent than these reports suggest.[19]

A fairly negative missionary report on the revival in Christian Pettah more than a year later (June 1861) confirms this suggestion and the account displays interesting parallels to developments in later Pentecostalism. It referred to "the apparent assumption of miraculous gifts" and "an unhealthy state of spiritual excitement," including the frequent use of prophecies, tongues, interpretations, visions, and the introduction of outward rules such as wearing white clothing and the appointing of Apostles, Evangelists, and Prophets—all given by revelation of the Spirit. Another missionary spent a week with Arulappan and reported on the manifestations of "a great shaking, attended with certain 'gifts', viz. speaking with tongues, seeing of visions, interpretation of tongues and prophecy" and even writing in the Spirit, something that later occurred in the Azusa Street revival. Unlike the pentecostal revival, however, physical healing seems not to have been a feature of Arulappan's movement, at least as far as these accounts reveal. Henry Groves reproduces a report from the *Madras Church Missionary Record* in which "a deeply interesting revival of spiritual religion" is described "with the same physical emotions" that had marked the "Ulster Revival." However, in this case, the missionaries had succeeded in keeping "in check" the "painful manifestations."[20]

A CMS missionary writing on the revival amplified what were regarded as the manifestations needing correction:

> The whole number of the persons affected hardly exceeds one hundred, or perhaps, including the congregations connected with Mr. Arulappen..., one hundred and fifty....both in the case of Mr. Arulappen's congregations and also in that of one or two congregations in other parts of Tinnevelly, to which the movement extended, there have been cases of excesses, which...shew an unhealthy excitement which should have been checked. For instance, the newly awakened have fancied that they could speak in tongues, have seen visions, to which they have attached great importance, have given utterance to prophecies, etc. But in the congregations connected with ourselves...all such tendencies were checked in the first instance.[21]

At least one of the CMS missionaries, a Mr. Gray, was not as sure about this "checking," and expressed cautious support for the revival movement. He expressed fear that he might "by my own deadness and coldness...throw a chill upon the blessed work." He continued:

> Some of the revived believers expected that the signs mentioned in Mark xvi. would follow believers now, even as in primitive times. But the Missionaries exerted themselves to remove these expectations.

We should not wonder, however, if some of the converts should reason thus. What God is now doing in the midst of us was altogether beyond the expectations of Missionaries and other Christians: who can say what manifestations the Spirit of God will or will not make of his power?[22]

Besides the reported speaking in tongues, prophecies, visions, and revelations, other common revival manifestations reported by the missionaries included loud sobbing and crying, falling down, swaying back and forth, and rolling the eyes. This revival was primarily a local Indian movement initiated by an independent Indian preacher that spread to other Christian congregations where CMS missionaries were working. One of them, the Reverend A. B. Valpy, expressed "his firm conviction, that the blessing which has been vouchsafed to us in this district is mainly owing, under God, to the efforts of the party of native Christians." He also believed that some CMS missionaries had carried their "scepticism and mistrust" too far.[23]

He exhorted his fellow missionaries:

There was evidently a belief in the power of the Holy Spirit to work in this land even as he had been doing in Ireland and in America; and there was special prayer made for a revival of religion. It came. There was a baptism of the Holy Spirit which filled the members of this [Arulappan's] church with a holy enthusiasm; and caused them to go everywhere preaching the gospel, in demonstration of the Spirit and of power.... Let us not put our views of decorum and of order above the mighty operations of the Spirit.... we can no more expect men to act under such circumstances in accordance with ordinary rules of decorum, than we could expect men aroused from their beds by an earthquake to avoid every demonstration of a noisy or alarming character. Perhaps it behoves us all, to surrender our very imperfect views of the power and majesty of the Holy Spirit, and prepare for something grander, more awful and revolutionary than we have yet witnessed.[24]

Notwithstanding these remarkably prophetic expressions of support, it seems that many, but not all, of the CMS missionaries sought to suppress the "excesses" of this revival. Arulappan died in 1867 and within a decade most of his churches had joined the CMS. Christian

Pettah, however, remained a separate independent church. Followers of Arulappan were actively responsible for an outbreak of revival in Kerala in 1873–75 among Syrian Orthodox and CMS churches led by Brahmin converts Justus Joseph and his brothers Matthew and Jacob, among others. Among the Syrians this revival led in turn to the foundation of the Mar Thoma church. As in Arulappan's revival, this movement was also accompanied by physical and emotional phenomena including speaking in tongues, causing concerns for missionary observers. And it was among Groves's Brethren churches in South India that the first pentecostals were found, some with direct links to the earlier revivals.[25]

The connections between Arulappan's revival movement and Pentecostalism are not only phenomenological. Four decades later, in 1908, the pioneer of Pentecostalism in Europe, T. B. Barratt of Norway, arrived in Bombay for a two-month stay at the missionary retreat at Coonoor. Barratt was invited and financed by Anthony H. Groves, a tea planter in the Nilgiri hills, son of Henry and grandson of Anthony Norris Groves, Arulappan's one-time mentor. Among other things, Barratt discovered that his Indian interpreter Joshua had received Spirit baptism, with glossolalia, in 1897, evidence that speaking in tongues continued in India long after the time of Arulappan and prior to the pentecostal beginnings in North America and Europe. And Barratt was to report on and be amazed by another revival taking place further north.[26]

Pandita Ramabai (1858–1922) and the Mukti Revival

Born in North India two years before Arulappan's revival started, Pandita Sarasvati Ramabai was one of the most famous Christian women India has ever produced. She was a reformer, Bible translator, social activist, and leader of another Indian revival movement in her Mukti Mission from 1905 to 1907. Ramabai is significant in both the origins of Pentecostalism and in its acceptance among the wider Christian community. Her revival movement was given prominence in reports in the emerging pentecostal press. The details of Ramabai's life have been adequately covered elsewhere. Her rejection of British colonialism remained with her all her life—like most educated Indians, she believed in Indian nationalism, stimulated by the British rulers' repression of and arrogance toward Indian social structures, causing determined Indian resistance. She spent three years visiting the Western world and favorably commented on women's rights in

American society, while criticizing that society's shortcomings. In 1895 she established a mission on a farm she had bought at Kedgaon, near Pune, and her work shifted from a religiously "neutral" charity to an overtly evangelical Christian one. This mission was given the name "Mukti" ("salvation") and its main purpose was to provide a refuge for destitute girls and young women, particularly those who had been the victims of child marriages and had become widows, and those rescued from starvation. By 1900 it had almost 2,000 residents. Ramabai believed that Hindu women could find complete freedom only by converting to Christianity. Her mission aimed to provide a totally supportive environment for its large community trained in income-generating skills, but her overtly evangelistic aims brought her into conflict with the Hindu majority. In 1904 Ramabai began her personal translation of the Bible from Hebrew and Greek into Marathi, a process that took eighteen years, almost to the end of her life. In 1907 the mission newsletter *Mukti Prayer-Bell* stated that Mukti was a "purely undenominational, evangelical, Christian Mission, designed to reach and help high caste Hindu widows, deserted wives and orphans from all parts of India," who would receive "a thorough training for some years" after which they would "go out as teachers or Bible women to work in different Missions." Ramabai had a team of seventy, including twenty-five volunteer Western workers. Minnie Abrams, a "deaconess missionary" in the Methodist Episcopal Church since 1887, joined Ramabai in 1898 and was a significant bridge between Ramabai and the emerging global pentecostal network until Abrams's untimely death in 1912. Abrams was to be the international publicist for the revival that ensued.[27]

In about 1894 Ramabai had an experience described as "the blessing of the Holy Spirit," when, she wrote: "I found it a great blessing to realise the personal presence of the Holy Spirit in me, and to be guided and taught by Him." She saw her need to be "filled with the Spirit" and professed to "enter on a new experience of God's power to save, bless and use." Thereafter she identified increasingly with radical evangelicals, Keswick "higher Christian life," and Holiness movements, and these revivalist networks promoted her work.[28]

Ramabai attended and addressed the Keswick convention in 1898, where she asked for prayer for an outpouring of the Spirit on Indian Christians:

At that time the Lord led me to ask those present to pray for an outpouring of the Holy Spirit on all Indian Christians....I requested

God's people to pray that 100,000 men and 100,000 women from among the Indian Christians may be led to preach the Gospel to their country people.... Since that time God wanted me to pray and expect great things of Him.[29]

After hearing of the Welsh revival and a revival conducted by R. A. Torrey in Australia in 1904, she dispatched her daughter Manoramabai and Minnie Abrams there. In January 1905, Ramabai instituted an early-morning daily prayer meeting, when women would meet and pray (in her words) "for the true conversion of all the Indian Christians including ourselves, and for a special outpouring of the Holy Spirit on all Christians of every land." The numbers gradually increased from seventy to 500 and Ramabai wrote that in July 1905 "the Lord graciously sent a Holy Ghost revival among us, and also in many schools and churches in this country." Her Bible school became the hub for all-night prayer meetings and the noise of girls weeping and praising God, many speaking in tongues and prophesying. Ramabai explained: "Some have laughed at us, for we have become fools. The Spirit-filled girls cannot suppress their sorrow for sin or their joy in salvation. They burst into loud crying and laughing, they shake, they tremble, some of them dance with joy and almost pray simultaneously in loud voices." One visitor commented, "It was impossible to hear what anyone was praying about in the volume of sound which arose and which might continue for an hour or more at a stretch." Even Manoramabai "on more than one occasion, when close to me, prayed for a long time aloud though the words were absolutely incomprehensible." Manoramabai explained that she "knew perfectly well all the time what she was praying about, and those who had this gift testified to the spiritual help derived, saying that they had never been able to give God praise or worship in such a satisfying way till they did so in tongues."[30]

The revival spread to other parts of the region. Students of the Zenana Training Home in Pune who attended Ramabai's meetings took it there. Its leader Sunderbai Powar later commented: "One can see the fruits of the Revival in the girls' conduct. They love each other and are anxious to win souls for Jesus. Some of the Biblewomen...are filled with the Spirit.... they stood on the road and began to give the message, an unusual thing for Indian women to do." A year later Manoramabai reported: "About the middle of August last year, the Lord began to call out praying bands of girls and women from Mukti to carry the message of salvation to those in other places." Abrams also led teams for revival meetings in surrounding places. She took eleven young women to an orphanage at Telegaon and found that similar phenomena followed them with miraculous healing and great interest among the Hindu population. As one periodical observed, Ramabai's "Praying Bands" of young women were going "in every direction to scatter the fire that has filled their own souls" and the result was that "many parts of India are hearing of the true and living God." The revival lasted for a year and a half and resulted in over a thousand baptisms at the school, confessions of sins and repentances, prolonged prayer meetings and the witnessing of some 700 in teams into the surrounding areas, about a hundred going out daily, sometimes for as long as a month at a time. These "Praying Bands" spread the revival wherever they went and some remarkable healings were reported.[31]

It was not only in Mukti that revival was taking place, however, for reports were coming from other parts of India, including Tamilnadu, where ecstatic phenomena were reported among the Brethren churches in 1905, and in Kerala, Andhra, and Karnataka. The revival movement in northeast India in the Khasi Hills also received international publicity. But it was the Mukti revival that grabbed the attention of the Western evangelical world, and especially that of emerging Pentecostalism. References to the revival are plentiful and clearly situate it within the new movement. The Azusa Street revival's newspaper *The Apostolic Faith*, Alexander Boddy's *Confidence* in Sunderland, England, and the Stone Church in Chicago's *The Latter Rain Evangel* had major articles on the Mukti revival, attesting to the importance placed on it by early pentecostals. The first report of the revival in India in *The Apostolic Faith*, entitled "Pentecost in India," commented: "News comes from India that the baptism with the Holy Ghost and gift of tongues is being received there by natives who are simply taught of God.... Hallelujah! God is sending the Pentecost to India. He is no respecter of persons."[32]

The report to which this refers was carried by *The India Alliance*, the periodical of the CMA in India:

> Those who are following through the papers the reports of the revival movement in India cannot but be struck with the likeness of many things in the revival to apostolic times and events, and the records frequently read like a continuation of the Acts of the Apostles. Some of the gifts which have been scarcely heard in the church for many centuries, are now being given by the Holy Ghost to simple, unlearned members of the body of Christ and communities

are being stirred and transformed by the wonderful grace of God. Healings, the gift of tongues, visions and dreams, discernment of spirits, the power to prophecy and to pray the prayer of faith, all have a place in the present revival.[33]

Significantly, this report states that speaking in tongues occurred in the Bombay area before news of Azusa Street had reached India; and the first missionaries to India from Azusa Street, Albert and Lillian Garr, only reached Kolkata (Calcutta) three months after the report. The first direct report from Mukti from neighboring Methodist missionary Albert Norton said that in about September 1906 they had heard of the gift of tongues being received by "Christian believers in different places and countries." He had visited Mukti a week earlier, where in a prayer meeting he had seen young women speaking in tongues, but "it closely resembled the speaking of foreign languages." On the previous weekend he had again visited the Mission where he described "some 24 different persons had received the gift of tongues." This was "abundant evidence that God was working in a wonderful way" and that "those speaking in tongues gave evidence that their souls were flooded with blessing from God." They were "waiting on God for the bestowment of all the Spirit's gifts which He has for us."[34]

In September 1907 *The Apostolic Faith* published a letter from the Garrs, who mentioned that Ramabai and her daughter had been "tarrying" for the Spirit, who had come to them, a number of her teachers, and 300 "native girls." This issue ran another report on the revival titled "Manifestations of the Spirit in India" taken from a "published report from the Mission at Mukti." It refers to frequent scenes of various phenomena experienced in the revivals in "Assam and India," including trembling, shaking, loud crying, and confessions, unconsciousness in ecstasy or prayer, sudden falling to the ground twisting and writhing during exorcisms, and "joy unspeakable" manifested by singing, clapping, shouting praises, and dancing. The report warns against those who would "suppress these manifestations" and thereby grieve the Holy Spirit and stop the work. The writer was Minnie Abrams, who exhorts:

> We do not need to worry over these manifestations, nor seek to suppress them....we have seen over and over again during the past fifteen months, that where Christian workers have suppressed these manifestations, the Holy Spirit has been grieved, the work has stopped and no fruit of holy lives has resulted....The writer

testifies that she herself has, in the silence of the midnight hour, alone in her room without a sound in the house, been shaken from her innermost being, until her whole body was convulsed and filled with joy and consciousness that the Holy Spirit had taken posses-sion of every part of her being. No one had greater prejudice against religious excitement than she, but every time she put her hands upon the work at Mukti to suppress joy or strong conviction, or reproved persons being strongly wrought upon physically in prayer, the work of revival stopped and she had to confess her fault before it went on again. We have learned that God's ways are past finding out, as far above ours as the heavens are above the earth.[35]

In the *Mukti Prayer-Bell* of September 1907 Abrams gives prominence to speaking in "unknown tongues" and an outline of the "creed" of the Mukti Mission. The creed states that the "baptism of the Holy Ghost, giv-ing power for service, is given with the gifts of the Spirit as recorded in 1 Cor. 12:4–11" and that these doctrines are "accepted and taught by all of the Mukti staff of workers." This was one of the earliest statements of what became accepted pentecostal theology, whereas the "initial evidence" of tongues was only enshrined in American Pentecostal denominational dogma in 1918. It is unlikely that Los Angeles had any influence on what happened at Mukti, even if Ramabai and Abrams had heard of Azusa Street before that, which is also most unlikely. Abrams's own account of revivals specifically links the Mukti revival with those in Wales and north-west India, she sees the Korean (1907) and Manchurian (1910) revivals issuing from these same sources, and the Los Angeles and European pentecostal revivals as connected but separate movements. A reading of early pentecostal historians like Stanley Frodsham confirms this view. It is best to see the Mukti and Azusa Street revivals (together with the 1909 Chilean revival) as formative events contributing toward the emergence of Pentecostalism.[36]

Ramabai herself was a sympathetic and involved participant in this revivalism. The January 1908 issue of *The Apostolic Faith* carried a report directly from the *Mukti Prayer-Bell,* in which Ramabai wrote that she was "not aware that anything like the present Holy Ghost revival, has ever vis-ited India before the year 1905," and that many had "stumbled" over the manifestations and criticized the revival. Ramabai was "convinced more and more" that those given the gift of tongues had been "greatly helped to lead better lives" and were more effective in prayer and evangelism as a result. A couple of months later, Ramabai's "Stray Thoughts on the Revival" gave a clear indication that Ramabai thought that revivals were the means by which the Holy Spirit was creating a contextual form of Indian Christianity. This revival was to proceed according to the will of the Spirit, who knew perfectly well how to work in harmony with the Indian psyche to "suit their nature and feelings," and would be hindered by "foreignised" Western ideas of decorum. These ideas were shaped by Ramabai's background in philosophical Brahmanism and her resistance to all forms of imperialism.[37]

The Mukti mission was visited by several Western pentecostal leaders, including T. B. Barratt, who, in 1908, spoke to 1,200 young women in an assembly there and was awestruck by the simultaneous praying he had heard among them. After they had dispersed to classes, some remained "lying prostrate on the floor, praying and speaking in tongues." In January 1909 the American healing evangelist Carrie Judd Montgomery and her husband George spent two days at Mukti and reported that 400–500 of the girls at Mukti had "been baptized with the Spirit and speak with new tongues." "None can doubt," George wrote, "that the Latter Rain as a great flood has been poured out at Mukti," and that "all the workers there are baptized with the Spirit and speak in tongues." Both Mukti and the neighboring Daund mission run by Albert Norton were main centers for pentecostal mission, Norton referring to Daund as "one of the mother colonies for pentecostal work in India." Minnie Abrams was a prominent speaker in several pentecostal conventions during her furlough in the United States in 1909 and 1910. Abrams outlined her views on Spirit baptism in an article titled "The Scriptural Evidence of Pentecost" and wrote that the "outpouring of the Holy Ghost" on the Christian and Missionary Alliance had "greatly strengthened our hands at Mukti." Mukti operated as the main center in India for the spread of Pentecostalism—much as Los Angeles or Oslo did in the West. Visitors from all over India and Sri Lanka received Spirit baptism at Mukti or in other centers like Bombay. The Mukti revival was of international significance and its importance for the pentecostal missionary movement worldwide cannot be underestimated. Ramabai was a pioneer of an independent Indian Christianity in the tradition of Arulappan. The Indian revival movements were to result in an unparalleled missionary outreach of Indian Christians. Ramabai died in 1922, less than a year after her daughter Manorambai's death. Although she never considered herself a "pentecostal" in the contemporary sense, her impact on global Pentecostalism was considerable.[38]

The Mukti revival had at least five far-reaching consequences. First, the leaders of the Azusa Street revival in Los Angeles saw the Indian revival as a precedent to the one in which they were involved, a prototype. Frank Bartleman, eyewitness and chronicler of the Azusa Street revival, some two decades after that revival wrote about the origins of the pentecostal movement: "The present world-wide revival was rocked in the cradle of little Wales. It was brought up in India, following; becoming full-grown in Los Angeles later." Pentecostalism, he thought, was the outgrowth of two earlier revival movements: the Welsh Revival of 1904–05, a Holy Spirit revival movement that brought several thousands to Christian faith, and the Mukti revival in India. But Bartleman also implied that these earlier revivals represented the birth and adolescence of the "world-wide restoration of the power of God." However, the Indian revival was a "full-grown" pentecostal revival that took place before word of the Los Angeles happenings reached India. It is more likely that these various revivals were simultaneous rather than sequential. In other words, the connections between these various revival movements were incidental, though they certainly fed on one another for sustenance.[39]

Second was Mukti's impact on the beginnings of Latin American Pentecostalism. Abrams contacted her friend and former Bible school classmate in Valparaiso, Chile, May Louise Hoover, with a report of the revival in Mukti in a booklet she wrote in 1906 titled *The Baptism of the Holy Ghost & Fire*. In its second edition later that year, she included a discussion of the restoration of speaking in tongues (the first published pentecostal theology of Spirit baptism), and 30,000 copies were circulated widely. As a result of Abrams's booklet and her subsequent correspondence with the Hoovers, the Methodist churches in Valparaiso and Santiago were stirred to pray for a similar revival that began in 1909. Willis Hoover became leader of the new Methodist Pentecostal Church. It is also significant that one of the leaders of the Indian revival and an acquaintance of Ramabai, Shorat Chuckerbutty, was the woman who prayed for Alice Luce, CMS missionary in India at the time, to receive her pentecostal baptism. Luce was a pioneer both in her work among Hispanic pentecostals in the southern United States and Mexico, and in being the first to promote the "indigenous" church principle that was to affect pentecostal missions so profoundly.[40]

Third, both Ramabai in her ministry and the revival she led demonstrated an ecumenicity and inclusiveness that stand in stark contrast to the rigid exclusivism of subsequent pentecostal denominations. She often alluded to divisions in the church and the need for unity. Although there were obvious limitations to this with Ramabai's increasing identification with conservative Evangelicalism, her earlier inclusivity was undoubtedly a result of the pluralistic context of India and Ramabai's indebtedness to her own cultural and religious training in Brahmin philosophy and national consciousness.

The fourth feature of both the Mukti and Christian Pettah revivals was the prominent role given to women, who carried the pentecostal message out into other parts of India in the years that followed. The revivals empowered the marginalized, little-educated women who lacked formal ordination or acceptance in either Hindu reform circles or Western-dominated Christian circles. Notwithstanding these disadvantages, the revival movements enabled them to live productive lives and they imparted a sense of identity and dignity to many others. These revivals were to characterize Pentecostalism throughout the global South. This was another case of Pentecostalism's early social activism, in which the Mukti revival and Ramabai herself were pioneers without precedent.

Last, these indigenous revival movements were, indirectly, resistance movements against foreign forms of Christianity. This was not lost on the missionaries themselves. One of them, in the wake of the Manchurian revival, wrote perceptively, although slightly peeved by what had moved out of his control:

> A "revival" is almost always partly a protest.... It is protest against foreign theology, against the domination of foreigners and foreign-trained men.... The desire is to drive out of power all those of whom they do not approve or, if necessary, to start an independent church.[41]

Forces had been set in motion by these revival movements that were to take Christianity in the majority world in a direction that none of these missionaries would have ever anticipated. These were the first showers; the storm was yet to come.

Other Revivalist Movements

There were other figures who might be regarded as precursors of Pentecostalism. Chinese pastor Xi Shengmo (1835–96), whose name means "Overcoming Demons," was well educated and from a wealthy family in

Shanxi province. He ran opium refuges throughout the province in which his own Chinese medicines were used for the treatment of addiction (using a formula revealed to him by the Holy Spirit), and he was renowned for his gifts of exorcism and healing with revelatory dreams and visions. During his lifetime he wrote some 100 hymns set to popular Chinese tunes. He was ordained by the founder of the China Inland Mission (CIM), Hudson Taylor in 1886, but Xi was never under the authority of the CIM and was criticized by one missionary acquaintance for his "tendency to exalt things Chinese" and for his "not a little under-estimation of the foreign mission-ary." Xi may be just one example of other preachers in China and elsewhere for whom divine healing and deliverance from demons were essential parts of Christian ministry in the late nineteenth century. Divine healing and exorcism were rarely part of the Protestant missionary establishment's practices, and it was only with the advent of the pentecostals in the twen-tieth century that this practice became widespread. In the words of Daniel Bays, Xi "prefigured some of the independent Chinese church leaders of the twentieth century."[42]

The "Korean Pentecost" of 1907–08 commenced at a convention in Pyongyang under the Presbyterian elder Sun Ju Kil and followed an earlier revival that had begun among Methodist missionaries in Wonsan on the northeast coast of Korea in 1903. None of these events seemed to have had any direct influence on international Pentecostalism at the time, although they did not escape notice. Canadian Methodist missionary Robert Hardie, one of the leaders of the 1903 revival, described his own experience as "baptism of the Holy Spirit." Missionaries who had visited the revivals in Wales and India visited Korea and inspired the Korean Presbyterians to expect a similar event. The Korean revival, like those in Wales and India, was part of the international holiness revivals characterized by emotional repentance with loud weeping and simultaneous prayer. Eyewitness William Blair likened the Korean revival to the Day of Pentecost in Acts 2, and the "Korean Pentecost" soon spread throughout the country—Blair recorded that "Christians returned to their homes in the country taking the pentecostal fire with them." This was a specifically Korean revival, whose features still characterize both Protestant and pentecostal churches in Korea today: prayer meetings held daily in the early morning, all-night prayer meetings, vocal simultaneous prayer, Bible study, and an emphasis on evangelism and missions. But beyond these features are more typi-cally pentecostal practices like Spirit baptism, healing the sick, miracles, and casting out demons. As was the case in India, national evangelists, especially Sun Ju Kil with his teaching of premillennial dispensationalism and later the Presbyterian pastor Ik Du Kim, famous for his healing and miracle ministry, took the revival movement in a more charismatic direction. Pentecostal papers also reported on the Korean revival, one comparing the revival to that of Wesley and noting the "extraordinary manifestation of power," then quoting the somewhat prophetic speculation that "it would not be so very wonderful if the Korean revival were to usher in such a religious awakening of the Orient as would transform the great Chinese empire and change the face of the whole missionary situation." Such an international "awakening" was part of radical evangelical parlance. By the end of the twentieth century, this prophecy had been fulfilled, perhaps not exactly as imagined. As late as 1911, reports from Pyongyang about "the greatest weekly prayer meeting in the world," with 1,100 in attendance, with one sixth of all Korean Christians training for the ministry, were being published in the pentecostal press. In 1923 the Korean Presbyterian Church, as a result of the manifestations of gifts of the Spirit, reversed its constitutional statement that miracles and healing had ceased.[43]

Soon after the Korean revival, similar revivals broke out in 1908 in Manchuria, North China—at the time, like Korea, under Japanese occupation—and in Fujian in southeast China among Methodists in 1909, when speaking in tongues was reported, and in 1909–10 in Shandong in northeast China. These revivals were directly inspired by the events in Korea, as one of the missionary leaders there, Jonathan Goforth, and a number of Chinese leaders, had seen the Korean revival. Significantly, Goforth visited a pentecostal church, Elim Tabernacle in Rochester, New York, in December 1909 to give a "stirring account of the recent outpouring of God's Spirit in China." It was reported that the congregation was "greatly encouraged and inspired to lay hold of God in a fresh way, crying to Him for even a mightier power that will sweep the earth and thus hasten the coming of our blessed Lord and Redeemer." Pentecostal missionaries in north China, including Bernt Berntsen, visited the revival meetings of Goforth there. The Christian and Missionary Alliance in Gansu province in western China experienced a revival in January 1908 in which a Chinese preacher called Brother Yong experienced Spirit baptism, spoke in tongues, and was reportedly effective in gifts of healing, prophecy, and casting out demons, a full four years before any of these missionaries turned pentecostal, according to one of them. CIM missionary James Webster reported that a Chinese pastor, after thanking the missionaries for bringing the gospel to China, remarked that "the Holy Spirit came down from Heaven. You could not send Him to us." The missionary replied that they could now take a "back seat" because it would "not do any longer for us to exercise lordship over God's heritage in China." The revival movement was once again recognized as the means by which the Spirit was creating an independent Chinese church.[44]

These various international revival movements were the soil in which local Pentecostalism grew and thrived, revivals that rapidly spread to other places. All over the world untold thousands of revivalists with no known Western connections were responsible for the spread of the pentecostal gospel. In the Ivory Coast and the Gold Coast (now Ghana), William Wade Harris, a Methodist-raised Grebo from Cape Palmas, Liberia, spearheaded a revival in 1914–15 that included many pentecostal phenomena including healing and speaking in tongues. This resulted in 120,000 conversions in a year, the largest influx of Africans to Christianity the continent had ever seen. It is quite possible that Wade Harris had encountered the pentecostal missionaries working in Liberia in his home region of Cape Palmas (especially as they began among the Methodists), but there were no recorded connections thereafter. These various charismatic revivals were not primarily movements from the Western world to "foreign lands" but, more significantly, they were movements within these continents themselves. In most cases the revivals were led by local leaders. It can be argued that the revivals independent of Western Pentecostalism in Korea, China, India, Chile, Nigeria, and the Ivory Coast were not specifically pentecostal revivals, but this depends on how "pentecostal" is defined. If the charismatic practices of healing, prophecy, speaking in tongues, other physical manifestations, and emotional prayer meetings are characteristics of Pentecostalism, then these revivals demonstrate that pentecostal origins are complex and varied, polycentric, and diffused.[45]

2

Origins and Organization

Revivalism and Relevance

The revival movements discussed in the previous chapter illustrate that majority-world Christianity could no longer be understood exclusively through the lens of Western churches or missionary agencies, but could express itself more freely and flourish by engaging with local contexts and local agendas. The life, work, and ministries of Arulappan and Ramabai and others like them enabled Christianity to take on local idioms that were to be further developed in independent churches. This was always heightened by the transforming power of the Holy Spirit, which enabled people of every language and culture to take the gospel to every nation. The primary motivation for the early expansion of pentecostal forms of revivalism was these revivalists' overwhelming sense of divine calling and empowerment to proclaim their personal testimony to the whole world. The transnationalism of revivalist Christianity had just begun. How this worked out and accelerated in different contexts is the subject of this and the following chapters. But first it is necessary to return to questions of causes and origins. Pentecostalism has grown most rapidly in those areas of the world where a pluralistic religious environment is the norm—including such "Christian" countries as the United States or Ukraine, or where well-established Protestant missions were operating and there was a ready acceptance of the pentecostal message of power to overcome an evil spirit world—such as in the regions of the sub-Sahara, Indonesia, and China. There were several reasons for this. I will deal with some of them here, including the multiplicity of denominations and mission agencies that greatly facilitated the creation of new ones.

There were also other, more immediate causes, however. Not least of these was racism and colonialism, which were significant factors in the formation of independent churches throughout the global South. Although independent churches were seldom directly the products of secession from missionary churches, they were major catalysts for a fire that only needed a spark to set it ablaze. The earliest independent churches in Nigeria, Ghana, and South Africa arose partly out of nationalist feelings and a desire for African self-expression and freedom from missionary control. The same pattern was to be true of independent churches across Asia and particularly in China, where a strong anti-colonialism and rising nationalism were prevalent in the early twentieth century. The various independent pentecostal churches were complex symbolic systems, expressions of cultural protest against and resistance to colonial domination. Many Africans turned to less conventional forms of Western Protestantism such as Pentecostalism and the healing movement. These provided the basis for new churches to emerge as what social anthropologist Jean Comaroff calls (in the South African context) "a more radical expression of cultural resistance." The oppressed people directed their disaffection against the more tangible colonialism of the mission churches, for repudiating the established churches was also a symbolic rejection of the larger social system. In particular, the "key metaphor" of healing emphasized "the reintegration of matter and spirit, the practical agency of divine force, and the social relocation of the displaced." The outcome of this was that these movements had drawn together "everything that had been set apart in the black experience of colonialization and wage labor." These churches were not overtly political but formed a systematic counterculture that attempted both to encompass and to transform alienating structures of power and control. They were a creative response to the breakdown of traditional society, providing security and order in new social groupings. Whether the pentecostal pioneers were aware of this or not, the new movements they helped form affected profoundly the allocation of power and influence within their communities.[1]

However, an overemphasis on reaction to colonialism and racism may lead to reductionism, where religious causes are not given enough attention. The growth of independent pentecostal churches should be seen also and primarily as the result of a proclamation of a message addressing communities' tangible needs, a local response to the Bible. Instead of being *objects* of foreign mission reacting to that mission, indigenous pentecostal leaders were in fact the *subjects* of their own mission, actively involved in their own initiatives. The English Catholic historian

Adrian Hastings wrote that African independent churches should be seen in a continuous rather than a discontinuous relationship with missionary churches, precisely because they sought to reproduce what they saw as important in missionary Christianity. The process was primarily one of conversion to their cause, not of secession from the missionary churches. Although this is certainly an important observation and there were more similarities than differences between pentecostal and older churches, these considerations should not distract from the fact that pentecostal churches introduced many innovations to Christianity that the foreign missionaries had been unable to accomplish within the confines of their Western cultural paradigms. Harold Turner wrote that the prophet-healing movements in Africa were fundamentally spiritual and religious movements, and should be studied and evaluated in religious terms. Although we may not make an arbitrary or superficial distinction between religious and nonreligious factors in the emergence and growth of Pentecostalism, of the many factors accounting for their emergence and continuing growth, none are more significant than the religious ones. David Bosch writes of the "superficial, impoverished gospel" preached by Western missionaries that "did not even touch on many facets of the life or struggle of the African" and answered questions that Africans were not asking. "Salvation" was seen exclusively as the "saving of souls" from moral sins, so that Christianity was perceived as a religion with a list of taboos. This inability to be relevant to the daily struggles of ordinary people left people profoundly disillusioned with the form of Christianity that people had embraced after being persuaded by the missionaries to forsake their popular folk religions. This failure was especially acute in the area of sickness and healing, where the older missions' response was to simply provide medical facilities when they had the resources. No religious solution was given to the problem of sickness, and even the advent of medical missions tended to secularize healing to the realm of Western medical expertise and outside the sphere of religion. This created a vacuum that was later filled by the prophetic and pentecostal movements. In these and most communities in the majority world, religion could not be separated from the whole of life's experiences, and sickness and affliction were also religious experiences. These were to a large extent health-oriented communities, and in their pre-Christian religions, the most prominent rituals were those for healing and protection. Because healing and protection from evil are also prominent practices in the liturgy of many pentecostal churches and are important elements in their evangelism and church recruitment—especially in the early stages of their development—the pentecostal message of healing and deliverance proved popular in many of these communities.[2]

African theologians have pointed out that many African Christians felt that the church was not interested in their daily misfortunes and tangible problems. One of the greatest attractions provided by the pentecostals is their open invitations to bring local anxieties and paranoia about witches, sorcerers, bad luck, poverty, illness, and other kinds of misfortune to the church for relief. Daneel's research among Shona "Spirit" churches in Zimbabwe demonstrated the preponderance of religious causes for the appeal of these movements, highlighting such factors as adaptations to African rituals and customs, prophetic practices in detecting and removing malignant medicines and wizardry, and especially the practice of healing and exorcism. As a consequence of these and many similar situations throughout the majority world, new indigenous pentecostal leaders responded vigorously to what they experienced as a void left by rationalistic, older forms of Protestant Christianity that had initiated what amounted to the destruction of their ancient spiritual values, even if this had taken place unwittingly. Pobee and Ositelu write that African "Pentecostal" churches "reflect an African dissatisfaction with a Christianity that is too cerebral and does not manifest itself in acts of power in the Spirit and Spirit possession." The main characteristics of these churches, they argue, are their emphases on receiving a conscious experience of the Holy Spirit, healing and exorcism, their insistence on personal testimony, and their function as a "protest movement" against what they call "the North Atlantic captivity of the Christian faith." Indigenous pentecostal missionaries in the majority world proclaimed that God was not only in the business of "saving souls," but was also addressing physical affliction and deliverance from all kinds of oppressive forces and structures, providing answers to felt human needs. It was especially the message of healing from sickness, deliverance from the oppression of evil spirits, and the possibility of receiving the enablement of the Spirit to cope in a hostile spirit world, that was indeed good news. This was a religion that offered solutions to all of life's challenges, not only the so-called spiritual ones.[3]

To a large extent, independent pentecostal churches were created to address the problem of both foreignness and irrelevance. Their founders were convinced that they were providing a more genuine form of Christianity, for they believed that any religious institution that did not cater to daily life experiences would be spiritually empty. Powerful men and women throughout the global South, charismatic leaders who attracted followers through their preaching and healing attributed to the power of the Holy Spirit, founded many new pentecostal churches in the early twentieth century. This concept of a man or woman "of the Spirit" was a leading factor in the origin and growth of African independent "churches of the Spirit." Some of these leaders, like Garrick Braide in Nigeria, Wade Harris on the coast of Ghana and the Ivory Coast, and Simon Kimbangu in the Congo, did not intend to found new churches but were part of unanticipated mass movements toward Christianity all over Africa at the time, for which the foreign missions were unprepared. These leaders were seen as better able to meet the felt needs of the people than the foreign missionaries had been. But these movements were not so much secessions from or reactions to the mission churches as they were mass conversions or African "revivals," and the followers of these revival leaders and prophets only later organized themselves into denominations. In particular, the pentecostal churches that have arisen in the twentieth century, both new and older ones, have attributed their emergence to the work of the Holy Spirit. Among the most significant causes for the growth of Pentecostalism is their derivation from original, creative attempts to relate their "full gospel" in a meaningful and symbolically intelligible way to innermost needs. In so doing, they have succeeded in creating places where local people can be "at home." Comaroff reminds us, however, that these "religious" factors can only be understood with reference to the inclusive symbolic systems in which they arise. Not only did the emphasis that pentecostals place on the Spirit seem to "accord with indigenous notions of pragmatic spirit forces," but also it served to "redress the depersonalization and powerlessness of the urban labor experience." This may explain why pentecostal churches have succeeded in cities, at least from this sociological perspective. But the significant religious factors should not be overlooked in discussing the rise and development of Pentecostalism throughout the global South. However, we should not assume that these were the only causes, nor should we separate them from their larger context. Throughout the twentieth century, new Christian movements with radically different messages and orientations have arisen to challenge older ones. Nostalgic notions of the old, the traditional, and the rural should not be seen as more "authentic" or more "contextual" than the new, the modern, and the urban.[4]

Pentecostalism expanded rapidly in the global South during the first half of the twentieth century through the feverish efforts of many fragmented and missionizing groups. Pentecostal missionaries from the

global North differed in many ways from conventional Protestant missionaries, especially in their fierce independence, their sharing of a supernatural
worldview, and their conviction that their experience of the Spirit was all they
needed to evangelize the nations. In China, for example, they tapped into
what Daniel Bays describes as "the supernatural aspects of Chinese popular religions of the time." This was to characterize many forms of Chinese
Christianity thereafter, and Pentecostalism "with its radical egalitarianism
and its provision for direct revelation from God" for ordinary, unlearned
believers, as well as its anti-hierarchical stance, encouraged the formation of
independent churches. But the missionaries themselves were often assert-
ively independent of ecclesiastical organizations, a fact that could hardly
pass unnoticed by the local believers they influenced. As W.W. Simpson,
veteran missionary to China turned pentecostal, commenting on his resignation in 1913 from the Christian and Missionary Alliance (CMA), put it:
"While in the C.M.A. I had naturally conformed to their ways; now I was free
to do as the Lord wished. This vision was the Lord's instruction to do just
like the early preachers did from Pentecost onward." Inevitably, such subjective conclusions about the Lord's wishes sometimes led to autonomous
and misconstrued decisions made without regard to anyone else, often pre-
sumptuous and arrogant, forming the seeds of schism. The consequent rise
of independent denominations and frequent and sometimes scandalous
divisions within Pentecostalism soon made it the most diverse and fragmented movement within world Christianity. Curiously—but perhaps not
unexpectedly—it was this very fragmentation that caused its growth, while
it confounded any possibility of a distinct pentecostal identity.[5]

The pentecostal and healing missions from which independent
churches emerged were themselves undergoing a process of fission,
inherent in the ecclesiological structures of these groups that saw every
congregation as an independent unit. The result was considerable confusion, so that the new Christians saw a multiplicity of denominations as
the norm, and the creation of many more new ones was but a natural
consequence. Hastings considers the entire African independent church
movement to be "clearly a very Protestant movement," emerging and continuing from a string of denominations and secessions in Britain and the
United States. The tendency for Catholics to be more resistant to schism
might be partly attributable to their rigid, central hierarchical system,
which, before Vatican II did not favor the ideal of an "indigenous church."
They also had a different attitude toward the Bible, which for them did
not exist as an independent source of authority apart from the church

and therefore apart from the European missionary priest. Since Vatican II, Catholic spirituality, with its focus on and prayer for the unity of the church, has also attributed to a resistance to schism.[6]

Questions of Origins

The seeds of pentecostal transnationalization can also be found in the early years of the century. Most pentecostal groups in these years had not yet emerged as fully fledged denominations and were in competition with each other in the global religious market. But these various groups were united in their conviction that they had a mission to share their special message with the world. The pentecostal revival resulted in a category of ordinary, untrained, often ignorant people named "missionaries" who were "called" in the various revival movements they were part of, and who spread out to every corner of the globe within a remarkably short time. Many of the early missionaries were independent and had none of the financial backing provided by Western mission agencies. Most of them fully intended to go permanently to the countries they were called to and some died there. The Western missionaries who went to the majority world not only reproduced the many denominations of the West, but in some cases, actually created separate denominations. This was glaringly obvious in Africa, where almost every Protestant missionary group established itself and no comity agreements were observed until much later. Various mission groups competed with and even slandered one another, had different qualifications for membership and leadership, and different disciplinary regulations. Consequently, it was relatively easy to switch membership from one denomination to another.[7]

The many different factors that might account for the *origins* of Pentecostalism must always be distinguished from those that might explain its subsequent *growth*, as they are not usually the same. It is undoubtedly true that the earliest independent pentecostal denominations formed as revival movements that were reacting to the dry formalism and rationalism of the older churches. Independent churches in the majority world seceded from Western-dominated forms of Christianity for similar reasons. Many of them felt that the older churches had "lost the Spirit" and their new churches were created to restore the practice of gifts of the Spirit. But this does not explain why some of these movements continued to grow profusely among those who had never belonged to any other church. None of the causative factors can be isolated from the others, as a wide number of different causes can result in the emergence of a particular form of Pentecostalism, and equally as many reasons exist to explain its subsequent growth. As far as the expansion of Pentecostalism in the global South is concerned, it is necessary to view the question of causation within the macro-context of colonialism during the late nineteenth and early twentieth centuries. It is not always easy to distinguish between what might be considered "background" factors from the more proximate "immediate" causes.

To illustrate this again with reference to Africa, the twentieth century was one of rapid social change, with industrialization and urbanization and a transition from a pre-colonial stage through a traumatic colonial one to an equally traumatic post-colonial political order. The situation was particularly aggravated during the colonial era with the imposition of discriminatory laws that created migratory labor, the loss of land, alienation, and impersonal mass housing. When the full impact of colonialism was felt, it resulted in a sense of oppression, disorientation, and marginalization that left people seeking to form new relationships in smaller social groups, where they could really belong and regain some sense of human dignity. It was in this situation that pentecostal revival movements were born. The independent churches that formed early on provided what has been described as a "place to feel at home." This was most noticeable in South Africa which had the largest settler community on the continent and the deliberate social engineering of apartheid. But residential, educational, and social segregation existed almost everywhere in Africa during European colonization, rendering Africans second-class citizens in their own land. Worse, this discrimination and segregation also extended to the churches, many of whose leaders accepted uncritically the sociopolitical status quo and the paradigms of colonialism. As a result, little attempt was made to give African church leaders any real authority. Hastings writes of the racism present in the mission churches, where "even able and experienced [African] ministers remained second-class members of the Church, always inferior to the most junior missionary recently arrived from Britain." Comaroff describes the white Protestant leaders in South Africa who retained "strict paternalistic control over black congregations" which was "paradigmatic of hierarchical state structures at large."[8]

It will readily be seen how the question of origins is a complex one. By far the most widely publicized theories on the origins of Pentecostalism posit that it is a "made in America" religion. Stated simply, the theory is that Pentecostalism originated in the United States and expanded from there to the rest of the world. It is therefore an American religion in both its origins and its heart. This seems to fit its more recent forms, such as the "prosperity gospel," which sees wealth and capitalism as signs of God's favor. Most theories place the beginnings of Pentecostalism in nineteenth-century American radical evangelicalism, especially in the fringe groups within the holiness movement and among disenchanted Methodists. Depending on the position of the particular historian or hagiographer, global Pentecostalism was either born in the Church of God movement in the North Carolina Appalachian hills in the 1890s, in Charles Fox Parham's Apostolic Faith in Topeka, Kansas, in 1901, or, most commonly, in the Azusa Street revival in Los Angeles, 1906–09. The primacy of Azusa Street as the cradle of Pentecostalism over other American claims was established in the 1970s largely through the influence of Walter Hollenweger and his doctoral researchers in Birmingham. There had been a persistent racial bias against Azusa Street as a place of origin in white pentecostal historiography, because this was an African American mission to which whites and Hispanics flocked and where, in the oft-quoted words of eyewitness Frank Bartleman, "the color line was washed away in the blood." Hollenweger and his doctoral researchers set out to correct that bias, and did so successfully.[9]

The first quarter of the twentieth century was the formative period of Pentecostalism, before denominations were really established, and of central importance to this period was the Azusa Street revival. There the African American preacher William Joseph Seymour led twelve-hour-long services every day for three and a half years. People flocked there from all over North America and Mexico, and missionaries visited from far-flung countries and left as independent pentecostal missionaries. There is a direct connection between the Azusa Street revival and many of the first pentecostals who rapidly spread out to China, India, South Africa, and the Middle East, but these were by no means the only connections. Seymour was described as a meek and gracious man who even allowed his critics to speak to his congregation and advertised the meetings of his rivals. Seymour was spiritual father to thousands of early pentecostals in North America and for three years the revival was the most prominent center of Pentecostalism on the continent, further promoted by Seymour's periodical *The Apostolic Faith*, which reached an international circulation of 50,000 at its peak in 1908. People influenced by this revival started several new pentecostal centers in the Los Angeles area—by 1912 there were at least twelve. Hundreds of visitors came to see what was happening and to be baptized in the Spirit. Many of them began pentecostal centers in various other cities. People came from Latin America and Europe and missionaries came from Asia and Africa, and they went back with the "baptism" to their various countries. Pentecostal missionaries were sent out from Azusa Street to over twenty-five nations in two years, first to China, India, Japan, Egypt, Liberia, Angola, and South Africa. This was no mean achievement and the beginning of what is arguably the most significant global expansion of a Christian movement in the history of Christianity.

So, Seymour's Apostolic Faith Mission at Azusa Street was the most prominent and significant center of American Pentecostalism and was predominantly a black church rooted in African American culture. Hollenweger wrote that the main features of its spirituality were an oral liturgy, a narrative theology and witness, the maximum participation of the whole community in worship and service, the inclusion of visions and dreams into public worship, and an understanding of the relationship between body and mind manifested by healing through prayer. These expressions were a fundamental part of early Pentecostalism and remain in the movement to this day. Bartleman wrote of Azusa Street as the "American Jerusalem," the place from which Pentecostalism was expanding to the ends of the earth. Hollenweger wrote of the need to determine the origins of Pentecostalism from a theological or ideological perspective. Writers began to assert the important role of this predominantly African American church as the generator of pentecostal churches throughout the world. Cecil M. Robeck Jr. has definitively established the significance of Azusa Street and its leader William Seymour in global pentecostal history. There have been several theories on the origins of American Pentecostalism, and most of the recent ones place Azusa Street squarely at the center, although this has not gone unchallenged. But the question of origins has often been influenced by the ideological presuppositions of its propagators. Joe Creech refers to the "central myth of origin for almost every pentecostal denomination" that has placed Azusa Street in the middle of American pentecostal historiography and has overlooked or minimized other important centers of pentecostal expansion. Histories of Pentecostalism usually begin with American pioneers like Parham and Seymour and then emphasize the beginnings of Pentecostalism in other countries with reference to mostly white male missionaries sent from the United States or other Western countries. For example, the Canadian John G. Lake is credited with the founding of Pentecostalism in South Africa, the Americans Alfred G. Garr and George Berg with India, the Swedish Americans Gunnar Vingren and Daniel Berg and Italian American Luigi Francesconi with Brazil, British missionary William Burton with the Congo, and so on.[10]

Without underestimating the important role of these pioneers, it remains true that many historians have ignored, overlooked, or minimized the vital role of thousands of national workers and women in the global expansion of early Pentecostalism. A theory of origins in Los Angeles in 1906, while certainly having merit as far as some parts of the world are concerned, must be balanced by the equally convincing case of multiple, often unconnected religious and cultural origins. The macro-context must not be lost. Seen from this perspective, Pentecostalism is neither a movement with distinct beginnings in the United States or anywhere else, nor a movement based on a particular theology; it is rather a series of movements that have taken several years and several different formative ideas and events to emerge. Pentecostalism in its origins and causes is a multicentered and variegated phenomenon, best seen as historically related, revivalist movements where the emphasis is on the experience of the Spirit and the exercise of spiritual gifts. This more nuanced view will help us dispel the tendency to treat North American forms of Pentecostalism as normative, it will maximize our understanding of the impact and influence of local leadership in comparison to that of Western missionaries, and it will enable us to better understand the contextualization of the pentecostal message in different cultures, nations, and contemporary contexts. The many various revival movements worldwide were part of a series of events that catalyzed the emergence of worldwide pentecostal movements. A more nuanced, multicultural, and polycentric perspective on pentecostal origins will better reflect global realities and place different forms of Pentecostalism within their local contexts. Whatever the influence of American Pentecostalism and the Azusa Street revival might have been on world Pentecostalism then, there were other important forces in several regions giving the emerging movement a local character that tempered some of the globalizing forces at work. The stream of revivalist missionary fervor at the beginning of the twentieth century became a catalyst in many parts of the world for the acceptance of pentecostal ideas. The new movement was actually an extension of the evangelical missionary movement and was to become a major player in the remarkable transformation of world Christianity within a relatively short period.

The first issue of the Azusa Street revival newspaper revealed the essence of the pentecostal missionary thrust. "Many are speaking in new tongues," it declared, "and some are on their way to the foreign fields, with the gift of the language." In this way God was "solving the missionary problem, sending out new-tongued missionaries on the apostolic faith line, without purse or scrip, and the Lord is going before them preparing the way." The "missionary problem" was how to get enough missionaries out all over the world in the shortest possible time without any unnecessarily irritating delays like theological preparation and language learning. Pentecostals believed they had this short-cut to missionary preparedness. They continued the revivalist emphases of the movements out of which they emerged, convinced that they were involved in a worldwide revival that was preceding the imminent coming of Christ. They used biblical texts from the Acts of the Apostles (Acts 2:4 in particular) to proclaim that the evidence of their receiving the Spirit was to speak in new tongues— for some this meant speaking the languages of the nations without the need for prior study. Charles Parham, William Seymour, and many of the first American pentecostals believed they had been given foreign languages through the experience of Spirit baptism so that they could preach the gospel throughout the world. Hundreds did just that and went out believing that they would immediately be able to preach in the languages of the nations. Most of these newly-gifted missionary linguists made haste to travel to China, India, and Africa with a language they would later discover they did not have. Apart from isolated instances when it was claimed that they had actually spoken in known languages, most admitted that they were unable to speak any local languages and some returned home, thoroughly disillusioned.[11]

Early pentecostal missionaries followed their revivalist compatriots in thinking of "mission" as "foreign mission" (mostly cross-cultural, from "white" to "others"), and they were mostly untrained and inexperienced. Their only qualification was the baptism in the Spirit and a divine call; their motivation was to evangelize the world before the imminent coming of Christ—and so evangelism was more important than education, "civilization," or charitable works. In common with the missionary ethos of the day, pentecostal workers from the Western world usually saw their mission in terms of moving from a civilized, Christian "home" to a Satanic and pagan foreign land, where sometimes their own personal difficulties, prejudices (and possible failures) in adapting to a radically different culture, living conditions, and religion were projected in their newsletters home. These newsletters were written for the primary purpose of raising financial and prayer support, and sometimes they were remarkably frank. The missionaries went out, like many other missionaries before them, with a fundamental conviction that the Western world was a Christian realm, that they were sent as light to darkness, and that the ancient cultures and religions of the nations to which they were sent were heathen, pagan, and demonic, to be conquered for Christ. This was part of their evangelical conviction that "heathen idolatry" was a manifestation of rebellion against the true God. In this they were no different from their evangelical compatriots. Of course there were political and social factors facilitating the early growth of Pentecostalism, but the primary motivation of the first pentecostals was religious and eschatological.

The first two decades of the pentecostal movement were marked by feverish and often admirable and sacrificial missionary activities. The first American missionaries that went out only five months after the Azusa Street revival began were self-supporting and most of them were women. John G. Lake, a Canadian evangelist and former elder in John Alexander Dowie's Zion City, traveled to South Africa from Indianapolis in 1908 with Thomas Hezmalhalch, himself an Azusa Street convert. After arriving in Johannesburg they established the Apostolic Faith Mission, now the largest classical pentecostal denomination in that country. In 1909 the message was taken from the pentecostal movement in Chicago of William Durham (who became pentecostal at Azusa Street) to South America, first to Italian communities in Argentina and Brazil by Luigi Francesconi. Then in 1910, two Swedish Baptist immigrants who also had connections with Durham, Gunnar Vingren and Daniel Berg, began what became the Assemblies of God in Brazil, now the largest non-Catholic denomination in Latin America and the largest Assemblies of God in any nation. These and many others were all important figures in the early spread of Pentecostalism.

Despite all these important connections, to focus on the United States in the debate on the origins of Pentecostalism is, in my view, to miss the point and distort the facts. The previous chapter established the Mukti Mission as one of the most important early formative centers of Pentecostalism, and it shares this importance with Azusa Street. But Pentecostalism did not arise in a single event, place, or phenomenon; it was a movement that crossed national and ethnic boundaries and resulted in a plethora of different types of revivalist Christianity in the twentieth century. Stepping back a little in history, as we did in the previous chapter, will reveal that "typically" pentecostal manifestations of healing, tongues, and prophecies were evident in nineteenth-century Christianity in several countries. By 1905, Western evangelical periodicals were reporting on revivals in Wales and India, heightening expectations that these revivals would spread worldwide as a sign of the last days. Elisabeth Sisson, a former missionary who was soon to join the pentecostal movement, wrote of the Welsh revival as the beginnings of a worldwide revival on "all flesh," the "latter rain" prophesied by the prophet Joel. Minnie Abrams wrote of a whole sequence of interconnected revivals, from Torrey's meetings in Australia in 1903–04, to the Welsh Revival and the Indian revivals, and from Mukti to Korea, Manchuria, and the rest of China. Holiness periodicals like J. H. King's *Live Coals* and A. B. Crumpler's *The Holiness Advocate* reported on the series of revivals in India, Bartleman documented the influence that the Indian revivals had on their expectations for Los Angeles, and *The Apostolic Faith* declared only months after the beginning of its own Azusa Street revival, "Pentecost has come and is coming in India, and thank God in many other places." During the decade following, revival movements were occurring in China, West Africa, and East Africa that were quite independent of Western pentecostals and resulting in vibrant new churches developing along their own historical trajectories.[12]

Classical Pentecostal Denominations

Pentecostalism did not begin as a denomination or schism from other Protestant churches but rather as a hodgepodge of assorted individuals who shared a common experience of Spirit baptism and were largely rejected by their fellow Christians. At first, they were opposed to creating new denominations, but as their ostracism increased, their attitudes hardened and they sought ways to work together. Over time, denominations began to arise. In North America, the holiness movement had given birth to a multiplicity of new churches in the late nineteenth century, and it was in this pluralistic milieu that Pentecostalism arose. Between 1895 and 1905, over twenty holiness denominations were set up, including the Church of God (1886), the Christian and Missionary Alliance (1887), the Church of the Nazarene (1895), and the Pilgrim Holiness Church (1897)—thus creating a precedent for the further fragmentation that was to occur. However, the oldest form of American Pentecostalism, the Holiness ("three-stage") pentecostals began in existing church organizations and emerged as pentecostal denominations in the first decade of the twentieth century as the Church of God in Christ, the Church of God (Cleveland), and the Pentecostal Holiness Church. These churches held that a distinct experience of sanctification was needed in addition to conversion and Spirit baptism. "Finished Work" ("two-stage") pentecostals were stimulated by the preaching of William Durham in Chicago, who taught that salvation was a complete process that included sanctification and was followed by Spirit baptism. The scattered remnants of Baptists, Christian and Missionary Alliance, Dowie's Zionists, and other independent evangelicals with a "Finished Work" experience coalesced in 1914 to form the Assemblies of God. This new movement, which eschewed denominationalism, underwent its first major schism in 1916, when the Oneness pentecostals left eventually to form the Pentecostal Assemblies of the World and later, the United Pentecostal Church. The process of schism and proliferation was set in motion in American Pentecostalism and was to multiply thousands of times throughout the world. Other major denominations would be formed in the next thirty years, but in many countries, new national denominations were to spring up that often dwarfed the American-originating ones in size and influence.[13]

Several different American pentecostal denominations trace their origins to Azusa Street, including the largest: the Church of God in Christ (COGIC) and the Assemblies of God (AG). However, in the case of COGIC, the denomination itself was constituted in 1897 by African Americans Charles H. Mason (1866–1961) and C. P. Jones, former Baptists who had embraced the Holiness position of entire sanctification. Mason visited Azusa Street in 1907 and received Spirit baptism, after which the denomination split over the issue of tongues as evidence and Jones organized the Church of Christ (Holiness), while Mason was elected overseer of COGIC. Because COGIC was already an officially registered church in 1907, Mason issued preaching credentials to much of the American pentecostal movement. Many of the first leaders in the AG had Mason's credentials and COGIC had an equal number of black and white ministers and members until the founding of the AG in 1914. Mason had considerable abilities and organized his church with bishops and overseers in most regions of the United States; the church grew tenfold between 1930 and 1960. After a seven-year dispute following his death, Mason was eventually succeeded as presiding bishop in 1968 by his son-in-law J. O. Patterson, who remained in office until his death in 1989. During Patterson's tenure, the church again grew tenfold to become the largest pentecostal denomination and second largest African American denomination in the United States.

The Assemblies of God (AG)—which began an aggressive missionary thrust after its organization in Hot Springs, Arkansas, in 1914—and its independent "district councils" and associated national denominations— collectively constitutes the largest pentecostal group in the contemporary world. The AG in Brazil is by far the largest of the AG denominations, and several other large denominations seceded from there too. The AG's connections to Azusa Street are more indirect than those of COGIC. With its strong emphasis on local and regional government, the AG was created to counter the extreme individualism developing in Pentecostalism— whether it succeeded ultimately in eliminating individualism is doubtful. It appears that the invitation to attend the founding convention was issued only to white, mostly southern pentecostal leaders, with the exception of G. T. Haywood from Indianapolis, who later became the presiding bishop of the first Oneness denomination, the Pentecostal Assemblies of the World. Charles H. Mason attended only as a guest at the Hot Springs convention and preached to the gathering of over 400 preachers. Many missionaries already serving overseas sought affiliation with the new movement, which initially resisted adopting either a constitution or a statement of faith. It was inevitable that in such a highly individualized and subjective environment, conflict would arise, and two early doctrinal controversies split the AG. The "Oneness" or "New Issue" controversy had been brewing since a convention in the Los Angeles area in 1913, but in 1916 open hostility resulted in the secession of the non-Trinitarian group. Oneness pentecostals reject the traditional Christian doctrine of "separate but equal" Persons in the Trinity and believe that Jesus is the revelation of God the Father and that the Spirit proceeds from the Father revealed in Jesus. Unlike the traditional notion that Jesus is the human name of Christ, in Oneness teaching Jesus is the New Testament name of the one God of the Old Testament (Yahweh), who reveals His immanence in the incarnation of Jesus and His transcendence in the presence of the Spirit.[14]

In 1918 another debate took place over "initial evidence" in which healing evangelist and AG Executive member F. F. Bosworth was forced to resign. Bosworth argued that speaking in tongues was one of the gifts of the Spirit but did not necessarily constitute the initial evidence of Spirit baptism. As a result of these and other disputes the AG became more rigid on doctrinal issues and formulated a "Statement of Fundamental Truths" in 1916, eventually enshrining the doctrine of the Trinity and "initial evidence" as essential teachings of the denomination. Gradually there was a shift to centralization at the headquarters in Springfield, Missouri. In 1929 the denomination adopted its first constitution and Ernest Swing Williams (1885–1981), a former convert of Azusa Street, became its first general superintendent, a post he held until 1949. In 1942 the AG joined the newly formed National Association of Evangelicals (NAE), a move that was to identify the denomination increasingly with conservative evangelicalism. Thomas Zimmerman (1912–91), general superintendent from 1959 to 1985, was one of the most significant AG leaders who stressed church growth and identification with Evangelicalism; he presided over the AG's steady transition to a middle-class denomination. The Pentecostal Assemblies of Canada (PAOC) began as a Oneness denomination in 1919 but joined the AG the following year, a move that caused the Oneness pentecostals to leave. In 1925 the PAOC separated from the AG in order to pursue its own missionary policy, and PAOC missionaries established national churches in many parts of the world, sometimes in the same regions in which AG missionaries were operating. The AG continued to expand worldwide, particularly through its Division of Foreign Missions in the post-colonial period. In thirty years (1960–89) as its executive director, J. Philip Hogan (1915–2002) presided over the growth of the AG worldwide from 3 million in 1960 to an estimated 30 million in the 1990s. When asked to give the reason for this tenfold growth, Hogan replied:

> The concept of the indigenous church has been one of the major keys in the growth of Assemblies of God foreign missions. The Division of Foreign Missions has continued the vision of our founding fathers that we would produce national churches that are self-supporting and self-governing. Most of the pioneer missionaries had the idea of producing national churches. We were able to build on that principle, and that's one of the reasons why there are 30 million people today in the Assemblies of God around the world. In the beginning we never set out to build an American or a Western organization, but to build indigenous churches.[15]

Another international pentecostal denomination is the Church of God (CG, Cleveland, Tennessee), a holiness church with roots in the Christian Union founded by R. G. Spurling in 1886 in Tennessee. A revival in this movement in Cherokee County, North Carolina, in 1896 was accompanied by healings and (according to some reports) speaking in tongues by

130 people, many of whom were Cherokee Native Americans living in the Appalachian hills. Some CG historians link this event with the emergence of their denomination, but some of the early events are obscure. In 1902 the church became the Holiness Church, and in 1907 was named the Church of God when the headquarters moved to Cleveland, Tennessee, under Ambrose J. Tomlinson (1865–1943). In 1908 the CG became pentecostal when G. B. Cashwell, who had received Spirit baptism at Azusa Street, brought this experience to Cleveland. In 1909 Tomlinson became the CG's first General Overseer and the church's first missionaries were sent to the Bahamas the following year. In 1920 the denomination's Assembly accepted the proposal that Tomlinson, "General Overseer for Life" since 1914, be given unrestricted control. Resulting tensions led to Tomlinson's expulsion from the church and his founding a rival Church of God in 1923, while the leadership of the CG passed to Flavius J. Lee. A protracted legal battle between the two Churches of God in Cleveland over property and the name of the church ended only in 1952, when it was declared that Tomlinson's faction would be known as the Church of God of Prophecy (CGP). When A. J. Tomlinson died in 1943, his son Milton A. Tomlinson (1906–95) became general overseer of the CGP, a position he held until 1990. The CGP has been perhaps the most integrated classical pentecostal denomination in the United States and has remained true to the conservative ethical principles of the Tomlinsons, resulting in the withdrawal of many middle-class white Americans in the 1990s. In contrast to the CGP, in 1926 the black and white congregations in the CG were segregated and there is a separate black CG organization in Florida to this day. The CG and CGP underwent further splits, so that ten separate smaller denominations emerged. The CG joined the NAE at its inauguration in 1942, but the CGP did not join. As a result of the extensive work of both the CG and the CGP in the Caribbean and the migration of Caribbean people to Britain, there the CG is called the New Testament Church of God (NTCG), and the NTCG and the CGP have been the largest black-led denominations in Britain.[16]

The Pentecostal Holiness Church (PHC) formed as a result of a merger between two Holiness groups: the Fire-Baptized Holiness Church founded by Benjamin Irwin in 1895, and the Holiness Church of North Carolina founded by Ambrose Crumpler in 1898. When Irwin resigned suddenly from the Fire-Baptized leadership in 1890, his assistant Joseph H. King (1869–1946) took over. A further merger took place in 1915 when the Tabernacle Pentecostal Church (founded in 1898 by N. J. Holmes) joined the denomination. G. B. Cashwell, a minister in Crumpler's church, began preaching the pentecostal message to all three groups, who rapidly accepted it. Crumpler did not, and he resigned from the Holiness Church, after which Cashwell became leader. In 1909 the name of the Holiness Church was changed to Pentecostal Holiness Church, and the merger with the Fire-Baptized church was completed in 1911. J. H. King was general superintendent of the church from 1917 until his death in 1945, and in 1937 his title was changed to Bishop. The PHC joined the NAE in 1943. Bishop J. A. Synan, father of the well-known pentecostal historian Vinson Synan, was leader of the church from 1950 to 1969. One of the best-known ministers in the PHC was the evangelist Oral Roberts (1918–2009), who began his tent campaigns in 1948 but left the denomination to join the United Methodist Church in 1969. The church added the prefix "International" to its name in 1975.[17]

Pentecostal denominations in Europe emerged even more slowly. In a matter of months after his return to Europe from his pentecostal experience in New York, Norwegian Methodist T. B. Barratt was holding meetings in Sunderland, England. Barratt was the founder and prime motivator of early Pentecostalism in Europe. The new teachings he brought back to Norway from his Spirit baptism experience were unacceptable to his bishops and he was eventually forced to leave the Methodist Episcopal Church and found a fellowship of independent churches. Barratt also drew large crowds to his meetings throughout Europe. He sent missionaries to Sweden and Germany, and went himself to visit the Middle East and India. He wrote to the Hoovers in Chile, encouraging them (and all he came in contact with) to establish self-governing, self-supporting, and self-propagating churches. Unlike the hierarchical Pentecostalism that was to develop in North America, Barratt's churches and those planted by many missionaries from Europe were strictly independent and congregational. Barratt submitted himself to baptism by immersion by the Swedish Baptist, later pentecostal pastor Lewi Pethrus in 1913. Barratt's ministry also had a social impact by caring for the poor, the homeless, children, and the elderly; and he was a prolific writer, especially in his periodicals. By 1910, Norwegian pentecostal missionaries had already gone to India, China, South Africa, and South America.[18]

In Sweden, Norway, and Finland Pentecostalism quickly grew in size until it was second only to the Lutheran state churches. Barratt made several visits to Sweden, and Lewi Pethrus's Filadelfia Church in Stockholm was the largest pentecostal congregation in the world until the 1960s when churches in Chile and Korea overtook it. Pethrus (1884–1974) became pentecostal after visiting Barratt in Oslo in 1907. Opposition from his home denomination occurred gradually, until he and his Filadelfia Church were expelled from the Baptist denomination in 1913. Pethrus remained Baptist in ecclesiology, a strong advocate of the independence of the local church with no outside interference or denominational organization. This principle has influenced Scandinavian pentecostal churches and missions all over the world. For forty-seven years Pethrus pastored the Filadelfia Church, which had over 6,000 adult members. His output was prodigious. During that time he established a rescue mission (1911), a publishing house (1912), a Bible school (1915), and a secondary school (1942); he edited a daily Christian newspaper *Dagen* (1945), wrote some fifty books, and established a bank (1952) and a radio station broadcasting in twenty-three languages from North Africa (1955). He was probably the most influential pentecostal in Europe during his lifetime and was open to ecumenical contact of various kinds.[19] Pentecostalism expanded to most countries in Europe. The AG in Portugal, planted by missionaries from Brazil, was to become the largest non-Catholic denomination there until about 2000, when the Brazilian church of Edir Macedo, the Universal Church of the Kingdom of God, had become larger. Portuguese AG congregations were also established wherever Portuguese people had migrated, in places like Johannesburg, South Africa.

There were several factors at work preparing the way for Pentecostalism to enter Britain. England was the home of the Keswick Conventions, which had taught a distinct baptism in the Spirit as "enduement with power," a sudden experience of spiritual power for witnessing. The Welsh Revival (1904–05) followed this teaching and brought an estimated 100,000 people into Christian churches in Wales. Its leader Evan Roberts had an ecstatic experience of "baptism in the Spirit." Many leading British pentecostals like George and Stephen Jeffreys, and Donald Gee were converted through this revival, and Anglicans Alexander Boddy and Cecil Polhill, leader of the Pentecostal Missionary Union, visited it. Although a rift developed between pentecostal and holiness groups, especially through the opposition and writings of the influential Jessie Penn-Lewis, the influence of Keswick and the Welsh Revival on the emergence of British Pentecostalism was considerable, creating an expectation for revival throughout Britain and Europe. The leader of Pentecostalism in Britain, Alexander A. Boddy (1854–1930), vicar at All Saints in Monkwearmouth, Sunderland, since 1886, visited the revival under T. B. Barratt in Oslo in early 1907. He compared it to the time when he had been with Evan Roberts during the Welsh Revival but said that the scenes in Norway were "more supernatural." Boddy believed that "very soon we shall witness the same in England." He invited Barratt to preach in his parish in September that year. When Barratt accepted and held special meetings in the church hall, many of the people who had gathered received Spirit baptism. Boddy's church became the most significant early pentecostal center in Britain, and he provided the leadership and direction that shaped its future. Annual Whitsun (Pentecost) conventions from 1908 to 1914 drew pentecostals from all over Britain and continental Europe, including Barratt and leaders from the Netherlands and Germany. Boddy edited the widely influential periodical *Confidence* (1908–26), which reported on the Pentecostal revivals all over the world and expounded the doctrine of Spirit baptism and spiritual gifts. Although Boddy was acknowledged leader of British Pentecostalism before World War I, he remained an Anglican minister until his death. From his church the Pentecostal Missionary Union for Great Britain and Ireland (PMU) was formed in 1909, and led by Cecil Polhill (1860–1938), a former missionary (since 1885) to southwestern China with the China Inland Mission. Polhill was baptized in the Spirit during a visit to the Upper Room in Los Angeles in early 1908. Through an inheritance, he was now a wealthy landowner and avid supporter of pentecostal missions. He bought a large house in London to hold pentecostal services and organized annual conventions that lasted through the war years.[20]

William Oliver Hutchinson, a Baptist preacher who had received Spirit baptism in Sunderland in 1908, opened the first purpose-built pentecostal hall in Britain in the same year, the independent Emmanuel Mission in Bournemouth. Hutchinson founded the first Pentecostal denomination in Britain, the Apostolic Faith Church (AFC), in 1911. It is likely that former Congregationalist preacher in the Welsh Revival, George Jeffreys (1889–1962), received Spirit baptism at Emmanuel Mission in 1910. The AFC became increasingly a personality cult around its leader and imbibed British Israelism (the belief that the British and related people were descendants of the lost tribes of Israel) and other teachings rejected by most early pentecostals. Daniel P. Williams led the first secession of most of the Welsh congregations to form the Apostolic Church of Wales in 1916. James Brooke was to lead another secession from the AFC in 1926 to form the United Apostolic Faith Church. The AFC would fall into obscurity and the other two British Apostolic denominations would remain small in Britain, but they performed significant work overseas,

especially in Africa. The healing evangelist Smith Wigglesworth (1860–
1947) received Spirit baptism in Boddy's church and became an international preacher. George Jeffreys was founder of what would become
the Elim Pentecostal Church and his brother Steven Jeffreys became
an evangelist in the Assemblies of God. George Jeffreys was trained at
the PMU college in Preston in 1912–13 under Polhill's sponsorship. One
of his fellow students was William F. P. Burton, founder of the Congo
Evangelistic Mission. Successful evangelistic meetings held by George
and Stephen Jeffreys in South Wales in 1913 put the Jeffreys brothers
on the national stage. George Jeffreys has been described as the greatest British pentecostal evangelist ever, whose meetings attracted many
thousands with remarkable healings and great numbers of conversions,
especially in the 1930s. British pentecostals experienced significant
growth during their first forty years.

George Jeffreys founded the Elim Evangelistic Band in Belfast,
Northern Ireland, in 1915, renamed the Elim Pentecostal Alliance in
1918, after which a central council governed the organization. Jeffreys
remained in Ireland until 1921, only making occasional visits to Britain,
and by this time there were twenty-two churches in the region. Jeffreys
did not intend to form a denomination and discouraged proselytizing,
but the nature of the movement led inevitably to denominationalism.
After 1921 Jeffreys began planting churches in England and Wales and
moved his headquarters to London; a number of churches joined Elim.
From 1926 until the 1990s, Elim held its annual Easter Convention
in the Royal Albert Hall in London (then seating 10,000), and Aimee
Semple McPherson was the first invited guest speaker. In 1929 the Elim
name was changed again to Elim Foursquare Gospel Alliance, apparently
being inspired by McPherson's movement. From 1934, Jeffreys began to
lose his tight control over the Elim leadership and his support of local
church government versus the centralized system that had developed.
The British Israel theory espoused by Jeffreys led to his resignation from
Elim in 1939 and a schism, when the Bible Pattern Church Fellowship
was created. The majority of ministers and members remained in the
Elim movement, but it took a long time to recover. In more recent years,
the Elim Pentecostal Church (as it is now known) has had to adjust to
the challenges posed by the Charismatic movement and to the question
of the authority of the local church, but has emerged, along with the
Assemblies of God, as the largest classical Pentecostal denomination in
the United Kingdom.[21]

The Assemblies of God in Great Britain and Ireland (AGBI), distinct from its namesake in the United States, emerged in 1924 as a congregational association of autonomous churches under the chairmanship of J. Nelson Parr (1886–1976). These assemblies were highly suspicious of the centralized control in the Elim movement, and George Jeffreys was not invited to be part of the new group. Parr, baptized in the Spirit in Boddy's church in 1910, issued the invitation to a meeting of fourteen leaders in Aston, Birmingham, in 1924 when the AGBI was formed, with the seventy-four assemblies that joined the association guaranteeing autonomy to each local church. The AGBI specifically declared itself pacifist, another reason for the break with the patriotic Anglicans Boddy and Polhill, and like its American counterpart (and unlike Elim), also preached the doctrine of the "initial evidence" of tongues. In 1925, following the departure of Polhill and Boddy, the PMU joined to become the missionary arm of the AGBI. Donald Gee (1891–1966), a pastor in Leith, Edinburgh, was chairman of the AGBI from 1948 until his death in 1966. His overtures to nonpentecostal churches and his support of David du Plessis's ecumenical efforts earned him the opposition of the American AG. Gee traveled internationally and was the organizer of the European Pentecostal conference held in Stockholm in 1939 (the first such meeting since Amsterdam, 1921) and the first World Pentecostal Conference (WPC) in Zürich in 1947. A prolific author, he was also the first editor of the WPC's periodical *Pentecost* and one of the most influential pentecostal leaders of his time.[22]

With the mass immigration of people from the West Indies to Britain after 1951, African Caribbean pentecostal churches were set up and grew remarkably during the 1960s. The main churches had links with the Caribbean and the United States, but many new independent churches were also formed, resulting in a great variety of churches among African Caribbeans, and later in the African communities in Britain. Later migrations after 1960 resulted in a number of West African pentecostal churches being established in Britain (especially Nigerian ones) and elsewhere in Europe. Black Pentecostal immigrants felt unwelcome in British churches partly because of the cultural differences between the community-oriented Africans and African Caribbeans and the more reserved and individualistic English, but also because of the incipient racism present in British society. The first New Testament Church of God was formed in Wolverhampton in 1953 by Oliver Lyseight, A. D. Brown and G. S. Peddie. By 1961 there were already eighty African Caribbean churches in Britain, mostly Pentecostal, and this was before the period of their greatest expansion. They have been extremely influential within the British church context. Since the 1960s, African-led denominations have expanded in Britain and throughout Western Europe and North America. Most of them have retained their African identity and provided places to be at home for African migrants. Some of these African-led congregations are among the largest in Europe.

As the various pentecostal denominations organized themselves in the early twentieth century, there was always an emphasis on moving out, establishing new congregations, and supporting missions, which were seen as an essential function of and inseparable from the church. From the 1920s onward, the classical pentecostals and the independent denominations founded in the global South began their steady expansion. Some were far more successful than others depending on the means and the volunteers available. The American AG, for example, because it succeeded in winning experienced missionaries for its cause, quickly established itself as a global movement with agents throughout the global South. By the outbreak of the Second World War in 1939, the Assemblies of God in its various forms was the largest pentecostal denomination in the world, even though its growth had been modest. By 1951 it had an estimated 318,000 members worldwide. The growth thereafter can only be described as astonishing. By the 1990s it was the largest or second-largest Protestant denomination in over forty countries. By the end of the century many of its most prominent leaders were from the majority world. Estimates of its combined membership for 2010 exceeded 60 million, the vast majority (some 85 percent) of which were in the global South. Everett Wilson describes the first ever meeting of the World Assemblies of God Fellowship in Seoul, Korea, in October 1994, an association which at its founding had sixty autonomous and loosely affiliated national groupings of churches and now has 150. The venue in Seoul was "10,000 miles and culturally half a world away from the Midwestern town of Springfield, Missouri." Although the largest, the AG is but one of many pentecostal churches that has expanded into many countries worldwide. The Church of God (Cleveland) states that it has a "presence" in nearly 150 countries; and the Foursquare Church claims to operate in nearly 140 countries. But it is not only from the West that this expansion occurs. Within these denominations there is expansion from the South to other parts of the globe, and denominations founded in Africa, Asia, and Latin America plant congregations in the global North as well as elsewhere in the South.[23]

The earliest pentecostals understood their movement in eschatological terms, the divine breaking into history of a movement of the Spirit to revive a dead church, evangelize all nations, and prepare for the imminent second coming of Christ. Since the first academic studies on Pentecostalism, writers have speculated on the causes for its emergence and growth. A great many opinions on the subject are highly selective, subjective, and reductionist, depending on what particular interest or experience they reflect. It is necessary to adequately examine the religious and theological factors in the remarkable expansion of Pentecostalism. Contemporary Pentecostalism, whether in its "classical," "charismatic," or "neocharismatic" form, has spread all over the world and has affected every type of Christianity. Christianity will never be the same again.

Missions and Migration

The Context of Missionary Expansion

We have seen that pentecostal and revivalist Christianity is inherently expansionist or "missionary." The missionary enthusiasm was founded on religious convictions and a sense of eschatological destiny. The Holy Spirit had been given in power in the revival of these last days to enable the preaching of the pentecostal message to the ends of the earth. In this chapter I trace some of the ways in which this enthusiasm played out on the world stage by looking at some central actors and prominent areas of activity in early Pentecostalism. Although the early pentecostal missionaries talked of the "heathen" in contrast to the "civilized" nations of the North, their focus on human depravity knew no geographical boundaries and only a "born-again" conversion experience and a radical break with the past could save individuals from inevitable doom. These missionaries were often regarded by colonial authorities as independent religious mavericks, and unlike most other foreign missionaries, their links to colonial powers were often tenuous as they had no official recognition for many years. Few of them set up mission compounds, but when they did, they were usually in close proximity to the communities among whom they worked. Some, in contrast to many of their Protestant counterparts, deliberately chose to live in "native" houses or were forced to do so because of lack of funding; some immediately began living and working with orphans in these houses and setting up rudimentary schools. Pentecostal single women missionaries in India lived with Indian women workers. All these things endeared them to those who were suffering under colonial racism and gave local Christians opportunities to break free from what were often regarded as colonial churches. The creation of independent churches in sub-Saharan

Africa, China, and India (inter alia) was one of the consequences of these developments, and most of these churches were pentecostal. In short, Pentecostalism had a global orientation from its beginning. As one pentecostal newspaper remarked, God was "picking people up everywhere, out of all nations and out of all denominations."[1]

Catholic missionary priests generally had much greater authority and higher qualifications than Protestant missionaries. The high entrance requirements and commitment expected of Catholic priests, including celibacy, tended to insulate them from rival authorities. By contrast, Protestant churches encouraged a local ministry requiring only a minimum of theological training, a feature that favored the emergence of indigenous and independent churches. In addition, the greater emphasis placed by Catholics on ritual made this form of Christianity attractive to many Africans whose customary religions abounded in many different kinds of rituals. Independent churches seceding from Protestant churches in Africa often became more like Catholics in their emphasis on ritual, as well as in episcopal ecclesiology. But even more important, Catholic missionaries were more accommodating toward traditional customs (including ancestor rituals), which often were assimilated into the church in modified forms, whereas Protestant missionaries tended to confront and reject what they considered "pagan" customs. Marthinus Daneel thinks the reason is theological; Catholic "natural theology" has greater flexibility than Protestantism, which emphasizes "the total corruption" of human nature and stresses the need to make a "radical break with paganism and hence with traditional values."[2]

Hundreds of pentecostal missionaries set out from North America and Western Europe, especially Britain, Scandinavia, and the Netherlands. By 1914, only eight years after the Azusa Street revival, there were Western pentecostal missionaries in over forty countries in Asia, Africa, Latin America, and in some Pacific and Caribbean islands. The cultural and religious contexts of these missionaries must be given serious consideration in any discussion of the changing nature of Christianity during the twentieth century. Although they were not as closely associated with colonial governments as their more "respectable" and generally better-educated Protestant counterparts were, and although their attitudes and activities were probably not as greatly influenced by imperialism and colonialism, pentecostal missionaries who hailed from the same background did not escape these dangers. Their Christocentric message was very similar to that of their evangelical contemporaries, but like them, these missionaries living and working in the zenith of European colonial expansion and imperialism were beset by a host of problems, presuppositions, and prejudices on the mission field.[3]

Standardization of pentecostal missionary practices occurred gradually and the printed periodicals played a vital role, facilitating the early missionary migration and the rapid globalization of Pentecostalism. Often the only link with any form of organization was through these periodicals, which served a fourfold function. First, they provided missionaries with information on their home bases (such as they were) and the movement's progress worldwide. Second, they were the means of disseminating information about the work of the missionaries to a much wider audience than the local church that produced them. This was aided by the promotion of conventions at which the missionary cause was highlighted and missionaries on furlough promoted their work and appealed for more workers and funds to support them. Third, the periodicals were a channel for raising funds for the support of the missionaries, and they published regular accounts of donations given for this purpose. Many of the early periodicals saw the promotion of pentecostal missions to be one of the chief reasons for their existence. Fourth, and perhaps most important, they were the means by which a pentecostal meta-culture was formed in these early years, a meta-culture that was laid down for posterity and would shape the next century of pentecostal expansion. As this developed it would include not only missionary methods, doctrines, and practices, but would extend to encompass almost everything in community life, including matters of appropriate dress, food and drink, rites of passage, marriage customs, burial practices, and attitudes to the state. A radical break with the past was demanded; and converts were shown how to make it.[4]

Missionaries in China and India

Asia, and particularly China, was a favorite destination for early Pentecostal missionaries. Several missionaries went out to Asia from Azusa Street. Among the first were Alfred G. Garr (1874–1944) and Lillian Garr (1878–1916), former pastors of a congregation of the Burning Bush in Los Angeles, a holiness church that merged with Azusa Street for services early in the revival. Baptized in the Spirit at Azusa Street and reported to have received "the gift of tongues, especially the language of India and dialects," the Garrs were both supposedly able to speak Bengali—and in Lillian's case, also Tibetan and Chinese. They left Los Angeles in July

1906 and arrived in Calcutta that December with an African American assistant, Maria Gardner, and their young daughter Virginia. Although disillusioned with their lack of any divinely given language abilities, they were invited to hold nightly meetings in William Carey's old Baptist church. A British military captain donated enough money to the impoverished Garrs to sustain them during their entire time in India. Lillian, in her first report to *The Apostolic Faith* in March 1907, wrote that thirteen or fourteen missionaries and other workers had received Spirit baptism. The Garrs continued to work on the Indian subcontinent amid controversy because of their dogmatic stance linking Spirit baptism with speaking in tongues. They moved to Bombay in March 1907 and visited Mukti Mission and the missionary retreat station in the hills at Coonoor. By September these restless itinerants were in Colombo, Sri Lanka. The focus of their ministry was on reaching missionaries with their message because these missionaries—unlike the Garrs—knew the customs and languages of India. "The only way the nations can be reached," they declared, "is by getting the missionaries baptized with the Holy Ghost." This became a strategy for many pentecostals in foreign countries who could not speak local languages and it resulted in a rapidly developing network of interconnected missionaries who spread the pentecostal message throughout the world with astonishing rapidity. Most of these came from evangelical faith missions like the Christian and Missionary Alliance (CMA) and the China Inland Mission (CIM), but sometimes missionaries from older denominational missions were affected.[5]

China, with one third of the estimated world population at the time, was regarded as the most important place for Western missionaries. There were very few Christians there, despite a century of Protestant missions. Pentecostal periodicals made regular pleas for more missionaries to China, declaring that a million Chinese were passing into eternity every month. Although the Garrs were among the first to arrive in Hong Kong, they were preceded by two months by the first pentecostal missionaries to China, T. J. and Annie McIntosh, who had received Spirit baptism through the ministry of Gaston B. Cashwell after the latter's return to the American South from Azusa Street. McIntosh believed that he had been given the Chinese language while speaking in tongues and after a revelation, set sail with his wife and daughter for the Portuguese colony of Macao, arriving there in August 1907. McIntosh's letter to Cashwell the day after his arrival mentioned a welcome meeting in which twenty-five missionaries and "five or six Chinamen" were present; but two weeks later, there was resistance to McIntosh's teaching from the missionaries and greater numbers of Chinese were attending pentecostal services. A report in September "from missionaries in Macao, China" mentioned that "some of the Chinese Christians have received the baptism with the Holy Ghost and are speaking in new tongues." Four months later Cashwell reported that seventy people had received Spirit baptism thirty days after the McIntoshes arrived in Macao. Like the Garrs, McIntosh also reached out to other missionaries, and reported that "Pentecost has come" to the South China CMA mission in Wuzhou (in Guangxi province) as a result of two missionaries who had attended meetings in Macao and numbers of Chinese who had also "received their Pentecost" there. Like the Garrs, the McIntoshes had an itinerant ministry and traveled widely in the vicinities of Macao and Guangzhou (Canton). In Guangzhou they reported that within a month some seventy people in Macao, Guangzhou, and Wuzhou had received Spirit baptism, including fourteen missionaries. The McIntoshes received increasing criticism, particularly because they were young and inexperienced and were not able to speak Chinese despite their original claims to do so.[6]

After nine months in China, the McIntoshes met with severe opposition from a CMA missionary and left for Palestine and the United States in May 1908. But before they left, Annie Kirby, Mrs. McIntosh's aunt, and Mabel Evans arrived to assist them in Macao. On the departure of the McIntoshes, Kirby and Evans moved to Guangzhou with an experienced missionary, Fannie Winn (who spoke Chinese), where they worked with Chinese leaders. Once in Guangzhou, Kirby, Evans, and Winn established a work with a Chinese leader called "Brother Ho," then moved two miles across the city to stay with a Chinese woman, Ho Si Tai, who fitted out a chapel for them in the house they rented from her. They spent most of their time in evangelistic work, holding two street meetings and two services in the chapel every day. Kirby and Evans would draw in crowds by singing with a portable organ and Winn would then preach in Chinese. This was a method used frequently by Western evangelical missionaries at this time. Within a year the three women returned to the United States, apparently never to return to China.[7]

The Azusa Street newspaper also reported other pentecostal activities among CMA missionaries in Macao and Wuzhou, where a number of Chinese Christians had been baptized in the Spirit. The CMA annual report for 1907 reflected on the need for a revival in China, "a mighty outpouring of the Holy Spirit" that would "awaken her out of this fearful sleep of death," that would "mean the bestowal of the old Pentecostal power and gifts promised so long ago, but lost for all these centuries." Then it described what had happened in Wuzhou in September 1907:

> The Spirit fell in a quiet Saturday night meeting and, without there having been any special exhortation or request in prayer on this line, a number "began to speak with other tongues." It was an entirely new experience, but a blessed one to many, both foreign and native brethren and sisters, old and young. The features and manifestations of these meetings were very similar to those of which we have read in various parts of the world. It seems as though the Holy Spirit is falling on the children of God simultaneously in all parts of the world, often without the intervention of a human leader.[8]

Carrie and George Montgomery's tour of South China and India in 1909 was mainly to visit CMA missions, and they had relatively little contact with the independent pentecostal missionaries there. After arriving in Hong Kong, they proceeded up river to Guanzhou and Wuzhou, where among other places they visited two "Bible schools" (one for "boys" and one for "girls"), where the students were trained as Bible teachers. Once or twice on this brief journey, Carrie Montgomery refers to those "native workers" who had particularly impressed her. There were likely hundreds of these Christian workers assisting the foreign missionaries and making a great impact on the local people. In Wuzhou they met a remarkable but unnamed Chinese Christian woman who was one of the teachers in the girls' school, who together with "many of the girls in the school had received their Pentecostal baptism." According to the missionaries, through the "great spirituality" of this woman many girls in the school had become "so deeply spiritual." The Montgomerys then visited Guangzhou, where they "found great prejudice against the Pentecostal movement," because there had been "so much wildfire and fanaticism." It is possible that this prejudice was occasioned by the visits of the McIntoshes to that city, for at this stage the Montgomerys were still leaders in the CMA, which took a moderate line on spiritual gifts and did not teach "initial evidence" as did the missionaries emerging from Azusa Street. The Montgomerys then returned to Hong Kong and made a brief visit to Macao before leaving for India.[9]

The Garrs and Maria Gardiner arrived in Hong Kong in October 1907 at the same time as two women from Seattle, May Law and Rosa

Pittman. They were directed to the American Board (Congregational) Mission where the first pentecostal services were held with the help of a Chinese schoolteacher, Mok Lai Chi (1868–1926). These four missionaries were augmented in October 1908 by two more American women, Cora Fritsch and Bertha Milligan, who had both spent a year in Japan. Fritsch, only eighteen when she arrived in Japan, was to spend four years in South China before she died of malaria, and she and Milligan later worked in Guangzhou, where Milligan was still working in 1920. The meetings in the American Board mission went on daily for a month and were interpreted by Mok Lai Chi, who soon became leader of this Pentecostal Mission, an independent church that exists to this day. *The Apostolic Faith* reported that "a glorious revival" broke out and later, that "a good many of the Chinese" had "received their Pentecost and are singing, praying, and praising in new tongues." Law and Pittman contracted smallpox and were quarantined in an offshore boat but recovered. Opposition from the American Board missionaries mounted; they were ejected from the building and moved to the much smaller venue of Mok Lai Chi's Morrison English School. A Shanghai missionary periodical said that Hong Kong had been disturbed by the "Pentecostal church," a sect whose aim seemed "rather to pervert Christian Chinese than to convert the heathen." Within six months, about a hundred people in South China had become pentecostal. In Hong Kong, some thirty people met regularly at Mok's school.[10]

These were hard times. Lillian Garr gave birth to a stillborn child and in March 1908 their invaluable assistant Maria Gardner and three-year-old daughter Virginia died of smallpox within a day of each other. After these tragic events the Garrs spent two months in Japan and returned to America, where they itinerated for over a year on behalf of the Chinese church. They were back in Hong Kong in October 1909 to open a missionary home, but left three months later and spent almost a year in India. They returned to Hong Kong for another year during which time their son was born. The Garrs left permanently for the United States in December 1911 to engage in church planting and healing evangelism until Lillian's premature death in 1916. Garr affiliated with the AG and sat on its executive board for a while but soon after resigned to work independently. The Garrs also influenced a young Canadian missionary couple, Robert and Aimee Semple (later McPherson), who arrived in Hong Kong in 1910. Robert Semple died of malaria after ten weeks, and Aimee and her new-born baby Roberta were left to return to North America.[11]

Because there were no organized pentecostal denominations during the first few years of pentecostal missions, some attempts were made to coordinate the activities of the various independent missionaries. One of the earliest attempts was that of the Pentecostal Missionary Union for Great Britain and Ireland (PMU), constituted by Cecil Polhill, Alexander Boddy, and others in Boddy's vicarage in Sunderland in January 1909. Although this organization was relatively small, it represents Pentecostalism in its formative stage and the inner dynamics of pentecostal missions. Polhill was the driving force behind the PMU ideologically, administratively, and financially. He attempted to create a pentecostal mission society exactly after the model of the society he belonged to, the China Inland Mission. Polhill, aristocratic owner of Howbury Hall in Bedfordshire, was one of the famed "Cambridge Seven" young men who had gone to China as evangelical missionaries. In 1888 Polhill went to work with the CIM in Sining in Gansu, thirty miles from the northern Tibetan border. Nineteen years later he returned to England after his father's death to manage his estate and on his journey via Los Angeles, he received Spirit baptism in the Upper Room mission and became pentecostal. A considerable amount of his personal finances went into supporting the Missionary Training Schools he created and the PMU missionaries sent out from February 1909, most of whom went to Yunnan province in southwestern China. The early PMU cooperated with the CIM, followed CIM policies, and used Polhill's CIM contacts in China. Thirty-six of the sixty PMU missionaries went to China, twelve went to India, nine to Africa, and three to South America; thirty-six of the sixty were women. Most came from various scattered congregations in Britain associated with the emerging pentecostal movement, but some were from Anglican and other churches, and some from Ireland. Some hailed from the pentecostal church established by Gerrit and Wilhelmina Polman in Amsterdam, which continued to send financial contributions for the PMU missionaries, as did other pentecostal assemblies in Britain and Ireland, and (until the outbreak of war) a church in Breslau, Germany. The first meeting of the PMU Council published the resolution that its candidates would go to a house purchased by Polhill in London for a Bible School for "some months study." No salaries were guaranteed and candidates were either to support themselves or get the help of their local "Pentecostal Centre." By November 1909 the PMU Training Home in London with A. M. Niblock as principal had eleven men attending classes. Two months later a separate training center for women was opened in London under the capable leadership of Eleanor Crisp.[12]

Seven young missionaries, five men and two women, arrived in Hong Kong in October 1910 and traveled on to Shanghai. These were Percy Bristow, Frank Trevitt, Amos Williams, John McGillivray, John Beruldsen, and his two sisters Christina and Thyra Beruldsen. In Hong Kong the four men visited the Pentecostal Mission, where they described a prayer meeting of about thirty Chinese and eight American missionaries led by J. H. King, later presiding bishop of the Pentecostal Holiness Church. In Shanghai they were met by CIM workers and visited a pentecostal mission where they found four Canadians and about a hundred Chinese. From Shanghai the party dispersed to a Scandinavian Alliance mission in Suan-hwa-fu, Hebei, in the north and to the independent mission of Mr. and Mrs. Stanley Smith (another of the Cambridge Seven) in the west in Shanxi for language learning. In a short time the Smiths had received Spirit baptism. Two of the missionaries, Trevitt and Williams, went to the Tibetan borders farther west; others worked in North China and were eventually endorsed by the American AG; and one left the PMU after a theological controversy to work with Stanley Smith. The mission in Suan-Hwa-fu became independent of the Scandinavian Alliance in 1913 and operated a school for children and a street chapel. Most of the PMU missionaries operated in Yunnan province, and the PMU was amalgamated with the British Assemblies of God in 1925, a year after that denomination was formed.[13]

The caliber of these first and somewhat forgotten missionaries is seen in the story of Frank Trevitt (1881–1915). A mechanic from Birmingham, he received Spirit baptism and healing from tuberculosis (the disease of which he would die seven years later) at Emmanuel Hall in Bournemouth, the first independent pentecostal congregation in Britain. Trevitt, his Welsh companion Amos Williams, and the two other men in the party disturbed the PMU Council with an announcement of their engagements to four Scottish young ladies without seeking the required permission. The Council took swift disciplinary action and forbade them to marry at least until 1915. The reasons given for this decision were that the PMU was in its infancy and that other mission organizations adopted a four-year restriction. Trevitt and Williams protested desperately against the decision, wondering "if there hasn't been a mistake made as to the four years of waiting" and arguing that "a man has very little influence over the natives if un-married," backed by pleas to Scriptures, circumstances, and culture. Their petitions fell on deaf ears; but their fiancées, sisters Maggie and Lizzie Millie from Stirling, were allowed to enter the Women's Training Home in London. Trevitt and Williams thoroughly imbibed the focused Polhill vision for Tibetan people and worked in very difficult circumstances on the Tibetan border, often walking many miles in remote and mountainous terrain and taking many days to reach a village. A man with limited formal education, Trevitt's first task was to learn Tibetan, which he seems to have taken to with relish. He was a flamboyant but difficult character and was frequently involved in controversy, earning the ire of his organization not only on the issue of his marriage but also in his strained relationships with other missionaries. Trevitt and Williams itinerated around China against the wishes of the PMU Council, who on at least one occasion ordered them to return to their station. But because of their obstinacy the Council resolved to further delay the sending out of the Millie sisters to China. The women were sent to a separate station in Yunnan in April 1914 and told to wait twelve months. By this time Trevitt's tuberculosis had reappeared. He was hospitalized in Hong Kong and died after a year of intense suffering. Tragically, his death occurred within weeks of their long awaited double wedding in Hong Kong in 1915, and Williams died suddenly of smallpox as the newly married couple were on their journey to their mission station in the interior. The young widows Maggie Trevitt and Lizzie Williams continued to serve in southwest China for another ten years.[14]

The PMU (probably Polhill himself) gave their sometimes wayward son Frank Trevitt a moving tribute, summing up what he and many like him were all about:

Certainly, if to no one else, the Baptism into the Holy Ghost, with signs following, made all the difference in the world to Frank Trevitt. Seven years were added to the life of the worn, emaciated consumptive given less than six months to live; glorious, strenuous years; tested, difficult times, including the ups and downs of life on the Chinese border, with two languages to cope with for the young mechanic, and with the strain of revolution and the white wolf perils. Well done, Frank Trevitt—we believe he has earned the Master's "Well done." You did bravely, Friend. Enthusiastic to a point, sometimes beyond discretion, it is an undoubted fact that the Lord signally used this dear Brother, both in the Homeland, and during his stay in China. There was a fire, a life, an enthusiasm, a faith about him that carried things through, and secured victory. Many owe healings to him under God, many baptisms in the Holy Ghost. He was faithful, too; no looking back, thank God; even to the last, with him, it was "Tibetward."[15]

Other missionaries were not as strictly managed as those in the PMU and seemed to go wherever opportunities opened. The CMA encouraged spiritual gifts in its early years, including speaking in tongues, and it was only when controversy erupted over tongues as "initial evidence" that the organization began to retreat from the pentecostal movement. Pentecostal manifestations had come to the south China CMA mission in Wuzhou through two missionaries who had attended meetings in Macao. Numbers of Chinese had also "received their Pentecost" there, and this was also reported in pentecostal papers and by the missionaries themselves in a CMA newsletter. At that stage, the CMA welcomed such manifestations of spiritual power.[16]

After pentecostal phenomena broke out in a CMA convention in Taozhou, Gansu, in 1912 during a visit by Trevitt and Williams, Otilia and William W. Simpson (1869–1961), a missionary in China from 1892–1949, became pentecostal, although the Simpsons had experienced speaking in tongues among the Chinese four years earlier, which they had denounced as demonic. They passed on their pentecostal experience to many CMA churches in southwestern Gansu, their testimony was published in the CMA's *Alliance Weekly*, and Simpson also shared his experience at neighboring CIM missions. Soon after his Spirit baptism, Simpson prayed for Chinese workers to have the same experience and wrote that as a result, the spiritual life of the churches had improved, "pastors, teachers and evangelists are much more enthusiastic and fervent in their labors, and conversions are more frequent and thorough than formerly."[17]

The CMA annual report at the end of 1912 (written by Simpson) was very positive about this pentecostal revival:

> We praise the Lord that He is working with us and confirming His Word with these same mighty signs as of old. Many cases of instantaneous and remarkable healings have occurred.... More than thirty have received the Holy Spirit accompanied by speaking in tongues and prophesying.[18]

Because of his insistence on speaking in tongues as "initial evidence," Simpson's relations within the CMA soured; he resigned in 1914 and applied to join the PMU. His letter to them described the support he was getting from CMA Chinese churches, but his mission committee had "just plainly ordered us off the Field, but the Churches have petitioned the Board to retain us." He wrote, "If they uphold me they will have to remove the opposers from the field and permit the work to be entirely Pentecostal, and if they go against me the great body of the Churches, all the really spiritual ones, will join me in an independent Pentecostal work." He resigned from the CMA in 1914 "because they required us to subscribe to unscriptural teaching about the Baptism in Holy Spirit." Simpson was probably typical of such controversial pentecostals, traveling among CMA and CIM stations praying for missionaries and Chinese pastors to be baptized in the Spirit, claiming to have visited all the CMA mission stations and that "nearly all" the Chinese leaders had received Spirit baptism "according to Acts 2." He was never accepted into the PMU, but the resulting tensions in China and India among CMA missionaries brought about a major secession from the CMA at this time, with many CMA ministers and missionaries joining the newly formed AG.[19]

In Shanghai, Simpson visited the Door of Hope rescue mission for prostitutes where Antoinette (Nettie) Moomau (1872–1937) had held meetings. Most of the leaders and workers at the Door of Hope had received the pentecostal experience through her ministry. Moomau, a Presbyterian missionary in China since 1900 who received her Spirit baptism at Azusa Street while on furlough in 1906, was the first pentecostal missionary in Shanghai and one of the first in China. She had established the Apostolic Faith Mission among influential Chinese people in the city, and she remained in the area until her death in 1937. Simpson was in Shanghai for a while and helped open a new mission in Nanjing where Chinese preacher Nathan C. S. Ma (Ma Zhaorui) and his wife were working; this couple ran a girls' school and industrial orphanage that continued for many years. Ma was also an influential preacher in the Shandong Revival in the 1930s.[20]

Simpson reported that six out of nine Norwegian missionaries had been Spirit baptized, so that "the entire mission is practically Pentecostal," and that several Chinese workers in Gansu (including three pastors) would leave the CMA. He asked Polhill if the PMU could take on the entire work, but the PMU realized the sensitivity of this and did not do so, and by 1915 Simpson was courting the new American AG. In a printed circular distributed to various missionaries, Simpson wrote that he hoped "to carry the Pentecostal Baptism and the faith once for all delivered to the saints all over Northern and Central China, to every part of Mandarin speaking China where Pentecost has not fallen before I get there." In January 1915 CIM director D. E. Hoste (like Polhill a member of the famed "Cambridge Seven" and who went to China in 1885) wrote to Polhill to complain about Simpson's "propaganda," as Simpson had named Polhill and Boddy, among others, as character references. Polhill now had a serious dilemma, as he was a member of the CIM Board and several other missionaries in China had already left the CIM and the CMA to become pentecostals. Polhill published a formal statement in July 1915 "to let his position be known," and would have "no sympathy with any propaganda" if pentecostal missionaries entered smaller towns in China occupied by the CIM unless invited by CIM missionaries. He believed that PMU missionaries, and particularly Simpson, had followed his policy. He would take responsibility for Simpson as long as he carried out these conditions and Polhill would deplore any pentecostal missionary who did not. However, Polhill also distanced himself from the recent anti-pentecostal stance of the CIM.[21]

The opposition by established evangelical missions was now firmly in place. Simpson returned to the United States in 1915 and for two years led the newly established Bethel Bible School in Newark, New Jersey. He returned to China in 1918 after the death of his wife, married another missionary, Martha Merrill, in 1925, and made his base in Minzhou, Gansu. He traveled throughout China as an AG missionary and worked with Chinese leaders in establishing congregations and beginning Bible training schools for preachers. His writings brimmed over with confidence in the progress of his work. By January 1920 he reported that there were ten "Assemblies" with about 300 "Spirit-baptized saints spread over three counties," and twenty-four students in his Bible school. There were several full-time Chinese preachers in Simpson's mission, all of whom had already been Christians in other churches for several years. Simpson reported 400 baptized in the Spirit and a total of 1,000 people connected with the AG in the province of Gansu. He was committed to creating and encouraging Spirit-filled Chinese leaders, which became his life's work. He later reported "some 50 odd students from five provinces, Mongolia and Manchuria." He remained in China (with a break during the war from 1940 to 1945) until the Communist takeover in 1949, when he returned to the United States at the age of eighty. His itinerant preaching and teaching all over China was done on foot and by train, and he assisted in the training of Chinese ministers, both men and women, in Gansu, at the Truth Bible Institute in Beijing from 1935 to 1940, and after the war in remote, northwest China.[22]

Simpson's aim was simple, as he wrote in 1941, after he had been unable to return to China because of the war:

> The Lord enabled our national co-workers to keep His work going with His presence and blessing. His unerring guidance has led me to devote much time to training them in the Word and work during many years and in many places. China must be evangelized by Spirit-filled and led Chinese, not by American missionaries. The Chinese soon learned self-government, self-support, self-propagation and thus became indigenous Assemblies.[23]

It was this commitment to training national workers that was one of Pentecostalism's strengths. Most of the training programs were easy to access and so the transition to leadership was relatively simple and rapid. Such was the remarkable determination of these early pentecostal missionaries and it is no wonder that today a significant proportion of China's burgeoning Christianity is pentecostal in nature.

Robert F. Cook (1880–1958) and Anna Cook, former Baptists, first encountered Pentecostalism and joined the Upper Room Mission in Los Angeles in 1908. There they met A. G. Garr and the first pentecostal missionary to South India, George Berg, during his furlough in Los Angeles in 1912. The Cooks and their two young daughters left the following year for India with Berg, who was to leave India in 1914. After a month with Berg in the hills, the Cooks set up base first in Bangalore and then, after a disagreement with Berg, moved to Kovilpatti village in the Tirunelveli district in 1914, where they lived in a small room in a house shared with three Indian families under unsanitary conditions. They reported crowds of people coming to their meetings as well as remarkable healings and exorcisms. An Indian Christian gave them an acre of land on which they erected a chapel. They had eight Indian preachers assisting them— some of whom had previously worked with Berg. The Cooks and their teams preferred to travel third class rather than use coaches reserved for Europeans—probably as much out of necessity as conviction—and they used the opportunity to preach and sing to a captive audience. They used the limited funds they raised to recruit and support their Indian workers, but the Great War brought increasing financial pressures on them. They moved back to the safe garrison of Bangalore before taking furlough in 1915, when Charles Cumine, an Anglo-Indian, took charge of the mission. Cumine went on a tour of Kerala with Cook in 1916–17, and was still the main leader with Cook in 1920. Anna Cook died of typhoid in 1917 and the following year Cook married Bertha Fox, a missionary who had worked near Bangalore with a Mukti Mission worker, Mary Bai Aiman. For a while the Cooks were loosely affiliated with the AG and lived in Doddaballapur, Mysore, where they opened the Berachah Orphanage. They moved to Kottarakkara, Kerala, in 1922 and started a Bible school, opening a building for it in 1927 in Chengannur with the financial assistance of Essek W. Kenyon, the forerunner of the Word of Faith movement. This became Cook's headquarters and was named "Mount Zion."[24]

The Cooks were missionaries who engaged with Indian pentecostals on an equal basis but were also involved in various subsequent secessions. Pentecostalism in Kerala was already progressing in the 1920s with little expatriate supervision. More Indian evangelists and leaders, especially from Brethren or holiness backgrounds, became pentecostal. On his return from furlough in 1926, Cook sided with the Indian leaders in a dispute with the AG missionary Mary Chapman, who had insisted on the registration of church buildings with the AG before finances could be given. Cook formed the Malankara Pentecostal Church of God and left the AG in 1929, eventually affiliating with the Church of God and remaining in India until 1950. Several Indian preachers associated with Cook were instrumental in starting independent pentecostal churches, including K. E. Abraham, who joined Cook in 1923 and worked with him as a teacher in the Bible school.[25]

Cook refers obliquely to him and the schism he led:

In 1930, while the revival was still on, one of the leaders of the fellowship, a young man became vain and lifted up with pride because of his ability. 1 Tim.3:6. He thus became prey to the National spirit, which was prevalent in India at that time. Four other workers and a number of our fellowship followed him....we could well refute the accusation these workers flung in the teeth of the European missionaries and could affirm that we were NOT foreign paid servants.[26]

Apart from its negative reference to Indian nationalism, the last comment refers to the fact that by 1930 Cook was not affiliated to any denomination and only joined the Church of God (Cleveland) in 1935 after a visit by its missionary leader J. H. Ingram, who enthused about "the great mass movement to the Church of God here in India." Ingram marveled that he had "actually captured fifty-eight Pentecostal churches, pastors, deacons, and all…the combined membership will run near four thousand." Cook himself wrote to Ingram that the decision to join them had been made because he believed that this was "a body that would consider Indians co-equal in the carrying on of the work with us." It is revealing that the very capable leader K. E. Abraham was never ordained by Cook but by Ramankutti Paul of the Ceylon Pentecostal Mission in 1930; but it could also be that Cook was disinterested in hierarchical leadership and did not practice ordination. Cook refers to the secession by Abraham and his associates "on the supposed grounds that the missionaries were lording over the native church and controlling it." He declared that this was "a false accusation" because they had decided "to confer full liberty on assemblies, workers and members of the church" and "The missionary was to be only a co-advisor." Cook estimated that the secession split his membership (about 7,000 at the time) in half. The secessionists founded the Indian Pentecostal Church in 1934, now with the AG the two largest pentecostal denominations in India, and from which further secessions have ensued.[27]

Missionaries in Africa

As in China and India, pentecostal missionaries went to certain countries in Africa early. Liberia was a favorite place for African American missionaries, who perhaps were encouraged by the contemporary "Back to Africa" movement advocating emigration to Africa by the children of slaves. But missionaries did not find Liberia an easy place to live in and several soon returned to the United States. First, there was considerable unrest among the native Liberians, especially in the Cape Palmas area where the Grebo people lived. An insurrection against the Liberian government took place in 1909 and escalated into full-scale war in 1910. For much of the twentieth century there was extensive exploitation of native Liberians by the settler Americo-Liberian minority. Slavery was outlawed there only in 1936, and indigenous Liberians were denied voting rights. The famous Liberian prophet William Wade Harris, before his call to the ministry while in prison, was jailed for planting a British flag in Monrovia because he believed that British protection was better than the Americo-Liberian oppression that his fellow Grebos were suffering.[28]

Pentecostal missionaries with connections to Azusa Street started arriving in Liberia in 1907. *The Apostolic Faith* reported that African American evangelist Lucy Farrow, who had first accompanied Seymour to Los Angeles from Houston, would be in the first party of Azusa Street missionaries who left for Africa, as would Julia Hutchins, the African American woman who had first invited Seymour to Los Angeles and then barred him from her church. Within a few weeks of their arrival in Liberia, seven Azusa Street missionaries, Mrs. Cook, Mrs. Lee, and the whole Batman family of five, died of tropical fever. *The Apostolic Faith* did not announce their tragic deaths, which soon became a source of great embarrassment and criticism for the new Apostolic Faith movement. Some holiness periodicals used the deaths as proof of the "delusion" taught at Azusa Street and charged Julia Hutchins with "kidnapping" a young Kru girl from Monrovia because she had returned to the United States with an African child. Farrow returned after seven months in Johnsonville, Liberia, where she worked among the native population, reporting that twenty had "received their Pentecost" and that she had been able to speak and preach two sermons in the Kru language. The paper concluded the report on Farrow by saying that some of "the heathen" had spoken "in English and some in other tongues." The paper announced that the Lord had shown Farrow when she was to go, told her the time she was to return, and provided the fare in time. Farrow returned safely and was preaching in Virginia and the southern states. She continued to work at Azusa Street for a few months before returning to her home in Houston.[29]

Other early African American missionaries to Liberia were Mr. and Mrs. Frank Cummings, Church of God in Christ missionaries who went there in 1907, and Edward and Mollie McCauley, leaders of the racially mixed Apostolic Faith congregation in Long Beach, California. With an associate named Rosa Harmon, the McCauleys arrived in Monrovia in November 1907 and established a thriving work there among Kru people. Canadian John Reid visited Monrovia briefly on his way to Cape Palmas in December 1908 (where he soon afterward died) and reported how he stumbled upon the Apostolic Faith Mission hall, met McCauley, and learned that he had 145 members. Rosa Harmon reported 154 Kru members the following year. On an overnight stop in Monrovia in October 1913, global traveling American preacher Daniel Awrey reported a thriving, "large congregation in the Apostolic Faith Church" less than two months before his own death from malaria at the pentecostal mission near Cape Palmas. He was by no means the last pentecostal missionary to die in Liberia. Altogether, ten missionaries died of tropical diseases in the first eight years of the mission in Cape Palmas. Others returned home.[30]

Things were a little easier for missionaries in the temperate highlands of the South. Thomas Hezmalhalch (1847–1934), John G. Lake (1870–1935), Jacob Lehman, and others began the Apostolic Faith Mission of South Africa (AFM) in Johannesburg in 1908, the largest pentecostal denomination in the country today. Hezmalhalch was an itinerant holiness preacher in his sixties who received Spirit baptism at Azusa Street. He was involved in a pentecostal church in Indianapolis and a new outreach in Zion City, Illinois—where he became acquainted with Lake. Lake was a former elder in Zion City who had received Spirit baptism through the ministry of Parham there in 1906. The team was identified with the pentecostal work in Indianapolis and sent from there to South Africa. Because of his seniority, Hezmalhalch was regarded as leader of this group and became the first president of the AFM, although Lake was the more charismatic. Lily and Jacob Lehman were returning missionaries who had been six years in southern Africa (Lehman had gone to Bulawayo, Southern Rhodesia, in 1901); they were able to speak Zulu and had received Spirit baptism in Indianapolis. With hardly enough funds for the voyage, the pentecostal missionary party of seven adults and seven Lake children sailed third class for South Africa via Liverpool in April 1908.[31]

The Zionist connections of the American missionaries proved fortuitous. Pieter L. le Roux, an Afrikaner and Dutch Reformed missionary working in Wakkerstroom near the Natal border, had joined Dowie's Zionist movement in 1902 or 1903 and become an elder, together with some 400 African fellow-workers and converts. They were baptized in 1904 by Daniel Bryant, Dowie's appointed Overseer for South Africa, and the movement reached 5,000 in a year. Le Roux was to become the first South African president of the AFM, a position he held for over thirty years. Bryant, on his return to the United States in 1906, had become disaffected with Dowie's successor Wilbur Voliva and left the movement. He had also encouraged his followers to seek a deeper baptism in the Spirit. It seems that his disaffection had spread to his South African followers, who welcomed the Zionists-turned-pentecostals with open arms. The Zionists in the Wakkerstroom area were the source out of which a whole series of African Zionist denominations emerged throughout southern Africa. Two of the Zulu leaders associated with le Roux were Daniel Nkonyane and Fred Lutuli, both of whom already had hundreds of followers of their own by 1905 and were to found significant independent Zionist churches after breaking with the AFM in 1910.[32]

Lake wrote effusively to his supporters of how God had "wonderfully blessed" their work so that "manifestations of the Spirit have been intense in their power and depth of character beyond anything I have known." Daily meetings with packed audiences with instant healings, people falling to the ground "under the power," and other manifestations of the Spirit were reported. Back in North America these events were regarded as the most remarkable of the reports from pentecostal missionaries anywhere. Lake wrote that "Johannesburg was never so religiously stirred before," and that he was receiving so many enquirers that he had "hardly been able to eat, let alone sleep." The services began in an American Congregational "native" church in Doornfontein, an area inhabited mainly by "Coloured" (Afrikaans-speaking, mixed race) and African people. This soon became too small, and the pentecostal team was given the unrestricted use of the 500-seat Zion Tabernacle. Lehman observed "the prejudice that exists with the white people against the natives" and that because of the whites coming to the meetings, "the natives became timid and were crowded out." The Zion Tabernacle's larger capacity had seemingly solved the problem temporarily, soon becoming the Central Tabernacle of the AFM. In May 1909 Lake was about to depart for the town of Volksrust for a conference with the "native preachers under our baptized brother, Elder le Roux," who had joined the AFM with "thirty-five native preachers ministering to five thousand people." Lake wrote that there were now "at least fifty thousand" people for whom the AFM was responsible. Lake opines that because the white South African missionaries working with them already spoke "Dutch" (Afrikaans) and "native languages," and because they did not "live in the luxurious way that the Americans have been accustomed to," they were "a better class of missionary than the average foreign missionary." He asked for support for these workers, which would be "worth as much in the extension of the Kingdom of God as twenty American missionaries would be." While these statements might not have endeared Lake to his American readers and fellow-missionaries, he seems to have won the hearts of many Afrikaners with his anti-British views (perhaps gleaned from Dowie in Zion City) and his sympathy with the Afrikaners' plight since the recent Anglo-Boer War.[33]

South African Pentecostalism was very quickly segregated. Although the very first meetings in the Zion church in Johannesburg were integrated, within a few months segregation was practiced. This led to a whole series of secessions from 1910 onward. In a letter to his American supporters, Lehman commented on the "very unsatisfactory" arrangements in the

Zion Tabernacle and the "terrible barrier of race distinction" that "could be our greatest difficulty." This had caused the "native work" in Johannesburg to be independent of the "white work" from March 1909. Lehman thought that "no one else had the burden of the natives of Johannesburg on their hearts," and he secured a separate hall rented by the Africans themselves. He worked for a time with the rival Pentecostal Mission and continued his work in the mine compounds and hospitals around Johannesburg for eleven years. Lake and Hezmalhalch returned to the United States briefly in September 1909 and visited Durham's mission in Chicago as well as Azusa Street and the Upper Room in Los Angeles. During 1910 the two missionaries fell out, with Hezmalhalch being influenced by other missionaries who had charged Lake with financial irregularities. There were also rumors of exaggerated reports made by the missionaries. Lake, however, continued to get the support of all the Afrikaner and African AFM workers. The Upper Room, Lake's largest financial supporter, published a full vindication of Lake in November 1910, stating that they were fully satisfied with Lake's integrity. The AFM executive wrote a letter of support for Lake, stating that the accusations were "petty jealousies" that South Africans were ignoring. Hezmalhalch was dismissed from the presidency and returned to California, leaving Lake in charge. This event marked the first denominational schism in South African Pentecostalism, with Lake and most Afrikaner pentecostals in the AFM and most of the other foreign missionaries in the Pentecostal Mission. Lake returned permanently to the United States in 1913, when le Roux took over as president of the AFM, and the organization was dominated by Afrikaners thereafter.[34]

The history of the AFM and its relationship with apartheid is a painful one. The Pentecostal Mission under the American George Bowie and British immigrant Archibald Cooper in Middelburg included Henry and Anna Turney's mission and Lehman's work in Johannesburg. This group split again into the Full Gospel Church and the Assemblies of God, and eventually into further factions. The Full Gospel Church affiliated with the CG in 1951 to become the Full Gospel Church of God. The Assemblies of God in South Africa divided several times and exists in various independent groups today. In 2002, three of the major factions reached an accord, but a decade later this had not yet become organizational unity.[35]

Some Western pentecostal missionaries founded independent national churches. One of these was William F. P. Burton (1886–1971), who became a pentecostal in 1911 and trained under Thomas Myerscough in Preston and at the PMU training school in London. As David Maxwell observes, "The sense of certitude and absolutism that came from his dramatic conversion and profound experience of the Holy Spirit led to dogmatism and irascibility." Controversy followed his unorthodox and independent ways and brought him into conflict with the PMU Council. After pastoring churches while waiting for doors to open, Burton sailed for Africa in 1914, spending a year in South Africa and Lesotho before being joined by his friend James Salter. They headed north to the Belgian Congo in 1915 together with two Pentecostal Mission workers, George Armstrong and Joseph Blakeney. Their mission came to be known as the Congo Evangelistic Mission (CEM) from 1919, although it was only officially organized in 1922, when Salter became Home Director in England. Arriving in Elizabethville (now Lubumbashi), they proceeded to their first mission station at Mwanza Kasingu among the Luba people, but Armstrong died of malaria before their arrival and Blakeney left to return to South Africa a month later. Burton and Salter together began the urgent task of language acquisition and after a month were trying to preach in Kiluba, but they recognized their great limitations. By the end of 1915 they were joined by two American women sent from Johannesburg, who established a new station south of Mwanza but left the mission in 1917 because of ill health. After a few months at Mwanza, Burton and Salter were joined by a group of fourteen emancipated Bekalebwe slaves who had become evangelical Christians in Angola, led by a former slave raider, Shalumbo Kisoka. They immediately joined up with the new mission and Shalumbo became its first African evangelist, working there for the next twenty years preaching and healing, resulting in much of its early success. Burton soon recorded that each of six "native evangelists" held two to six meetings a day in six to eight villages a week, with an average weekly attendance of 6,300 people.[36]

In 1917 Burton constructed a chapel and school building at Mwanza, partly in reaction to Catholic opposition. There was a possibility that villages won for Pentecostalism would be taken away from them—so it was necessary to teach the Christians in these villages "to read, put Testaments in their hands, and send them out." This underlined the urgent need for the mission to train "native evangelists," he wrote. The stage was set for the multiplication of mission stations after the model of the older missions. In 1918 Burton married a South African, Helen (Hetty) Trollip, and returned with her to Mwanza. By this time there were three new missionary "recruits" from South Africa (two women and one man) and two Americans, making a total of six, who immediately set out to learn the language. By 1920 Burton himself had written down a Kiluba vocabulary of 15,000 words. He would later institute a strict regime by which any missionary who could not preach in the local language after six months in the field would be sent home. By 1922 there were fifteen white missionaries and between thirty and forty African evangelists in the mission. By 1925 the number of missionaries had reached thirty and there were 100 African evangelists. A Bible school for the training of workers was started at Mwanza and the "most promising" of the young evangelists who had already proved themselves in the different stations (as Burton put it) were trained there for two years. Many of the African evangelists in the CEM were severely persecuted for their faith, being opposed by chiefs and witch doctors, and they were lashed and beaten, imprisoned, and poisoned. But the work of the CEM continued to grow. Burton operated on the principle of training African workers, always under white supervision. As he reported in 1925, "The great needs are Spirit-filled native evangelists, and a few white workers to superintend and help them." But he was not unaware of the benefits of having African leaders, and his accounts of the work of such leaders in the Congo and South Africa provide uniquely fascinating stories of African initiatives in the early years of Pentecostalism. Nobody else from this era provided much information on African leaders, but Burton wrote books about some of them. As former PMU colleague Percy Corry put it in his foreword to one of these books, these accounts were "a revelation of what can be done by consecrated, Spirit-filled, native leaders." They showed the "indigenous church" as "directed and encouraged by Spirit-filled leaders, and as such it must command attention." This was an example of what God could do "if we allow Him to use us in a similar way in our own lands and to the people at our very doors."[37]

Burton's method was to select the best young men from the different stations who had shown the ability to evangelize and lead a church. Not more than forty at a time, "with their wives," were selected for the central training school, run by Burton himself, in the first years of the CEM. The course lasted for about two years and its primary purpose was "to make them Bible-lovers and to encourage them in personal holiness and fellowship with God. Brilliance of preaching and leadership are secondary to this." They accompanied the missionaries on their itinerating to learn on the job. A photograph of two of the CEM's "native overseers," Kangoi and Ngoloma, published in 1922, had the revealing caption, "These men now take practically the same place and responsibility with regard to the young native churches as the white missionaries." It continued, "If anything occurred necessitating the withdrawal of white workers, the native church would still have steady godly men to whom to look for help and direction." Unfortunately, Burton did not follow through on this remarkably enlightened vision. Almost forty years later, the CEM was still directed by an all-white Field Executive Council and had sixty-five European missionaries working in fourteen mission compounds. Two missionaries were killed in the Congolese civil war, and Burton and his missionaries were evacuated in 1960. The result of this seeming setback was that ten years later the churches left behind and now led by Africans had more than doubled in membership.[38]

There is no doubt that Burton was an unusual, even unique, pentecostal missionary. He had benefited from a public school education in England. By profession an engineer, he was an extremely talented person, an adept linguist, author of many books, and accomplished in building, art, poetry, photography, surveying, and cartography. He wrote books about the mission, about the southeastern Congo and its inhabitants, and about the things he had learned there. His ethnographic books on and photographs and paintings of Luba society and landscapes all received wide recognition. But his somewhat unorthodox methods seldom met with the approval of the Belgian colonial authorities, who saw African religious enthusiasm, with its tendencies toward independence, as dangerous, even subversive. They saw Burton's emphasis on divine healing as detrimental to their own desire to further medical science, and his criticism of the migrant labor system increased the tensions. They much preferred the orderly Catholics, with whom Burton had several clashes. Nevertheless, the remarkable Burton remained at Mwanza for forty-five years in all, directing his mission until 1960 when the civil war that followed independence forced him into retirement in South Africa at age seventy-four. The church formed by his converts eventually became the Pentecostal Community of the Congo, now a vibrant denomination of half a million that has weathered the ravages of continued civil war in that troubled region. Burton, like those indomitable pentecostal missionaries in other parts of the world, was a rugged individualist and somewhat maverick, but he was totally committed to the task he felt called to do and the people to whom he had been sent. He represents a shift from the heady eschatological pressure of the pentecostal missionaries who went out before the First World War, a shift that was evident in the more settled missionary methods practiced by pentecostals for the next half century. The institutionalization of pentecostal denominations was taking place and would be accompanied by further schism and proliferation.[39]

Missionary Strategies

The most significant event for Protestant Christianity in the first half of the twentieth century, contemporaneous with the birth of Pentecostalism, was the birth of the ecumenical movement, a series of events beginning with the great World Missionary Conference held in Edinburgh in June 1910 and culminating in the formation of the World Council of Churches in Amsterdam in 1948. It is not the purpose of this book to go into detail about these pivotal events, but there were remarkable similarities between the aspirations of the leaders of the Edinburgh Conference and those of the fledgling pentecostal movement, throwing into perspective the distance that later developed between these two global movements. In his opening address at Edinburgh, Archbishop of Canterbury Randall Davidson used eschatological language to prophesy that those at the Conference might well experience in their lifetime "the Kingdom of God come with power." The chairman of the Conference, American evangelist John R. Mott, believed that Christianity stood at the dawning of a new age of global expansion where the opportunities presented by the political, economic, and religious contexts were unprecedented: "the day of God's power," he called it. None of these Edinburgh participants would have reckoned on an obscure revivalist movement on the fringes of Christianity at the time as being a major contributor to the realization of these prophecies. For their part, the new pentecostals and radical evangelicals hardly noticed the Edinburgh event; they were not invited to attend and their work was unrecognized, but these were still very early days. But then, neither were the Catholics nor the various Orthodox bodies invited. This great missionary conference was notoriously underrepresented by anyone outside the Western world—only nineteen out of 1,215 delegates, of which eighteen were from Asia, only one from Africa, and none at all from Latin America. Very few people at the Edinburgh conference would have heard of Pentecostalism, and those that had would have written it off at best as an eccentric and over-emotional sect, or at worst as a dangerous heretical movement. Certainly no one would have anticipated its enormous role in the future of world Christianity. There is no evidence that the 1910 Conference had any significant influence on pentecostal missions, despite its emphasis on evangelism (its motto was "the evangelization of the world in this generation"). Pentecostals were not yet organized into structures, and the Edinburgh conference did not foresee the massive transformation in the nature of the church that was to take place during the twentieth century in which Pentecostalism played a major role.[40]

The Conference made various inaccurate assumptions, such as that Christianity would not flourish without white missionary control. Providentially, Pentecostalism gave the lie to that assumption and contributed significantly to the reshaping of Christianity from a Western to a predominantly non-Western phenomenon. Things did not turn out in the way that the Edinburgh Conference anticipated.[41]

Brian Stanley observed:

> The measure of missionary success enjoyed by Christianity in the century that followed arguably owed rather little to the priorities set and the objectives enunciated at Edinburgh. The Christian faith was indeed to be transfigured over the next century, but not in the way or through the mechanisms that they imagined. The most effective instrument of that transfiguration would not be western mission agencies or institutions of any kind, but rather a great and sometimes unorthodox miscellany of indigenous pastors, prophets, catechists, and evangelists, men and women who had little or no access to the metropolitan mission headquarters and the wealth of dollars and pounds which kept the missionary society machinery turning; they professed instead to the simple transforming power of the Spirit and the Word.[42]

The editor of the Atlanta pentecostal periodical *The Bridegroom's Messenger,* Elisabeth Sexton, referred to the conference in a 1910 editorial as "undoubtedly the greatest missionary gathering the Christian world has ever known," but doubted whether any activity "not representing the fullness of the Gospel, with full redemption in Christ Jesus for body, soul and spirit" would achieve the expected outcome. She felt that concessions made "regarding heathen religions in recognizing certain moral good in them" would "dishonor God and weaken the cause of Christ." She reiterated her conviction that the only "equipment for effectual missionary service" was "Holy Ghost power" and "uncompromising faithfulness to the full Gospel truth." Without this there was "little hope for great results for God as the outcome of this great missionary conference." Her commentary illustrates some of the fundamental issues developing in pentecostal circles that were to make it highly suspicious of and largely uncooperative with the wider Christian world. In addition, some of the differences between the missionaries represented at Edinburgh and those of the emerging new movement are obvious. The former emphasized careful strategic planning; the latter stressed spontaneity and reliance on the leading of the Spirit with the confirmation of "signs and wonders." The former were willing to recognize the good in other faiths; the pentecostals based their appeals for missionaries on the utter darkness they perceived to be in the "heathen" nations and their religions, and assumed that these nations desperately needed the Christian gospel. At an address to a Chicago pentecostal audience in 1910 intended to spur people to volunteer for missionary service, Minnie Abrams titled her talk "The Midnight Darkness of India's Superstition" and spoke of her first impressions in Bombay of "these masses of people all in awful darkness and bowing down to idols."[43]

Western pentecostal newspapers were filled with such descriptions of the darkness, depravity, and suffering of the "heathen" nations to which their missionaries had ventured. This was a fairly stereotypical view of most radical evangelicals at the time and was not peculiar to pentecostals, but seeing other religions as spiritual entities to be confronted placed pentecostal missionaries at some advantage over their more rational Protestant counterparts. Pentecostals believed in a spiritual universe that included good and evil forces, and although they tended to see these in dichotomous terms, unlike most of the Protestant missionaries pentecostals entered into the world of other religions addressing many central human aspirations, especially the need for spiritual power to overcome evil and suffering. There was one more positive commentary on the Edinburgh conference more than two years later by Cecil Polhill, leader of the PMU, who thought that the conference was "evidently ordered in the Plan of God" and its reports brought the church "face to face with the world's needs in detail" while they concentrated on the "unparalleled opportunity" and the "Church's responsibility." He drew special attention to the "Report of the Commission for Carrying the Gospel to All the Non-Christian World" and highlighted its emphasis on the unprecedented opportunities for evangelization. But he said that the Church had not responded to these calls and that the pentecostal movement had arisen to rectify this grave omission.[44]

The tendency of Western pentecostal missionaries was to encourage local leadership and autonomy, even though this was not unqualified. But because of this, pentecostal churches became national churches rapidly and developed their own momentum without further help from foreign missionaries. This was particularly the case in the AG, where the influence of the concept of planting "three-self," "indigenous" churches was considerable. On occasions in the early pentecostal literature there are glimpses into how rapidly indigenization took place. AG missionary George Kelley wrote from Sainam in South China in 1920 about one of their missions, which had "assumed the support of all the workers and the work as a whole, with the exception of the preacher." Elders and deacons had been ordained and the work had "a desire to be wholly self-supporting" the following year. Although the pentecostal missionary newsletters focused on the activities of the Western missionaries, now and then we get glimpses in the early years of the multitude of "native helpers" who were doing most of the work in evangelism and church-planting. At the beginning of the twentieth century, these local workers outnumbered foreign Protestant missionaries by at least six to one. In Pentecostalism the ratio was probably much higher, but the national workers were often not recognized and many were driven to begin their own movements. But the growth in conversions and whatever success these missions had was largely due to the efforts of these local preachers. This emphasis on local leadership was the legacy of pentecostal missions, who ultimately raised up national leaders who were financially self-supporting and whose new churches were nationalized much sooner than older mission churches had been. In many countries, however, it was the denominations and independent churches founded by native people that became significant in the spread of pentecostal ideas. Some of these national churches were established after secessions from foreign-led pentecostal churches, and some were founded by the initiatives of native-born leaders who believed they had been empowered by the Spirit to establish new movements among their own people.[45]

It is widely acknowledged that the Anglo-Catholic missionary in China, Roland Allen (1868–1947) was a radical, provocative mission strategist far ahead of his time, who tirelessly advocated a post-Western Christianity and mission methods that focused on local talent. While he was undoubtedly influenced by his predecessors Henry Venn, Rufus Anderson, William Taylor, and John Nevius, Allen went much further than they did in advocating a truly "indigenous church" completely independent of foreign influences. What resonated so much with those pentecostals who, directly or indirectly, came in contact with his principles, was his focus on mission as being primarily the work of the Spirit. Allen constantly emphasized that the Holy Spirit who came at Pentecost was a Spirit who both empowered and motivated ordinary believers to propagate the gospel. He opposed the mission station model because it perpetuated the missionaries' foreign culture and their permanence. He believed in the spontaneous expansion of "indigenous," local churches as a result of a proper understanding of the role of the Holy Spirit and that of the missionary. His best-known work, *Missionary Methods: St Paul's or Ours?* was first published in 1912 and a second edition appeared in 1927—but as he predicted, it was only years after his death that his critique came to be appreciated.[46]

How telling, for example, are these words that struck chords in pentecostal hearts:

> [St. Paul] was always glad when his converts could progress without his aid. He welcomed their liberty. He withheld no gift from them which might enable them to dispense with his presence.... He gave as a right to the Spirit-bearing body the powers which duly belong to a Spirit-bearing body. He gave freely, and then he retired from them that they might learn to exercise the powers which they possessed in Christ....
>
> To do this required great faith; and this faith is the spiritual power in which St Paul won his victory. He believed in the Holy Ghost...as a Person indwelling his converts. He believed therefore in his converts. He could trust them.[47]

Allen's books on indigenization were already circulating in pentecostal circles as early as 1921, when Alice Luce (1873–1955), an AG missionary to Hispanic Americans from 1916, wrote a series of three remarkable articles on Allen's teachings entitled "Paul's Missionary Method's." Luce was a CMS missionary in India when she was attracted to Pentecostalism through the ministry of the Indian woman Shorat Chuckerbutty, who laid hands on her for Spirit baptism in 1910. Although she acknowledged the important contribution to her thinking of Allen's book *Missionary Methods* (which she read while in India), she could not remember the name of its author. Luce wrote that her initial pentecostal experience had taught her that "there is such a thing as doing an apostolic work along apostolic lines." She was surprised at how very quickly the "heathen" were able to recognize "the difference between those who went to them with a hidden sense of their own superiority and those who really had the spirit of a servant." She wrote how important it was to declare the equality of all nations before God and to train "native workers," the only ones who would ever accomplish the evangelization of their own nations and who had "many advantages over the foreigner." Paul's aim was to found everywhere a "self-supporting, self-governing and self-propagating church," with trained leaders who were independent of the foreign missionary and became missionaries in their own right. Although it might be necessary for new churches to have "foreign supervision" for a long time (here she differed from Allen), this was only because of maturity and experience and had nothing to do with nationality or race. Once there were "spiritually qualified leaders" in the national church, the foreign missionary must "be subject to them, and to let them take the lead as the Spirit Himself shall guide them."[48]

In the 1950s the AG mission strategist Melvin Hodges (1909–1988) through his widely influential book *The Indigenous Church* (1953) not only emphasized creating "indigenous churches," but also stressed church-planting—a fundamental principle of pentecostal mission strategy. Hodges was undoubtedly indebted to both Allen's and Luce's ideas in framing his own missiology. But the influence of Hodges on AG missions in the mid-twentieth century contributed further toward their commitment to national leadership and establishing theological training institutes (often called "Bible schools") and in-service training structures throughout the world. This in turn resulted in the much more rapid growth of national pentecostal churches. Hodges was a missionary in Central America who articulated what had always been at the heart of pentecostal growth in different cultural contexts. He said that the aim of all mission activity was to build an "indigenous New Testament church" that followed what he termed "New Testament methods." He emphasized that the church itself (and not the evangelist) is "God's agent for evangelism." The role of the cross-cultural missionary was to ensure that a church became self-governing, self-supporting, and self-propagating—thus he enthusiastically embraced and enlarged a "three-self" policy of church planting, the main theme of his book.[49]

Significantly, he introduced an emphasis on "indigenization" that was lacking in the earlier works on the subject by nineteenth century mission strategists. The foundation for this was the Holy Spirit:

> There is no place on earth where, if the gospel seed be properly planted, it will not produce an indigenous church. The Holy Spirit can work in one country as well as in another. To proceed on the assumption that the infant church in any land must always be cared for and provided for by the mother mission is an unconscious insult to the people that we endeavor to serve, and is evidence of a lack of faith in God and in the power of the gospel.[50]

Hodges's views had a profound impact on the subsequent growth of the AG, which prescribed the reading of *The Indigenous Church* to future missionaries. But of course, attaining "three-selfhood" does not guarantee real contextualization unless the "three selfs" are no longer patterned on foreign forms and are grounded in the thought patterns and symbolism of the popular culture. Yet, Pentecostalism's religious creativity and spontaneously contextual character were characteristics held as ideals by missionaries and mission strategists for over a century. "Indigenization" was automatically and, so it seemed, effortlessly achieved by pentecostal churches long before this goal was realized by older missions. For Hodges (and again, with echoes of Allen), the foundation for mission and the reason for the continued expansion of Pentecostalism is the "personal filling of the Holy Spirit" who gives gifts of ministry to untold thousands of common people, creating active, vibrantly expanding, and "indigenous churches" all over the world.[51]

Despite using "us" and "them" language, Hodges had remarkable insights:

> We have not understood that the members of the Body of Christ are scattered in all lands, and that we, without them, are not made perfect. We have thought of the temple of the Lord as complete in us, of the Body of Christ as consisting of us, and we have thought of the conversion of the heathen as the extension of the body of which we are the members. Consequently we have preached the Gospel from the point of view of the wealthy man who casts a mite into the lap of a beggar....
>
> We have done everything for them except acknowledge any equality. We have done everything for them, but very little with them. We have done everything for them except give place to them. We have treated them as "dear children" but not as "brethren."[52]

William Burton discussed the principle of indigenization in a 1933 publication, stating that the idea first found prominence among pentecostal missionaries at about the time of the Great War. He wrote that "white missionaries" were "a mere passing phase in the introduction of Christianity to a heathen people" and that native Christians were given "from the very commencement, the responsibility for the support and propagation of the young church" (significantly, Burton also mentions self-government, thus supporting the "three-self" principle). Burton's own mission, however, was governed by white missionaries until they were forced to leave the Congo in the 1960 civil war, opening up the way for national leaders to take the denomination much further than the missionaries had been able to.[53]

Despite the exhortations that so greatly influenced the policies of pentecostal missions, there are still areas of world Pentecostalism dominated physically, financially, and ideologically by foreign Western missionaries. Pentecostal missiological writing is sometimes limited by an ideology that sees the mission enterprise in terms of successful procedures and strategies. It appears that the ideal of a "three-self" independent church was slow in being realized in many of the expatriate mission efforts, with only occasional exceptions. By the middle of the century, among denominations planted by Western pentecostals, the great majority of converts in the majority world remained objects of mission and marginalized. Fortunately, these same converts are now beginning to produce scholars who challenge the presuppositions of the past and are not content to follow foreign mission ideologies and strategies blindly. These missionaries placed their emphasis on aggressive evangelism and church-planting, and the training of indigenous leaders was to further this emphasis. Social uplift was of secondary importance and only a few engaged in this sort of activity in the early years. But the stage was set for a profound change in the nature of world Christianity itself in the latter half of the twentieth century.

4

Women and Family

Women Leaders from the North

The majority of pentecostals are women—by most estimates the proportion is three to two, and in some countries it is probably higher—and women have been the main bearers of the pentecostal message worldwide. Ramabai, Minnie Abrams, Aimee Semple McPherson, and Carrie Judd Montgomery were no token women, nor were they only outstanding individuals with exceptional talents. That they were indeed, but because they were women in male-dominated societies, their contributions to Pentecostalism were all the more remarkable. In this chapter I will make a deliberate attempt to illustrate both the importance of leading women pioneers and the issues faced by ordinary women participants in Pentecostalism. Unfortunately, it is all too easy to privilege hierarchical leadership roles in studies such as this, and consequently to obscure the very important leadership roles exercised by those women who are never accorded the privileged offices reserved for men. After a discussion of the role of women leaders and founders in pentecostal movements both in the global North and the South, the latter part of this chapter considers what is an even more profound and less ostentatious area of the liberation of women in Pentecostalism: their role in the pentecostal family.

From its beginnings, the widespread phenomenon of women with charismatic gifts throughout Pentecostalism resulted in a much higher proportion of women in ministry than in most other forms of Christianity. Leadership and participation were based on the fundamental pentecostal belief in the priesthood of all believers and the empowering and legitimizing experience of the Spirit that is available to all, irrespective of gender. Women were prominent because inspirational leadership was privileged over organizational leadership. Like men, women could exercise any spiritual gift, testify to their experiences, and witness through music, prophecy, song, and many other forms of participation in the services—and in most cases, they did so more than men did. The spiritual leadership of women in Pentecostalism accorded well with the prominence of women in many pre-Christian religious rituals in Africa and parts of Asia, contrasting again with the prevailing practice of older churches, which barred women from entering the ministry or even from taking any part in public worship. No observer of pentecostal activities will fail to notice that most of those involved are women, even though the leadership is often male. But in spite of all the practical involvement of women with personal charisma and authority in pentecostal churches, these churches were not yet ready to come to terms with the theological implications of women in ministry. There were loud, male, conservative voices in pentecostal denominations advocating restrictions.

The late nineteenth and early twentieth century was an important period for changing social and religious expectations on the role of women. By the 1880s, evangelical training schools for missionary women were being founded in the West, women were accepted into Bible schools like those of D. L. Moody in Chicago, A. J. Gordon in Boston, and A. B. Simpson in New York, and pioneering women like Phoebe Palmer, Catherine Booth, Carrie Judd Montgomery, and Maria Woodworth-Etter were preaching in mass meetings. These women inspired the early pentecostals and some, like Montgomery and Woodworth-Etter, joined the fledgling movement, where they were free to exercise their healing ministry but did so in independent organizations that pentecostal denominations could choose to ignore if they were so inclined. The example of these pentecostal women and those who went as missionaries to Africa, Asia, and Latin America deeply influenced communities in which they served, and women leaders emerged all over the world, often subjected to patriarchy, but setting precedents for leadership that reverberated in the years to come. There were many examples, and only a few can be given here. Carrie Montgomery's periodical *Triumphs of Faith* was a significant vehicle for giving expression to women from its beginning. The majority of articles published there were written by women. One in 1886, entitled "Should Women Prophesy?" gave a spirited defense of the rights of women in ministry.[1]

During the Charismatic movement in North America, Kathryn Kuhlman (1907–76) was the most prominent healing evangelist, but other American leaders included inner healing writer and Charismatic Agnes

Sanford (1897–1982), Jesus People leader Linda Meissner, and more recently, prosperity preachers Marilyn Hickey (b.1931) and Joyce Meyer (b.1943). Jackie Pullinger (b.1944) began work among Hong Kong prostitutes, drug addicts, and gang members in 1966 and continues to rehabilitate and provide homes for 200 destitute people in her St. Stephen's Society. Her solution for drug addiction is prayer and the power of the Spirit, and her center does not use medication. Heidi Baker (b.1959) is a prominent and influential contemporary missionary in Mozambique with an earned PhD. She is a preacher with an extensive social welfare and healing ministry she runs with her husband Rolland called Iris Ministries, who (among other things) has issued calls for Americans to reject "superstar" ministries.[2]

The remarkable and sudden surge in the number of missionary candidates offering themselves for overseas service from the 1890s onward was partly attributable to changing attitudes toward single women becoming missionaries in Western Protestant, and especially evangelical, circles. Most of these missionary candidates were women who came from societies where their role was rapidly changing from a purely domestic one to one in which women—at least middle-class women—could embark on certain professional careers. These women had volunteered for one of the few careers available in an ecclesiastical world that was still very much male dominated. Published figures indicate that by 1900, 45 percent of the Protestant "foreign missionary" force was already female. John Alexander Dowie, whose Zionist healing movement had so much influence on early Pentecostalism, was a strong supporter of women in ministry. In 1903 he replied to a letter from Alexander Boddy, who had asked Dowie why his leaders, men and women, dressed up like Anglican bishops. Dowie, for all his shortcomings, was a fervent believer in a Christian egalitarianism that made no distinction between sexes, races, or social groups. Dowie used the opportunity to defend the ministry of women. His women leaders wore the same "costumes" as the men because he believed that "God has not only called men but women to the ministry, and what would apply to the robing of a man would also apply to that of the woman." He wrote that the Bible taught "neither male nor female, but that all are one in Christ Jesus." Women were called to the office of prophetess and so "God is no respecter of persons, and I, therefore, feel that women whom God has called should be ordained." Boddy's own position on women's ordination was unclear, but he was a minister in the church establishment that at the time did not ordain women, perhaps because of its relationship with the Catholic order of deacon, priest, and bishop. His wife

Mary Boddy, however, was highly influential in early British Pentecostalism and came into the pentecostal experience before her husband did.[3]

However, "free church" and independent pentecostals had no such qualms. The Azusa Street periodical *The Apostolic Faith* had established the precedent that it was "contrary to the Scriptures that woman should not have her part in the salvation work to which God has called her." The author, probably William Seymour, wrote that men had "no right to lay a straw in her way, but to be men of holiness, purity and virtue, to hold up the standard and encourage the woman in her work, and God will honor and bless us as never before." After all, the foundation for this ministry of women was the Spirit: "It is the same Holy Spirit in the woman as in the man," the author declared. In the Old Testament, women were only allowed into the "court of the women and not into the inner court" and the anointing oil (signifying the Holy Spirit) was only poured on male kings, priests, and prophets. But all this changed when "all those faithful women" were together in the upper room at Pentecost, when "God baptized them all in the same room and made no difference." The result was that "all the women received the anointed oil of the Holy Ghost and were able to preach the same as the men." The event of Spirit baptism first given at Pentecost had demolished all gender discrimination. However, there was an ominous qualification to this apparent freedom: "No woman that has the Spirit of Jesus wants to usurp authority over the man." Unfortunately, the initial enthusiasm for women ministers was later modified further by Seymour when the Mission's constitution declared "Women may be ministers but not to baptize or ordain in this work." In part, this may have been a reaction to the hurt Seymour suffered after the defection of his leading women Florence Crawford and Clara Lum and the end of his *Apostolic Faith* periodical in 1908. But it is a reflection of the ambiguity with which pentecostal men and women approached the issue, having been immersed in a strongly patriarchal form of Christianity that was difficult to challenge.[4]

Nevertheless, North American pentecostal history is full of women pioneers. The controversial Florence Crawford (1872–1936) and the African American preacher Lucy Farrow (1851–1911) were prominent leaders in the Azusa Street revival. Crawford was founder of the Apostolic Faith Church in Portland, Oregon; and Farrow was William Seymour's mentor, possibly his pastor in Houston, Texas, and the most significant leader at the beginning of the revival in Los Angeles. There were several prominent American pentecostal healing evangelists who were women. The best known were Maria Woodworth-Etter, Carrie Judd Montgomery, and the enigmatic Aimee Semple McPherson. These pioneers were the trickle that became a flood in the later history of Pentecostalism.

Probably the most famous of the American pentecostal woman involved in church leadership was the colorful and controversial Aimee Semple McPherson (1890–1944), founder of the Church of the Foursquare Gospel in 1927, now known as the Foursquare Church. Born in a Canadian Salvation Army family, she became pentecostal in 1907 and was ordained by William Durham in Chicago with her evangelist husband Robert Semple in 1909. The Semples first accompanied Durham on his preaching tours and then went to Hong Kong as missionaries in 1910. When Semple died of malaria after two months in Hong Kong, his young widow returned to Los Angeles, married Harold McPherson in 1911, and began an ecumenical, interdenominational preaching and healing career of the "Foursquare Gospel," another term for "full gospel" but a fourfold rather than fivefold one that omitted sanctification as a distinct experience. In mass meetings all over the country, she used bold and innovative methods including flamboyant advertising, showering handbills from an airplane, driving a "gospel auto" on which slogans were painted, using dramatic illustrations in her (partially acted) sermons, and becoming the first woman to preach on the radio. "Sister Aimee," as she was known, was an enormously talented public speaker, writer, musician, and administrator—and a media star. She was ordained in the Assemblies of God in 1919, but left in 1922 over the question of ownership of church property. She and McPherson separated in 1918 and were divorced in 1921. In 1923 she opened a 5,300-seat building in Los Angeles called Angelus Temple, a building still in use. She opposed racism, fought against crime and poverty, encouraged women to enter the ministry, and began a campaign against drug trafficking. Her disappearance through kidnapping to Mexico in 1926 and her spectacular reappearance a month later was an event shrouded in controversy and great media publicity. Even her death in 1944 from an accidental overdose of prescription medication was controversial. She left behind a membership of 22,000 in more than 400 churches and 200 overseas mission stations, and a Bible college founded in 1923 that had trained 3,000 preachers. Aimee McPherson was the prototype of a new kind of American pentecostal leader; these individuals were able to use and adapt the prevailing popular culture of their day for their own purposes. McPherson's Life Bible College had far more women than men, and she saw this as a vital part of her war against gender discrimination and male prejudice in Christianity. However, there was even some ambiguity about her views on women in ministry, for at Angelus Temple she allowed only male elders, one of whom would sit with her on the platform and preside with her in baptisms and communion.[5]

Aimee's son, Rolf McPherson (1913–2009), took over as president of the denomination, a post he held until 1988. During his time in office the Foursquare Church became one of the fastest-growing pentecostal denominations in the world. Large congregations like Angelus Temple and the Church on the Way in Van Nuys, California, led by Jack Hayford have continued their founder's vision of changing with the times, especially in adapting to the challenge of the rapidly growing new Charismatic churches with their modern worship styles. The Foursquare Church joined the National Association of Evangelicals in 1952, and it has maintained its founder's commitment to mission, helping the poor, disaster relief, and the ministry of women. Some 40 percent of the Foursquare ministers internationally are women, probably a higher proportion than in any other pentecostal denomination.[6]

Histories often credit the origins and development of pentecostal movements worldwide to men. The first histories of the movement exhibited not only what Wacker terms a "white racial bias," but also a "persistent gender bias" in which the role of women leaders was ignored. Sometimes the wives of pentecostal leaders play a more important role than their husbands do, though their work is often unrecognized. Three examples among many are Marie Burgess Brown in New York, Ellen Hebden in Toronto, and Margaret Idahosa in Nigeria. But women have always played an important part in Pentecostalism, often in striking contrast to other denominations. Their role in the pentecostal transformation of world Christianity, however, has been ambiguous, unrecognized, and neglected, if not entirely overlooked. Women played significant roles in the beginnings of Pentecostalism. Seymour's core leadership team was fully integrated with women and men being responsible for various aspects of the work—and more than half these leaders were women. Lucy Farrow was the person who initiated the conversion of William Seymour to Pentecostalism and arranged his transfer to Los Angeles, and she led the first party of Asuza Street missionaries to Liberia. Lucy Leatherman was similarly involved in the introduction of T. B. Barratt, pioneer of Pentecostalism in Europe, to Pentecostalism; and she and another woman prayed for his Spirit baptism. Minnie Abrams in India sent her booklet to Willis Hoover, which sparked the Chilean pentecostal movement. Antoinette Moomau was founder and leader for many years of the first pentecostal church in Shanghai, China. Mukti Mission founder Pandita Ramabai—arguably the most significant woman involved in early Pentecostalism—and the revival movement she led were almost completely ignored by historians because she did not start a Pentecostal denomination or believe in the American-originated doctrine of speaking in tongues as "initial evidence" of Spirit baptism, and perhaps also because her revival was not in the Western world. These are cases where the influence of women has far exceeded the impression left by the written histories.[7]

Lucy Leatherman, from Greencastle, Indiana, was a physician's widow and the first pentecostal missionary in the Middle East. A former student at A. B. Simpson's Missionary Training School in Nyack, New York, she had received Spirit baptism through the prayers of Lucy Farrow at Azusa Street, where she believed she had spoken Arabic and was called to evangelize Palestinian Arabs. Her testimony was published in *The Apostolic Faith* and evokes a mystical experience:

> While seeking for the baptism with the Holy Ghost in Los Angeles, after Sister [Farrow] laid hands on me, I praised and praised God and saw my Savior in the heavens. And as I praised, I came closer and closer, and I was so small. By and by I swept into the wound in His side, and He was not only in me but I in Him, and there I found that rest that passeth all understanding, and He said to me, you are in the bosom of the Father. He said I was clothed upon and in the secret place of the Most High. But I said, Father, I want the gift of the Holy Ghost, and the heavens opened and I was overshadowed, and such power came upon me and went through me. He said, Praise Me, and when I did, angels came and ministered unto me. I was passive in His hands, and by the eye of faith I saw angel hands working on my vocal cords, and I realized they were loosing me. *I began to praise Him in an unknown language.*
>
> In a few days, while on my way to church, I met a lady and two little children. She was talking to her children in a language that sounded like the words God had given me. I spoke a sentence to her, and she said, "What you say means God has given Himself to you." She is from Beirut, Syria, and speaks Arabic. Eight years ago, in A.B. Simpson's missionary school at Nyack, New York, I heard the Macedonian cry to go to Jerusalem, but it is to the Arabs. I am told there are more Arabs than Jews there, and God has been speaking to me and asks me if I would be willing to go with Him to the wild Arab of the desert. Anywhere with Jesus I will gladly go.[8]

This remarkable older woman, together with Maud Williams, who had received Spirit baptism in Toronto under the ministry of Ellen Hebden, met T. B. Barratt in New York and introduced him to the pentecostal experience. Leatherman ministered in four continents and at least ten countries, no mean feat for a woman in those days. She traveled from country to country in the Middle East, sending back reports to several pentecostal papers. She was among the first group of missionaries reported as having left Los Angeles for Jerusalem in August 1906. Leatherman was responsible for the first pentecostal congregation in Asyût, Egypt, the place later made famous by the orphanage of her younger contemporary Lillian Trasher. Leatherman organized a conference in Ramallah, Palestine, with about 300 attendees, where an Egyptian from Asyût, Ghali Hanna, received Spirit baptism and started Pentecostalism in Egypt. Leatherman undertook an arduous and lonely journey, sometimes by mule in mountainous regions through Syria and Galilee, and she held meetings in Beirut. She then left for Egypt to see Ghali's work and reported a "great revival" in which "multitudes" had been "saved, sanctified and baptized with the Holy Ghost and fire." A world traveler, Leatherman left Egypt in February 1909 and moved eastward through Arabia to India, visiting missions in the Pune area (including Mukti) and meeting up with Carrie and George Montgomery on their round-the-world tour. She moved via Hong Kong and Shanghai (where she visited two pentecostal missions) to Yokohama, Japan. Her ceaseless activity had taken its toll. She grew very ill and spent months in Japan resting. But from there she went to Manila in 1910, where she preached to American military personnel. The report in *The Upper Room* in Los Angeles described her as "this brave woman whom God has made a pioneer in the Gospel." By 1911 she was on her way back to Palestine, and en route in Britain she preached in pentecostal conventions. Working in Beirut, Jerusalem, and returning to Asyût in 1913, Leatherman returned home for a short visit in 1916, having spent two dangerous years in the Middle East during the war. She soon traveled again, this time to South America as a missionary of the Church of God, which she had joined during her time in the United States. She ministered among fledgling pentecostal communities in Chile and Argentina until 1922, when she returned to the United States to be hospitalized at the end of her life, probably dying soon after her return.[9]

Lillian Trasher (1887–1961) founded an orphanage in Asyût, Egypt, in 1911. She arrived there as a young woman in 1910, devoted her life to this work, and seldom returned to her homeland. Because of her health she returned to the United States in 1955 for the first time in twenty-five years, only to spend the time raising funds for her orphanage. It was a measure of her commitment and stature that by 1917 all the expatriate pentecostal missionaries in Egypt had left after the outbreak of war—all, that is, except Trasher, who was then caring for some fifty orphans. She remained there through the Second World War and continued working with Egyptian orphans for over fifty years until her death in Egypt in 1961. One of the remarkable things about her work from the beginning was the recognition, esteem, and support she received from the Egyptian government and the financial support she received from Egyptian people, Muslims and Christians alike. They saw this work as theirs and readily helped Trasher put up buildings when needed. She is thought to have cared for over 8,000 Egyptian children during her lifetime, and at the end of her life there were 1,200 housed in the orphanage. The Lillian Trasher Memorial Orphanage now houses 650 and Lillian Trasher is buried in its grounds.[10]

Most records indicate that there were significantly more women involved in early American pentecostal missions than there were men. The influential Stone Church in Chicago under former Zionist elder William Hamner Piper was one of the greatest supporters of missions in the early American pentecostal movement. In 1919, for example, this church sent donations to thirty-two single women and twenty-six men. This did not include the missionary wives; if they were included, at least two thirds of the missionaries would have been women. Wacker also observes that half the traveling pentecostal evangelists were women. The training schools at that time had a majority of women, and the First World War had reduced the number of men applying even further—especially in Britain, where the men's training school for the PMU had to close and its conscientious objectors were sent to labor camps. In the United States, too, one of the best-known and best-equipped schools, Rochester Bible Training School in New York State, had ten women and four men in the class of 1917–18, whereas two years later there were seventeen women and three men. Of course, one reason for this could be that the School was attached to Elim Tabernacle, a prominent independent pentecostal congregation led by the three Baker sisters.[11]

Many pentecostals were still reluctant to allow women to teach men, because their conservative church backgrounds encouraged a literal reading of Paul's injunction that women must not be allowed to teach or have authority over men. The first person who received the pentecostal experience in Britain in January 1907, eight months before Pentecostalism was introduced by T. B. Barratt in Sunderland, was a woman: Catherine Price, who continued weekly pentecostal meetings in her home in Brixton, London. The principal of the women's training school for the British PMU was the remarkably capable Eleanor Crisp (1856–1923), who remained in this post for the entire life of the institution, 1910–22. She was the only woman on the PMU's ruling Council and a frequent speaker at pentecostal conferences in Britain.[12]

Women Leaders in the South

Women played an enormous role in early Pentecostalism as leaders and missionaries throughout the world, even though they faced enormous prejudice in their task, both socially and theologically. Pentecostal women leaders, like Pentecostalism itself, come in many hues and shades. Only a few women expressed their opinions on the ministry of women publicly in these years. It was still too sensitive a subject, and those women who were in ministry just got on with the job. They often led the way, founding and leading congregations, running mission bases, and taking responsibilities that put them on an equal footing with men. They were also soon to discover the ways in which women were even more oppressed in some countries than they were in the North, which affected converts and church attendees. Christianity had a distinct advantage when it was seen as the great equalizer, the religion that offered women freedom from harsh oppression—particularly in India where it was often contrasted with Hinduism and Islam. This contrast often appeared in the writings of Western women missionaries. One remarked that the Hindu women of India "were sunk in degradation from which only the Gospel of Jesus Christ can save them" and that the Muslim men similarly were "appalling" in their "oppression and degradation of women." In particular, the practices of *purdah* (a lifelong seclusion that barred women from education or employment), child marriage, and the caste system came in for heavy criticism. Women missionaries spoke of the plight of the village women in Palestine with "bright intelligent faces," who had been raised with the belief that they were "as truly beasts of burden as the donkeys" and that donkeys were "often better cared for."[13]

In China there were far more men attending Christian services than women. One missionary explained: "Here in China as in other heathen lands the women have hard work to do and consequently have not the same liberty as the men," implying correctly that the men did not have the same level of hard work. Sometimes the liberation of women was couched in purely esoteric terms. PMU missionary Ethel Cook expressed how women were empowered in China because "some of the simple women are being taught by visions and dreams occasionally," giving an example of a woman who "knew God had given her His Spirit—and she certainly had a real quickening touch of God upon her." Missionary May Kelty found opposition to the ministry of women among Argentine men and commented wryly about how she wished they would "interpret all the Scriptures as literally as those concerning women speaking in the church." Generally speaking, the women in Pentecostalism accepted that their authority was given them by the indiscriminate and equalizing power of the Spirit—and consequently they did not see the need to challenge cultural assumptions or even the traditional scriptural interpretations regarding their role.[14]

One of the most prominent women in the early development of Pentecostalism worldwide was, of course, Pandita Ramabai. As we have seen, although her considerable contribution to the cause of Indian women was well known, her influence on early Pentecostalism was almost unrecognized until recently. Her seeming acquiescence to the Indian caste system by focusing on "high caste" women in the early years of her mission has elicited criticism, but after her move to Kedgaon in 1896 she concentrated on helping lower-caste famine victims, and her later years were spent promoting "the gender-egalitarian impulse of Christianity and its compassion to sinners, especially the rehabilitation of 'fallen women.'" She too counteracted virulent male prejudice, not only from fellow Indians. American evangelical leader and Keswick speaker A. T. Pierson criticized speaking in tongues during the revival at Mukti in 1907 as accompanied by "indecencies" and committed by "hysterical women." Ramabai vigorously contested these comments, writing in her *Mukti Prayer Bell* newsletter that some of the young women in the Praying Bands were speaking in tongues, for which she "praised God for doing something new for us." She wrote that she would not try to stop the work of the Spirit, was "not aware that anything like the present Holy Ghost revival, has ever visited India before the year 1905," that "mountains have been made out of mole hills," and the reports of hysteria were "greatly exaggerated." Ramabai did not believe that the "tongue movement" was "of the devil, or is confined to a few hysterical women" (as Pierson had charged), but was convinced that those given the gift of tongues had been "greatly helped to lead better lives." For his part, Pierson had concluded that the present-day manifestations of tongues, including what he had seen among Welsh delegates at the 1905 Keswick conference, were "Satanic disturbances" and "imitations by the Devil of true tongues speaking." Ramabai had this perceptive comment about Western criticisms of the revival:

> Why should not the Holy Spirit have liberty to work among Indian Christian people, as He has among Christians of other countries? And why should everything that does not reach the high standard of English and American civilization, be taken as coming from the devil?...I see that God is doing great things for us and among us....what has happened here, during this revival, is not an imitation of anybody. Had these people who have come under the power of the Holy Ghost been mere imitators, they would certainly have shown their inclination toward that way before the revival came.[15]

Behind these comments was not only Ramabai's sympathy for the revival movement, but also her underlying nationalism, defense of women in ministry, and desire for an Indian church moved by the Spirit in an Indian way. As Meera Kosambi puts it, Ramabai "repeatedly attempted to indigenize Christianity and transform its alien cultural trappings into a more recognizable Indian garb." In the same article Ramabai wrote about the gift of tongues, which she said was "certainly one of the signs of the baptism of the Holy Spirit" and for which there was "scriptural ground." However, in common with some other early pentecostals, Ramabai found that "there is no scripture warrant to think that the speaking in tongues is the only and necessary sign of baptism of the Holy Spirit." But she wrote that gifts of healing, tongues, prophecy, and other gifts were "not to be discarded" but should be sought after. She ended this ten-page exhortation by witnessing to the physical manifestations happening:

> I have seen not only the most ignorant of our people coming under the power of revival, but the most refined and very highly educated English men and women, who have given their lives for God's service in this country, coming under the power of God, so that, they loose [sic] all control over their bodies, and are shaken like reeds, stammering words in various unknown tongues as the Spirit teaches them to speak, and gradually get to a place, where they are in unbroken communion with God. I, for one, do not dare to put them down as a few ignorant and 'hysterical women.' I wish all of us could get this wonderful and divine hysteria."[16]

Ramabai went on to declare her belief that "there is no effectual remedy of all the evils prevalent in this country, except in a Holy Ghost revival moving both Indian and foreign Christian people." Quoting the words of Christ, "How much more shall your Heavenly Father give the Holy Spirit to them that ask Him," Ramabai concluded: "We have been asking our Heavenly Father to give us the Holy Spirit and not evil spirits. He has answered our prayer. We praise Him, we bless Him, we magnify His Holy Name, and we thank Him with all our heart." Ramabai thereby defended the Indian pentecostal manifestations against the prevailing criticisms of Western evangelical leaders.[17]

Spiritual, moral, and societal leadership was no longer confined to ordained and hierarchically appointed clergy, nor even restricted by caste convention and Hindu conservatism, but was in the hands of the most ordinary of Christians empowered by the Spirit, indeed those of Pierson's "ignorant women." These women were now leading public prayer, mission, and social reform. Ramabai herself was an Indian woman who resisted both patriarchal oppression in India and Western domination in Christianity. Or as Abrams put it, Ramabai "demonstrat[ed] to her countrymen that women have powers and capabilities which they have not permitted them to cultivate." The Mukti pentecostal revival was pre-eminently a revival among women and led by women. Ramabai both influenced and attracted other women into active Christian ministry, not only her own countrywomen but also foreigners like the independent Methodist missionary Minnie Abrams, who had a profound impact on early Pentecostalism with her booklet *The Baptism of the Holy Ghost and Fire* (1906). This was the first theological defense of the pentecostal doctrine of Spirit baptism; it sparked the pentecostal revival led by her friends the Hoovers in Chile. Abrams was a champion of women's ministry in the pentecostal movement. In 1910, during leave in the United States two years before her death, she reported on the Laymen's Missionary Convention that she had attended in St Paul, where she was told that "the evangelization of the world was a man's job." She wrote that although she was "only one little woman," "many a woman has undertaken a man's job in connection with her own and carried it through to success." She thought that even if "the evangelization of the world is a man's job, you cannot do it without the women." In recruiting women for her pioneering new mission in India, she wanted those who had "been a success at home...educated and cultured women," but above all "women full of love and the Holy Spirit...women willing to settle down and plod, and hammer away until the rock breaks...who do not know what it is to be defeated in that which they undertake." Unlike the PMU, which, following CIM policy, wanted all their applicants (especially the women) to be under thirty in order to withstand better the rigors of language learning and missionary work, Abrams had quite the opposite opinion, preferring them to be "at least thirty years of age for this pioneer work."[18]

There were other notable older women among early pentecostal missionaries. Lucy Farrow was already in her mid-fifties when she introduced William Seymour to the pentecostal doctrine of Charles Parham and arranged his move to Los Angeles. Annie Murray, who was in charge of a mission home in Bombay from 1910 until her death two years later, was an older blind woman who would never have been accepted by any of the established mission societies because of her age and disability. Many early indigenous pentecostal leaders were women. They could not fail to have been impressed by the examples set by the Western women missionaries who worked among them and by indigenous pioneers like Ramabai. Ramabai's organization produced scores of female Indian missionaries who traveled the length and breadth of India. The pentecostal revival in Mukti in 1905 was an Indian movement among Indian women, with the participation and observation of a small number of expatriate missionaries. This remained the main source of Indians working in pentecostal missions for at least a decade, and by 1910 there were 125 young women training in the Mukti Bible school to become full-time Christian workers. Western pentecostal periodicals particularly noted the enormous contribution made to Christian mission by the three Indian Brahmin women: Ramabai, Soonderbai Powar, and Shorat Chuckerbutty. One declared that "the best work done in India to-day" was "upon purity principles of faith and prayer, and no leaders there are more mightily anointed than many of the native women," who were "women of peerless purity and power, the Deborahs of the darkened Empire." Each of these women was a "Spirit anointed prophetess of purity and faith principles" who had exposed herself to dangers on behalf of the "oppressed and perishing." These Indian women were outspoken in their demands for equality in an unjust society, and of course, they had had the shining example of Pandita Ramabai who had led the way.[19]

Soonderbai Powar was one of the most critically outspoken on the subject of the oppression of women in India. She wrote that Indian women were never free but were forced to be obedient to men throughout their lives, first to their fathers, then to their husbands, and finally to their sons. Their obedience was forced and was not "drawn by tender love and chivalrous attentions." She blamed this bondage squarely upon Hinduism, which she stated was "a religion that has drawn out all that is selfish in man and made him see as his god nothing but his own ugly self; that has made woman nothing but a soulless animal to be used for the pleasure of man." At a convention in Rochester, New York, in 1918 one of Ramabai's American assistants spoke of the contribution such Indian women had made to Pentecostalism. She pointed out that they were "so filled with the Spirit and so taught of God" that expatriate missionaries (such as Alice Luce) had "received Pentecost through their gracious ministry" and had "been willing to learn the deeper truths of God through their words and holy examples." Luce (1873–1955), a CMS missionary in India since 1896, had received her Spirit baptism in 1910 through the hands of Shorat Chuckerbutty, a Bengali Brahmin Christian who ran an orphanage and school in Allahabad, where a pentecostal revival was taking place and daily services were held in which many were reported converted and baptized in the Spirit. Both Luce and Agnes Hill, then general secretary of the YWCA in India, had visited Chuckerbutty's center "and received the baptism in the Holy Spirit through the prayers of an Indian woman, glory to God for the great sisterhood there is!" reported Hill a few years later. Luce was later to move to the United States and join the AG, where she became a missionary and Bible college principal among Hispanics in San Diego from 1926 until her death.[20]

The Hong Kong Chinese evangelist Kong Duen Yee (1923–66), born in Beijing and an actress in over seventy Chinese films, was a controversial leader. Better known by her stage name Mui Yee, she lived only seven years after she became a pentecostal in 1959, when she was reportedly healed. She gave up acting and established the Christian Charismatic Evangelistic Team, which in 1963 became the New Testament Church in Hong Kong. In Singapore, the former Brethren elder Goh Ewe Kheng had become pentecostal in Kong's meetings. His Church of Singapore became a respected and large Charismatic church in the city, with Goh becoming chair of the Evangelical Fellowship of Singapore in the mid-1990s. Kong led many revival meetings in churches in Hong Kong, Taiwan, Malaysia, and Singapore and was heavily critical of other churches, especially those that did not accept her teaching of Spirit baptism accompanied by speaking in tongues. She called on people to leave their churches and form independent churches in association with the New Testament Church, which she said was the only true church. After her death from tongue cancer in 1966, her daughter

Ruth Cheung took on the leadership of the church until she renounced the extremes of its teachings and moved to California. The new leader of the organization from 1976 was Elijah Hong, a former AG member who joined Kong in Taiwan in 1965 and propagated even more radical millenarian teachings from his Mount Zion New Testament Church. The church continues in this part of Asia and in the Chinese diaspora but is marginalized by other Chinese churches. In Taiwan, Hong is considered by the church to be the prophet Elijah, "God's Chosen Prophet of All Nations"; members believe they are "spiritual Israelites"; and that a mountain in southern Taiwan is Mount Zion, the new Jerusalem on which Jesus will alight at his second coming. The New Testament Church still considers Kong its founder, and Mount Zion is actually home to 300 people who operate a large organic farm and to which church followers make pilgrimages from other parts of the world.[21]

There are more recent examples of pentecostal women who have defied the odds in male-dominated societies. South Korea has two eminent ones, both originally from North Korea. After she fled with her family to South Korea, Jashil Choi (1915–89) attended the Assemblies of God Bible school in Seoul and started a small congregation in her house. This became the tent church of which her future son-in-law David Yonggi Cho became pastor in 1958. By the 1980s, it was the largest congregation in the world. Choi is not often recognized as the force behind Yonggi Cho's early success, but Cho himself refers to her as "my spiritual mother, and my greatest benefactor." In 1973 Choi also founded the well-known prayer center near the demilitarized zone, associated with Yoido Full Gospel Church and now including her name in its title, Osan-ri Choi Jashil Memorial Fasting Prayer Mountain. Her daughter and the wife of Yonggi Cho, Sunghae Kim, who has a doctorate in music, for several years has been the president of Hansei University in Gunpo, the denomination's university. Another influential pentecostal leader is the founder, in 1970, of the Foursquare Church in Korea, Seen Ok Ahn (b.1924). She may not have had quite the worldwide impact of Choi and Yonggi Cho, but nonetheless she has established a chain of congregations, a theological college, a prison ministry, and six independent Christian schools with 8,000 students and a staff of 400 in her home city of Daejeon.[22]

A prominent African independent church with many thousands of members is the St. John's Apostolic Faith Mission of South Africa, founded by Mokotudi Christina Nku (1894–1988), a former member of the Dutch Reformed Church. As a young woman she began to have revelations, including, during a serious illness, a vision of heaven in which she believed God told her that she would not die. These mystical visions and her subsequent healing legitimated her calling as a religious leader in a male-dominated society. Women had always played prominent roles as religious leaders and healers in African societies. Further visions established Christina Nku's reputation, and later she had a vision of the large church with twelve doors that she would build. She met Elias Nkitseng of the Apostolic Faith Mission in 1918 and she and her husband Lazarus Nku were baptized in 1924. They did not remain in the AFM long, as its president P. L. le Roux apparently objected to "some of her more elaborate displays of prophetic rapture."[23]

Nku established the St. John's Apostolic Faith Mission in 1933, becoming well known as a healer and attracting thousands into her church. The twelve-door church known as the Temple, which she built in 1952 in Evaton, southwest of Johannesburg, was the largest independent church building in the Gauteng urban area. Although the "Apostolic" name of the church implied continuity with the pentecostal movement, her healing rituals brought increasing distance between her and the white-led pentecostal denominations. In particular was the use of blessed water, as she prayed over water in thousands of bottles and buckets, which was distributed to the faithful for healing. Nku is a somewhat ambiguous example of female leadership. In the growth and development of St. John she was assisted by her husband, who became a bishop, and by Elias Nkitseng. But Nkitseng died in 1948 and Lazarus Nku was killed in a railway accident in 1949. Nku began to rely increasingly on her son Johannes, whom she made a bishop and eventually gave the senior male position of archbishop. Male leadership, even if token, was more acceptable to male-dominated African society and the church accommodated itself to this prevalent opinion. During her leadership Christina Nku, who was better known as MaNku ("Mother Nku"), established schools for children and self-development programs for youth and adults in her church. This directly benefited the community in the years of apartheid and functioned as a response to a system that oppressed the poor African majority.

With her advancing age, MaNku's grip on the church began to wane and Johannes Nku and Petros John Masango (1908–84) were opposing candidates for archbishop in 1970. When Masango won the election, MaNku announced that Masango would only occupy the office until the following year when she would appoint another archbishop. She followed this announcement by expelling Masango and declaring that she would not take orders from any bishop, who had "no authority in this church in my lifetime," and no new constitution would be valid without her written approval. Masango announced that a conference would be held in his home in Swaziland and not, as usual, at the Temple in Evaton. He and Johannes Nku also differed sharply on the issue of polygamy, which the latter supported. Johannes Nku resigned from the church and went into business, eliciting sharp criticism from his mother. The differences between MaNku and Masango became so sharp that they resulted in protracted litigation in the Supreme Court, with the final ruling in 1971 declaring Masango lawfully elected archbishop. Masango broke all ties with the Nku family in 1972 and established himself as "founder" of the church, the one from the east prophesied by MaNku, with his own special place for baptisms dedicated at Katlehong in eastern Gauteng in 1983. Despite this rift, Masango was a capable leader and by the mid-1970s the main faction of St. John had some 50,000 members. Masango remained archbishop until his death in 1984, by which time the church estimated its membership to be over 100,000 throughout South Africa. After Masango's death there was another bitter and prolonged struggle for control of the church between several factions, and Jacob Maragu became archbishop of the main faction in 1997. When Maragu died in 2005 he was succeeded by his wife. By 1997 the church MaNku had founded existed in three major factions and several minor ones, and in 2006 attempts were made toward the reunification of five of the thirty-nine factions, facilitated by the South African Council of Churches. One of the major factions is led by MaNku's grandson. Her autocratic leadership notwithstanding, Christina Nku was undoubtedly one of the most remarkable women the South African pentecostal movement has produced.[24]

Possibly the two most prominent contemporary African pentecostal women are firmly within the "Word of Faith" prosperity camp. Archbishop Margaret Idahosa (b.1943) took over the Church of God Mission International in Benin City, Nigeria, after her husband Benson Idahosa's death in 1998. She leads a congregation in a building with a capacity of 5,000, holds several services weekly, and runs a private university, a group of Christian schools and hospitals, and an influential international ministry to encourage women in Christian leadership. In Nairobi, Kenya, Bishop Margaret Wanjiru (b. 1961), born in poverty, is a remarkable leader who was a street hawker and cleaner before she started her own business. She confesses to having been a witch before her conversion in 1990 and she was for many years a single parent. In 1993 she founded Jesus Alive

Ministries, which is now a megachurch in Nairobi that claims 20,000 members and promises its followers prosperity, success, and deliverance from all evil powers. She was one of the first African pentecostal women to enter politics, becoming a member of parliament for the constituency in which her church is located in 2007. She was appointed Assistant Minister for Housing in 2008, but lost her seat in an election in August 2011, but was back as Assistant Minister soon after. Kenyans were fascinated by the soap opera over her first marriage that played out on the national media in 2007–08, resulting in a court injunction against her pending marriage to a South African pastor. The drama ended with the even more dramatic death of the man who claimed to be her first husband and the father of her children. This event would engender enormous respect for Wanjiru as a victim who had overcome a deliberate attempt at character assassination. As the pentecostals would put it, she had defeated the devil.[25]

The Gender Paradox in Pentecostal Families

Several studies show that Pentecostalism gives women significant advantages, particularly bestowing moral autonomy in the family and challenging notions of masculinity and patriarchal hegemony. This is what sociologist Bernice Martin has termed the "Pentecostal gender paradox." We have seen how, on the one hand, women are often denied hierarchical positions of leadership in pentecostal churches. But on the other hand, women lead the way in gifts of the Spirit, and in the words of Martin:

> In societies characterized by a tradition of male dominance [women] have been enabled to institute a family discipline, sanctioned and effectively policed by the church community, which puts the collective needs of the household unit above the freedom and pleasures of men and which has called an end to the long-tolerated double standard of sexual morality.[26]

There have been many emotionally charged debates in pentecostal denominations on the question of women's rights to leadership, almost always based on what male functionaries consider the incontrovertible biblical support for exclusively male leadership. The last international conference in Sunderland, England, in 1914 spent much time debating the topic of "Woman's place in the Church," and by today's standards their discussion would be considered archaic and reactionary. All the published opinions were those of men, except for that of Wilhelmina Polman, the wife of the Dutch pentecostal leader, whose stated position was as conservative as was any of the men's. Even today, many women married to conservative pentecostal men toe the party line and submit themselves to their husbands "as unto the Lord."[27]

Across the Atlantic, E. N. Bell, first chairman of the American AG, a former Baptist pastor and a bachelor, wrote about the role of women missionaries on the eve of the formation of the AG in 1914. He believed women were "recognized in the New Testament only as 'helpers in the gospel,' as Paul puts it." He stated that women missionaries should not itinerate alone but find permanent work in a station "under the proper oversight of some good brother whom God has placed in charge of the work." Although he reluctantly admitted that "God has blessed" the work of women who had opened up stations of their own and that he had "never objected to this," he found "no scriptural precept or example for such independent leadership by women." The early AG continued this reactionary trend. Its first General Council in 1914 adopted a resolution on "Rights and Offices of Women" to recommend that "we recognize their God-given rights to be ordained, not as elders, but as Evangelists and Missionaries, after being approved according to the Scriptures." These positions were regarded as subservient in the denomination. However, women delegates—and there *were* a handful present—were not allowed to vote on this or on any other resolution. Women were permitted to become assistant pastors in 1920, but this was simply a response by the male AG Council to a need for pastors to leave their wives in charge of congregations when they itinerated. Grant Wacker traces "the tortured story of women's credentialing as ministers in the infant Assemblies of God," where restrictions on women's authority in this and other American pentecostal denominations increased during the years following the First World War. Only beginning in 1935 could women become pastors and, even then, only with significant restrictions.[28]

Such restrictions did not reflect the reality of the prominent role played by women pastors, founders of churches, and missionaries in early Pentecostalism. There were actually very few restrictions on women as missionaries, because somehow the patriarchs in their wisdom had decided that this was a position less threatening, perhaps because it was less authoritative within their organizations. The geographical distance of the women missionaries from the church headquarters may have made it more acceptable—but after all, these women also had received the gift of the empowering Holy Spirit, the only qualification for being sent. Consequently, the practice of pentecostal missions and the stated position of the supporting churches did not always harmonize. But this was a time when women were still not fully enfranchised, higher educational opportunities were still denied them, and a general patriarchal attitude prevailed globally. Although the degree of gender discrimination has improved since then, pentecostal denominations in the West still struggle with these unresolved issues and are characterized by "a hierarchical male clergy and a high degree of institutionalism." Some organizations have yet to rethink decisions and actions limiting this most important ministry of women, who form the large majority of the church worldwide.[29]

Yonggi Cho in Korea appointed women as leaders in his thousands of home groups; throughout the world, women assume leadership and pastoral roles in such groups where the bulk of church development and nurture occurs. Pentecostal churches also have strong women's organizations that run in parallel with the structures dominated by men and where women's influence and authority often equal or exceed that of men. Pentecostalism would not have grown as it did without their ministry and support. Nonetheless, even in those churches where only male leadership is allowed, to conclude that these churches are home to dominant men and subordinate women is a gross oversimplification. Pentecostalism, with its recognition of the empowering gifts of the Spirit available to all—and often, to women far more than to men—means that women actually have many ways to exert influence and authority in the churches. However, this neither excuses nor justifies patriarchal notions, attitudes, and actions of pentecostal leaders. Religious ideology since time immemorial has been used to reinforce and mystify male patriarchy and female subordination, and Pentecostalism is no exception.[30]

Gender issues in the study of Pentecostalism have recently received more attention, especially from social scientists. Social anthropologist Elizabeth Brusco has led the way in this area with her 1995 study of evangelical women in Colombia. At first glance, many pentecostal churches reinforce traditional male dominance in the family and the church. Miller and Yamamori discovered only one congregation led by a woman in several years of field research; and Crumbley discovered severe restrictions on women in leadership in the three Nigerian Aladura churches she studied. Brusco described her first experience of a pentecostal service, a Hispanic congregation in New York where the women "ran almost the entire service from the floor" while "four men dressed in business suits sat on the stage." This is not an unusual scenario, and men are often given "up front" places of prominence in pentecostal congregations even though much of the activity is conducted by the women. Women are singled out for disciplinary action in congregations by male leaders often for the most trivial of reasons—a study in Brazil recorded that 90 percent of disciplinary cases were of women members. However, this is only one side of the story, for as Brusco observes, to understand the worldwide appeal of Pentecostalism to women it is also important to understand its "aggressive focus on the family, on marital and parental roles and responsibilities, that results in a discernible shift in the domestic life of converts." Women convert to Pentecostalism for the same reasons that men do: healing, spiritual nourishment, and community acceptance; but to this must be added the significant attraction of being "somebody" in a society where you are "nobody," and the benefits of "effectively addressing the problems resulting from machismo, especially that of the male abdication of family responsibility."[31]

Brusco's research in Colombia demonstrates the dominant feature of machismo in Latin American societies, defined as "arrogance and sexual aggression in male-to-female relationships" and "the alienation of men from the household," resulting in a polarization between male and female roles, rendering women invisible. In these and many other societies, women justifiably see their men as the main source of family income but do not have any control over that income, and so are often forced to find alternative means. The dissolution of the family is seen as the worst possible tragedy leading to financial ruin. Machismo is not only detrimental to women; several studies show that it is also detrimental to upward social mobility for men because it encourages a profligate and dangerous lifestyle. Machismo is not confined to Latin America, however; it is found in varying degrees in all societies worldwide and wherever women are subservient to men. Conversion to Pentecostalism does bestow a sense of dignity and value on women, but this is not the only benefit. Brusco shows that pentecostal women take their role as mothers and wives seriously and that this has had the effect of supporting a dominant and positive female position as moral leaders in the family and of reattaching men who had detached themselves from family responsibilities. This she terms the "domestication of men," because women are usually the first to convert to Pentecostalism and often bring the male members of their families with them afterward. The result is as follows:

> The ascetism required of evangelicals brings about changes in the
> behavior of male converts, particularly in relation to the machismo

complex in Latin America. Drinking, smoking, and extramarital sexual relations are forbidden. By redirecting into the household the resources spent on these things, such changes have the effect of raising the standard of living of women and children who are in varying degrees dependent on the income of these men.[32]

This has the effect of reforming gender roles in such a way as to enhance female status. Martin describes this as men being "returned to the home," and argues that there is an "implicit deal" in which greater sexual equality is tolerated by the pentecostal church leaders "as long as women are not seen to be publicly exercising formal authority over men." She suggests that it suits both women and men for this gender paradox to remain unresolved and that women gain more from the paradox than men do. Women are universally regarded as the morally superior partners in a marriage and consider it their job to constantly reform their husbands. Once converted, the men are subjected to teachings about their lifestyle, their family responsibilities, and conjugal fidelity. One study of two pentecostal churches in the greater Durban area of South Africa showed how Pentecostalism challenged male notions of masculinity and male understanding of the husband as "head of the home." The men in these churches exercised leadership in the family and church only by permission of the women, and on becoming pentecostals they began to see that Christ's example should be followed by men serving their wives and children. Mark Cartledge found from research into "godly love" in the Church of God (Cleveland) that "the mother is the key player" in the pentecostal family, particularly with regard to "socializing 'born again' experiences" and ensuring "the Pentecostal identity of the family." The men looked to their wives for spiritual leadership and guidance, whereas the women usually look to family members other than their husbands. This placed marriage at the center of "Pentecostal socialization." Through its emphasis on conversion and holiness, Pentecostalism often creates a different type of man, a domesticated man, and thus obliquely offers a sociopolitical critique resulting in the empowerment, liberation, and equality of women. Well, almost.[33]

Of course there are limitations to the extent of this liberation, for hegemonic masculinity is still a feature of many societies. Pentecostalism seldom directly challenges patriarchy or the power structures that render women unequal, and sometimes it deliberately legitimizes these structures. The discourse of pentecostal women is often radically different when they are in the presence of men. Yet, it is often the women to whom the men look for spiritual guidance, the women who lead in prayer and gifts of the Spirit in church gatherings, and ultimately it is the women to whom their husbands look for spirituality. Often the women are the first to convert to Pentecostalism and their husbands are sometimes either passive followers or do not join the church at all. The result is that women take the lead in the spiritual direction of the home in many pentecostal families. A study of women's participation in a pentecostal church in La Paz, Bolivia, argues that a contradiction between the teachings and ideals of the church and the reality of their family life has never been completely resolved. While Pentecostalism legitimizes male authority, it also modifies harmful behavior toward women. This unresolved paradox suits both the men and the women in the commonly accepted ideological characterization of male and female roles.[34]

Several studies of Latin American Pentecostalism have demonstrated how husbands' behavior changed after conversion and how this improved women's lives in the family. One study points out that women's emancipation in Pentecostalism is predominantly practical. Women bring their husbands to faith to try to alter habits like smoking and drinking, and after conversion their sexual aggression and arrogance toward women has to change in order to suit a pentecostal lifestyle. This study argues that family life and a husband's responsibility to his wife and children are essential in pentecostal communities. Other studies suggest that Latin American Pentecostalism might best be viewed as a women's movement, for it provides a survival mechanism for many women and a potent force for change in the face of severe gender inequalities, transforming both male and female roles. Men no longer make autonomous decisions, for as Brusco points out, although the husband may continue to be regarded as the head of the family, "his relative aspirations have changed to coincide with that of his wife." Brazilian women researchers have cautioned against a Western feminist interpretation positing contradictory male and female roles in Pentecostalism, because pentecostals see adherence to strict moral codes not as oppression but as "proof of the liberation of the individual."[35]

This chapter has focused on the role of women in Pentecostalism and how they have a significance often denied them in the larger culture. While women do not always have easy access to hierarchical leadership roles in pentecostal churches (with a few notable exceptions), their role as leaders of, participants in, and controllers of the pentecostal congregation and especially of the pentecostal family is of enormous importance. This feature in a Christian movement that is predominantly female goes a long way toward explaining its proliferation during the twentieth century. Outward leadership of women is the consequence, not the cause, of the liberation of women in Pentecostalism, and to focus on the absence of the hierarchical leadership of women is to miss what is really going on. To be sure, this is paradoxical and, on the face of it, women are not liberated from the larger embedded structures of patriarchy in church and society. But because liberation often takes place through the reordering of relative participation in the most intimate sphere and in the basic building block of the larger society—the family—the liberation of women in pentecostal churches is all the more profound and transforming. But there is still some way to go.

5

Bible and Community

The Bible in Pentecostal Practice

The various revivals at the beginning of the twentieth century started a wave of anticipation across the Christian world for a worldwide revival that had never been seen before, one that would result in unprecedented missionary activity across the globe. These are my central assumptions: (1) the Azusa Street revival in the United States and the Mukti revival in India were part of a wider series of revivals in the first decade of the twentieth century that facilitated the early promotion of pentecostal beliefs and values throughout the world; (2) missionary networks, especially that of the CMA, were instrumental in spreading Pentecostalism internationally; (3) pentecostal periodicals not only spread Pentecostalism but were the foundation of the meta-culture that arose and influenced all forms of Pentecostalism worldwide; and (4) these revivals were part of a series of formative events in the emergence of a new international missionary movement that took several years to develop a distinctive identity.

New forces were pushing for autonomy from Western colonial control, and these extended to the churches planted by Western missionaries, including pentecostal ones. These forces were aided by the propensity of the movement toward schism, its flexibility and adaptability in a variety of cultures, the political movements toward independence from colonialism, the liberation that Pentecostalism offered especially to women, the religious continuity between Pentecostalism and popular religion, and the social and economic forces that made its expansion outside the Western world inevitable. In this chapter, special attention is given to the majority world's discovery of the Bible, a source of authority independent of Western missionaries. Although we have explored the role of Western missionaries in the early expansion of Pentecostalism, they were hardly the driving force for long. The hegemony of Western missionaries ceased early on.

The Bible, and pentecostal interpretations and uses of it, were of primary importance to the expansion of Pentecostalism in the global South. Walter Hollenweger dedicated his first tome, *The Pentecostals,* to the pentecostals who taught him "to love the Bible" and to the Presbyterians who taught him "to understand it." His implied slighting of pentecostal biblical scholarship notwithstanding—although perhaps fair when he wrote it—Hollenweger knew that pentecostals were devoted to the Bible. In some cases, it was the only book they read. The first pentecostals always appealed to the Bible and their literal and pragmatic interpretation of it to justify their sometimes controversial practices. These justifications were often couched in fundamentalist language. Writing in 1926, AG leader Stanley Frodsham asserted:

> There are thousands of Pentecostal assemblies on the earth today. We have never known of a Modernist among them. All believe in the plenary verbal inspiration of the Bible. All teach repentance toward God and faith in the Lord Jesus Christ, and salvation from sin through the all-blotting-out blood of Jesus Christ. All believe there is healing through the stripes of the Crucified One.... Everywhere a life of practical holiness is taught. All are looking for the near and pre-millennial coming of the Lord Jesus Christ and, needless to say, they all believe in receiving the Holy Ghost just as He was originally received on the Day of Pentecost.[1]

This belief in "plenary verbal inspiration" as the source of pentecostal teaching and practice still dominates global Pentecostalism today. In his second book on the subject of the worldwide shifts in Christianity, *The New Faces of Christianity: Believing the Bible in the Global South,* Philip Jenkins concentrates on the implications of the shifts in Christian demography for the teachings and practices of the Christian faith. As his subtitle suggests, one of the most significant factors in the growth of Christianity in the South has been the approach to "believing the Bible." Jenkins points out that the interpretation of the Bible in the South is conditioned by the cultural contexts of agrarian, tribal, animistic, and economically impoverished communities. These conditions, Jenkins writes, are similar to those that prevailed in the ancient Near East, and therefore the Bible has a greater immediacy in the global South than it does in the prosperous West. All this makes "southern" understandings of the Bible very different from those found in the Western world.[2]

For many years, the primary objective of Protestant mission schools was to enable people to read the Bible in their own language. The translation of the Scriptures was often the first literature to appear in a local language. Great authority was given to the printed word and people were now able to compare the message of the missionaries with that of the Bible. They weren't always in harmony. The Bible therefore became an independent source of authority. Soon, the missionaries were being criticized for not being biblical enough. Because of the authority given to the vernacular Bible in all areas of life, most pentecostals throughout the world interpreted it in a very literal and fundamentalist way. They saw practices or customs in the Bible closely resembling their own, and it seemed to them that the Bible was much more sympathetic to their own traditions than the missionaries had led them to believe. For example, despite the missionaries' almost universal condemnation of polygamy, many biblical heroes were polygamists. The missionaries disapproved of ancestor veneration, but the long lists of ancestors in the Bible seemed to legitimate Africans' concern that the "living-dead" continue to be honored. The new churches created in Africa in the early twentieth century used Bible verses to justify their practices and found new prohibitions there that were taken literally, from the Old Testament in particular. But for this reason, too, African churches often rejected witchcraft, magic, and ancestor veneration as means of solving problems. Western Protestant missionaries had also rejected these rituals, but for quite different reasons. Whereas their worldview saw these practices as "ignorant superstitions" to be systematically obliterated by education, Africans saw them as real social problems that were manifestations of evil spirits and sorcery, and they proclaimed a more radical solution. In this they appealed to the Bible, and created what Hastings suggested amounted to "a sort of biblical-African alliance" against the more rationalistic and inflexible Western Christianity. In the vernacular Bible, Africans had an independent source of authority abounding in symbolic healing practices and exorcisms not unlike their own. In short, the Bible seemed to lend much more support to traditional African customs than to the imported cultural customs of the European missionaries.[3]

Pentecostalism as a whole also identifies its beliefs with the biblical worldviews. It becomes therefore an attractive option for those most in sympathy with a supernatural worldview. The biblical literalism found in pentecostal churches is consistent with their roots in holiness, healing, and other radical evangelical and revivalist movements. Pentecostal missionaries all used the Bible to justify everything they did and believed in, but they also pointed to a God who continued to do the things God did in the Bible's pages. These things—miracles, healings, deliverance from evil spirits, prophecy, and speaking in tongues—all reminded their hearers of the needs addressed by their traditional and oral religions, but the pentecostal missionaries' claims seemed more powerful in meeting those needs. Furthermore, it took neither great learning nor a foreign missionary to demonstrate a present, intervening God—women and men in whom the Spirit had come could do the things that Jesus, Peter, or Paul had done. And so they went out and did them, and their message attracted greater numbers of their own people.

Pentecostals usually interpret the Bible through a "plain reading" that makes use primarily of the normal or customary understanding of the literal words, and most use a vernacular translation in so doing. Of course, "plain reading" does not always lead to uniform understandings, and pentecostals attach multiple meanings to the same texts depending on their own contexts. Lamin Sanneh has pointed out the significance of Bible translations for local people's enthusiastic discovery of Christianity. The adoption of local names for God, for example, "opened the way for indigenous innovation and motivation in the religious life," and the translations "helped to bring about a historic shift...by pioneering a strategic alliance with local conceptions of religion." This was preeminently the case with pentecostals, who use a precritical method of reading the Bible, common to all ordinary readers in the world who have not been trained in critical methods. This is not necessarily a disadvantage or a slavish literalism— the Bible is usually applied to a real-life community and situation. Local pentecostal missionaries and evangelists, armed with the powerful tool of their vernacular Bibles, were able to present a biblical message that spoke both attractively and effectively to the contexts of their compatriots. However, this approach to the Bible is drawn through the filter of personal experience; and pentecostal preachers have an uncanny ability to relate biblical narratives to real-life situations. In Latin America, prior to Vatican II, the laity were discouraged and even prohibited by the Catholic Church from possessing and reading the Bible. But pentecostals make it a priority for converts to own and read the Bible for themselves, empowering common people (and especially women).[4]

In common with conservative evangelicals and fundamentalists, pentecostals have a high view of the Bible (usually referred to as "the Word of God"), which is understood as fully authoritative and is taken literally. All pentecostal teaching is based directly or indirectly on biblical texts, and these are everywhere accepted in a precritical sense. Importantly, however, pentecostals do differ from fundamentalists in that the text does not have authority *in itself*—rather, it is the Bible as interpreted by the inner working of the Spirit that is authoritative. As one early pentecostal writer put it, "The Spirit works with and through the Word....If [we] neglect the reverent study of Scripture, we cut ourselves off from the very vehicle through which God's Spirit enters human spirit." British biblical scholar Andrew Davies points out that for pentecostals, the Bible is read not only for the knowledge it conveys "but to meet God in the text, and to provide an opportunity for the Holy Spirit to speak to our spirits." Pentecostals rely on direct revelation from the Spirit in addition to biblical sanction—and sometimes, revelation replaces text as a direct authority. In pentecostal history, revelation and personal experience were almost always measured by reference to the Bible as the final arbiter in questionable practices. Thus pentecostals have two reciprocal sources of authority held in tension: reading the Bible affects praxis, and the experiences that follow influence the understanding of the Bible. In his book *Pentecostal Spirituality,* Church of God theologian Steven Land argues consistently that "Pentecostalism cannot and should not be simply identified with a rationalist or scholastic type of evangelicalism." He points out that "Protestant fundamentalist scholasticism has so subjugated Spirit to the Scriptures that the only significant function of the Spirit is to witness to the Bible which is interpreted by human reason." On the contrary, as Pentecostal Holiness leader G. F. Taylor put it in 1920, Spirit baptism "is a key to many portions of the Word....To properly comprehend this truth is to find a key that will unlock many obscure passages of the Word." Or as AG leader D. W. Kerr said,

> The words of Scripture are holy things, but we may become so enslaved to the mere letter of scripture that the life and spirit of the words have no longer any life-giving power in us nor through us....The Holy Spirit, as we are being filled with Him, will illuminate our whole being with light....the living Word dwelling in us, will so illuminate the written Word as we read it, that all things will be as clear and plain to our understanding, as they were to those who wrote them.[5]

Davies argues that despite the apparent dogmatism of pentecostals, the experiential focus of pentecostal worship means that the Bible is interpreted through a spiritual encounter rather than by a literal exegesis. Archer shows that the "narrative criticism" used by pentecostal communities in interpreting the Bible is "story telling," by which "the Bible is not reduced to propositions but instead functions as it was intended to—as stories that grip and shape the readers while challenging them to infer from the narrative a praxis-orientated theology."[6]

Although the vernacular Bible played such a prominent role in the expansion of Pentecostalism, it was only as its message was contextualized and understood by its hearers that it took hold. As Sanneh points out, Christianity (and therefore Pentecostalism) is a translated, intercultural, and adaptable religion; and the only way that it can be communicated to people is through the medium of their own language and culture. Pentecostalism thus becomes a local religion and takes on the context of its followers, not only in the way that they understand the text, but also in their appropriation of language and cultural symbols in their worship—in fact, in the totality of their experience. The Argentinean Catholic theologian Severino Croatto lists three factors that affect the way people understand the Bible. He points out that in addition to the "privileged locus" of "the interpretation of *texts*" (the first aspect), hermeneutics must also take into account that "all interpreters condition their reading of a text by a kind of *preunderstanding* arising from their own life context" (the second aspect), and that third, "the interpreter *enlarges* the *meaning* of the text being interpreted" (italics in original). Ordinary pentecostals are not really interested in the first aspect, but they inevitably enlarge the meaning of the Bible for themselves out of their own contexts. In general, and despite the recent scholarly associations for pentecostal studies and pentecostal biblical scholars aplenty, pentecostals worldwide do not usually have a sophisticated articulation of theological beliefs. Their understanding of the Bible is conditioned by their presuppositions arising out of real-life situations and their perception of how the Bible speaks in these contexts, which inevitably enlarges its meaning for them.[7]

This is why pentecostal preaching is often filled with personal narratives and testimonies that are related to the text that is read. At a grassroots level the personal testimony becomes the primary tool for evangelization; believers tell their stories of conversion and healing in order to persuade others to become believers. The relating of testimonies is still a prominent feature of many pentecostal church services. Another Latin American scholar, Carlos Mesters, writes that when the "common people" read the Bible a "dislocation" occurs and "emphasis is not placed on the text's meaning *in itself* but rather on the meaning the text has *for the people* reading it." Although Mesters refers to the "base communities" in the Catholic Church, in many parts of the world (including Latin America) pentecostals have run "base communities" for a century, minorities of people protesting against marginalization and oppression often engineered in the name of the state. Pentecostals have a "concordistic" approach to the Bible: they take the Bible as it is and look for common ground in real-life situations. On finding these "correspondences" they believe that God is speaking to them personally. As pentecostal scholar Kenneth Archer puts it, pentecostals "re-experienced" the biblical text by removing it from its original context and placing it within their own, thereby giving the text new meaning.[8]

The Bible in the Majority World

The connection between the Bible and everyday life lies at the heart of the appeal of the pentecostal message. This can be illustrated by reference to Africa, where, in keeping with the strong sense of community, members of pentecostal and independent churches usually hear the Bible being read in the community of the local church, and during celebrations of communal worship, where it is often directly related to real problems encountered by that community. This interpretation of the Bible as it is prayed, sung, testified, danced, and preached in worship services implies a hermeneutics from the underside of society, where ordinary people, like the people Mesters describes in the base Christian communities of Brazil, have "found the key and are beginning again to interpret the Bible... using the only tool they have at hand: their own lives, experiences, and struggles." The experience of the Spirit common to pentecostals means that the Bible is used to explain the working of the Holy Spirit in the church with supernatural "gifts of the Spirit," especially healing, exorcism, speaking in tongues, and prophesying. There are many differences among the various pentecostal churches in the practice of these gifts because of their different understanding of the same texts. A reciprocal relationship between the Bible and the Spirit occurs: not only does the Bible explain the experience of the Spirit but, perhaps more important for pentecostals, the Spirit enables people to better understand the Bible. The experience of the Spirit becomes a self-authenticating key in the hermeneutical process. Anglican charismatic John McKay explains that when pentecostals make choices and decisions the "conviction of their essential rightness is based on revelatory experience, the confirmation of the Word, and their own corresponding faith, not on experimental investigation or argument, and consequently is much more absolute."[9]

One major attraction of Pentecostalism for people in the majority world is that, probably above all other considerations, pentecostal churches give biblical answers for "this worldly" needs that prevail in poor societies, like sickness, poverty, hunger, oppression, unemployment, loneliness, evil spirits, and sorcery. In any given pentecostal congregation one will discover testimonies of healings, deliverance from evil powers, the restoration of broken relationships, success in work or business ventures, and other needs that were met, usually through what was seen as the supernatural intervention of God through his Spirit—including the use of agents of the Spirit like evangelists, prophets, and other gifted church leaders. These experiences will usually be backed up by scriptural support. The Bible thus becomes a source book of supernatural answers to human needs. But because of the subjective ways in which it is understood, in some pentecostal and independent churches the Bible is used as a rationale for practices that other Christians would not consider biblical. However, the fact that people are contextualizing the Bible themselves is significant. Among many African independent churches there is real appreciation for the "African-ness" of their understanding of the Bible—and because these churches are founded and led by Africans who have read and interpreted the Bible for themselves, they are seen as specifically geared to fulfill African aspirations and meet African needs. Most pentecostals also read the Bible literally as an ethical rule book, and because of this have rigid opinions on matters like total abstention from alcohol and tobacco, abortion, homosexuality, and divorce; some pentecostals even have rules against eating pork, using cosmetics and jewelry, and especially in prescribing what clothes women should and should not wear. All these legalistic taboos are justified by referring to the Bible.

On a more positive note, in much of the majority world the Bible is interpreted to include all of life's problems, which has particular relevance in societies where disease is rife and access to adequate health care is a luxury. The prevalence of sickness and affliction therefore becomes a hermeneutical key with which the Bible is unlocked. "Salvation" becomes an all-embracing term, usually meaning a sense of well-being evidenced in freedom from sickness, poverty, and misfortune as well as in deliverance from sin and evil. Healing is seen as an essential part of the biblical revelation, and to support this, reference is made to Old Testament prophets, Christ himself, and New Testament apostles who practiced healing. In many independent Spirit churches in Africa, the healing offered to people sometimes relies heavily upon symbols, especially sprinkling by holy water, a sacrament in many churches providing ritual purification and protection. In most other pentecostal churches, the emphasis is on the laying on of hands with prayer, but anointing oil is also used as a symbol of the Holy Spirit. Symbolic healing practices are also referred back to the Bible, where Jesus used mud and spittle to heal a blind man, Peter used cloths to heal the sick, and Old Testament prophets used staffs, water, and various other symbols to perform healings and miracles. Salvation is understood as deliverance from the evil forces aligned against people. The methods used to receive this salvation and the perceptions concerning the means of grace sometimes differed, but the Bible is believed to reveal an omnipotent and compassionate God concerned with all the troubles of humankind. Bishops, prophets, ministers, evangelists, and ordinary church members exercise the authority that has been given them by the God of the Bible reinforced by the power of the Spirit to announce the good news that there is deliverance from sin, from sickness and barrenness, and from every conceivable form of evil, including oppression, unemployment, poverty, and sorcery.

Any discussion of the Bible in Pentecostalism must also consider the emergence of prophets, especially in Africa, where they are seen as continuing in the biblical prophetic tradition and providing an innovative alternative to traditional diviners. Their pronouncements are accepted as revelations from God, but they are not usually accorded the authority of Scripture. The prophets are the ones to whom God's will is revealed and through whom God's power is manifested. The Spirit gives the prophets the power to heal sickness and overcome evil. This understanding of the present dynamic of the Holy Spirit, common to pentecostals everywhere, presupposes that there is a personal and omnipotent power that bears witness to the word of God. In this regard, prophets demonstrate Croatto's third aspect of interpretation by enlarging the meaning of the biblical text. Prophetic practices must not only deal with the *results* of evil; they must also reveal and remove its *cause*. For this reason, church members consult prophets in a way similar to the consultation of traditional diviners. Sometimes the revelation of the cause is by itself sufficient to guarantee a solution to the problem and the supplicant is satisfied. Diagnostic prophecy is the most common form of prophecy in most Spirit churches in Africa, for the overriding concern of the prophets is with the context of evil and suffering. Their revelations become one of the major attractions for outsiders.

Prophecy often becomes an extremely effective form of pastoral therapy and counsel, mostly practiced in private—sometimes a moral corrective when it identifies wrongdoing, and often an indispensable facet of Christian ministry. It can become an expression of care and concern for the needy; and in some cases, might actually bring relief. Prophetic healing therapy in African churches should not simply be equated with pre-Christian healing and divination practices. The many parallels between the *forms* of the old practices and those of the new prophetic ones do not mean that the *content* of prophecy is the same. The parallels are often the very features that make prophetic healing rituals so significant to so many people. The similarities are sometimes the greatest strengths for people seeking meaningful solutions to their problems, for whom prophetic healing practices represent both a Christian and an African approach to the problem of pain and suffering. As revealers of God's will from the Scriptures and dispensers of God's power through the Spirit to meet human needs, African prophets become agents of salvation. The Spirit gives revelations and the ability to overcome many African problems, which brings salvation from pain, fear, and suffering for many people. Of course, human error is inevitable in healing practices. In many pentecostal healing services, sick people often go away unhealed, and so-called miracles are claimed which eventually prove to be no miracles at all.[10]

Without doubt, the Bible plays a very important, although not an exclusive role, in pentecostal practice worldwide, and pentecostals see the Bible as their ultimate authority for faith, practice, and ethics. Preaching is a very important function of pentecostal liturgy, and this must also be seen to be based solidly on the Bible. So the sermon usually begins with a reading from the Bible and is often interspersed by phrases like "the Bible says" to reinforce the message. Although preachers often stray a long way from the biblical passage, preach in an anecdotal fashion, and sometimes do not make a conscious effort to explain the Bible at all, the Bible is given pride of place. The interpretation of the text is conditioned by the context and for a disadvantaged people, preaching often centers on salvation here and now, and on material security that offers health, wealth, and influence in community and public affairs. Through the Bible people learn about God and discover the means by which God speaks today. The Bible provides the basis and the conditions for living, and those who follow its instructions will be enabled to overcome all kinds of difficulties, in this life especially. In some cases, it is not the Bible alone but those charismatic leaders who interpret it correctly and declare this interpretation to the faithful who have ultimate authority. But even when it is interpreted for the ordinary members by leaders, the authority of the Bible itself is never questioned. Preaching must always be founded on what the Bible says, either directly or implicitly. In the formerly colonized world, African, Asian, and Latin American people themselves, without the help of Western missionaries (who represent former colonial powers), have discovered in the Bible their own freedom from oppression. They have discovered that, contrary to previous assumptions, the Bible does provide answers to questions that ordinary people are asking. The translation of the Bible into the vernacular has brought about a discovery of its relevance, its applicability to human aspirations and needs, and its bearing on issues that were often left unaddressed or inadequately attended to by traditional religions and older forms of Christianity.

Education and Bible Schools

Western pentecostal congregations sent out missionaries to various parts of the world in the early twentieth century, or gathered independent missionaries already in the "field" under their wings. Even though there was a rather chaotic flurry of mission activity in early Pentecostalism, these missionaries did not just appear miraculously. They went through a process of calling from many different walks of life, preparation, training (in some cases), sending, and learning before they actually began the work that they believed they had been called to do. In most cases these missionaries led the advance of Pentecostalism, but things rapidly changed. By the late twentieth century, many of the denominations established by missionaries had local leadership. In some cases, like that of the Assemblies of God in Brazil and the Apostolic Church in West Africa, the churches planted by Western missionaries and developed by local leaders grew many times larger than the Western denomination itself. In some cases, like that of the Zion Christian Church in South Africa, the Church of Pentecost in Ghana, the Indian Pentecostal Church, and the Methodist Pentecostal Church in Chile, among others—schisms from missionary-planted churches resulted in much greater growth. Protestant mission history has many examples of churches that expanded much more rapidly when the foreign missionaries departed.

The focus on training indigenous leadership came out of the pentecostals' background in evangelical missions, where training "native workers" was a principle long advocated. Pentecostals began to see the need to train talented local people. A pentecostal missionary in Egypt from Azusa Street, A. H. Post, wrote that the Spirit baptism of Egyptian workers for active service was one of the most encouraging signs of the mission there. He made a plea for the training and support of these workers, saying that because "they know the language and the customs and notions and ideas of the people...the right native man can win more souls to Christ than the American missionary can personally." PMU missionary Ethel Cook wrote from Yunnan, China of "the pressing need for more workers—native helpers of established character especially—to preach amongst the different tribes Peoples." As we have seen, W. W. Simpson established several Bible schools after his return to China in 1918 and his Truth Bible Institute in Beijing was a leading center for the training of Chinese pentecostal leaders. George Berg made training workers a priority in India, and even though he returned to the United States under a cloud of suspicion about his moral and financial integrity, his trained workers—some of whom assisted Robert Cook and other foreign missionaries—were pillars in South Indian Pentecostalism. Cook established a Bible school in Kerala in 1922 that was committed to training Indian missionaries and sending them out to neighboring Indian states. "The great advantage of a native missionary," he later wrote, "is that he knows the language and can thus give clear expression to his thoughts." He went on, "He knows how to move with his people and accustom himself to the environments. He is at home in any village on tour and is also accustomed to the climatic conditions."[11]

PMU leader Cecil Polhill, who was keen to implement a policy that would transfer the task of evangelization and church leadership to local people, published a significant article in 1917. He outlined an in-service training course for local church leaders in which these leaders would be gathered from local churches to a central place where they would be trained for two-week periods. He quoted from a CMS periodical to "emphasize the supreme fact that the natives themselves must be the chief factor in evangelization." Every missionary should be "the means in God's hands of sending out in a very short time numbers of well taught spiritual converts as missionaries to their own countrymen." Polhill used further quotations to drive home his point about the "tremendous limitations" of "foreign evangelists" who are "makeshift." The following was very important advice that, had it been followed for the rest of the twentieth century, might have made all the difference to the growth and maturity of national pentecostal churches:

> All Christians ought to be missionaries; but in a most real sense the best missions are home missions....he is likely to do the least permanent good while it is he that controls the situation. So long as the native workers are his agents, his helpers, his nominees, the whole venture takes on a foreign aspect, Christianity itself appears as a foreign faith, and suffers under all the prejudice and suspicion which things foreign usually evoke The larger advance will come when we have discharged our function as foreign missionaries by establishing in the several non-Christian lands indigenous, self-propagating churches, and have committed to them—either with or without subordinate assistance from us—the completion of the work of evangelization.
>
> Is not that day far nearer in not a few of our fields of work in Asia and Africa than we as yet commonly recognize? The Christians are reckoned by their thousands and tens of thousands. In nature and temperament they are far better qualified than we to present the message to their fellow countrymen. Intellectually they are often fully our equals. Spiritually the power that works in us is the power that works in them also. Have we had sufficient faith and courage to transfer to them the burden of responsibility and initiative, assured that as we do so the Holy Spirit of God will endue them with new love and wisdom, and supply to them that steadfast and keen initiative which we perhaps think they lack at present?[12]

These ideas did not catch on quickly in pentecostal denominations. Seldom did foreign missionaries consider Africans and Asians by temperament "far better qualified," by intellect "fully our equals," and having the same spiritual power. Expatriate missionaries continued to see themselves as the indispensable focus of the work and attempted to control local preachers, often with disastrous consequences. As a result, their entire mission ventures, as Polhill had warned, took on "a foreign aspect" and their converts became objects of suspicion and prejudice. Such attempts as were made to follow Polhill's advice were few and far between. In the PMU, operating in southwest Yunnan, Chinese preachers were put in charge of stations; in fact, because most of the foreign PMU missionaries lived in two main "safe" centers, local preachers usually staffed the outstations. The PMU Council declared its commitment to providing for "a new supply of Chinese evangelists" because the ultimate goal of the mission was "to raise up men and women out of the natives to evangelize and carry on the work," and "missionary work always fails unless it succeeds in reaching the natives to become workers."[13]

It took a while, but with support from gentle agitators like Polhill and Alice Luce—and, in the field, such as W. W. Simpson in China, Robert Cook in India, Gerard Bailly in Venezuela, and J. O. Lehman in South Africa—gradually the idea grew that investment in "native workers" was more important than increasing the numbers of foreign ones. Unfortunately, attitudes and policies did not improve quickly. The AG, in its second Missionary Conference in Chicago in 1918, resolved to recommend that "the ordination of native workers be discouraged except where the matter can be arranged for and looked after by the proper committees on their respective fields and districts." The reason for this draconian move was an instance of a "native" who had "attempted to assert authority over the missionary." The same conference recommended that no money should be sent directly to "native workers on the field." This distrust was perpetuated for decades thereafter.[14]

In their revivalist beginnings and conviction of the imminent return of Christ, pentecostals did not consider theological training of much importance, and most of their early preachers had little or none at all. Some of the first missionaries who went out were untrained and lacked financial backing from any organization. Most were without any theological or practical missionary training. Many believed their work should be continued until they died in the field (which many did) or until Jesus returned—whichever came first. The early pentecostals generally put priority on the calling and empowerment of the candidate rather than on age or education. As *The Latter Rain Evangel* put it in 1911, many of those pentecostal workers who had gone into the mission field "would never be accepted by boards, but God called them and they have obeyed Him." In the words of one commentator, "it was generally agreed that the historic denominations had lost their spirituality in direct relationship to their emphasis on education." Pentecostals were opposed to "an education that destroyed faith or reduced dependence on the Holy Spirit." In my own experience, pentecostals would speak derisively of "theological cemeteries"; and it would take at least half a century before pentecostals began to have reputable higher education institutions. The emphasis in pentecostal leadership was on the spirituality of the leader rather than on intellectual abilities or ministerial skills. This was the legacy of the evangelical "Bible schools" and "missionary training schools" instituted in the late nineteenth century, which often provided no more than rudimentary short courses in Bible study where the Bible was the only textbook. Early pentecostals believed that God had called "persons of average ability" who had been baptized in the Holy Spirit and were specially called to "become soul-winners in foreign lands." They were called from many different walks of life, and usually underwent preparation, sometimes training, sending, and learning, before they actually began the work.[15]

The first pentecostal training courses were generally of about eight months' duration, after which trainees were sent out into the field. Early pentecostal conventions made one of their chief activities the motivation and recruitment of new missionaries. Earnest appeals were made for young people to offer themselves, citing great needs in these exotic foreign places and often stating how much the people there were looking forward to the arrival of Western missionaries. The motivation for these hundreds of mostly young people who offered themselves for "foreign service" was the spiritual needs of the "heathen" world. Levi Lupton, a prominent pentecostal leader until his fall from grace though marital difficulties in 1910, planned his new Missionary Faith Home in Alliance, Ohio, to be "from one to three years careful, practical training, and real study of the Word of God." In Rochester, New York, Elizabeth Baker and her four sisters founded the Rochester Bible Training School in 1906 just before they became pentecostal. This school closed in 1924 to make way for Elim Bible Institute, but had a two-year program with a strong missionary emphasis, and fifty graduates became overseas missionaries. The great majority of graduates were women. These were the first significant American pentecostal centers for the training and sending out of missionaries. Whatever few training schools were put in place by pentecostals followed similar aims and patterns of the more radical and rudimentary schools, with an emphasis on thrusting out workers into the "harvest fields" as soon as possible, for the Lord's coming was near.[16]

Although Pentecostals were not as thoroughly immersed in Western theology and ideology as other missionaries were, they soon realized that if the Spirit had not given them the languages of the nations in which to preach their gospel they had better learn those languages themselves. So, great effort was put into language learning. By 1928 William Burton of the CEM had instituted a rule specifying that any missionary who could not preach in the local language within six months would be sent home. The PMU made it a compulsory condition for further service in the field, and would also recall its missionaries if they did not make satisfactory linguistic progress. The PMU also provided rudimentary training for its candidates but stated initially that their qualifications had simply to be "a fair knowledge of every Book in the Bible, and an accurate knowledge of the Doctrines of Salvation and Sanctification," and candidates "must be from those who have received the Baptism of the Holy Ghost themselves." There was no shortage of applications, and entrance requirements were soon made more stringent, including a required two-year training period. Candidates who were accepted for training mostly came from working-class occupations and had only an elementary or primary school education. In their admission policies, the PMU followed the established practices of other mission societies like the CIM. But unlike many other pentecostal groups at the time, the PMU did take its training programs very seriously.[17]

The first pentecostal missionary in Venezuela, former CMA member Gerard Bailly, worked for several years to establish the first pentecostal Bible School for Latin Americans at the Hebron mission station outside Caracas in 1909, where pentecostal pastors from that country and Puerto Rico were trained. Bailly did not charge fees and the school was self-supporting, with students employed in farm and other duties in the mission. Bailly made a plea for support, referring to the drain on missionary funds involved in preparation, equipment, travel, and language instruction. He declared that the "principal solution to the problem" was the "properly equipped native." Bailly later cautioned that "scriptural submission one to the other" should "not interfere with the free workings of a scriptural native church or pretend at a colonial government or lording it over God's heritage." These were remarkable insights for 1915, as Bailly envisaged a Venezuelan church "free from denominational and foreign trappings" that was "brought forth into national and spiritual birth in pentecostal manifestations and sovereign workings of the Holy Ghost." He was later responsible for assisting in the beginnings of such an independent Venezuelan church. In the United States in 1926, Alice Luce founded the first Spanish-language pentecostal Bible school in San Diego for the AG, which opened one in Mexico City two years later.[18]

Western pentecostal missions contributed generously toward the establishment of "Bible schools" and in-service training structures throughout the world, resulting in the more rapid growth of indigenous churches. An AG survey conducted in 1959 revealed that half the budget of the Missions Department and half its missionaries were committed to theological institutions. However, the fundamental flaw of these structures was that they were Western models foisted onto the rest of the world, remnants of the colonial past of cultural imperialism and ethnocentrism. Pentecostal missionaries from Europe and North America thought they knew what sort of training people needed in Africa, Asia, and Latin America in order to become ministers after the model of the West; and at least in Africa, they even provided suits and ties to their students to try to recreate their particular view of respectability. It is clear that the alliance between Evangelicalism and white classical Pentecostalism in the United States from 1943 onward had a profound effect on Pentecostal theological education. Pentecostals found themselves drawn into the evangelical-ecumenical dichotomy pervading North American evangelical Christianity. Pentecostals were in danger of losing their distinctive experience-oriented spirituality as they uncritically adopted evangelical and fundamentalist models of education. As Henry Lederle points out,

It is an irony of recent ecclesiastical history that much of Pentecostal scholarship has sought to align itself so closely with the rationalistic heritage of American Fundamentalism...without fully recognizing how hostile these theological views are to Pentecostal and Charismatic convictions about present-day prophecy, healing miracles and other spiritual charisms.[19]

Pentecostal Bible colleges became prime generators of this new pentecostal fundamentalism, and Western pentecostal denominations gave priority to exporting this theological education to the majority world. The rest of the world suffered from the great malaise in Western theological education, as missionary educators from Europe and North America unconsciously spread their presuppositions, paradigms, and ideological prejudices in Asia, Africa, Latin America, and the Pacific. Hwa Yung points out that the many theological institutions that have sprung up all over Asia have been "conditioned by the methodologies, agenda, and content of Western theology." He says, "This approach must be changed if the Asian church is to come to terms more adequately with its own identity, context, and mission." The independence of India in 1947 began a domino-like fall of colonies culminating with the first democratically elected government in South Africa in 1994. The end of colonialism gave rise to a new and strident nationalism, and more recently there has emerged a continentalism that emphasizes human dignity. The recent emergence of an "Asian Pentecostal theology," an Asian pentecostal theological society, and increasing numbers of Asian, Latin American and African pentecostals pursuing doctorates in theology are but a few examples of the changing times. Pentecostal churches in the majority world now develop their own theological paradigms that challenge and transform Christian spirituality throughout the world. Western models of theological education often do not take enough notice of the specific, local, religious, social, and cultural contexts that surround people in the majority world. Because it was also assumed that local leaders would be trained using Western methodologies, little thought was given to understanding how the Christian message might be communicated in other cultures and contexts that are multiethnic, pluralistic, and urbanized. Sometimes, insensitive and imperialistic attitudes on the part of dominant foreign missions have tended to stifle protest and constructive change.[20]

The various Bible schools that were eventually developed throughout the world shaped the future leadership of pentecostal denominations. Because the primary focus of these schools was on indoctrination rather than theology, graduates emerged bearing standardized doctrines, practices, and administrative structures they had learned during their limited period of training. They passed on a particular Western church culture that sometimes clashed with local cultures overseas. Internally, there were still leaders uncomfortable with the new emphasis on the need for education prior to service in a pentecostal ministry. Some pentecostal and charismatic organizations continue to insist on charisma rather than education as the essential prerequisite for Christian ministry. In the 1960s, Swiss sociologist Lalive d'Épinay contrasted the remarkably successful pentecostal pastors in Chile with little or no education, with the "complete stagnation" of the Methodists and Presbyterians whose pastors were well educated. This made him "less confident of the benefits of theological education, and even of the method of training in the developed countries which we impose on Protestants in the developing nations." He stated that the educational methods of the West were simply "not suitable for the needs in Chile." There, because North American missionaries had instituted theological education to avoid the "excesses" and "ignorant fanaticism" of Pentecostalism, Chilean Pentecostalism had a "strong anti-theological, anti-academic prejudice."[21]

But in more recent years, pentecostal theological colleges, liberal arts colleges, and even universities have been established in various parts of the world with government accreditation. The Church of Pentecost, for example, opened Pentecost University College near Accra, Ghana, in 2003. This was inaugurated by the President of Ghana and accredited by the University of Ghana, Legon. It had almost 3,000 students in 2011 and offered degrees in business administration, information technology, and theology. Its rector has a PhD from the University of Durham and its chancellor, also chairman of the denomination, has a PhD in theology from the University of Birmingham. The burgeoning unregistered house church movement in China is predominantly pentecostal in nature and its ministers are mostly not well educated. One of the largest groups, claiming to represent 7 million Chinese Christians, realized the need for training and began the first long-term Bible School training center in 1994, providing free training for students who must first prove their calling. By the following year there were eighty students in the Bible School, but the school was closed and ten of the students imprisoned. The movement persisted and had more than fifty training centers all over China by 2010. Bible Schools and theological colleges continue to be a prominent part of leadership training and take many forms, from short-term, part-time evening courses to fully fledged universities offering graduate study. Such is the changing world of pentecostal education.[22]

The drastic transformation in Christian demographics has so far made little impact on Western conservative evangelical theological education, however, which continues to be the leading model in pentecostal seminaries across the globe. Latin Americans, Africans, and Asians have an increasing sense of self-identity, and although Western theology has adjusted to the particular challenges of post-modernism, feminism, and religious pluralism, presuppositions remain. The rise of post-modernism has profoundly challenged the autonomous rationalism and empirical skepticism of Western education but has not yet shaken the foundations of the theology taught in pentecostal seminaries. The theology that is generally exported from the West, observes Andrew Walls, is a "heavily indigenised, highly contextual theology...a way of making peace between Christianity and the European Enlightenment, of translating Christian affirmations into Enlightenment categories." Characteristic of this is the literary-historical method of approach to Scripture that is almost universal in the West. Such theological methods were foreign to the Western church for centuries. Walls shows how all theological disciplines actually represent "a series of choices related to the cultural and religious history of the Western world." However, the southward movement of world Christianity has both "opened up untold fresh possibilities for theology" and "vastly multiplied the resources available." But the Western hegemony remains in theological institutions and their curricula. If the "non-Western" world is given any attention, it is usually placed in the context of Western churches and missions. One wonders how much longer this state of affairs can continue with the increasingly strident voice of majority world theologians.[23]

The nature of church leadership is a fundamental historical difference between the mission of pentecostal churches and that of older churches. In pentecostal practice, the Holy Spirit is given to every believer without preconditions. One result is that the dichotomy between "clergy" and "laity" does not usually exist. Until comparatively recently, pentecostals have had no tradition of formal training for "ministers" as a class set apart. Pentecostal leaders are those whose primary qualification has been a "call of God" and an ability to preach effectively. This is still the case. Many of the most successful pentecostal churches today are led by people with little or no training in theology. A strong emphasis on charismatic leadership is a feature of Pentecostalism today and is accompanied by inevitable problems (especially the emergence of dictatorial leaders), but it results in churches that are often well organized and where the emphasis is on hearing the "word of God" relevant to the daily needs of the hearers.[24]

We have explored the role of the Bible, its interpretation, and education in biblical studies in the spread of Pentecostalism worldwide. The Bible is applied to local contexts in a way that makes use of plain readings of the text, enlarging the meanings of the text by frequent recourse to experience-based narratives, and undergirded by a literal approach that is common to the various forms of Pentecostalism. The result is a multiplicity of interpretations, which indirectly or directly leads to schism. In particular, the Bible is applied to a supernatural worldview that finds many parallels with the biblical record and this in turn transforms the Bible into a textbook for human felt needs. This has sometimes led to tensions between local interpretations and those imposed by international organizations from the West, "universal" interpretations that are often propagated through the Bible schools. Nevertheless, for all their shortcomings, pentecostal educational facilities had the advantage of training a new breed of leaders able to sustain the growth of the movement in the developing post-colonial world. Experiencing the Bible being taught, sung, and danced in community is a central part of what it means to be pentecostal. How reading the Bible in these different pentecostal ways is linked to the main themes of the pentecostal message is the subject of the following chapter.

Pentecostals in Community and the Public Sphere

The history of Pentecostalism cannot be isolated from its characteristic practices. It almost goes without saying that pentecostal congregations are where community interaction happens. This is also where beliefs and values are formed, and pentecostal worship—especially prayer—is at the center of pentecostal communities. Steven Land observes that "the dimension of praise, worship, adoration and prayer to God" is the "most compelling characteristic" of Pentecostalism. The pentecostal worship service exists in many different forms, but this central activity lies at the heart of what Pentecostalism is all about. Here too, the Bible plays a prominent part. Pentecostal liturgy differs in different parts of the world, but the most essential common features are first, praise and prayer with singing, music, and often dancing (sometimes called the "worship time"); second, a central role given to biblical preaching; and third, usually individual prayer for needs at the close of the service. The observer able to attend public pentecostal events anywhere will immediately be aware that though the music and language are different, the spirituality is the same, something that Harvey Cox calls "primal spirituality," which touches the inner recesses of human nature. Pentecostal rituals exhibit a worldview that presupposes that worship is about encountering God, including a faith in an all-powerful God who is *there* to meet human needs. One does not need to look much further than this to explain Pentecostalism's attraction to the outside world, and this is also the fundamental change that Pentecostalism has facilitated in other forms of Christianity through the Charismatic movement. Pentecostal liturgy is often described as "lively" and is contrasted to that prevailing in more traditional churches. Traditional churches for their part have embraced some of these "lively" features in their own liturgies—only one of the transformations taking place in Christianity as a whole.[25]

Pentecostals would call their spirituality being "open to the Holy Spirit," and their invitation is to "come to church" expecting to "meet with God." Their worship is also participatory and spontaneous; their music is often contemporary, and there is usually a call for participants to "come to the front" (the "altar call") to receive prayer and counsel. Preaching is often anecdotal and entertaining, but the effective preacher will also be convincing and will elicit a response. The preaching is the high point of the service and the congregation wants to leave feeling that they have been "fed," empowered, and equipped for the week ahead. Different patterns of ministry, the central ordinances of baptism (usually by immersion of adult believers) and communion (almost always a simple remembrance of the death of Christ rather than celebrating a sacrament), the emphasis on vocalized, spontaneous prayer, and other ritual observances are all part of the pentecostal community, from which it reaches out into the local community. As Mark Cartledge observes, the pentecostal communities in their central rites of worship "form communal identity and assist members in negotiating the issues of everyday life." Pentecostalism, because of its inherent flexibility and spontaneity, takes on many of the characteristics of the society in which it is found. It taps into local cultural and religious traditions and thereby renders pentecostal worship more accessible.[26]

For pentecostals, Christian worship is a joyful experience to be entered into with the whole person: body, mind, and spirit. This free, exuberant worship is not merely a cultural trait of Africans or Latin Americans. One has only to be at a European football match to see that Europeans can exhibit the same qualities. A new emphasis on the role of the Spirit in the worship, work, and witness of the church is one of the main reasons for this infectious enthusiasm. The experience of the Spirit's presence is seen as a normal part of daily life and is brought to bear upon all situations. God's salvation is seen in different manifestations of God's abiding presence through the Spirit, divine revelations that assure us that "God is there" to help in every area of need. As Ghanaian theologian Asamoah-Gyadu puts it, referring to African Pentecostalism,

> One of the major contributions of African Christians, particularly Pentecostals and charismatics, to Western Christianity is the attention it draws to the fact that Christianity is about experience and that the power of God is able to transform circumstances that Western rationalist theologies will consider the preserve of psychology and scientific development.[27]

These holistic, ecstatic, and experiential religious practices are found throughout the world. The antiphonal, boisterous singing; simultaneous and spontaneous prayer; and rhythmic dance are found throughout global Pentecostalism, emphasizing the freedom, equality, community, and

dignity of each person in the sight of God. The experience of the power of
the Spirit is for Pentecostals a unifying factor in a global society still deeply
divided and can be the catalyst for the emergence of a new society where
there is justice for all and hope in a desperately violent world.

Many pentecostal churches seek to provide for the holistic needs of their
members. For this reason, some churches in South Africa form funeral
societies, bursary funds for the education of their children, and assist
members in financial distress. Some of these churches have "welfare committees" responsible for feeding and clothing the poor and the destitute. As
anthropologist Martin West points out, independent churches in Soweto
"meet many of the needs of townspeople which were formerly met by
kin groups on a smaller scale in rural areas." West's observation from the
1970s is still appropriate. He lists several ways in which the social needs of
church members are met in an urban setting. The congregation as a voluntary association provides its members with a sense of family, friendship
(providing support groups in times of insecurity), protection in the form
of leadership (and particularly charismatic leadership), and social control
(by emphasizing and enforcing certain norms of behavior); it also helps
in practical ways like finding employment, giving mutual aid in times of
personal crisis, and affording leadership opportunities. The churches thus
provide for their members "new bases for social organisation."[28]

Pentecostal and charismatic churches see themselves as God's people,
called out from the world around them with a distinct mission. They have
a sense of identity as a separated community whose primary purpose is
to promote their cause to those outside. "Church" for them is the most
important activity in life, and Christianity is brought to bear upon every
situation. For migrant pentecostals in Europe, their churches have practical functions; these can cover obtaining a visa to remain in the country,
receiving help in finding employment, dealing with racism and rejection,
finding financial help, receiving advice regarding marriage and family
affairs, or being healed from sickness and other afflictions seen as attacks
by Satan. In short, the church is a caring, therapeutic community and at
once a refuge from the storms and difficulties of a new life and an advice
center for every possible eventuality. Many European churches, influenced
by their individualistic and secular society, have largely lost this sense of
therapeutic community and belongingness that is so much a central characteristic of pentecostal Christianity.

There has also been increasing pentecostal involvement in politics and
in the public sphere. Pentecostal ideas on what constitutes a "Christian"

society in recent times are influenced by the controversies surrounding laws on abortion and sexuality in particular, but also by support for the death penalty and for the state of Israel. In this they have not been notice-ably different from the wider evangelical movement, and these notions are always supported by biblical reference. It is difficult to draw conclusions about contemporary pentecostal attitudes to politics, which can best be described as ambivalent. Many political leaders have been known to con-sort with pentecostals, who are an increasingly influential opinion-forming group. Frederick Chiluba (1943–2011), president of Zambia from 1991 to 2002 and a former labor union leader, declared Zambia a "Christian nation" and was known to have had a pentecostal experience. He preached in pentecostal churches and had several pentecostals in his government and as advisers. The political activities of the pentecostal bishop Margaret Wanjiru in Kenya were profiled in the previous chapter. Eduardo ("Eddie") Villanueva (b.1946) is the founder and leader of one of the largest non-Catholic denominations in the Philippines, the Jesus is Lord Church, which began in 1978 and is the largest pentecostal church in the country with over a million members and branches among expatriate Filipinas in other parts of Asia, Europe, and North America. He unsuccessfully stood as a candidate in the 2004 and 2010 presidential elections, and although he polled only 6 percent of the vote in 2004 and 3 percent in 2010, he remains a hugely influential figure in Philippine politics. Two of his sons are also in politics. His pentecostal identity in a strongly Catholic country probably cost him votes, especially when his opponents charged him with wanting to convert all Filipinos to Pentecostalism. Villanueva, who was a Marxist activist in his pre-Christian days, has a strong reputation as a campaigner against government corruption and calls for justice for the poor. Mike Velarde of the powerful El Shaddai organization has played an important role in mustering support for political candidates from his mil-lions of followers but did not support Villanueva in his candidacy.[29]

Social and political issues among pentecostals will continue to be debated and in such a fast-moving and changing movement it is difficult to draw precise conclusions. In fact, as Joel Robbins has pointed out after surveying the literature, "the way Pentecostalism shapes political attitudes and practices is at this point utterly inconclusive." Kalu takes sharp issue with Gifford's analysis of Ghanaian Pentecostalism making pentecostals "divine pool players" who are not motivated to work hard. He charges that Gifford's portrayal is "from only the perspective of its enemies" and is in contrast to the views of sympathetic African scholars. There is a sense in which pentecostals have preferred to get on with the job of involvement in society rather than making theoretical statements about it. The exceptions have usually been the more outlandish opinions expressed in national media. There are problems and ingrained hard-line attitudes to be sure. But as Miller and Yamamori have demonstrated, pentecostals are increasingly involved in "community-based social ministries," with a "balanced approach to evangelism and social action" that reflects the mature development of Pentecostalism "from being an otherworldly sect to a dominant force in reshaping global Christianity."[30]

Like many other religious movements in the 1990s, Pentecostalism was affected by the sudden fall of the Iron Curtain, especially in Central and Eastern Europe. But it is more difficult to establish the influence of the dramatic events of 1989–91 on the growth of Pentecostalism in the South in the last decade of the twentieth century, except in an indirect way. We have seen that its accelerating growth was already set in motion in the 1970s and has continued unabated ever since. Undoubtedly, the forces of globalization and the movement toward a "universal culture" were at work in this shift in religious demographics. Pentecostalism was also fast becoming an alternative meta-culture within an even larger global culture in an increasingly polarized world, and offered membership in a global religious community that was more accessible than the elusive wealth of the West. The end of the Cold War stopped the race for power and influence between the United States and the Soviet Union that had brought large amounts of money and dependency to prop up dictatorships in the southern continents; this meant that poverty accelerated and nations and peoples placed high value on international connections. This was particularly the case in Africa, where entrepreneurial religious leaders found that religion was a way to attain an affluent lifestyle—here, Pentecostalism's potentially anarchistic ecclesiastical structures offered freedom to run an independent church like a large and highly successful corporation. Thousands of independent charismatic churches were formed in Africa's cities, in some notorious cases forming grist for the mill of media reports and accusations of manipulation and exploitation. In forgotten parts of African cities where personal ambition for a better life was usually unrealized and bitterly disappointing, international contacts were given priority. The easiest international connections to obtain were religious ones, and the most successful preachers who were financially prosperous and attracted the largest numbers were those who could demonstrate and establish such links. Pentecostalism with its transnational and multicentered networks and ability to recreate itself in any cultural context was poised in the 1990s to provide these global connections. At the same time, pentecostal churches in the North were anxious to establish their own credentials as "international" organizations and needed the churches of the South to increase their own standing, often to their own considerable financial advantage. Thus, the dependency was entirely mutual.

Historically, what has happened to world Christianity in the twentieth century could also be described as a pentecostal reformation. Vinson Synan calls the twentieth century "the century of the Holy Spirit." Christianity as a whole has been profoundly changed by Pentecostalism's conviction that the emotions, music, and dance, and especially the exercising of spiritual gifts, are important both for meaningful Christian worship and for attracting people to Christianity. The transformation of worldwide Christianity into a more holistic and emotional spirituality stands in stark contrast to the doctrinal, intellectual emphasis of the European Enlightenment-influenced Christianity that prevailed well into the twentieth century. But this rapid expansion of pentecostal forms of Christianity has also come at a price. Traditional Christian churches have, as we have seen, resisted change; multiple and cascading schisms have occurred; and pentecostals have been accused of proselytism. Indeed, many pentecostal converts originate in other churches, even if their membership was nominal, as was mostly the case with Catholic converts in Latin America and in the Philippines. In some countries, like Eritrea, Greece, or Russia, pentecostals have come into open conflict with dominant forms of Christianity. In Eritrea this has resulted in severe persecution, as pentecostals are not among the four religions officially sanctioned by the government. They have been severely harassed and banned since 2002 and are arrested, incarcerated, and ordered to "return" to Eritrean Orthodoxy. Eritrea is reportedly one of the worst countries in the world for religious persecution and a new purge of pentecostals started in December 2007 and again in May 2011. As a result, pentecostals must meet secretly in small groups and in constant fear of harassment and arrest.[31]

Pentecostalism's aggressive evangelism also affects its relationships with other religions. Most pentecostals will affirm a theological exclusivism that proclaims no "salvation" outside of explicit Christian faith. This sometimes brings about a violent reaction from other religionists. This is most evident in India, where Hindu extremists burn down churches and persecute Christians; but it is especially prevalent in those Islamic countries where conversion to another religion is outlawed. Five pentecostal pastors in Iran were killed near the end of the twentieth century, including the leader of Iranian pentecostals, Haik Hovsepian Mehr, who lost his life in 1994. Nigerian historian Ogbu Kalu argued that Pentecostalism exhibits a "lack of a viable theology of dialogue in an increasingly pluralistic public space." Pentecostal rhetoric against Islam in Nigeria, he claimed, amounts to the "demonization of Islam." Pentecostal entrepreneurs from the south have moved into Muslim cities in the north to attempt to convert Muslims. Violence and intolerance results from the contesting religious fundamentalisms found in countries like Nigeria. Kalu concluded that multiculturalism and a tolerant religious pluralism are only workable in worldviews where religion has been relegated to the periphery. In most parts of the world where Pentecostalism flourishes, religion is at the heart of popular worldviews and conflict is inevitable. Nevertheless, a better understanding of other religions rather than a confrontational attitude will go some way toward easing tension.[32]

6

Full Gospel

Savior

It is impossible to fully understand the expansion of Pentecostalism in the global South without a consideration of its central ideologies or theological emphases. It was inevitable that the driving force behind and leadership of the movement would pass swiftly to local leaders, given the principles and features of the early pentecostal missionary movement. Without a true translation of the message into the thinking of the people, the work of the foreign missionaries would never really be effective. When missionaries discovered they could not automatically speak the local languages with the help of the Spirit, their only option (if they stayed) was to use interpreters and train locals. Very early on, indigenous leaders took up the baton and so began a swift transfer of leadership that was unique in the recent history of Christianity. Sometimes these leaders interacted with foreign missionaries as part of a pentecostal denomination; but increasingly, new movements arose in the South with little foreign missionary participation or none at all. The revivals in the first decade of the twentieth century had resulted in feverish missionary activity in the decades that followed among new Christian groups that had arisen in various parts of the world. Fundamental to the expansion of these revivalist movements was a conviction that the Holy Spirit had been poured out upon the earth to enable witnesses in every nation to spread the good news to the ends of the earth. Pentecostalism was missionary by nature and its mission was first and foremost evangelism. Its missionaries' fundamental task was proclamation, and most of these missionaries set out to establish churches wherever they went.

Because of the missionary nature of Pentecostalism, and because its missionaries instilled this orientation in their converts from the beginning, evangelism snowballed. This was combined with the experience of the Spirit and a particular form of premillennial eschatology that declared that the second coming of Christ would soon bring the end of the world as we know it. These believers did not share the confident hope in the benefits of Western civilization that characterized older Protestant churches. In the words of Albert Norton, veteran pentecostal missionary in India, Western civilization had entered "the dark shadow of the greatest national apostasy in all the history of mankind." The missionary task was urgent, and before the cataclysmic eschatological events accompanying the return of Christ, the power of Pentecost would be restored to the church. What were popularly termed "signs and wonders" would enable the Christian gospel to be preached all over the world. These missionaries were also convinced that the power of the Spirit had been given them to enable them to preach this gospel, and that this was the fundamental reason for their going far beyond their homes in their northern "Jerusalem" to the "ends of the earth." Their message spread rapidly, as messengers fanned out into a world dominated by Western colonial powers, where previously difficult-to-reach areas were being opened up by new and faster transportation and communication links.[1]

The concept of evangelism in pentecostal practice was inherited from late nineteenth-century radical evangelicals and differed significantly from that of older denominations. Simpson's "Fourfold Gospel" of "Jesus Christ: Savior, Healer, Baptizer and Soon Coming King" remained an important concept in Pentecostalism—with regeneration, divine healing, holiness and/or baptism in the Spirit, and the premillennial second coming of Christ the essential constituents of the pentecostal message. This "full gospel," as it came to be known in Pentecostalism, included a message of a personal, experiential, and exclusive salvation from sin through a "born-again" or conversion experience; an instant, distinctive experience of holiness following conversion known as sanctification (among Holiness pentecostals); the practice of healing the physically sick through prayer and laying on of hands; the baptism in the Spirit empowering for witnessing (often characterized by the "evidence" of speaking in tongues); and a sense of the imminent, premillennial return of Christ. Fundamental to all activities was the conviction that this "full gospel" had to be preached, modified by different pentecostal groups but foundational to their theology and practice.[2]

It is sometimes assumed that pentecostals so overemphasize the Spirit that their Christology is obscured. However, the focus of pentecostals in seeing Jesus as Savior is always Christocentric—"coming to Jesus," "receiving Jesus"—and a lifestyle conversion and a radical break with the past or the "world" is a prominent part of their "full gospel" proclamation and implicit theology. In fact, some suggest that as a result of their central Christology, Pentecostals might have a limited Trinitarian framework. Be that as it may, Pentecostals identify with the evangelical "born again" movement whose essential message is that "Jesus saves," expressly declaring the life-altering nature of Christian conversion, and the invitation to "sinners" is "Let Jesus come into your heart." This is expressed in the popular songs that form part of pentecostal worship worldwide and in the testimonies of radical change that are expected of pentecostal believers. I have stood in the blazing sun by the banks of a river in tropical Africa and watched baptisms by immersion of scores of new converts. The converts first must testify one by one of their conversion experience by stating what sort of life they have been "saved" from. The testimony will include a list of deeds thought to be unacceptable to Christian practice. Sometimes the pastor prompts the candidate if the list of sins is not long enough. The emphasis is always on a radical break with these past deeds after receiving Christ. This "born-again" conversion experience is the most important, foundational part of pentecostal experience and without it no other experience in the "full gospel" is possible. But the Christological emphasis continues: Jesus is also seen as the one who heals, the one who makes holy, the one who empowers believers by giving the Spirit, and the one who will soon return to reward the faithful and bring judgment to a decadent world.

This was the essential thrust of the message that was to be translated into the contexts of the peoples in the global South. The "full gospel" was intrinsically part of it. In continuation with the emphases of the various revival movements it emerged from, the power of the Spirit in pentecostal thinking is always linked to the command to preach the gospel to all nations. Pentecostal preachers had to proclaim this gospel everywhere with attendant signs that demonstrated the Lord's presence, especially that of healing the sick. The task of proclaiming the full gospel was also given urgency in view of the impending return of Christ. *The Bridegroom's Messenger* declared that the world was about to end and Christ had sent the new Pentecost to prepare for His coming. The nations of the world had to be evangelized through the power of the Spirit—with "signs following" before this cataclysmic event occurred—by missionaries "speedily propagating the word of truth in all nations before He comes." The power to preach the gospel and evangelize all nations permeated the activities of the missionaries and their converts, but not to the exclusion of all other activities. Pentecostals saw their task made both easier and more effective by the power of the Spirit. This view sometimes brought them into sharp tension with more experienced evangelical missionaries who had labored at individualistic evangelism for many years with limited results. The conflict became even sharper when newly Spirit-baptized missionaries and their converts declared that the previous efforts of the older missions had been virtually futile, and that they had found that the freedom of the Spirit gave them faster and more efficient methods than those of the bureaucratic machinery of established mission societies. W. W. Simpson described his evangelistic task in China as follows:

I know by practical experience and actual work that the evangelization of the Heathen can be carried on now exactly as in the days of Peter, Paul and Philip. This knowledge had revolutionized my whole work and methods, I now see the complete evangelization of China in the course of two or three years as a practical possibility within our grasp. Not by opening large mission stations and establishing extensive plants and institutions and cumbering the work with elaborately organized machinery, not by boards and committees and high sounding phraseology, not by suasive [sic] words of wisdom and discussions and councils, but by the foolishness of preaching in the demonstration of the Spirit and the power is the work to be done.[3]

It is no wonder the established missions were threatened by this sort of propaganda. There were other emphases linked to the pentecostal priority of evangelism, not least of which was the importance of sustained prayer. Writing about a new pentecostal team that had arrived in Johannesburg in 1908, W. J. Kerr explained the importance of prayer in the missionaries' strategy. They had emphasized "the necessity of much prayer, and most of the meetings are largely prayer meetings, either before or after the usual gospel service." It was customary for the workers to be in a back room of their meeting place "for one or two hours either praying with people, or waiting on God for His blessing," he wrote. It would be a mistake, however, to conclude that this "spiritual" kind of evangelism was the only activity pentecostals were engaged in. What is quite remarkable about the first missionaries was their occupation with rescue missions, famine relief, feeding the poor, and especially the creation of orphanages and schools to care for the many destitute children they came across. It was not just a case of preaching the full gospel and leaving their converts to take care of themselves. Looking after the physical needs of their converts and of needy children was an integral part of the gospel they proclaimed. This continued to be a characteristic of the many indigenous movements that emerged.[4]

Healer

The full gospel proclaimed that Jesus was the Healer from sickness and all forms of disease. This was in direct continuity with the divine healing movement at the end of the nineteenth century, one of the most important influences on early Pentecostalism and another expression of the popular beliefs on the fringe of Christianity out of which it emerged. Despite all the divisions that were later to erupt in Pentecostalism, divine healing remained constant. It is also likely that above all else, healing is the main reason for the appeal of Pentecostalism in the global South. Like the earlier advocates of divine healing, even though they suffered from severe illnesses and many of their earliest missionaries died from tropical diseases, pentecostals remained unshaken in their conviction that physical divine healing had been restored to the church in the worldwide revival of the last days. Healing was both an indispensable ingredient of their message and the means by which the nations would be brought to faith in Christ. Pentecostals believed that "signs and wonders" would follow their preaching in fulfillment of Christ's Great Commission. Healing and miracles are still prominent in pentecostal practice, especially in the majority world. Indeed, in many cases, the ability of a preacher to heal is the primary cause of church growth. Recent studies have emphasized that healing, more than any other factor, is the single most important category for understanding the expansion of Pentecostalism during the twentieth century.[5]

In the nineteenth century, divine healing became more acceptable within Protestantism. Figures like Johann Christoph Blumhardt (1805–80) in Bad Boll, Germany, and Dorothea Trudel (1813–62) and her successor Samuel Zeller (1834–1912) in Männedorf, Switzerland, operated centers for healing through prayer. The fame of Blumhardt and Trudel reached the English-speaking world in the second half of the century. Among those who were influenced and involved in healing by prayer were Charles Cullis, an Episcopalian physician, and the CMA leader A. B. Simpson, whose missionaries played a major role in early Pentecostalism in China and India. The healing movement gained momentum toward the end of the century and developed international networks. The "International Conference on Divine Healing and True Holiness," held in London in 1885, marked one of the high points in the healing movement and brought together leaders from several, mostly Western countries. The conference chair was William Boardman (1810–96) and the speakers included A. B. Simpson and Elizabeth Baxter (1837–1926). John Alexander Dowie (1847–1907), the controversial founder of Zion City near Chicago, has been regarded as "the father of healing revivalism in America," although there were several earlier figures. His Christian Catholic Apostolic Church was founded in 1895, placing Dowie in the tradition of the Scottish Presbyterian revivalist Edward Irving (whose followers became the Catholic Apostolic Church), and forming a link between Irving and Pentecostalism. Dowie's radical eschatology was still premillennial but included a strong missionary orientation and an emphasis on healing; his end-time restorationism and his acceptance of people from all walks of life became prominent motifs in Pentecostalism. In 1904 Dowie declared himself "First Apostle," and the following year Zion City went bankrupt, after which Dowie suffered a stroke and died in disgrace. Several Zion leaders became Pentecostals, and Dowie's influence extended far beyond North America. His Zionist movement was one of the most important formative influences on the growth of both Pentecostalism and of "Spirit" churches in Africa. Millions of "Zionists" attend celebrations at African "Zion Cities" in southern Africa, where healing, prophecy, and speaking in tongues are often the main activities. The Faith Tabernacle in Philadelphia was founded by a former Zionist and was an important influence on early West African Pentecostalism. Some leaders in the healing movement taught that divine healing was possible without medical assistance and some, like Dowie and some early Pentecostals, rejected the use of medical science altogether. Although this was not the view of the majority, the rejection of medicine was also a feature of early Pentecostalism and independent churches throughout the majority world.[6]

The presence of healing gifts sometimes broke down barriers of gender and race. Some of the prominent American healers were women, such as the African American Elizabeth Mix, who prayed for the healing of the Episcopalian woman Carrie Judd Montgomery (1858–1946) from an incurable disease. Montgomery published a monthly periodical, *Triumphs of Faith,* which began in 1881 and continued for almost seven decades; it was "devoted to faith-healing and to the promotion of Christian holiness."[7] Many of the articles were on healing and were written by women, and some leading ministers in the healing movement like her friend Elizabeth Baxter were featured. Montgomery was one of the most prominent American healing evangelists and bridged the gap between the healing and holiness movements and Pentecostalism when she became pentecostal in 1908. Montgomery's early views of physical healing were clear and included the rejection of medicine. These views were to typify pentecostals through much of the twentieth century. Maria Woodworth-Etter (1844–1924) was a tent evangelist who traveled around the United States in radical evangelical circles, and before the rise of Aimee Semple McPherson, she was the most popular featured speaker in early American Pentecostalism. Healing ministries were often the most effective ways to reach people with the Christian message, and this distinguished pentecostal missionaries from those from older missions. One of the earliest pentecostal missionaries in Shanghai, Antoinette Moomau, based her extensive ministry on prayer for the sick, writing:

> I believe I am safe in saying that whenever there is a case of healing, there are always one or more families reached simply through that testimony that Jesus is able to heal the sick. Many times the power of God comes upon these sick ones the first time they are prayed for, and in a short time they receive a clear experience of salvation.[8]

Healing evangelists have always been part of the pentecostal movement in the North, from Carrie Judd Montgomery, Aimee Semple McPherson, and Smith Wigglesworth in the earliest years of the movement to Kathryn Kuhlman and Morris Cerullo in the 1970s, through to Benny Hinn and German evangelist Reinhard Bonnke from the 1980s onward. Healing evangelists are long established in pentecostal circles in Latin America (Carlos Annacondia in Argentina), Asia (John Sung in China, Yonggi Cho in Korea, and Bhakt Singh and D. G. S. Dhinakaran in India), and Africa (William Wade Harris and Garrick Braide in West Africa and Engenas Lekganyane in South Africa in the 1910s, Joseph Babalola in the 1930s, and Benson Idahosa in the 1980s in Nigeria, among many others). A massive increase in membership among Argentine evangelicals during the 1980s was particularly the result of Annacondia's campaigns. He and compatriots Omar Cabrera, Hector Giménez, and Claudio Freidzon were responsible for the rapid growth of pentecostal churches in Argentina, where divine healing has become the sine qua non for church growth and their central practice.

The Argentine movement had international repercussions. Freidzon was a key figure in the development of the "Toronto Blessing" that commenced a year after Canadian Vineyard pastors John and Carol Arnott visited his church. Argentine pentecostal congregations are now among the largest in the world.[9]

Pentecostal denominations have sometimes had an uneasy and ambiguous relationship with international healing evangelists, who usually operate independently. Their healing campaigns, which contributed to the growth of Pentecostalism in many parts of the world, developed in North America after the Second World War and had their peak in the 1950s. David Harrell considers the period 1947–58 to be the period of "the great healing revival" in the United States that "dwarfed the successes of earlier charismatic revivalists; it had a dramatic impact on the image of American pentecostalism and set off a period of world-wide pentecostal growth." This may be overstating the case, for it does not account sufficiently for the efforts of indigenous and denominational pentecostal leaders. At first, healing evangelists enjoyed support from most pentecostal denominations, but some were embroiled in controversies that embarrassed the denominational leaders and caused them to distance themselves from these healers. Indeed, many of these evangelists themselves found it more expedient to work independently and reported remarkable healings and miracles in their campaigns. William Branham (1909–65) and Oral Roberts (1918–2009) were the best known and most widely traveled. Branham's sensational healing services, which began in 1946, are well documented. He was the pacesetter for those who followed before he became involved in doctrinal controversies that continue among his "Branhamite" followers. A. A. Allen (1911–70) died an alcoholic. Tommy Hicks (1909–73) was responsible for revival meetings in Buenos Aires in 1954 at the behest of President Juan Perón, which 400,000 people were reported to have attended. T. L. Osborne (1923–) had large crowds at his campaigns in Central America, the Caribbean, Indonesia, and East Africa. By 1960, Oral Roberts had become the leading pentecostal evangelist, increasingly accepted by mainline denominations, and one of the most influential pentecostals in the emergence of the Charismatic movement. His moving from the Pentecostal Holiness Church to the United Methodist Church in 1969 marked the end of the relationship between healing evangelists and denominational pentecostals, who were becoming increasingly critical of the evangelists' methods, particularly their fund-raising and often lavish lifestyles. Sometimes the emphasis on the "miraculous" has led to shameful showmanship and moral decadence, exaggerated and unsubstantiated claims of healing, and triumphalism.[10]

However, pentecostals regard "signs and wonders" to be such an indispensable part of their evangelism that without them their preaching is powerless. They consider this evidence that the apostolic power is as available as it had been in the time of the New Testament. These ideas were promoted in pentecostal periodicals. Elisabeth Sexton wrote that unbelievers would be convinced by "the supernatural manifestation of His power in His saints" and that the world had the right to expect signs to follow their ministry. William Burton in the Congo wrote that Christ's command to heal the sick had never been withdrawn. His apostles continued his healing and miracle ministry to the end of their lives. The present days were "apostolic days" and God was still sending apostles to the nations of earth. Jesus had given the example of a method of evangelism and he expected it to proceed in like manner, with "signs following" just as had happened from the beginning of his mission. Early twentieth-century pentecostal newsletters and periodicals abounded with testimonies to physical healings, exorcisms, and deliverances from evil spirits. Healing was an evangelistic door opener for pentecostals by which the full gospel was demonstrated in a physical and personal deliverance. Pentecostal missionaries and especially the healing evangelists expected miracles to accompany their evangelism, and as McGee put it, they "prioritized seeking for spectacular displays of celestial power." The "signs and wonders" promoted by healing evangelists have led to the rapid growth of pentecostal churches in many parts of the world. Harrell considers the independent American healing evangelists responsible "more than any other single force" for bringing "the message of God's miraculous power to the masses in the Third World."[11]

But while it is true that Roberts, Osborne, Hicks, and in recent years Reinhard Bonnke have been major players in popularizing healing evangelism, there were long-established traditions of healing evangelism initiated by indigenous preachers throughout the sub-Sahara, and from India to China. In many cultures of the world, healing has always been a major attraction for Pentecostalism and independent churches, and it has not had to overcome the anti-supernaturalism of rational enlightenment thinking prevailing in the West. In many rural African and Asian cultures the religious specialist had extraordinary power to heal the sick and protect from evil spirits and sorcery. The proclamation of healing and miracles related directly to those who saw the pentecostal message as powerfully able to meet human needs. Numerous healings reported by pentecostal preachers confirmed to them that God's Word was true and that God's power was evidently present—with the result that many were persuaded to become Christians. As Burton put it, healing belonged to the missionaries' credentials, and above all the "signs" promised in Mark 16, "again and again, we lay hands on the sick in the Name of Jesus and they recover, whereas the witch doctors' fetishes could not, in some cases, heal them." Furthermore, in contrast to the traditional healers who charged for their services, pentecostals offered their healing power for free. Burton wrote that healing was "the very foundation of pioneering missionary work." It was, in effect, this power confrontation with traditional healers that won converts. This healing activity was played out in many different contexts and occasions, often spreading much quicker through native agency. A missionary in South Africa wrote in 1909 that God was "doing marvelous things amongst the native people." When Africans got saved and healed, they also had "faith in God for the salvation and the healing of others." He continued, "It goes like wildfire from one to another. It is the ministry of healing that carries the Gospel. Missionaries without faith for healing do not amount to much here. There are plenty of them here now who cannot touch the people." Another early pentecostal described divine healing as "one of the greatest powers we have" and the means by which people were "brought to Jesus." He declared that he "could fill a fair sized newspaper with detailed accounts" of people "completely healed in answer to prayer."[12]

But it was not always power and glory for pentecostals. Some doubted the authenticity of the many reports of healing and some were later proved to have been exaggerated. Occasionally, cases of failed healings were reported, many missionaries themselves succumbed to sickness, and some tragically died of diseases like smallpox and malaria in their adopted countries after only a short time; there is no evidence that they were any different from other missionaries. Some taught, like contemporary "faith" preachers, that all sickness is from "the devil" and does not belong to a Christian, so that when one "feels" sick one has the symptoms but not the sickness itself. Some were more philosophical in their approach to their own physical weaknesses. Lillian Garr, who died soon after her return to the United States from Hong Kong and who lost both her daughter and her domestic helper to smallpox soon after their arrival there, wrote of the loss of two children of other missionaries, who had to "give up" their children because God was preparing them for "higher ministry." As a result of their "double sorrow" they would "come forth as gold." As she nursed her terminally ill husband in China, PMU missionary Maggie Trevitt struggled with the conflict between her faith in divine healing and the tragic reality of her husband's tuberculosis. The couple did "not understand why deliverance does not come," she wrote. They had both "asked the Holy Spirit to search us and anything that was revealed we confessed it and asked for cleansing and forgiveness, but still deliverance is withheld and the Lord must have a purpose in it." Sadly, her husband died soon after this letter was written.[13] Burton struggled with the issue of taking quinine as protection against malaria after he discovered how many missionaries had died of malaria in southern Africa:

> The Apostolic Faith and Pentecostal Mission have 33 graves of splendid men and women who refused quinine and died. But now these malaria victims are dying, and of course some of the Spirit filled missionaries are taking quinine, and they don't die, and they ask me which gives God most glory? To take this stuff and live, or refuse it and die?[14]

These were the dilemmas faced by pentecostal missionaries. Healing is probably no longer as prominent as it once was, but in many parts of the majority world, the problems of disease and evil still affect the whole community. These mostly rural communities are health-oriented and in their pre-Christian religions rituals for healing and protection are prominent. Pentecostals responded to a void left by rationalistic forms of Christianity that had unwittingly initiated the destruction of familiar religious values. They preached a message that reclaimed biblical traditions of healing and protection from evil and demonstrated the practical effects of these traditions. So they became heralds of a meaningful message that offered to meet physical, emotional, and spiritual needs of people—solutions to life's problems and ways to cope in a threatening, hostile world. But too often, this message of power has become an occasion for the exploitation of those who are at their weakest.[15]

Arguably the most effective and best-known Chinese healing evangelist of the twentieth century, John Sung (Song Shangjie, 1901–44), was an independent itinerant revivalist preacher in the 1930s. He lived during a turbulent time in China; but this was also the time of the Shandong Revival, when spiritual gifts were accepted in many Protestant churches. Song drew thousands to his meetings and regularly prayed for the sick, anointing them with oil. Startling results were reported. Born in the home of a Methodist preacher in Xinghua, Fujian, in southeast China, Song went to Ohio State University, graduating with a PhD in chemistry in 1926. One eventful year in the United States included a semester at Union Theological Seminary, New York, when he burned all his theological books and renounced theological education. After a "breakdown" (which he always claimed was a mistaken diagnosis for a spiritual experience) and six months in a mental hospital, he returned home in early 1927. This was the period of the anti-Christian movement in China, but for the next thirteen years, until ill health overcame him, he devoted himself exclusively to evangelism and healing, bringing at least 100,000 to conversion (some estimates are considerably more) and revival to hundreds of churches. He had an indefatigable preaching schedule throughout China and Southeast Asia, including Malaysia, Singapore, Borneo, Indonesia, the Philippines, Thailand, Vietnam, and Burma. Wherever he went, his diary recorded hundreds of conversions and healings from all kinds of afflictions. His hundreds of meetings (usually three a day with two hours of preaching in each service) were characterized by drama and emotion, including theatrics and vivid illustrations on the platform, vigorous clapping, spontaneous prayer in unison, and free-flowing tears. Song dressed in an informal long Chinese shirt and often appeared disheveled, with his hair falling over his forehead. His stern revivalist preaching appealed to common people, demanded repentance from moral vices, and was accompanied by revival songs, emotional scenes of people repenting with loud cries and tears, and exorcising demons. Numerous cases of healing in Song's ministry were reported, with overwhelming numbers of people lining up for prayer for healing and exorcism in his meetings. Wherever he went he set up evangelistic teams to continue the work he had started and hundreds of these teams operated throughout China and Southeast Asia. He became an international figure, but his many critics charged him with fanaticism, emotionalism, and even insanity.[16]

Although Song cautioned against what he saw as pentecostal excesses and had an ambivalent relationship with pentecostals, his ministry most certainly was characterized by pentecostal phenomena and he preached in pentecostal churches. He was a healing evangelist who not only was baptized by immersion in 1932 in Hong Kong, regularly prayed in tongues (a gift he first received in March 1934), and prayed for the sick during every campaign, but he also exercised a gift of knowledge and prophecy in the course of his preaching. With the gift of knowledge, he would speak out about personal details of people in his audience without contact with them beforehand. He was also reported to use predictive prophecy, and his diary records his occasional visions. These were also features of later pentecostal healing evangelists. His view on tongues was that it was the least of the gifts, but that every Christian should be filled with the Spirit. Like pentecostals, he saw this as an experience subsequent to conversion, prayed for people to receive the experience, and taught that it should be accompanied by receiving love and at least "one of the 9 gifts of the Holy Spirit (1 Corinthians 12:8–10)." He was also a conservative fundamentalist who sometimes used questionable exegesis and allegory, an outspoken critic of "liberal" theology, and one who believed that Western missionary control was a hindrance to the Chinese church. He wrote in his diary that only after the missionaries had gone and Western funds stopped would the Chinese church really grow. He made his views known clearly, declaring: "I feel that most of the [church] organizations set up by Westerners do not last long. The churches that God blesses are those built by Holy Spirit-inspired Chinese." He held annual Bible Conferences for church leaders; the one in Beijing in 1937 was attended by 1,600 delegates. Song prophesied that there would be a great revival in China after the missionaries left and after the Chinese church had suffered greatly. In spite of his often searing outbursts against Western missionaries, Song was welcomed in Western-founded churches (usually evangelical ones), and occasionally he was invited by the missionaries themselves. His effective ministry was regarded by many as preparing the Chinese church for the rigors of the impending Japanese war and the repression under Communism that was to follow. Song suffered from recurring tuberculosis and in 1940 was forced to give up his heavy traveling and preaching schedule when diagnosed with cancer. He died in 1944 at the age of forty-two after several major operations. His funeral service was conducted by his friend and well-known Beijing independent church pastor Wang Mingdao. Song's impact on Chinese Christianity was enormous. Not only was he spiritual father to many thousands of Chinese Christians, but his style of integrating emotional prayer with fundamentalist evangelism is now dominant in Chinese Protestant Christianity.[17]

The full gospel continues to be a central part of Pentecostalism's attraction in the majority world, even in its much modified forms, but nowhere is this more evident than in its proclamation of Jesus as Healer. Indeed, in many parts of the world, divine healing is part of all Christian belief and permeates Catholic, Protestant, Pentecostal, and Independent alike. In May 2005 the World Council of Churches (WCC) Commission on World Mission and Evangelism convened an international conference near Athens on the theme of reconciliation and healing. Although the conference did not set out expressly to deal with physical healing in Pentecostalism, this was clearly an important topic. A series of preparatory meetings were convened in London and Accra in 2002, Santiago de Chile in 2003, and Bangalore in 2004, in which I was invited to participate. There and in Athens, pentecostals were represented and their views heard. Pentecostal scholars including Finnish scholar Veli-Matti Kärkkäinen and Ghanaian Church of Pentecost leader Opoku Onyinah helped in the planning of these consultations and worked in various capacities in Athens. The meetings in Accra and Santiago were specifically aimed at bringing together pentecostals and churches involved in the ecumenical movement, and a complete issue of *The International Review of Mission* was devoted to "Divine Healing, Pentecostalism and Mission," with reflections, reports, and papers from the meetings in Ghana and Chile. The January 2005 issue of the *International Review of Mission* dealt with the conference theme and the practices of healing familiar to pentecostals, and a series of preparatory papers were sent out before the Athens conference. In Preparatory Paper 11, "The Healing Mission of the Church," a WCC document gave attention to healing gifts and the world of spirits for the first time. Sections of this document affirmed pentecostal beliefs, declaring that "spiritual powers" had not received adequate treatment in earlier WCC documents and that "a narrow rationalistic world-view and theology" was challenged by the views of proliferating Christian churches outside the West. The manifold gifts of the Spirit—including healing by prayer and laying on of hands, and the exorcism of evil spirits—were part of the ministry of Christ and of the worldview of the New Testament. These were biblical practices according to the apostle Paul's list in 1 Corinthians 12, and were seen as being among many other approaches to healing within contemporary Christian traditions.[18]

Although pentecostals from thirteen countries constituted less than 5 percent of the participants at Athens, that was a larger number than had attended any previous WCC event. For several other reasons their participation had a high profile. The first plenary paper was presented by Korean pentecostal Wonsuk Ma, testimonies were given by Latin American pentecostals in plenaries, Ghanaian Charismatic Methodist theologian Kwabena Asamoah-Gyadu and I were "listeners," and pentecostal presentations in well-attended workshops and a remarkable pentecostal dialogue with Orthodox delegates took place. In his opening address, WCC General Secretary Samuel Kobia referred to the significance of Pentecostalism to ecumenism, speaking of changes in the global dynamics of Christianity not only in its geographical change southward but also in the flourishing of pentecostal spirituality, having "spiritual, moral, theological, missiological" implications. As a result, he said, "forms of expressing our faith that grew out of European culture are no longer normative." There were a few tensions felt by pentecostal delegates: a desire for more enthusiasm to be expressed in the worship, the Orthodox litany that felt particularly foreign to pentecostals from the South, and concerns about the discussions on religious pluralism and the role assigned to difficult Old Testament texts seeming to condone violence. Some of the pentecostal concerns were expressed in a joint statement drawn up and agreed on by nineteen participants at the close of the conference. Part of it read:

> In spite of the goodwill of many, we still feel that Pentecostals are often misunderstood, misrepresented, and even unfairly carica-turized. We admit that we Pentecostals are equally responsible for the mutual suspicion and misunderstanding....Considering that many of us will be critically probed by our own people because of our personal decisions to participate in this conference, we become aware of this difficult task of bridging the gap between Pentecostals and the wider Christian community. At the same time, we affirm our commitment to the spirit of church unity.[19]

The Athens conference did help break down some of the hostility and misunderstanding that had arisen between the pentecostal delegates and the Ecumenical Movement, but there are at least two qualifications that temper a too optimistic assessment. First, the vast majority of pentecos-tals were not represented at the WCC meeting. With notable exceptions like the Korean Assemblies of God and some Latin American pentecostal churches, official representation by pentecostal leaders and major pente-costal denominations in national ecumenical councils remains rare, espe-cially in the case of denominations in the North. Some still eschew such an affiliation and see this as an attempt to create a "world super-church" that will have apocalyptic consequences. Participation in ecumenical gatherings has often been by somewhat isolated individual pentecostal theologians and not by their denominational representatives. There is also resistance among some WCC members to enter into dialogue and involvement with pentecostals, who are still regarded as schismatic.[20]

Second, the pentecostal perception of "healing" is not as holistic as it is portrayed in WCC circles, at least at first glance. This was typified by a comment made on the first day to Wonsuk Ma, who was then a pentecostal missionary in the Philippines, by another Korean who remarked that Ma had presented a view of healing as "physical cure" rather than offering a "deeper," more comprehensive view of healing. Of course, the so-called holistic view of healing often excludes the "physical cure" or what pentecostals call "divine healing." Ma replied that the pentecostal context was often marginalized, but pentecostals also needed to learn how to respond to the scientific approach to healing and to expand the notion of healing beyond the merely physical. The difference between pentecostals and most other Christians used to be that pentecostals believed that the gifts of the Spirit continue in the time between the Ascension and the Second Coming of Christ, whereas most Protestant churches influenced by modernism and rationalism believed that the time of miracles had ceased. This dichotomy is no longer as sharp, for the ecumenical movement acknowledges the active presence of the Spirit in the church through spiritual gifts, and pentecostals admit that other forms of healing (such as medical science) are also part of the healing economy of God. At the conference Wonsuk Ma said that pentecostals represented the "poor," and that the "core" of their pneumatology was "empowerment for witness." Coming from the poor, their conversion to Pentecostalism resulted in some of them moving upward socially, which was seen as evidence of the blessing of God. Healings and miracles were interventions of God that were regularly expected in Pentecostal ministry.[21]

There is another side to healing as practiced in some forms of Pentecostalism, however. The preparatory paper also warned about the idea of a "power encounter" that leads to "a triumphalistic, aggressive presentation of the gospel," but that an urgent dialogue "for the sake of the churches' ministry of healing" seemed appropriate. A testimony of restoration from a failed marriage by the daughter of a pentecostal pastor in Argentina demonstrated that her church was a healing and reconciling community where she had found acceptance and forgiveness. The testimony of a blind man from Kenya told of a pentecostal evangelistic healing "crusade" and the seeming failure of anyone to get physically "healed" there, leaving him hurt and disillusioned. The tendency of pentecostals to believe that physical healing will always occur is contradicted by these "failures" and their own experience. This is one of the disturbing questions concerning divine healing seldom discussed by pentecostals and for which there are no easy answers. During a workshop, Opoku Onyinah said that the WCC statement of healing was very close to his own understanding as a pentecostal and as an African, for the pentecostal salvation is holistic and includes physical healing. Pentecostals are no longer opposed to medical science but believe that however healing takes place, God heals, whether through prayer or medicine. Pentecostals affirm that God is all-powerful and compassionate and is deeply troubled by the suffering in this world. Healing is not seen as an end in itself, but as a sign of God's kingdom rule, as a confirmation of the power of the gospel to bring people to faith. But healing should not become "anathema in the ears of persons with disabilities" but a real possibility for everyone to experience the loving grace of God in healing, whether or not the physical cure is achieved.[22]

Baptizer in the Spirit

The rapid growth of Pentecostalism can also be attributed to a factor called the "Missionary Spirit," the motivation and driving force behind pentecostal expansion. The central doctrine of Spirit baptism has gone through several modifications and controversies in the Western world. The kaleidoscope of pentecostal missionaries illustrates several principles. First, the gift of tongues received with Spirit baptism was often referred to as the "gift of languages" in early American Pentecostalism and became the primary reason for the sending out missionaries. *The Apostolic Faith* in Los Angeles revealed that the expectations of early American pentecostals were that this gift had been given to fulfill the commission "Go into all the world and preach the gospel to all creation." As a result,

> The Lord has given languages to the unlearned Greek, Latin, Hebrew, French, German, Italian, Chinese, Japanese, Zulu and languages of Africa, Hindu [sic] and Bengali and dialects of India, Chippewa and other languages of the Indians, Esquimaux [sic], the deaf mute language and, in fact the Holy Ghost speaks all the languages of the world through His children.[23]

Early American pentecostal periodicals abounded with testimonies to this divinely bestowed gift of languages; but soon it dawned on pentecostals that there was no shortcut to language learning and their missionaries were faced with the same difficulties of communication as any other foreigner. They began to talk of speaking in tongues as being primarily "unknown tongues" and the shift away from "missionary tongues" was rapid when faced with the challenges of life in a different country and culture. However, because the pentecostal missionaries took many years to become familiar with the languages of the nations, they depended much more on the "native helpers" than other missionaries did. The traditional missionary set out to master the language and thus become less dependent on local people, whereas the foreign pentecostal missionary could not succeed without indigenous workers.[24]

The primary motivation behind the belief in missionary tongues was the conviction that the Spirit had been given to evangelize all nations. As *The Apostolic Faith* put it, it was "the baptism with the Holy Ghost which is the enduement of power, that will make you a witness to the uttermost parts of the earth." Inquisitive people went on pilgrimages to Azusa Street and returned having experienced their own personal Spirit baptisms. Not all the early pentecostal missionaries were novices. Some were already missionaries who had spent some time in the "field," like George Berg in India, Bernt Berntsen and Antoinette Moomau in China, and Samuel and Ardell Mead in Angola. These had all traveled far to Los Angeles and returned to these countries as pentecostal missionaries. Berg had been a Brethren missionary in South India and on his return to India after visiting Azusa Street he began with Brethren mission contacts. Berntsen was a Scandinavian Alliance missionary and Moomau a Presbyterian one. Because they were convinced they also had a message for traditional Christians, many of the first pentecostal converts were from existing Christian missions and included other foreign missionaries. Nevertheless, the remarkable fact was that these untrained and (in most cases) inexperienced pentecostal missionaries were sent all over the world from centers like Los Angeles, Indianapolis, London, Oslo, and Stockholm, according to one estimate reaching over twenty-five nations in two years. T. B. Barratt observed in 1909:

> In heathen lands, among Missionaries, native preachers and Evangelists, as well as among the people, this Holy Fire is spreading, and will do so increasingly. It is said that some fifty thousand people have within two years been baptized with the Holy Ghost and have spoken in tongues. Thousands of God's people have been wonderfully blessed of God outside of this number.[25]

Of course, it was part of the legacy of Protestantism that the world outside the Americas and Europe was regarded as "heathen," the dark world to which they had been sent with the light of the gospel and Western "civilization." But for pentecostals, the biblical texts were more significant. They were as much convinced by Acts 1:8 ("But you will receive power when the Holy Spirit comes on you; and you will be my witnesses in Jerusalem, and in all Judea and Samaria, and to the ends of the earth") as they were by Acts 2:4 ("All of them were filled with the Holy Spirit and began to speak in other tongues as the Spirit enabled them"), often regarded as their defining text. Pentecostals believed that the command of Acts 1:8 was not an option; it was the only way that the Great Commission could be fulfilled and it had to be sought before it was too late and Jesus had returned. In 1908, Indianapolis pentecostal leader and later first General Secretary of the Assemblies of God J. Roswell Flower put it, "When the Holy Spirit comes into our hearts, the missionary spirit comes in with it; they are inseparable" and "carrying the gospel to hungry souls in this and other lands is but a natural result." The PMU's director, Cecil Polhill, expressed the conviction that for any revival to endure it must have "the true Missionary Spirit." He thought that the "Pentecostal Blessing must go right through the world" and was "the very best thing in the world for the Mission Field." The gift of the Spirit was a "Missionary Gift." His mission organization was founded on the conviction that "every true Pentecost means missionary service to the ends of the earth." Alexander Boddy, Anglican vicar and board member of the PMU, wrote that a true "Pentecost" meant "a growth of the Missionary Spirit," that "the indwelling Christ is an indwelling Missionary" who had sent pentecostals to go into the world. When they obeyed, "He goes with us in the power of the Holy Ghost to preach a great and a full Salvation for Body, Soul, and Spirit."[26]

This theological link between Spirit baptism and Christocentric mission has always been made in the pentecostal movement and was inherited by the first pentecostals from the earlier revival movements they had been part of. The point cannot be overemphasized: just as Spirit baptism is Pentecostalism's most distinctive doctrine, so mission and evangelism are Pentecostalism's most important activities. This is the primary reason for its tendency to expand wherever it can. The spread of Pentecostalism worldwide should be seen in this light. Pentecostalism as a whole does not depend on highly specialized clergy to perform its mission, for its fundamental conviction is that all of God's children who are filled with the Spirit are called to be God's messengers of the good news. Minnie Abrams explained that Spirit baptism should "make us world-wide" and "enlarge us," for Christ had said "that repentance and remission of sins should be preached in His Name to all nations, beginning at Jerusalem," which was "the program that He laid out for us." Christ had said that "He would endue us with power from on high that we might be able to do it." Abrams was probably the first to give a detailed exposition of Spirit baptism within a Holiness framework, and she linked spiritual gifts with missions. Pentecostals were given gifts of the Spirit in order to engage in service to others—this was their mission to the world. As she put it, the "full Pentecostal baptism of the Holy Ghost" had not been received unless someone had received both the fruit of the Spirit and the gifts of the Spirit as outlined in 1 Corinthians 12. These gifts alone "enabled the early church to spread the knowledge of the gospel, and establish the Christian church so rapidly." It was this exposition that was shared with her friends the Hoovers in Chile that led to the beginning of Pentecostalism in that country.[27]

This fundamental and inseparable link between Spirit baptism, spiritual gifts, and Christocentric missions remained the central plank of the whole structure of Pentecostalism from its beginnings. Polhill stated that every missionary needed the baptism of the Spirit with the accompanying spiritual gifts for the task. There had to be "a distinct seeking of the baptism for service for every missionary, and equally a clear receiving or manifestation, probably the speaking in tongues, accompanying which will be some distinct spiritual gift or gifts to each one." Only in this way, he wrote, would "the Gospel be presented to every creature in the shortest possible time." Reflecting on the expansion of Chilean Pentecostalism over two decades, Willis Hoover wrote that it was "the missionary spirit" that moved pentecostals to go to places where the pentecostal experience was not known. For this some were prepared to migrate to other towns, work at their trade, and "sow the Word of the Lord." Some became pastors as a result—to this day, Chilean Pentecostalism prefers tried-and-proven leaders who have shown their gifting in ministry rather than those theologically trained ones who have not yet proven their practical abilities. For pentecostals, the baptism in the Spirit is both the primary motivation for and only essential prerequisite for mission and evangelism. Although they did engage in all sorts of philanthropic activities, they had been empowered by the Spirit to go into the most distant parts of their world. That local leaders soon arose with the same single qualification meant that Pentecostalism indigenized quicker than older mission churches had.[28]

But pentecostals also used Acts to affirm that, for them, the primary purpose of the outpouring of the Spirit was to send countless witnesses for

Christ out to the farthest reaches of the globe. It could be argued that Acts 1:8 was their most important motivation for expansion beyond the Western world, for the power of the Spirit had been given for the express purpose of reaching out as "witnesses" beyond their "Jerusalem and Samaria" to the "uttermost parts of the world." Pentecostals also frequently used the disputed appendix to Mark's Gospel (16:15–18), in which Jesus commanded them to "Go into the whole world and preach the gospel to all creation," promising that the "signs" that would follow their faith included healing the sick, speaking in tongues, and casting out demons. It was this use of biblical texts to integrate their experience of the Spirit with their mission that resulted in thousands of transnational missionaries going out to plant churches and cause the fastest expansion of a new Christian movement in the history of Christianity.

Soon Coming King

The final declaration of the full gospel was the affirmation that Jesus Christ was the "Soon Coming King." A particular kind of eschatological expectation was a dominant theme in Pentecostalism in its early years, further adding to the urgency of world mission and evangelism. A shift from the optimistic postmillennialism of early nineteenth-century Protestantism to a pessimistic, premillennialist "secret rapture" dispensationalism swept through evangelical circles later that century. It was believed in these circles that Christ's coming could occur at any moment, when believers would be raptured from the earth and the rest of the world left to await judgment. The world was seen as evil beyond repair and the task of the believers was to snatch as many as possible out of the certain flames of hell. This shift occurred gradually in the Holiness movement toward the end of the nineteenth century. It was the result of several factors, but it was precipitated by the influential teaching of John Nelson Darby of the Plymouth Brethren in Britain. A monthly periodical, *The Prophetic Times,* commenced publication in 1863 and prophetic conferences like D. L. Moody's annual Prophecy Conference in Massachusetts (beginning in 1880) prominently advocated Darby's eschatological views. Popular evangelical preachers A. T. Pierson, A. B. Simpson, and A. J. Gordon all expounded premillennialism; eventually it was accepted by a majority of evangelicals, and it was a prominent theme of the Keswick conventions in England that commenced in 1875. With few exceptions, most of the Holiness movement, many evangelicals, and subsequently most early pentecostals accepted premillennial eschatology. The reasons for this were complex but include a pessimistic reaction to theological liberalism and the "social gospel" that increasingly came to dominate the main Protestant denominations. The complex and intricately detailed premillennial eschatological system was the product of a highly rationalistic and literalist approach to biblical passages, especially the Book of Revelation. As most Holiness groups gradually accepted the Keswick position of Spirit baptism for mission service through exposure to its teachers, they also accepted its eschatology with its stress on the coming of a new Pentecost and an imminent worldwide revival to usher in the return of Christ. The demise of postmillennialism, with its optimistic view of a coming "golden age" of material wealth and progress, was replaced by an increasingly pessimistic view that the world would get progressively worse until the return of Christ. Accordingly, the missionary task was to rescue individuals from certain peril rather than seek to transform society.[29]

But this premillennialism was not entirely pessimistic, for there was a certain tension between the negative view of the world and the very positive view of their place in it. This ambiguity was especially noticeable in Pentecostalism. The outpouring of the Spirit in the last days made mission and evangelizing the nations possible and almost guaranteed its success. Pentecostals believed that they were part of the greatest spiritual revival the world had ever known and their evangelistic work was a direct consequence. The differences between these various interpretations of biblical apocalyptic literature were vast. Postmillennialists held that Christ would return after a thousand year period and therefore they laid greater stress on social activism in order to make the world a better place. Their mission work included educational, philanthropic, and medical activities as well as evangelism and church planting, but church planting was given less attention. By contrast, premillennialists believed that because Christ's return was imminent, the world should be seen as a temporary place in which Christians were merely brief visitors. This premillennialist eschatology and ethic of "separation from the world" influenced pentecostal political views considerably. For decades, pentecostal faithful were exhorted to have nothing to do with politics. The political realm was part of the evil world system that would end at the coming of Christ. For the same reason, many early pentecostals were opposed to war and advocated pacifism. During the Great War of 1914–18 most pentecostals were conscientious objectors, holding that war was another evil consequence of the end of the age and that Christians should have no part in it. For most of them, the outbreak of the war was evidence that the end had come and that the world, of which they were certainly no part, was involved in a bloody conflagration that would lead to the final battle of Armageddon preceding the return of Christ. As believers, they would be snatched away from the world's conflicts, and therefore they should have no part in war. But in the years following World War I their pacifism changed radically, as pentecostals began to see governments in a more positive light and were influenced by prevailing warmongering cultures and a "just war" theology. Pentecostal chaplains joined the American army to minister to pentecostal soldiers fighting in Vietnam, Iraq, and Afghanistan. A minority, including the largest African American denomination, the Church of God in Christ, continued to be pacifist in official orientation and more recently, the Pentecostal Charismatic Peace Fellowship founded by AG minister Paul Alexander in 2002 became a lobbying group for pentecostal involvement in international social justice and opposition to war. This organization holds annual conferences and is now called Pentecostals and Charismatics for Peace and Justice. But for the majority of white North American pentecostals, their prevailing eschatology and membership of the National Association of Evangelicals caused them to be proponents of the so-called religious right.[30]

Pentecostal periodicals were full of exhortations about the imminent return of Christ. In many pentecostal circles, current events are taken as signs of the times, proof that the Lord would be coming back soon. Their mission work consisted particularly (but not entirely) of feverish evangelism and church planting, and together with most of the "faith missions," they began to propagate this eschatology. But we must remember that early pentecostal missions also had philanthropic and educational components, especially the creation of orphanages, schools, and rescue centers—Albert Norton's and Mark Buntain's rescue work in India, Mok Lai Chi's schools in Hong Kong, and Lillian Trasher's orphanages in Asyût, Egypt, being prime examples. Norton wrote disapprovingly of those missionaries who fraternized with European colonialists in their sports and amusements "to ignore and deny the existence of the sufferings of the poor." The evangelism of the pentecostals did not therefore obliterate all other concerns, although it must be said that all other activities were usually seen as subservient to the primary task of getting individuals saved and filled with the Spirit. The first pentecostals saw the soon coming of Christ as the prime motivation for the urgent task of preparing the world for this cataclysmic event. Prophecies, tongues, and interpretations and visions affirmed this expectation on almost every occasion. The second coming of Christ would occur when the Gospel had been proclaimed to every nation, they declared, and so it was necessary to engage in the most rapid evangelization possible. In 1911 W. W. Simpson, while still a CMA missionary and in the midst of the revolution against the Manchurian empire, wrote to Mok Lai Chi stating,

> Whatever may happen politically we hope to be able to remain here till the Lord comes which we believe is very soon....The work is in a very prosperous condition. The churches purified, revived and mightily baptized and filled with the Holy Spirit and all earnest in serving the Lord and eagerly waiting for the Lord's return....
>
> Tell all that in standing for the Latter Rain teaching I have been standing for the Truth of God and shall receive the Lord's "Well done" for it when He comes and that His coming is nigh even at the doors; for "this generation shall not pass away till all be fulfilled." "Look up and lift up your heads for your redemption draweth nigh." The best of us are not half earnest enough in expecting the Lord's soon return. Let all who believe the teaching practically get ready and join in the continuous prayer. "Even so, come Lord Jesus," and it will not be many days before He will come for those who love his appearing.[31]

Despite their optimism about their role in this end-time mission, pentecostals' view of the world around them, especially the religious world, was decidedly negative. The increase of "false prophets," the expansion of Islam, theological liberalism (especially "Higher Criticism," anathema to these premillennialists), and the spread of heterodox Christian groups like Mormons and Jehovah's Witnesses—all were signs of impending doom. In fact, for so many of these pentecostal missionaries and their children, the "soon coming of the Lord" was realized in their premature death through diseases—especially smallpox, malaria, and from 1918, the influenza epidemic. The preceding quotation also reveals that their belief in the imminent coming was linked to some apathy toward political events.[32]

There is evidence that these early eschatological emphases remained for much of the twentieth century in Pentecostalism, especially among its first constituency, the poor and oppressed. But with the coming of a new, middle-class, and prosperous form of Pentecostalism (including those aspiring to be so) in the last quarter of the twentieth century, a different approach to eschatology arose, if not a rejection of premillennial pessimism entirely. In many cases, the new emphasis was on "realized eschatology," God's kingdom present in the here and now, and not only evidenced by divine health but also through financial prosperity and success in this life. This shift also meant that the world was no longer a desperately evil place to be shunned and escaped. Many of these new pentecostals are world-affirming; education and economic success become priorities; and longing for a better life in the hereafter is replaced by a desire for a better life in the here and now. Indeed, the new emphasis continued the optimistic pentecostal trajectory that a good God desired good things for people, not just in the hereafter but especially in the here and now. This new emphasis was to reach its zenith in the prosperity gospel and spread worldwide in the 1980s. The particular eschatology still espoused in pentecostal churches, especially in the United States, includes a particularly undiscerning approach to biblical prophecy relating to Israel. This is sometimes called Christian Zionism and sees Israel's occupation of the Holy Land as the fulfillment of end-times prophecies and the oppression of Palestinians as its logical, justified outcome. Wild and speculative assertions as to the personality of the "Antichrist" and fantastic interpretations of obscure biblical texts all combine to create an ideology that is decidedly right wing and driven by world events, therefore changing regularly. Thus, the "scarlet whore" of the Book of Revelation, also identified with the Antichrist, has been variously identified in pentecostal circles with the Roman Catholic Church and/or the pope, the World Council of Churches, Germany, Russia, fascism, communism, and currently, militant Islam.

Pentecostals place primacy on evangelism, which includes signs of the Spirit's presence and the coming of the eschatological kingdom of God. These emphases have created distance and suspicion between pentecostals and other Christians that continues today, especially when pentecostals use a language of power and a tendency toward triumphalism in their evangelism, and neglect the role of suffering in Christian experience. The *charismata* of the Spirit are, for pentecostals, proof that the gospel is true. The "full gospel" is understood to contain good news for all life's problems, particularly relevant in those societies where disease is rife and access to adequate health care is a luxury. As Währisch-Oblau has observed in China, the need for healings is in direct proportion to the unavailability of medical resources and the breakdown of the public health system there. Prayer for healing is "an act of desperation in circumstances where they see few alternative options." That people believe themselves to be healed means that for them the "full gospel" is a remedy for their frequent afflictions; it therefore seeks to be relevant to human totality and to proclaim biblical deliverance from the real fear of evil. The methods used to receive this deliverance and the perceptions concerning the means of grace sometimes differ, but pentecostals believe in an omnipotent and compassionate God concerned with all human troubles and willing to intervene to alleviate them. They exercise the authority that they believe has been given them, reinforced by the power of the Spirit, to effect deliverance from sin, sickness, and oppression, and from every conceivable form of evil.[33]

7

Transformation and Independence

The First Pentecostals in Latin America

The global shifts and constant mutations that characterized Pentecostalism were strongly influenced by local factors. Independent churches with a pentecostal emphasis proliferated in the global South, and this expansion had repercussions for all of world Christianity, drastic changes that were unforeseen by the Edinburgh World Missionary Conference in 1910. But this was not just a geographical and cultural shift of center; it was at the same time a reformation of Christianity so fundamental that its reverberations extended much further than had the Protestant Reformation. The 1910 Edinburgh missionary conference had left Latin America out of the program altogether, regarding it (like all Europe), as already Christianized and therefore not needing missionaries. In stark contrast, pentecostals, like their evangelical counterparts, saw South America as the "neglected continent" and were stridently anti-Catholic. Their rhetoric described Latin America as a "Romanist" stronghold and their letters and reports abounded with allusions to the "darkness" and "delusion" of popular Catholicism in this region. They were at pains to point out that Catholicism was "Christopaganism" or "baptized paganism" and that such things as the burning of (Protestant) Bibles, the veneration of Mary and images, "pagan" religious festivals, and rampant immorality were evidence that South America was anything but a "Christian" continent. Furthermore, they pointed out, there were millions of indigenous Amerindians who were without any knowledge of Christianity. Evangelical Christians thought that South America had few qualified mission workers but was wide open to American missionaries in particular. Pentecostals, therefore, must grasp the opportunity so that God could "find faithful workers whom He can thrust forth into this most neglected field of the whole world, for truly the fields are white already unto harvest." Calls for increased missionary activity on the "neglected continent" went largely unheeded in mainline Protestant denominations, but in the second half of the century Latin America became the world stronghold of Pentecostalism. Some pentecostal denominations, like the Assembly of God in Brazil, were established several years before the major ones in the United States, from which they are sometimes erroneously presumed to have emerged, were even founded. The birth of Latin American Pentecostalism took place at a time when North American pentecostal denominations were still forming.[1]

The movement in the South therefore is quite different from that in the North, and we should not regard it as a North American creation or import, especially not in the case of the two most heavily pentecostal countries at that time, Chile and Brazil. In every Latin American country except Chile, where Pentecostalism began with a large number of established Methodist believers and an experienced minister, the movement had a very slow start. Nevertheless, by the end of 1910, Pentecostal missionaries were already operating in at least nine Latin American countries. Many of the first pentecostals in Latin America were Chileans. This is all the more surprising because so little coverage of the dramatic events in Chile and Brazil appeared in the English-language pentecostal periodicals, and these two areas of greatest expansion received almost no support from American churches. One reason is that, in the case of Chile, there was very little influence from the North. The origins of Pentecostalism there are associated with Willis C. Hoover (1858–1936), a revivalist minister in Valparaiso, a former physician who had been in Chile since 1889, pastor of the largest Methodist Episcopal congregation in Chile (700 strong) and a district superintendent. Like fellow pentecostal leaders T. B. Barratt in Norway and Minnie Abrams in India, he was a product of Bishop William Taylor's missionary zeal. There is some evidence that the Hoovers received pentecostal papers from the United States, but that these were only circulating after the Chilean revival began in April 1909. Hoover himself wrote that in 1907 his wife May Louise received a copy of Minnie Abrams's 1906 booklet *The Baptism of the Holy Ghost and Fire*, thus learning of the outpouring of the Spirit in India. Mrs. Hoover's subsequent correspondence with Abrams, her former fellow student in the Chicago Training School, kick-started the Chilean pentecostal revival. The Hoovers also made contact with a Swedish pastor in Chicago, Alexander and Mary Boddy in Sunderland

(and their paper *Confidence*), and others like fellow Methodist Barratt in Norway, thus learning of the pentecostal revival movement taking place in various parts of the world.[2]

The Methodist Episcopal Church in Valparaiso was stirred to pray for a "Holy Ghost revival," and in January 1909, daily prayer meetings "for the outpouring of the Holy Spirit upon our church" began. These meetings happened to coincide with the opening of a new church, the largest Protestant building in Chile at the time. By July 1909, after six months of prayer, the expected revival arrived in Valparaiso during one of these prayer meetings and many unusual and ecstatic manifestations occurred. These included weeping, uncontrollable laughter, groaning, prostration, rolling on the floor, revelatory visions, singing and speaking in tongues, with people repenting and confessing sins. There were more than 200 conversions in a year. Those baptized in the Spirit felt compelled to go out onto the streets to tell of their experiences, and this, together with the noise generated by the revival meetings, brought a hostile reaction from the civic authorities, the local press, and eventually from the Methodist hierarchy. In Santiago, some of the revivalists were arrested, including a young English-born former prostitute from Valparaiso, Nellie (Elena) Laidlaw, whom Hoover described as having "remarkable manifestations and gifts." She was refused permission to prophesy in two Santiago Methodist churches, prompting a majority of the members to resign and begin holding meetings in homes. Hoover's support for Laidlaw was his undoing as far as the Methodist Church was concerned and Hoover became the subject of a flurry of scurrilous reports. There were other positive and independent reports of this revival. A. B. Simpson visited Chile early in 1910 and preached to almost a thousand people in Hoover's church in Valparaiso. He wrote that Hoover was "the most successful missionary in Chile" and that the revival there was "accompanied by many of the remarkable manifestations which have come to our [CMA] work in India, South China and many parts of America," including simultaneous prayer, speaking in tongues and divine healing. Simpson warned that sending Hoover back to the United States "would break up the largest Protestant church in Chile and probably lead to the forming of an independent mission" and that "the gravest issues are hanging in the balance," especially if the Methodist Church were to "dismiss him or try to coerce his people." The warning went unheeded and in 1910, the Methodist Conference met in Hoover's Valparaiso church building and in the presence of his members, charged him with "scandalous" and "imprudent" conduct and with propagating teachings that were "false and anti-Methodist...contrary to the Scriptures and irrational...offensive to decency and morals" and involving "hypnotism." Presiding Bishop Bristol removed Hoover as district superintendent and told him that either he had to leave Chile or leave the Methodist Episcopal Church. The revivalists in Santiago decided to form a new church and the Valparaiso congregation officials and the majority of its members joined them. Hoover resigned in May 1910, stating that he was not separating himself either from Wesley or from Methodism. In the Valparaiso congregation, 450 of Hoover's 700 members and all the members of the two congregations in Santiago had already resigned. Hoover was invited to become superintendent of the new church, which was named Iglesia Metodista Pentecostal (MPC).[3]

Within the first year, Hoover's Valparaiso congregation received 150 new members. Five years later there were congregations of the new denomination in twelve different cities, some 1,200 members, and several other groups affiliated with the MPC. Chilean missionaries also planted MPC congregations in Argentina and Peru in the 1920s, and by 1925 there were fully self-supporting churches with some 3,000 members in forty towns across Chile. Significantly, this Chilean movement with origins in India was not connected to American pentecostal churches. Although Hoover was an American, his ejection from an American Methodist mission meant that he relied on local people for his support, infrastructures, and workers. As a result, the Methodist Pentecostal Church (MPC) was almost immediately a self-governing, self-supporting, and self-propagating church—probably the first in Latin America. Chilean Pentecostalism, like the movement at Mukti, did not follow American classical Pentecostalism's doctrine of "initial evidence," and taught that speaking in tongues was one of many manifestations of Spirit baptism. Many secessions have taken place in the MPC, the first when Carlos del Campo left to start the Iglesia del Señor (Church of the Lord) in 1913; and later the Iglesia Evangélica de los Hermanos Pentecostales (Evangelical Church of the Pentecostal Brethren). In time, Hoover would clash with the majority of the Chilean pastors in the MPC over the use of popular music and instruments in the church, among other things. Hoover led a secession himself in 1932 and founded the Iglesia Evangélica Pentecostal (Evangelical Pentecostal Church, EPC), which he led until his death in Santiago four years later. The vast majority of Chilean pentecostals belong to the family of churches with origins in the MPC.[4]

Manuel Umaña Salinas (1876–1964) became the pastor of the Santiago branch of the church in 1910 when the denomination was founded. After Hoover's resignation in 1932, Umaña became its first Chilean general superintendent (later called presiding bishop) until his death in 1964. It was the first time that a pentecostal church in Chile had taken the title of bishop for its leader—a declaration that Pentecostalism was a viable alternative to Catholicism for Chilean people. Under Umaña's leadership and slogan of "Chile para Cristo" ("Chile for Christ"), the church grew steadily, planting congregations throughout the country and sending missionaries to Argentina and Peru. During this time only the Catholic Church was given official recognition in Chile. All non-Catholic churches were regarded as heretical sects. But the MPC soon established itself as the largest non-Catholic denomination in Chile, one with a special appeal to the poorer masses. The Santiago congregation was soon the largest in the MPC, and in 1928 it moved to Jotabeche, where in the 1960s it claimed to be the largest congregation in the world with 150,000 members. The church claims to be true to the doctrines and principles of the Methodist church founded by John Wesley, but at the same time being truly pentecostal by giving wide latitude to the gifts of the Spirit "according to the Scriptures and especially the Acts of the Apostles, chapter 2." It maintains Methodist doctrines and practices, including infant baptism and episcopal structures.[5] The MPC entered into a "fraternal relationship" with the PHC in the United States in 1967, based on their common Wesleyan and pentecostal heritage.

From the 1940s until the 1960s, Bishop Umaña directed members to vote en bloc to attract political attention. There was a definite gap between the views of the denominational hierarchy and those of the ordinary members. Some pentecostals were leaders in rural labor unions and neighborhood social service associations organized by Eduardo Frei Montalva's Christian Democratic government in the 1960s. It is thought that more pentecostals than Catholics supported the left-wing government of Salvador Allende, although pentecostal leaders were publicly against it. Some demonstrated against the Pinochet regime and were exiled or killed. In 1990, a survey revealed that less than 15 percent of pentecostal respondents supported Pinochet's regime.[6] After the September 1973 coup installing Augusto Pinochet's military dictatorship, some pentecostals joined the interdenominational Committee of Cooperation for Peace to defend human rights, but as relations between Pinochet and the Catholic bishops deteriorated, Bishop Javier Vásquez Valencia with 2,500 other evangelical leaders had placed an advertisement in the national newspaper supporting the Pinochet regime. The MPC's biggest congregation was in Jotabeche, Santiago de Chile, one of the largest in the world at the time. Vásquez, who had been pastor of this congregation since 1965, invited Pinochet to inaugurate the new Jotabeche Cathedral in September 1975. An evangelical "Te Deum" followed the opening, taking on the role of a national dedication service previously filled by the Catholic Church.[7] The new tradition has continued and the Te Deum service is held in this cathedral every year, attended by the Chilean president and other political and military leaders. Vásquez was presiding bishop of the MPC from 1982 until his death in 2003. Questions have been raised about the MPC leaders' friendly relationship with the Pinochet government, as Pinochet's presence at pentecostal functions in the face of Catholic opposition seemed to legitimize his repressive regime. But the vast majority of pentecostal members in Chile represent the working classes and did not follow their leaders' example; most of them opposed Pinochet and supported the popular socialist politics of Salvador Allende before his overthrow in 1973. Young pentecostals who later resisted Pinochet's regime were harassed, tortured, and even killed. Pentecostal churches in the WCC like the Pentecostal Church of Chile were particularly targeted for persecution by the military junta.

Chilean evangelicals constituted more than 20 percent of the country's population in 2010, compared to 62 percent (and shrinking) for Catholics. This remains a source of tension and there is little dialogue taking place between pentecostals and Catholics. There are now over thirty pentecostal denominations deriving from the MPC, comprising over 95 percent of the Protestants in Chile, which has an astonishing 1,400 other pentecostal denominations. The MPC and the EPC are the largest, followed by the Evangelical Pentecostal Methodist Church, and the Pentecostal Church of Chile (PCC), together accounting for almost 2 million Christians in 2010, while the original Methodist Church had 30,000. The PCC was formed after a schism in the MPC in 1946. The PCC and the smaller Misión Iglesia Pentecostal (Pentecostal Mission Church), which split from the EPC in 1952, joined the World Council of Churches in 1961, the first pentecostal churches to do so internationally. Since 1999, as a result of pentecostal pressures, a law has been passed providing equality for all religions in Chile. In the same year a Charismatic bishop, Salvador Pino Bustos, attempted to run for president but failed to receive enough support to register as a candidate. But because pentecostals are such a significant religious minority in Chile, their role and influence in Chilean politics continue to be important and they are courted for political support.[8]

The largest and most prolific region of pentecostal activity in Latin America is in the enormous Portuguese-speaking country of Brazil, with probably the largest number of pentecostals in the world, some 15 percent of the total population according to reliable sources, some estimates reaching 21 percent—or somewhere between 30 and 40 million people in 2010. Including Charismatic Catholics and evangelicals would make these figures considerably higher. The two earliest forms of Pentecostalism there have common associations with the Chicago ministry of William Durham. Durham had prophesied that his associate since 1907, Luigi (or sometimes, Luis) Francescon (1866–1964), a former Waldensian and leader of the first Italian pentecostal church, would preach the pentecostal message to the Italian people. Francescon established congregations throughout the United States and in Buenos Aires, Argentina, in 1909. In 1910, he went to São Paulo, Brazil, with a small team to begin working among the large Italian community there, at that time over a million strong. He preached on the baptism in the Spirit to Italian Presbyterians and was expelled from their church. The result was the formation of a pentecostal denomination, Congregazioni Christiana (Italian for "Christian Congregations"), the first pentecostal church in Brazil. Around 1935 it began to adopt Portuguese in its services and attract native Brazilians, and it is now known by its Portuguese name Congregação Cristã, one of the seven largest Pentecostal denominations in Brazil.[9]

Two Swedish Baptists, Gunnar Vingren (1879–1933) and Daniel Berg (1884–1963) were responsible for the beginning of Pentecostalism in the state of Pará in northeast Brazil. Vingren, a graduate of the University of Chicago's Divinity School and pastor of a Swedish Baptist church in South Bend, Indiana, and Berg, a layman in Chicago, had both met Lewi Pethrus in Sweden. At a conference in Chicago they received separate prophecies that they should go to "Pará," a place they had never heard of. After discovering that this was in north-east Brazil, they travelled to Belém in 1910 and began prayer meetings in the cellar of a Baptist church pastored by a Swedish missionary. Some received Spirit baptism and began evangelism in their neighbourhood. A group of eighteen, a majority of the members, was expelled from the church in June 1911 and Vingren became their pastor. Berg and Vingren learned to speak Portuguese in six months and in three years they had over a hundred converts. In five years there were 400 pentecostals and ten churches in northern Brazil.

Berg assisted Vingren as a freelance evangelist, supporting the mission as a steel foundry worker, then as a shipping agent and colporteur distributing Bibles along the rail and riverboat routes, making converts as he went. In 1917 he reported 126 baptisms and eleven missions established along the Amazon River and its tributaries; two years later there were twenty-six assemblies and 500 people in the movement. As in other parts of Latin America, violent mobs were organized against the pentecostals and some were thrown into prison. Vingren and Berg adopted Brazil as their own country and the church was a Brazilian church from the beginning. Vingren made it clear that the work should grow through Brazilians going to other parts of the country—first to the Amazon interior, then farther south along the railroad and along the coast. As he put it, "There was not a missionary there when the Lord poured out His Spirit and started a big church."[10]

The resulting church was first called the Apostolic Faith Mission but registered in 1918 as Assembléia de Deus (AD, Assembly of God). The denomination grew rapidly, particularly through its practice of prayer for healing. Tragically, Vingren left Brazil in 1932 with stomach cancer and died in Sweden the following year. Brazilians quickly took over the ministry. Brazilian pentecostal missionaries were sent out very early in their history. In 1913 José Plácido da Costa (1869–1965), one of the first converts of Vingren and Berg, left Belém for Porto, Portugal, to establish the first pentecostal church there. He was followed by another Belém pentecostal, José de Mattos (1888–1958), in 1921. The first Portuguese congregation was established in the Algarve and pastored by de Mattos until 1938. Daniel Berg founded a congregation in Porto in 1934 and a Swedish missionary, Jack Härdstedt, started one in Lisbon. The mission to Portugal from Brazil and Sweden was soon followed in 1931 by Portuguese missionaries going to Portuguese territories and colonies abroad, the first to the Azores.

The AD spread to every state in Brazil, an independent movement with some support from Lewi Pethrus in Stockholm and missionaries from the Swedish pentecostal movement. Members were recruited initially from the lower strata of Brazilian society, and Pentecostalism appealed to Amerindian, black, and mixed race (mulatto) Brazilians, the majority in this and several other Brazilian pentecostal churches. Brazilian Pentecostals from Belém began evangelizing the Amazonas region and spread to the big cities of Recife, Rio de Janeiro, São Paulo, and Pôrto Alegre. They emphasized healing and establishing churches in cities, which experienced remarkable growth. In São Paulo 10,000 converts a year were baptized and the city now has over a thousand AD congregations. In 1930 the headquarters transferred from Belém to Rio de Janeiro, the Swedish leaders handed over the leadership to Brazilians (although the "pastor-president" was Swedish until 1950), and the AD became a national church independent of foreign missions. The church considers itself an independent church within the worldwide AG fellowship of churches. The AD has education and literacy programs for members; provident funds for unmarried mothers, the sick, and the orphaned; abundant printed literature from their own publishing house; and community projects like community centers, factories, schools, hospitals, old age homes, libraries, and day nurseries. It is the largest pentecostal denomination in the world and the largest Protestant church in Latin America. A significant schism in 1955 resulted in the formation of Igreja O Brasil Para Cristo (Brazil for Christ Church).[11]

Harvey Cox profiled the Afro-Brazilian woman Benedita Souza da Silva Sampaio (b.1942), a pentecostal born in poverty in 1943 who became a prominent politician in President "Lula" da Silva's ruling socialist Labor Party and governor of Rio de Janeiro state from 2002 to 2003. She was the first woman and the first Afro-Brazilian to occupy this office, and an ardent campaigner for black women's rights. Since then, the most prominent politician involved in the ongoing struggle to preserve the Amazonian rain forests from destruction is Marina Silva (b.1958), another Afro-Brazilian pentecostal born into poverty and illiteracy in Amazonia, but rising to become Minister of the Environment in Lula's government from 2003 to 2008. She left the Labor Party to fight the presidential election in 2010 on a Green ticket against Lula's hand-picked successor Dilma Rouseff, but came third with 19.4 percent of the vote. Her late entry still attracted impressive and rapidly rising support, and she remains an important figure in Brazilian politics.

Guatemala, which may be the most pentecostal country in Latin America, has produced two far-right presidents who were members of Charismatic churches: military dictator Rios Montt from 1982 to 1983, still a political force in this country, and Jorge Serrano from 1991 to 1993, now in exile in Panama. However, these two dictators represented the educated middle-class Charismatic elite and not the majority of Guatemalan pentecostals, over half of whom are Amerindians.[12]

Relationships between pentecostals and the Catholic Church in Latin America have not been easy. In the first place, they have been mutual antagonists: the pentecostals charge the Catholics with Christopaganism, persecution of pentecostals, and responsibility for the region's underdevelopment;

and Catholics see pentecostals as troublesome, even heretical sects. In reality, popular Catholicism and Pentecostalism have very similar belief systems and worldviews. But in 1992 Pope John Paul II warned against the "invasion of the sects" and the "ravenous wolves" that were threatening the Catholic hold on Latin America—yet Pentecostalism, more than Catholicism, is essentially a Latin American phenomenon. Studies have shown that Catholicism had proportionately far more foreign priests in Latin America—an astonishing 94 percent in Venezuela—than Pentecostal churches had foreign missionaries. Second, Latin America has changed rapidly in the twentieth century from being a predominantly Catholic continent to one where religious pluralism is a fact of modern life. The Catholic proportion of the population has been steadily decreasing and pentecostals command significant influence both socially and politically. Third, from the very start, Pentecostalism took on a Latin American character that contrasted with the old Latin liturgies of the Catholic Church. In the eyes of many, the Catholic Church had become the church of the middle and upper classes, a vestige of Spanish and Portuguese colonialism, while Pentecostalism represented ordinary, working-class people. And worst of all, pentecostals engaged in aggressive proselytizing of nominal Catholics, whom they considered not really Christians. Understandably, the Catholic Church has felt threatened by the remarkable pentecostal growth that has exploded the myth of a united Latin American Catholic culture. One of the common accusations made in the past was that the new "sects" were agents of the neo-imperialist United States. As many have pointed out, however, it is the Catholic Church whose leaders are "foreign." Nevertheless, one of the most remarkable reactions has been the "Pentecostalization" of the Catholic Church in Latin America, or what Andrew Chesnut calls "a Catholicized version of Pentecostalism." Some observers think that in 2010 there might have been almost twice as many Catholic Charismatics in Latin America as pentecostals—some 73 million.[13]

African Trailblazers

Pentecostalism has rapidly become one of the most prominent and influential religious movements across Africa. But the "Pentecostalization" of African Christianity cannot be understood without reference to the pioneers in the early years of the movement, particularly those leaders from whose work emerged what are widely referred to as "churches of the Spirit," independent African churches with a pentecostal emphasis.

The complex West African pentecostal history begins with African preachers, especially the Grebo Liberian prophet William Wade Harris and Garrick Sokari Braide (1882–1918), a popular Anglican revivalist preacher in the Niger River Delta of southeastern Nigeria. Braide preached about repentance, the destruction of fetish charms, and healing through prayer. He preached against the lucrative alcohol trade, was regarded as a threat to British rule and financial hegemony, and was jailed in 1916 for seditious behavior, succumbing to the influenza epidemic soon after his release. His disagreements with the Anglican church and subsequent imprisonment caused his followers to form the Christ Army Church in 1916, the first independent "church of the Spirit" in Nigeria, to be followed by many more, including the highly successful Aladura movement in southwestern Nigeria.[14]

William Wade Harris (1865–1929) had at least passing acquaintance with the Azusa Street missionaries who arrived in Liberia in 1907, some of whom worked in Harris's home district of Cape Palmas among Grebo Methodists. From 1913 to 1914 Harris began preaching in Côte d'Ivoire and on the west coast of Ghana about one true God, healing, and the rejection of practices associated with African religions. Harris and his companions were responsible for one of the greatest influxes ever seen of Africans to Christianity. Harris may have baptized 120,000 adult Ivorian converts in a year. In 1914, he was deported by French colonial authorities and village prayer houses set up by his followers were destroyed. Although he directed people to existing mission churches, thousands of his followers found themselves disagreeing with Methodist financial policy, their prohibition of polygamy, and the foreign liturgy that was so different from the African singing and dancing practiced by Harris. They organized themselves into the Harrist Church, which grew rapidly, although it became increasingly identified with the nationalist struggle, was severely persecuted by the French administration, and was only officially registered in 1955. Other churches in the Ivory Coast were to emerge in the Harrist tradition and Harris's influence was to be felt in neighboring Ghana.[15]

Ghana had its fair share of early charismatic preachers and prophets responsible for the rapid growth of Christianity in the early twentieth century, among whom were John Swatson, a disciple of Harris with a Methodist background who became an Anglican preacher, and the younger Sampson Oppong (d.1965), a converted fetish priest who became a Methodist preacher during the 1920s and 1930s. Both men exercised charismatic gifts of healing and both fell out of favor with their British ecclesiastical overseers and died in obscurity. The first "spiritual church" to emerge in Ghana was the Church of the Twelve Apostles in 1918, founded by Harris's converts Grace Tani and Kwesi John Nackabah. This new church followed Harris's emphasis on healing and the use of holy water, administered in healing "gardens," communal dwellings much like the American "healing homes" set up in the late nineteenth century. In 1938 the church considered affiliating with the Apostolic Church of Britain, but according to one account they withdrew when the Northern Irish Apostolic missionary James McKeown insisted that tambourines be substituted for calabash rattles, apparently seen as an attempt to deprive Africans of the power to ward off evil spirits.[16]

The four main classical pentecostal denominations in Ghana today are the Church of Pentecost, the Apostolic Church of Ghana, the Christ Apostolic Church, and the Assemblies of God. The first three have origins in the work of a remarkable Ghanaian, Peter Anim (1890–1984), regarded as the father of Pentecostalism in Ghana. The region had witnessed a major outbreak of the deadly influenza epidemic in 1918 and a concomitant economic recession, and Western medicine and mission-founded churches were unable to handle the crisis. Africans were convinced that the epidemic had an important spiritual dimension and set up a number of fellowships to pray for divine intervention. Anim came into contact with the publication *The Sword of the Spirit* of the Faith Tabernacle church in Philadelphia, and in 1921 received healing from guinea worm infection and protracted stomach ailments. Faith Tabernacle was an offshoot of Dowie's Zion City, which emphasized healing and baptism by immersion. Anim resigned from the Presbyterian church to become an independent healing preacher who gathered a large following, affiliating for a short time with Faith Tabernacle. Similar developments in Nigeria took place, where David Odubanjo became the leader of Faith Tabernacle. Relations between the West African and Philadelphia church deteriorated for three main reasons. First, in over four years none of the American leaders had ever visited West Africa, which cast doubt on their commitment. Second, there were doctrinal differences over speaking in tongues, already practiced by the Africans but rejected by the Americans, who like the Zionists in Chicago, considered it a satanic delusion. Third, in 1926 the Philadelphia church's leader, Pastor Clark, was excommunicated over his matrimonial affairs. Anim and the Nigerian leaders severed the connection with Faith Tabernacle in Philadelphia.

At the same time another periodical began circulating in West Africa, *The Apostolic Faith* from Portland, Oregon, a movement whose founder Florence Crawford was a leader in the Azusa Street revival. After the break with Philadelphia, Anim found the teachings of the Apostolic Faith in line with his own practices and took the name Apostolic Faith for his movement. In correspondence with Odubanjo, he discovered that Faith Tabernacle in Nigeria was seeking affiliation with the Apostolic Church in Britain to assist in addressing the difficulties the African leaders were having with the colonial administration. Anim and two of his leaders met the three British Apostolic leaders on their voyage from England and accompanied them from Accra to Lagos in 1931. According to Anim's own account, the Spirit baptism of some of his key leaders took place in 1932 during prayers in a village and quickly spread in what was called a "Holy Ghost Dispensation." Ghanaian scholars argue that Anim's organization was pentecostal before there was any missionary presence. Anim's organization affiliated with the Apostolic Church after a brief visit from their missionary in Nigeria in 1935. Anim negotiated for missionaries to be sent to Ghana to assist the growing number of churches and the Apostolic Church sent the McKeowns in 1937. Anim's contemporary James McKeown (1900–89) contracted malaria soon after his arrival and was taken to hospital for treatment, a position that Anim and his followers found deviating from their understanding of divine healing without the use of medicine. This conflict resulted in Anim and some of his followers withdrawing from the Apostolic Church two years later to form the Christ Apostolic Church (CAC). The CAC continued its opposition to the use of medicine well into the 1970s. After a short retirement in 1957 Anim continued as leader of the CAC in Ghana until his death at the age of ninety-four. The CAC suffered several schisms in its short history from which it never fully recovered, and it was soon overtaken by the rapidly growing and well-organized Church of Pentecost. Nevertheless, Anim remains the most significant and respected pioneer of Ghanaian Pentecostalism.[17]

In 1953, McKeown himself, on a visit to Britain, came into conflict with the Apostolic Church and resigned, whereupon the Church Council in Ghana declared him leader of the now-independent Gold Coast Apostolic Church, which, after Ghana achieved independence in 1957, became the Ghana Apostolic Church. Protracted legal battles between the British and Ghanaian churches over church properties ensued, and an attempt to have McKeown deported failed. In 1962 President Kwame Nkrumah intervened and ordered the Ghana Apostolic Church to change its name; thereafter it was known as the Church of Pentecost (COP). The opposing faction left the COP and joined the Apostolic Church, which was declared to legally own all properties acquired by the church before the split in 1953. Although McKeown was chairman of the COP, there was an all-Ghanaian executive council and Ghanaians took the initiative for the expansion of the church. This was an autochthonous Ghanaian church and McKeown's links with British Pentecostalism were at most tenuous. McKeown himself was a supporter of the principle of indigenization, stating that "it would be difficult to grow an 'English oak' in Ghana. A local 'species', at home in its culture, should grow, reproduce and spread; a church with foreign roots was more likely to struggle." On another occasion, he stated: "Who runs the Church of Pentecost? Ghanaians. You talk about my founding this Church, but I could never have done all that. The Africans did it."[18]

In 1971 the COP entered a cooperative agreement with the Elim Pentecostal Church in Britain, whereby Elim missionaries would assist the church in leadership training, radio ministry, and publishing. McKeown began to withdraw from his dominant role in the 1970s, when he would spend increasing time in Britain (especially after his wife remained there after 1974), and he finally retired and left Ghana in 1982 at the age of eighty-two. By this time the COP was easily the largest pentecostal church in Ghana. He was succeeded as chairman by Ghanaians: Apostle F. S. Safo (1982–87), Prophet M. K. Yeboah (1988–98), and Apostle Michael K. Ntumy (1998–2008). The COP went through twenty years of rapid growth, from 129,000 members in 1982 to 717,000 in 2002. The Pentecost Bible College developed into Pentecost University College in 2003 and was opened by J. A. Kuffour, at that time the president of Ghana. The first principal was Apostle Dr. Opoku Onyinah, a PhD theology graduate of Birmingham who was elected fifth chairman of the church in 2008. In 2011 the COP claimed to have 1.5 million members in Ghana, with ninety-six primary schools, six secondary schools, and seven hospitals and clinics. Furthermore, it now operated in over eighty countries worldwide.[19]

Parallel events took place in Nigeria. Testimonies of people who claimed that they were healed of influenza drew large crowds to join the fellowships in southern Nigeria, which organized themselves in 1918 under Anglican leader Joseph Shadare as *Egbe Okuta Iyebiye,* a Yoruba term meaning "Precious Stone" or "Diamond Society," to provide spiritual support and healing for victims of the epidemic. This group left the Anglican Church in 1922 over the issue of infant baptism; through Odubanjo's efforts, they affiliated with Faith Tabernacle, but severed the affiliation in 1925. In the same year, the Eternal Sacred Order of Cherubim and Seraphim Society was founded by another Anglican, Moses Orimolade Tunolashe (who became known as

Baba Aladura, a title used by subsequent leaders of this church), and the fifteen-year-old girl Abiodun Akinsowon (later called Captain Abiodun), for whom Orimolade was called upon to pray for healing. Orimolade had begun preaching in about 1915 after partially recovering from a long illness. This new movement emphasized prayer and so its followers were called *aladura* ("owners of prayer"), a term that distinguished them and stuck. Orimolade took the revival to other parts of Yorubaland, where the largest and most numerous independent churches of the Spirit in West Africa are now found.[20]

Faith Tabernacle experienced remarkable growth under the activities of the young Yoruba prophet Joseph Ayo Babalola (1904–59), who appeared on the Nigerian religious scene in the late 1920s. Babalola claimed he heard a divine voice calling him to become a prophet and evangelist, and as a result became an itinerant preacher, carrying a Bible, a bell, and "water of life" (holy water) which he claimed would heal all sicknesses. Initially operating from his local Anglican church, he was soon expelled because of his healing practices. He met Shadare, joined Faith Tabernacle in Ilesa in 1929, and played a leading role in a revival that began the following year, when it was reported that many were healed and believers had to renounce all evil practices and witchcraft. The church that Babalola helped establish became affiliated with the Apostolic Church after the arrival of British missionaries in 1932, but in 1939 it seceded after the missionaries objected to the use of "water of life" in healing rituals. For their part, the Nigerians disagreed with the missionaries using medicine and quinine for healing, which seemed to compromise their doctrine of divine healing. The CAC was constituted in 1941 and is now the largest Aladura church in Nigeria and one of the largest independent Spirit churches in Africa. It considers itself a pentecostal church and follows the Apostolic Church in both polity and theology but with significant modifications. The CAC proscribed polygamy and the use of all medicine, traditional and modern, but has more recently modified the medicine ban. It is the only church with roots in the Aladura movement to be accepted by other pentecostal churches. After the secessions in Ghana and Nigeria, the British missionaries and the Apostolic Church remained in both countries. By 1950 Aladura churches like the CAC and the Cherubim and Seraphim were at the center of Yoruba society and, despite numerous secessions, they are still a significant force in Nigerian Christianity. The churches of the Spirit in West Africa, though influenced by Western Pentecostalism, were birthed in an African revival marked by the rejection of pre-Christian religion. Many of the new pentecostal churches formed in this region today have roots in both the Aladura and the Apostolic Church movements, which remain important influences on African Pentecostalism as a whole.[21]

Sometimes the leaders and prophets of African churches of the Spirit were given biblical mandate as Moses figures, bringing their people out of slavery into the promised land, the new "City of Zion." This is seen most clearly in the churches in southern Africa, the most colonized and oppressed region in the continent. The historical links with early Pentecostalism are clear, and the Spirit churches there are usually referred to as "Zionist" and "Apostolic" churches. Their reading of the Bible portrays the Exodus as a deliverance from the old life of trouble, sickness, oppression, evil spirits, sorcery, and poverty. The new Israel incarnate in Africa is moving out of Egypt toward the new Jerusalem, the Zion of God, where all these troubles are forgotten. The people of God are the members of this new African church, which has been able to discover its own promised land. Zion, the new Jerusalem, the holy place is not in some far off foreign land at some distant time in the past, but present here and now in Africa. This idea was also influenced by the Zion movement of Dowie and his Zion City in Chicago. Most Zionist and Apostolic churches have a church headquarters where the founder or bishop lives, a healing colony to which members must make regular pilgrimages on holy days for church conferences. This African Zion is above all a place of healing, blessing, and deliverance—in short, the place where the imminence of God is keenly felt. It is also the place where the means of grace and the manifestation of God's presence in the sacraments are administered by the leader. The conferences of the church at "Zion" are therefore of the utmost importance. Members are expected to visit their Zion at least once a year, a pilgrimage following the Old Testament tradition of the annual journeys of the people of God to their holy place at regular festival times. Without such a pilgrimage, the process of receiving the message of God is incomplete. Through this journey members meet the leader and obtain his (it is usually his) blessing, especially through the sacrament of communion. The Easter Festival of South Africa's largest denomination, the Zion Christian Church (ZCC) at Moria (named after the mountain Moses ascended) in the northern Limpopo province is the annual highlight. Somewhere between 1 million and 2 million people, dressed in ZCC khaki, gold, and green uniforms, congregate there annually. The pinnacle of the weekend's activities is when Bishop Barnabas Lekganyane, resplendent in green and gold and marching at the head of a brass band, takes the podium to address the assembled and expectant multitude. As the grandson of the founder of the church, his word is regarded by his faithful followers as the word of God.[22]

The church's founder was Engenas Lekganyane (c.1880–1948), an evangelist in the Free Church of Scotland, born in Limpopo province. He met P. L. le Roux, the first Afrikaner leader in the Apostolic Faith Mission in Johannesburg soon after it was founded in 1908 by missionaries from Indianapolis. Lekganyane had suffered from an eye disease for some years, but had received a vision in which a voice told him that if he went to Johannesburg he should join a church that baptized by threefold immersion in water, and thereby find healing. He joined the AFM, was baptized, and became a member of a congregation near his home. A Zionist historian suggests that Lekganyane followed Elias Mahlangu rather than le Roux on his arrival in Johannesburg in 1912, and Mahlangu baptized Lekganyane, resulting in his healing. Mahlangu was an AFM preacher until about 1917 and the distinction between "Zion" and "Apostolic" was blurred at that time. Lekganyane first got his preaching credentials from the AFM, but in 1916 was ordained into Mahlangu's Zion Apostolic Church (ZAC) and he started a ZAC congregation in his home village of Thabakgone. This appears to have been a schism under Mahlangu, not the first in the AFM's short history. In 1917 Lekganyane prophesied the defeat of Germany by Britain, and when this came to pass his prestige as a prophet and "man of God" grew. Lekganyane became the leader of the ZAC in the Limpopo province, a powerful preacher who won many converts. He appears to have continued with Mahlangu for about three years, but differences between them soon emerged. Customs promoted by Mahlangu to which Lekganyane took exception included the compulsory wearing of white robes, growing beards, and taking off shoes before a service, practices now found in many Zionist and Apostolic churches but not in the ZCC. Lekganyane's final break with the ZAC came in 1920, when he went to Lesotho and joined Edward Lion's Zion Apostolic Faith Mission (ZAFM). Lion, whose original surname was Motaung ("lion person") had been a notable preacher and healer in the AFM, and the two leaders had much in common. Lekganyane was ordained as bishop of this church in the Transvaal, but again, differences emerged and around 1924–25 he founded the ZCC. Lekganyane had married a second wife, which was another reason for the break with Lion, who opposed polygamy. Lekganyane remained a strong admirer of Lion, and named his second son after him. He subsequently related how around 1920, he had had a revelation that a multitude of people would follow him. But as often happens in schisms of this kind, the main reason for Lekganyane's break with the ZAC and the ZAFM was a leadership power struggle.[23]

The ZCC grew rapidly. By 1925, when Lekganyane applied for government recognition, he claimed 926 adherents in fifteen congregations. The government, which looked at independent African churches with considerable suspicion, denied his application and did so again in 1943. In 1930 Lekganyane was involved in a dispute with his chief over the chief's mistreatment of one of his members and was forced to leave his home village. Church members raised the money to purchase a farm and gave it to Lekganyane as his personal property. This farm became Zion City, Moria. An early emphasis of Lekganyane's ministry was divine healing, and it was probably his reputation as a healer more than anything else that contributed to the rapid growth of the ZCC. He used to heal by personally laying on hands, but as the church grew this became impractical and he began to bless strips of cloth, strings, papers, needles, walking sticks, and water, to be used for healing and protective purposes. These symbolic ritual practices emerged in the latter part of Lekganyane's ministry, resonated with African healing practices, and are reasons for the present-day distance between the ZCC and pentecostal churches. Several miraculous incidents are attributed to Lekganyane in his later years. Believers testified that he had helped in obtaining employment, the blessing of harvests, and "rain-making"—a traditional sign of power for which Lekganyane was well known. Healing and miracles continued to be one of the main characteristics of Lekganyane's ministry. By 1942 the ZCC had about 27,487 members and had spread to Zimbabwe, Botswana, and the Northern Cape Province. A year later the membership was estimated by government sources to be between 40,000 and 45,000, and the ZCC had already become the largest independent church in southern Africa.

Lekganyane died in 1948 after a long illness, and there was a leadership crisis. He had not appointed a successor, and his two sons, Edward and Joseph, disputed the succession. After the traditional mourning period of a year, they formed two separate churches in 1949. The followers of Joseph (the minority faction) became the St. Engenas Zion Christian Church, while the majority of Engenas's people followed Edward in the ZCC. In beliefs and practice there is little difference between these two churches, and their Zion headquarters adjoin each other. Under Edward Lekganyane (1926–67) the ZCC continued to grow remarkably, so that by 1954 the membership was some 80,000. In 1963 Edward enrolled in the three-year course for evangelists at the Dutch Reformed Church's Stofberg Theological College, near his headquarters; he attended classes in his chauffeur-driven black limousine wearing his rather ostentatious diamond ring. It seems that the only difference he had with his teachers there was on the question of baptismal modes, Lekganyane favoring threefold adult immersion after the practice of the American Zionists and the AFM. He seems to have tried to move the ZCC in a more biblical direction, but not everyone in the ZCC was happy with his newfound friendship with the Reformed Church, some alleging that the church had "lost the Spirit" and was not as "powerful" as it used to be. Nevertheless, Edward was an effective leader. Two days after his sudden and premature death of a heart attack in October 1967, a leading article in the black newspaper *World* said that he had been "one of the most powerful leaders who have dominated the religious scene in this generation." His son Ramarumo Barnabas Lekganyane (b.1954) was only thirteen years old when his father died but was chosen as the new leader by a General Council of the ZCC at the Easter Conference in 1968. The ZCC was governed by a superintendent until 1975, when Barnabas was old enough to become bishop. The church grew rapidly and in 2001 the government census put ZCC membership at 5 million, twenty times the size of the AFM, the country's largest classical pentecostal denomination. There were another 8 million people in the thousands of Zionist and Apostolic churches that exist in South Africa.[24]

The ZCC attempted to play a role in the changes that took place in South Africa in the early 1990s. The church was known for promoting harmony and reconciliation, which may be the reason the three most influential political leaders in South Africa at the time (Mandela, De Klerk, and Buthelezi) were each invited to the Easter Festival in 1992 at Moria, when I attended. ZCC Bishop Lekganyane made an attempt to play a constructive role in the delicate political negotiations being conducted at that time, and thereby help promote peace during a period of violent strife. The bishop's sermon on this occasion was directed at the three leaders, lashing out at "warmongering" and inflammatory political speeches, saying that leaders as well as followers were responsible for the current carnage in the South African townships. He made a plea for peace and emphasized the role of the ZCC as a church of peace. Any political leaders ignore the ZCC at their peril, and this is probably why all three leaders accepted the invitation. Arguably, the largest crowd that any South African political leaders had ever addressed was there, perhaps as many as 2 million. The greatest applause that afternoon was given by the ZCC multitude to Mandela, who made reference in his speech to prominent African National Congress (ANC) officials who were members of the ZCC. The ZCC does not engage in political posturing, and like many other African churches does not align itself with political parties. The bishop prudently avoided any impression of taking sides in his sermon. The afternoon belonged to him and not to any of the politicians present—they were on his turf.[25]

The existence of enormous independent churches today has a lot to do with early pentecostal missionaries, who tapped into the new phenomenon of African independence particularly prevalent in institutionally segregated South Africa. American missionary Jacob Lehman wrote of a whole tribal community in the northwest of the country that had seceded with their chief from "a certain missionary society" because of exploitation by missionaries. Near Middelburg, Lehman and other pentecostal missionaries held services to welcome a group of secessionists into the pentecostal fold and John G. Lake visited an "Ethiopian" church conference seeking affiliation with the AFM. Lake wrote of a "native missionary," Paul Mabiletsa, who told Lake about a paralyzed woman healed through prayer. In 1920 Mabiletsa founded the Apostolic Church in Zion, which would become one of the larger Zionist churches. Lake also reported that twenty-four "native Catholic churches" and "five large Ethiopian churches" had decided to affiliate with the AFM in 1910 and that the "African Catholic Church," with seventy-eight preachers, joined in January 1911. In 1911 the "Ethiopian Church" affiliated with the Apostolic Faith Church. Clearly, many of the early pentecostal "converts" in South Africa were already members of Christian churches, especially African independent ones. But the flow went both ways. By 1915 there were several secessions from the pentecostals, especially from the AFM. African leaders likely felt marginalized by the white leadership. One Pentecostal Mission worker complained about African women who had "risen up refusing to acknowledge any authority in the church" and who were now "trying to establish a church of their own, with a native as leader." African churches of the Spirit are a long established tradition. Although many of these independent churches may no longer be described as pentecostal without further qualification, the most characteristic features of their theology and practice are overwhelmingly so. Pentecostal missions in South Africa were the unwitting catalysts for a much larger movement of the Spirit that was to dominate southern African Christianity into the twenty-first century. Similar links between foreign pentecostal missionaries and independent churches have been documented in West Africa, as the stories of Faith Tabernacle and the Apostolic movement demonstrate. The same links can be demonstrated in East Africa. The influence of these churches on African Christianity is pervasive.[26]

Asian Pioneers

There are many examples of pentecostal churches founded in Asia also. For example, it was thought that Pentecostalism in Sri Lanka began with the Danish actress Anna Lewini and former British soldier in India Walter Clifford, who arrived in Colombo in 1919 and 1923, respectively. From their work evolved the Assemblies of God and the independent Ceylon Pentecostal Mission (CPM), founded in 1921 by Alwin R. De Alwis (c.1890–1967) and Ramankutty Paul (1881–1945), a Dalit from Kerala. It was suggested that the De Alwis family became pentecostal as a result of Clifford's healing services. A perusal of early pentecostal papers, however, reveals that Alwin had been a pentecostal for at least ten years before Clifford arrived and was already leading a pentecostal mission. In fact, pentecostal missions were active in Sri Lanka long before Lewini and Clifford arrived, and its pioneers were Sri Lankans, including D. E. Dias Wanigasekera and Charles Hettiaratchy. There is also record of a Sri Lankan Baptist, J. J. B. de Silva, who became pentecostal, started an independent congregation, and assisted Anna Lewini. Ramankutty Paul returned to India in 1924 to establish the Pentecostal Mission with headquarters in Madras (Chennai). The first faith home (a commune where members dispose of all their private possessions and live together) was established in 1933 in Tuticorin, but it soon spread to other parts of India, Sri Lanka, and Malaysia, to which missionaries were sent in the 1930s. The CPM is an exclusivist sect where celibacy is encouraged for the increase of spiritual power, and Indian music usually accompanied by drums is used. Most independent Indian Pentecostal denominations have strict rules for members but none are as strict as those of the CPM, whose rules include dressing only in white traditional dress and opposition to all forms of jewelry, taking medicine, and the ordination of women. Celibacy is enjoined on all full-time workers who live in the faith homes, where compulsory prayer begins at 4 a.m. and strict obedience to the chief pastor, the head of the movement, is enjoined. After Paul's death in 1945, sole leadership passed to Alwin who remained as chief pastor until 1962; after disagreements over his leadership, the son of Ramankutty Paul, Freddy Paul, became chief pastor.

From the CPM came a whole string of secessions, including the Apostolic Christian Assembly, the Apostolic Fellowship Tabernacle of India, and the Maranatha Full Gospel Mission.[27]

K. E. Abraham (1899–1974), formerly a Syrian Orthodox school-teacher and ardent nationalist, was baptized by immersion in 1916 by K. V. Simon, leader of an Indian Brethren separatist group known as *Viyojithan* ("Separatist"). Abraham joined the pentecostal movement in 1923 through the ministry of C. Manasseh and influenced the emergence of Indian leaders thereafter. He worked with Robert Cook first in the AG and then in the Malankara Pentecostal Church of God, until separating from him in 1930. The reasons for the break with Cook are not clear but were connected to Abraham's own leadership aspirations and nationalist sympathies. Although there were many Indian pentecostal preachers, no Indians had been ordained until Pastor Paul of the CPM visited Kerala and ordained them. The two existing Pentecostal denominations were controlled by foreign missionaries, and the break revolved around the issue of funding for church buildings, which the missionaries controlled. Abraham emphasized the autonomy of the local congregation and stated that foreign missionaries were "non-biblical and non-apostolic." Abraham was fiercely nationalistic and, in the words of one of his biographers, "stood for national leadership, national churches, national missionary organizations and national administration...against the foreign domination...never wanted to sacrifice freedom for money." After three years with the CPM, Abraham, together with other Kerala leaders K. C. Cherian, P. T. Chacko, and P. M. Samuel, founded the Indian Pentecostal Church of God (IPC), which planted its first congregations in Tamilnadu, Andhra Pradesh, and Karnataka. Abraham started the Hebron Bible School to train Indian pastors. Contact was made and cooperation established with the Swedish pentecostal Filadelfia Church of Lewi Pethrus, and Abraham and Cherian spent eighteen months in 1936–37 itinerating in Sweden. The Swedish pentecostals with their emphasis on local autonomy gave unconditional financial support to the IPC in those early years. In Kerala, Pentecostal leadership has been dominated by people of Syrian Christian background. The IPC had the first of many schisms in 1953, when P. J. Thomas formed the Sharon Fellowship, formally registered in 1975. The IPC, with the Christian Assemblies of India and the Assemblies (Jehovah Shammah) are among the largest independent Indian Pentecostal churches, but there are growing, newer churches like the New Life Church and the Filadelfia Fellowship Church of India.[28]

From 1908 to 1917, a former schoolteacher in Hong Kong edited the first pentecostal newspaper outside the Western world. Mok Lai Chi (1868–1926) was born into a Christian family and attended an English school in Hong Kong until he went into government service as a translator in 1886. After some time living a profligate life "at large in the world," he repented and in 1892 began a school teaching English and shorthand. He is also recorded as being Chinese Clerk and Interpreter for the Registrar General in 1893. He was a deacon in the American Board Mission church, superintendent of a Sunday School, and secretary for the local YMCA, where he had done evangelistic work among the dock workers. He met Albert and Lillian Garr in 1907, interpreted for them in the Mission where they commenced services every night. Mok was baptized in the Spirit in November 1907, stating, "The Spirit spoke through me in the Mandarin dialect, the Hakka dialect, and an African tongue." His wife Alice Lena Mok followed a few days later. His four-page broadsheet was called *Pentecostal Truths* and contained articles mostly in Chinese, with up to a page in English. Many of the Chinese articles were translations of teachings published elsewhere in English, but Mok also wrote many articles in Chinese himself. Six thousand copies of the paper were printed and freely distributed throughout China and overseas in 1909 and had reached 8,000 by 1915. Although originally a monthly paper, during the war years only three issues were published, perhaps due to a shortage of donations. The first publication made front-page news in Azusa Street's *Apostolic Faith* in May 1908, with a report on how the paper started. It was a Chinese initiative from the start and Mok was in charge of its publication.[29]

Mok's description of its commencement, written from "The Apostolic Faith Mission, Hong Kong, China" shows his role:

> One day, Brother McIntosh told me that the Lord had spoken to him about starting a free paper, giving the name of "Pentecostal Truths," and asked me to pray about it. When I prayed the Lord spoke to me, commanding me to take charge of it. I said, "Lord, I am not a writer," but the Lord reminded me of what Moses said on Mount Horeb, and promised that He would make my brothers to help me. So in January, 1908, "Pentecostal Truths" made its first appearance with 1,000 copies. It has since increased to 6,000 copies each issue. It is a free paper, with three pages printed in Chinese and one in English. It reaches, as many other Pentecostal papers

do, many hungry souls, both in China and foreign countries. Besides the paper, we are publishing free tracts.[30]

In another letter, Mok said that he started the paper "without any fund and without any help whatever." In April 1909 the Hong Kong paper announced its aim as being "especially for proclaiming the truth of the baptism of the Holy Spirit to inspire the downcast Church," and that its content would be kept "simple but understandable to make sure that women and children can know and gain the heavenly blessings." By 1914 the paper seems to have shifted to a particular emphasis on "the fact of Jesus' imminent coming," and Mok exhorted his readers to "keep this paper to avoid regret," as soon, when Christ appeared in the sky, the paper would stop and his work would be finished.[31]

Mok Lai Chi was leader in what was first called the Apostolic Faith Mission, which was associated with the Garrs. The Garrs had a hand in persuading Mok to become pentecostal, and on their arrival in Hong Kong he already had a reputation as an influential Christian leader and respected director of the Morrison English School. A young American missionary, Cora Fritsch, writes of Mok as "the pastor" of the "dear band of [Chinese] baptised souls here" and "surely a chosen child of God, so devoted and consecrated to God. He gives all his time to the gospel work. Printing a paper as well as preaching and teaching school." Four days later she wrote that Mok took full charge of the services in the mission, and was a "highly educated Chinese" who "speaks and writes English almost as well as if he had been educated in America." The services were held in the "upper room" of a large house, the "Pentecostal Missionary Home" where the Garrs and other missionaries lived. But this building was far from where the "heathen" lived and too small for Mok's large family, so by April 1909 Mok had opened a new "mission hall to the heathen" in Wanchai, in the "slums of the town," filled with an attentive crowd of over 150 for nightly services. Four Chinese workers and at least some of the women missionaries helped him in this work, and were "living by faith." He reported on nightly conversions, with "idol-worshippers" coming to kneel at the altar, and that "cases of beri-beri, fever, sores, consumption, diarrhoea, dysentery, and other diseases have been miraculously healed by our Lord Jesus through the prayers of our little apostolic company." By April 1909 teams of Chinese workers were going out into the surrounding countryside taking *Pentecostal Truths* and tracts with them; a team of four women went to the villages on the mainland, with another two going farther into the interior. At the end of the year, the first two Chinese missionaries were sent out from Mok's mission to the Chih-Li (now Hebei) province in northern China. This is further evidence that the influence of Mok and his paper extended far beyond the confines of British Hong Kong.[32]

By March 1910 Mok had moved to a larger rented building with his family. It accommodated a women's English school with sixty-three enrolled, a kindergarten school for seventy-three children (these two schools did not charge fees), and rooms for counseling "seekers to come and tarry for their baptism." Missionary Anna Deane wrote that the church was "governed by the Chinese" and that Mok was its pastor with "all Chinese deacons." J. H. King, leader of the Pentecostal Holiness Church, was on a world tour in 1910 and spent a month in Hong Kong working with Mok, preaching every night with Mok interpreting. King spent his first night at "the mission of Rev. Mok Lai Chi far up the mountain side," and he gives us a description of this Chinese leader. He writes that he had "the air of a quiet, statue-like educated Chinaman, and his influence was strong and extensive among the Chinese." During this time Mok was visiting villages near Hong Kong on a regular basis to preach to the "heathen villagers," and he networked with several other Chinese preachers, including some of considerable means. By July 1910, Mok was disturbed by the divisions creeping into American Pentecostalism and wanted to ensure that future American workers would not cause divisions in China. He believed that it was the Chinese themselves who should evangelize China, but they needed teachers to train them in a Bible school, and English teachers to help in the school. Mok criticized missionaries who lived in luxurious houses with several servants, a lifestyle "higher than some of the leading European merchants," but this was not the case with native pentecostal missionaries. He dispelled the rumor that the Chinese required less food than foreigners, and said that Chinese workers needed adequate support. Garr wrote that they would leave Hong Kong as soon as the work was established and, significantly, that Mok Lai Chi was "the head of the work here."[33]

In 1910 Mok's paper explained (in Chinese) the relationship with the missionaries, declaring:

Hong Kong Pentecostal Mission is a Jesus church founded by Chinese themselves, not a branch of any foreign churches planted in my nation. Many genuine New Testament believers from many countries around the world always have correspondence with us. We love each other from our hearts and support each other.[34]

By 1913 the Hong Kong Pentecostal Mission was a totally independent Chinese church. The latest report we have of Mok's work in the overseas press was published in E. N. Bell's *Word and Witness* in November 1913, where Mok writes of a convention in August 1912 and ongoing conversions and water and Spirit baptisms. The Mission continued its daily activities, including a Chinese Bible class (with twenty students) five times a week for training workers, a Sunday school with 130 children "mostly from heathen families" and ten Chinese teachers, an English school and two "native workers," and the newspaper. It appears that this congregation met most of the costs of printing and postage for *Pentecostal Truths*, but that donations toward these costs from readers were also encouraged. The Mission was experiencing steady growth. By 1917 Mok reported that he was still running a weekday school that enabled him to support his family, and "two Pentecostal girls schools." The periodical may have stopped publication soon after 1917, as no later copies are known. However, there is evidence that Mok was involved in itinerating activities throughout the areas around Hong Kong, and was instrumental in founding other congregations in the area, one commencing in 1917 in Sun Yat Sen's birthplace Zhongshan, in which Mok held conventions, and existing today as the Yunfeng Pentecostal Church.[35]

In July 1921, Mok Lai Chi presented a petition to the Secretary for Chinese Affairs in the colonial government on behalf of 10,468 tenants (representing a substantial part of the population) against spiraling rents levied by Chinese landlords. Now fifty-three, Mok was still running the Pentecostal Mission and was recognized as a community leader, "representing Chinese tenants of the Colony." The tenants were also petitioning for proper legal representation on the Council. This may be the last written record of Mok Lai Chi. After Mok became ill in 1923, leadership of the Mission passed to his long-time co-worker Sung Teng Man, a civil servant and father of the present superintendent S. H. Sung, a businessman who took over after his father's death in 1958. The Mission opened two branch churches near Macau in 1916 and 1924, a branch in Kowloon in 1928, and one in Canton (Guangzhou) in 1934. Mok died in Hong Kong in 1926, but his independent Pentecostal Mission still exists today with two "Pentecostal Tabernacles" in Hong Kong and one in Vancouver, Canada. According to its present leader, the Mission has relied on part-time workers and leaders since its founding, it does not take up collections, and members spend an hour praying while kneeling in services. The leader of the first pentecostal church in China and undoubtedly a very influential pentecostal pioneer in his own right, Mok Lai Chi made an enormous contribution to Pentecostalism in China.[36]

No one knows how many Christians there are in China today, but most informed observers would venture at least 80 million, and some considerably more. The majority of these Christians probably belong to independent churches established since 1980. Although Western terminology is difficult to use after many decades of isolation and operating in secrecy, many, if not most of these churches exhibit pentecostal features or have been influenced by Pentecostalism. In pre-Communist times, independent pentecostal churches were flourishing in China. By the time Pentecostalism entered China there was an unprecedented growth in Protestant Christianity and revivalist expectations. The True Jesus Church (TJC) was the largest and most successful independent church to arise in early twentieth century China. Wei Enbo (c.1876–1919) was a member of the London Missionary Society and a silk trader who was reportedly healed from tuberculosis after encountering a pentecostal mission in Beijing in 1916. His contact with foreign missionaries was short-lived, and after a divine revelation he baptized himself by facedown immersion, took the name Wei Baoluo (Paul) and founded the International Assembly of the True Jesus Church in 1917 in Beijing. Wei was stridently anti-foreign missionary, preached about impending doom for Western Christendom, and attracted many followers from existing churches.[37]

Zhang Lingsheng (1863–1935), who had received Spirit baptism through an Apostolic Faith missionary in Shanghai in 1909, succeeded Wei after his death in 1919 from the tuberculosis from which he had been "healed," by which time the church had over a thousand members. It appears that Zhang had met pentecostal missionaries who had convinced him of the non-Trinitarian Oneness doctrine; the first pentecostal missionary in the region, Bernt Berntsen and his influential periodical *Popular Gospel Truths*, became Oneness in 1919. Zhang in turn had persuaded Berntsen to keep Saturday as the Sabbath, which practice Berntsen began to propagate in 1916. Zhang was to leave TJC in 1929. The TJC was a radically anti-foreign, exclusivist church that owed much of its early growth to the efforts of its preachers, including the Confucian scholar Gao Daling in Shanxi, and (Barnabas) Zhang Dianju (1882–1961), who traveled the length and breadth of South China on foot, reporting many signs and miracles, establishing churches and baptizing thousands. The church was particularly effective in converting members of the Seventh Day Adventist Church. An unsuccessful attempt to influence the National Christian Council of

China in 1922 resulted in further isolationism, and after the incident in Shanghai when British troops fired on unarmed protestors, their virulent anti-Western message became even more attractive. By 1929, the TJC was found throughout China, Taiwan, Singapore, Malaysia, and Hong Kong, its main attractions being deliverance from demons and opium addiction and the healing of the sick with holy water. The TJC had also suffered several secessions, including an attempt by Zhang Dianju to take over leadership, thwarted in 1930 when he was excommunicated. Wei Yisa, son of Wei Baoluo, and Gao Daling remained as leaders. By 1949 there were at least 700 congregations with more than 100,000 members in eighteen provinces, but the new government's opposition to religious sects had increased. In 1958 the TJC was banned, only able to recommence openly in 1980. In Taiwan it has been one of the fastest-growing churches, with over 28,000 members by 1968. The emigration of Chinese to Europe and North America resulted in the formation of the TJC in the West. During the Cultural Revolution, the church in mainland China, forced underground, grew rapidly. There may be at least 3 million TJC members in China today. TJC considers itself the only true church. Members observe the Sabbath and the Ten Commandments; both adults and children are baptized by immersion face downward in running water in the name of Jesus, after which a sacrament of foot washing is performed. Common pentecostal practices of speaking in tongues, trembling, singing, leaping, and dancing in the Spirit are found. The international leadership of the church is presently administered from Taiwan, but political tension between Taiwan and the mainland means that the mainland church remained isolated and has lost influence, especially with the recent rapid growth of house churches, congregations that meet in houses and are not registered with the government.[38]

One of the missionary couples W. W. Simpson recruited to the pentecostal cause in China was Leslie and Ava Anglin, Free Baptists who in the period following their pentecostal conversion established a community called the House of Onesiphorus in Tai'an, Shandong. With workshops, schools, and an orphanage with almost 500 destitute children in 1925, the Anglins eventually affiliated with the Assemblies of God. Their self-supporting community influenced Chinese pentecostal communities, in particular the Jesus Family founded by Jing Dianying (1890–1957) at Mazhuang, Shandong. Jing and others established a Christian savings society in 1921, a cooperative store attempting to meet the needs of the socially marginalized, followed by a silk reeling cooperative in

1926. Jing's contact with the Anglins led to his pentecostal experience there in 1924 and his expulsion from the Methodist Episcopal Church. Jing worked briefly for the House of Onesiphorus but in 1927 formed the Jesus Family, which grew with little contact with Western missions. Members renounced the world and their allegiance to natural families, committing themselves totally to the community; private ownership was forbidden; members had to live simply, work hard, and contribute to the community after the pattern of the early church. Family homes were established throughout China and by 1949 there were 127 self-supporting communities with over 10,000 members engaged in several different trades and educational courses. Although the Family first supported the Communist revolution in keeping with its own egalitarian principles, in 1952 Jing was arrested on several charges including imperialism and anti-Communism, and the Family was officially dissolved and repressed. Jing died of cancer five years later. In spite of this, the movement continued underground and in 1977, meetings resumed in Mazhuang. The old meeting place was restored by 1984, and a two-story hostel was started in 1988. Most Christian groups in central Shandong are of Family background, and their influence remains in other provinces. Apart from the strong sense of community, other characteristic Family beliefs that remain are early morning emotional prayer meetings with loud crying, simultaneous prayer and manifestations of the Spirit like speaking in tongues, trances, revelations through dreams, visions, and other means, hymn singing (Jing wrote many hymns), and sharing testimonies. Although these phenomena characterize pentecostal movements all over the world, in the Family these meetings last for at least three hours, and the regimented work activities revolve around the daily meetings. The Family suffered further repression in 1992, with several key leaders imprisoned and buildings demolished by the government.[39]

In 1929, a remarkable pentecostal revival occurred in Shandong in the wake of the anti-Christian movement and the chaos created by warlords and revolution. Initiated by a Norwegian independent missionary with pentecostal leanings, Marie Monsen, the revival exploded among Lutherans, Baptists, and Presbyterians after the creation of a grassroots Chinese pentecostal movement called the Independent Chinese Spiritual Gifts Society (SGS). Initiated by the Nanjing pentecostal Nathan (Zhaorui) Ma and organized by Presbyterians Yang Rulin and Sun Zhanyao, the SGS set out specifically to promote the practice of gifts of the Spirit. Emotional and ecstatic outbursts, speaking in tongues, "holy laughter," prophecies, healings, exorcisms, and public confessions were common in their meetings. The movement spread through the province and missionaries distanced themselves from it. Presbyterians in particular were affected; it was reported that two-thirds of Presbyterian pastors had joined the movement, but it soon spread to all the Protestant churches in the province. The revival reached other provinces like Henan, Manchuria, and Szechuan and was also influenced by the Jesus Family in Shandong. By 1936, SGS had organized itself into a separate denomination and opened its first church buildings in Qingdao and Jinan. The movement did not flourish during the Japanese occupation and subsequent civil wars, and although it continued to influence Chinese Christianity, many of its members joined the Jesus Family. SGS was finally dissolved in 1958.[40]

Independent Chinese churches were characterized by two things: pentecostal tendencies and conservative theology, characteristics that remain at the heart of Chinese Protestantism—especially, but not exclusively, those many groups that refused to join the government-recognized Three-Self Patriotic Movement. It has been estimated that half a million Chinese Christians lost their lives in the persecution that took place between 1950 and 1978, half of them during the Cultural Revolution that began in 1966. Many of these would have been members of the churches described here. All foreign missionaries left, and during these three decades Christianity became an underground Chinese religion with an apocalyptic emphasis. David Aikman considers how deeply Christianity penetrated Chinese society during the twentieth century. Many of the characteristics of the revivalist movements in pre-Communist China continued with the movements that emerged after 1980. Since the end of the Cultural Revolution, Deng Xiaoping's rise to power in 1978, and the subsequent relaxation of severe religious restrictions, China has been experiencing an unprecedented growth in Christian conversions dubbed "Christianity fever." The Chinese Protestant population was less than a million when Mao Zedong came to power in 1949. Today 50 million is a conservative estimate. The remarkable growth of Christianity in China is in no small part due to the efforts of the pioneers who established a vibrant Chinese Christianity that was not dependent on Western missionaries or organizations for sustenance. If recent reports are accurate, the majority of these Chinese Christians have pentecostal inclinations.[41]

The role of Pentecostalism and expatriate pentecostal missionaries in the early years of African, Indian, and Chinese independent churches and the links with some of its most significant leaders is an important historical fact that should not be glossed over by romanticizing "indigenous" churches without foreign influences. Nevertheless, there was indeed a very vigorous indigenous pentecostal movement at an early stage, and the growth and expansion of Pentecostalism in Asia and Africa was a direct consequence of this. From its beginning, Pentecostalism has been a highly migratory, missionary movement. Many pentecostals are unencumbered by ecclesiastical structures and hierarchies. With a sense of divine calling to do something important for God, they place primary emphasis on being "sent by the Spirit" and depend more on what is described as the Spirit's leading than on formal structures. People "called by God" are engaging in missionary activities in other countries because they believe that the Spirit directed them to do so, often through some spiritual revelation like a prophecy, a dream, or a vision, and even through an audible voice perceived to be that of God. The result is that pentecostals approach their ministry and involvement in the church with deep commitment, often with self-sacrifice and hardship in order to see their divine vision realized. Not all have the success they dream of, but their dedication to the mission of the church is impressive. The existence of vibrant African pentecostal churches in Europe since the 1990s has put pressure on European Christians to seriously reconsider the effectiveness, content, and relevancy of the church's mission. In its vigorous expansion, Pentecostalism as a whole sees the "world" as the space to move into and "possess" for Christ. Transnationalism and migration do not affect their essential character, even though their adherents may have to steer a precarious course between contradictory forms of identity resulting from the migratory experience. Pentecostals make full use of opportunities to proclaim the gospel in word and deed, in order to evangelize and minister to what they see as the felt needs of people, resulting in the growth of their churches.[42]

8

Charisma and Faith

The Charismatic Renewal

Classical Pentecostalism grew modestly during its first fifty years but gathered pace thereafter, becoming more noticeable to other churches and inevitably, coming in closer contact with them. After a period of isolation, some pentecostals began to interact with churches of older denominations in the 1950s. Many different factors contributed to the emergence of the Charismatic movement within mainline churches in the 1960s. Once again, it was the eruption of speaking in tongues in these churches that ignited the new fire. With the development of "non-denominational" Charismatic churches and organizations in the following decades, the term "Charismatic Renewal" was broadened to include all movements outside denominational Pentecostalism where spiritual gifts were exercised. The last quarter of the twentieth century was the time of unprecedented growth in global Pentecostalism, led by the rise of the mega-churches with their transnational networks and flamboyant, often controversial leaders. The international networks of the established denominations themselves soon helped spread the Charismatic movement. Contemporary Pentecostalism is very different from what it was a century ago. It is impossible to recount the multitude of events that brought about the massive shifts in world Christianity. But to analyze the more recent history of Pentecostalism, we must try to make sense of the bewildering mass of different movements that emerged about the middle of the twentieth century, affected by different contexts but eventually forming new transnational networks and coming closer together in emphases and ethos. This chapter traces only some of the major developments that began in the 1960s and transformed Pentecostalism from a relatively obscure and maligned sect to a transnational, global movement affecting all forms of Christianity today.[1]

Many observers assume that the Charismatic Renewal in North America began in the Episcopal Church in 1960 and in the Roman Catholic Church in 1967. The resignation of Dennis Bennett as rector of an Episcopalian parish in Van Nuys, California, in April 1960 is often regarded as the beginning of the Charismatic movement in the Western world. But this event, for all its significance, was the culmination rather than the beginning of a movement that had already existed for decades. Early Pentecostalism in Europe—unlike its origins among Holiness groups in North America—was a "Charismatic" and ecumenical movement, mainly, though not exclusively, in the Anglican, Lutheran, Reformed, Methodist, and Baptist churches. European leaders like T. B. Barratt, Lewi Pethrus, Alexander Boddy, and Jonathan Paul never intended to leave their denominations and some never did. They believed that their newfound pentecostal experience would renew and revitalize churches that had lost some of their vigor. The same was true of those involved in the revivals in India in 1905–07, in the Korean Pentecost in the Presbyterian and Methodist churches after 1907, in the revival among Methodists in Chile in 1909, among Anglicans in Nigeria from 1918 onward, and during the Shandong revival of 1929. Spiritual gifts, including speaking in tongues, had been experienced in mainline churches in India in 1905–07, in the Anglican church in England from 1907 to 1925, in German Lutheran and Reformed churches from 1907, in the French Reformed Church in the 1930s, among the Darmstadt sisters of Basilea Schlink from 1945, and in the Anglican healing movement, *Iviyo*, in South Africa among the Zulu in the 1940s—to give but a few examples. The North American events of the 1960s were not new, although they caught international attention.[2]

Other significant influences prior to 1960 helped change the attitude of older American churches toward the pentecostal experience. Once pentecostal denominations were drawn into the National Association of Evangelicals in 1943, a thawing of the frosty relationships between them and evangelicals took place. But this newfound rapprochement contributed toward the "evangelicalization" of white pentecostal denominations, which drew them into mainstream American society and had detrimental effects on their effectiveness as "protest" movements. Healing evangelists like William Branham, Oral Roberts, T. L. Osborne, and others in the 1940s and 1950s were either not affiliated to pentecostal denominations or operated independently of them; consequently, Christians outside these denominations were exposed to pentecostal experience. Beginning in 1955, Oral Roberts (1918–2009) brought the healing and pentecostal subculture into homes across the United States through his weekly national television program. His monthly magazine *Abundant Life* had a circulation of over a million and he became the best-known pentecostal in the world. In becoming a Methodist in 1965, he had committed the unpardonable sin as far as some classical pentecostals were concerned. This increased his distance from them while making him more acceptable to middle America. He became a local preacher in the United Methodist Church in 1968. The Graduate School of Theology at Oral Roberts University was headed by a Methodist theologian and became a recognized seminary for training Methodist ministers in 1982. Roberts's son Richard became head of his massive organization and university in 1993 until his resignation from the university in 2007 over alleged financial irregularities. Oral Roberts University recovered and, with the backing of Oral Roberts, appointed respected pentecostal scholar Mark Ruthven as its new president in 2007, two years before Oral Roberts died.[3]

There were even earlier influences. In 1948 a revival known as the "Latter Rain" movement began in Saskatchewan, Canada, and had an international impact, spreading across North America and as far as Ghana, contributing to the split in the Apostolic Church there and the emergence of the Church of Pentecost. The Latter Rain movement sought to return to the revivalism of early Pentecostalism, with the restoration of ministry gifts of apostles, prophets, evangelists, pastors, and teachers; it reported healings and miracles with new revelations from the Bible, declaring once again that this revival was the one promised in the Scriptures to precede the second coming of Christ. More than any other movement, it was the Latter Rain that influenced the more recent shift away from premillennialism through its emphasis on "dominion theology," which was more akin to postmillennialism. Because it stressed local church autonomy and anti-denominationalism, it conflicted with established pentecostal denominations and resulted in the resignations from these denominations of several prominent ministers. For a while, it even had the support of leading Swedish pentecostal, Lewi Pethrus. As a result of the Latter Rain, hundreds of autonomous churches sprang up all over North America, creating new networks that had nothing to do with established pentecostal denominations. Many of these churches continued into the 1960s and some of their leaders enthusiastically embraced and influenced the Charismatic movement and its aftermath, thus shifting Pentecostalism away from its narrow sectarian stance. The Latter Rain movement was a significant player in bringing about new shifts in pentecostal ideas and practices worldwide, particularly in the impetus it gave to congregational independence.[4]

Several mainline church ministers began speaking in tongues in the 1950s and promoted spiritual renewal thereafter. Richard Winkler, rector of Trinity Episcopal Church in Wheaton, Illinois, started the first Charismatic prayer meeting among Episcopalians in 1956 following his Spirit baptism and was featured in *Life* magazine for his ministry of exorcism. Presbyterian minister James Brown also received Spirit baptism in 1956 and began a similar meeting in his church in Parkesburg, Pennsylvania; Lutheran pastor Harald Bredesen (1918–2006) began a Charismatic prayer meeting in his church in New York in 1957 and was later the most popular spokesperson for the Charismatic renewal in the national media; and Episcopalian healing minister Agnes Sanford (1897–1982) spoke to many ministers about the baptism in the Spirit and was a major promoter of the Charismatic renewal in the 1950s. In 1951 the Full Gospel Business Men's Fellowship International (FGBMFI) was founded by Armenian American pentecostal and California millionaire dairy farmer Demos Shakarian (1913–93). This organization was backed by Oral Roberts, who spoke at its first and many subsequent meetings. The FGBMFI emphasized bringing the pentecostal experience to laymen and grew quickly. It admitted neither women nor church ministers into membership and was unashamedly capitalist in ethos. Soon it attracted men from both mainline and pentecostal churches, encouraging members to be active in their own churches. Thus FGBMFI brought Charismatic experience to mainline churches, and its annual conventions from 1953 onward featured all the leading independent healing evangelists and drew thousands. After the fashion of Rotary Clubs, FGBMFI's chapter meetings were held in plush hotel ballrooms and restaurants, a marked departure from the Pentecostalism of tents and storefront buildings. The FGBMFI helped finance Oral Roberts University and sowed the seeds for the "prosperity gospel" that would emerge in the 1970s, featuring some of the early "Word of Faith" preachers like Kenneth Hagin and Kenneth Copeland in its conventions. By 1972, the FGBMFI had some 300,000 members in the United States and had spread to more than a hundred nations. It had an influential monthly magazine, *Voice,* which publicized the Charismatic experiences of people from mainline churches, and a weekly TV program called *Good News* hosted by Shakarian.[5]

South African David du Plessis (1905–87), nicknamed "Mr. Pentecost," traveled around the world as an unofficial spokesperson for Pentecostalism in ecumenical circles. He was general secretary of the Apostolic Faith Mission of South Africa (AFM) in Johannesburg from 1936 until 1947, when he moved to Switzerland to help organize the first Pentecostal World Conference. According to his own account, du Plessis received a prophecy from English evangelist Smith Wigglesworth in 1936 that he would take the pentecostal experience around the world to mainline denominations. In 1948 he moved to the United States and affiliated with the Assemblies of God in 1955. His friendship with John Mackay, president of Princeton Theological Seminary and chairman of the International Missionary Council (IMC), brought him to the ecumenical movement. He addressed the IMC meeting in Willingen, Germany, in 1952 and the World Council of Churches (WCC) assembly at Evanston, Illinois, in 1954, after which he attended every WCC assembly until 1983. He was warmly received and his work brought many within mainline churches to a pentecostal experience. Because of their opposition to his ecumenical contacts and du Plessis's refusal to give them up, the AG withdrew du Plessis's credentials in 1962 and reinstated him only eighteen years later. His links with the WCC were objectionable to white American pentecostals in general and the AG in particular, since AG leader Thomas Zimmerman was also chair of the National Association of Evangelicals (NAE). But through the efforts of du Plessis, Roberts, Shakarian, and others, the wider Christian world was beginning to take notice of burgeoning Pentecostalism. Du Plessis was involved in organizing the Pentecostal-Catholic dialogue that began in 1972 and became an effective bridge between Pentecostalism, the ecumenical movement, and the Charismatic Movement in both its Protestant and Catholic forms.[6]

Increased national publicity for the Charismatic renewal occurred after an Episcopalian rector in Van Nuys (suburban Los Angeles), Dennis Bennett (1917–91) and his colleague Frank Maguire, vicar in Monterey Park, Los Angeles, received Spirit baptism in November 1959 together with many members of their churches. When Bennett spoke of his experience in a Sunday sermon in April 1960 these events became public knowledge. His testimony caused controversy and he was asked to resign, which he did formally in a pastoral letter explaining the compatibility of his Charismatic experience with Episcopalian teaching. The Bishop of Los Angeles, Francis Bloy, wrote to the parish banning speaking in tongues. One of the Charismatic members, Jean Stone, contacted the press and Bennett's story was reported in *Time* and *Newsweek*. Other Charismatics were encouraged to make themselves known, and the "Charismatic renewal" (a term coined by Stone and Harald Bredesen) or "Neo-Pentecostalism" was now in the open. Bennett was contacted by a sympathetic bishop in Washington State and appointed rector of a small, struggling church, St. Luke's in Seattle, which grew rapidly until it was the largest in the diocese and a place of pilgrimage for people seeking Spirit baptism. Soon Bennett was ministering to 2,000 people a week. His testimony was published as *Nine O'Clock in the Morning* in 1970 and became a best seller. Jean Stone (later Willans) began the quarterly magazine *Trinity* in 1961, which after the FGBMFI's *Voice* was the main publication promoting Charismatic renewal until it ceased publication in 1966.[7]

The Charismatic movement spread in the 1960s throughout the United States and Canada. Harald Bredesen and Lutheran pastor Larry Christenson (b.1928) from San Pedro, California, had received Spirit baptism at pentecostal meetings. Bredesen brought the Charismatic experience to students at Yale in October 1962, and a report in *Time* gave this event international publicity. Christenson, who related the compatibility of his Spirit baptism with the Lutheran tradition, visited Europe in 1963, was instrumental in the start of the Charismatic movement in Britain, and reported the presence of Lutherans in Germany who had spoken in tongues for sixty years. But Charismatics were not universally welcomed in their churches. The radical Episcopal bishop of California, James Pike, and Methodist bishop Gerald Kennedy positioned themselves against them. Pike forbade speaking in tongues in his north California diocese in 1963, warning of a "heresy in embryo" that was "dangerous to the peace and unity of the church." Conservative denominations like the Southern Baptist Convention, the Church of the Nazarene, and the Lutheran Church, Missouri Synod, expelled Charismatic ministers and congregations. Such resistance often caused Charismatics to leave and divide these churches, and precipitated the rise of independent Charismatic churches. Despite the opposition, Charismatic experiences in the older churches were encouraged by news reports and hundreds of popular publications—among the most influential were David Wilkerson's *The Cross and the Switchblade* (1963), and journalist John Sherrill's *They Speak with Other Tongues* (1964). Sherrill's was a pioneering book suggesting that middle America with its stately churches and comfortable lifestyles could embrace the pentecostal experience. Sherrill and his wife Elizabeth also collaborated with David Wilkerson in the writing of his book. Wilkerson (1931–2011) was a rural Pennsylvania AG pastor who started Teen Challenge, a rehabilitation center for drug addicts, in Brooklyn, New York, in 1958. Teen Challenge soon established other centers throughout the nation and internationally. Wilkerson gave credit for the remarkable success rate in providing deliverance for addicts to the experience of Spirit baptism that he urged on all his converts. *Reader's Digest* carried Wilkerson's story around the world and his book was made into a film starring pop singer Pat Boone, himself a Charismatic. Wilkerson established World Challenge in 1971, an international organization to coordinate his expanding ministry. In 1987 he resigned from the AG and joined up with his brother Don to found Times Square Church in New York; Don resigned in 1995 and this independent church has been led since 2001 by Carter Conlon. David Wilkerson died in a motor accident in Texas in April 2011.[8]

The Charismatic movement was further publicized by television broadcasts—particularly those of Oral Roberts and Pat Robertson (b.1930), a Southern Baptist minister and son of a US senator who resigned from the Baptists in 1987 to contend (unsuccessfully) for the Republican presidential nomination. Robertson, who has been known for his conservative and controversial sociopolitical pronouncements, founded media empire Christian Broadcasting Network (CBN) in 1960 and the CBN University, now called Regent University, in 1977. He publicly supported African dictators Sese Mobutu Sese Seke of the Congo and Charles Taylor of Liberia. He infamously called for the assassination of Venezuela's socialist president Hugo Chavez in 2005 and in 2010 suggested that Haiti's devastating earthquake was punishment because the country had made "a pact with the devil"; the fact that evangelicals make up 16 percent of the Haitian population, half of whom are pentecostal, seemed to have escaped him. Robertson has since retired from the presidency of Regent, which is now an independent Christian university with some of the best-qualified staff in pentecostal theology in the country, offering graduate degrees up to the doctoral level. Robertson is only one of many examples of US politicians with pentecostal connections; others include Republican vice-presidential candidate and former Alaska governor Sarah Palin, and John Ashcroft, former Republican attorney general, governor of Missouri, and son of an AG pastor. Such people are usually on the conservative, far right of the political spectrum.[9]

Paul Crouch (b.1934) founded Trinity Broadcasting Network (TBN) in 1973, now the world's largest Christian television network. There were many TV evangelists in the United States, including Jimmy Swaggart (b.1935) and Jim Bakker (b.1940), whose sensational falls in 1987–88 were a source of embarrassment for Pentecostalism that damaged its reputation, especially with the prominent media coverage exposing the various scandals. In 1988, Swaggart wept before a TV audience confessing unspecified sins, but refused to submit to rehabilitative discipline from his AG denomination, resigning instead. He continued in his multimedia Jimmy Swaggart Ministries, with his son Donnie Swaggart and grandson Gabriel Swaggart now playing leading roles. Bakker's Praise the Lord (PTL) empire declared bankruptcy and was sued for $56 million in back taxes. Bakker, also from an AG background, was imprisoned for fraud in 1989 and released on parole in 1994. He renounced his prosperity teaching two years later, began to teach on grace and restoration, and resumed a daily television broadcast in 2003. Baptist Charismatic Larry Lea and prosperity preacher Robert Tilton were also exposed by ABC News in 1990 for financial irregularities.[10]

The Charismatic movement in North America reached its peak at the 1977 Kansas City Charismatic Conference, hailed by its Catholic chairman Kevin Ranaghan as the most ecumenical mass gathering of Christians in 800 years. Although it revealed cracks in the façade of unity among Charismatics, this unprecedented conference that united some 50,000 Catholics, Anglicans, Protestants, and classical Pentecostals would never be repeated. But the Washington for Jesus prayer rally organized by Charismatic pastor John Gimenez of Virginia Beach drew an estimated 700,000 in April 1980, an event that placed evangelicals on the American political map as a substantial voting bloc. By 2010 there were an estimated 84 million pentecostals and Charismatics in the United States, some 26 percent of the population. With the growth of Pentecostalism came a growth in its intelligentsia and an increase in its ability to interact with outsiders. The creation of the Society for Pentecostal Studies (SPS) in the 1970s and formal dialogue between pentecostal representatives, mostly SPS members, and the Catholic Church (and later with other ecumenical church bodies) led to Pentecostalism being seen for the first time as a reasonably intelligent part of contemporary Christianity that needed to be better understood. SPS was predominantly North American in focus and membership and confessional in constitution; it included Protestant and Catholic Charismatic scholars. But by the 1990s SPS was developing an international membership and Pentecostal Studies in some universities had become a multidisciplinary subject in its own right.[11]

In Britain, the initial home of the Charismatic renewal was the Church of England. The first Anglican parish to become Charismatic was St. Mark's, Gillingham, Kent, in 1963 under John Collins, a former assistant at All Souls, and where David Watson (1933–84) was curate until his appointment as vicar to St. Cuthbert's, York, another center of the renewal. Early British Charismatic leaders were Anglicans David Watson, John Perry (vicar at St. Andrew's, Chorleywood) and Michael Harper; and Baptist pastors David Pawson (Gold Hill and later Guildford) and Barney Coombs (East Acton and Basingstoke). A curate in the evangelical All Souls Church in central London where John Stott was rector, Michael Harper (1931–2010), received Spirit baptism in 1962 and in 1964 established the Fountain Trust, the leading British organization promoting the Charismatic renewal, solidly ecumenical in vision and embracing all denominations. Harper first arranged a meeting of ministers for Larry Christenson's brief visit to London in 1963 and later that year for David du Plessis. Jean Stone and Dennis Bennett visited the United Kingdom in 1964 and 1965, respectively, and in all these meetings an increasing number of people were brought into the renewal. Harper organized a major international and ecumenical conference in 1971 at Guildford that had more than forty Lutheran and thirty Catholic delegates from different parts of Europe and North America, followed by biennial international conferences in Nottingham (1973) and Westminster (1975, 1977, and 1979), giving the movement a greater sense of identity and cohesion. Tom Smail (b.1928), then a Presbyterian minister, became director of the Fountain Trust on Harper's resignation in 1975 and served until 1979. He edited a journal, *Theological Renewal*—but the Trust and its journal closed in 1980 and Smail became an Anglican priest and vice-principal of a theological college. Harper left the Anglican church in 1995 over women's ordination and became an Antiochian Orthodox priest. The focus of the Charismatic movement in the United Kingdom now shifted from an ecumenical movement to denominational groupings.[12]

The Charismatic movement spread quickly in English-speaking Protestant areas like Australia, New Zealand, and Canada. In South Africa the movement began among Methodists in the late 1960s, and the head of the Church of the Province of South Africa (Anglican), the Archbishop of Cape Town from 1974 to 1981, Bill Burnett (1917–94) was the highest profile Anglican Charismatic, baptized in the Spirit in 1972 when he was bishop of Grahamstown. The Charismatic movement spread quickly in South Africa in the 1970s, especially among Anglicans and Baptists. Among many examples of the spread of the Charismatic movement in Africa are a popular Anglican healing center in Zimbabwe, the Charismatic Legion of Christ's Witnesses

(*Iviyo*) association within South African Anglicanism founded by Bishop Alpheus Zulu in the 1940s; a large Charismatic movement among Lutherans in Ethiopia and in the interdenominational "Big November Crusade" in Tanzania; multitudes of Ghanaian Methodist and Presbyterian Charismatics; and a large Charismatic movement in Nigerian Anglicanism.[13]

By the early 1980s the Charismatic movement in the West, especially in Protestant churches, slowed down as it became more acceptable within mainline denominations that attempted to accommodate it. In North America, major divisions emerged by 1977 and the closure of the Fountain Trust in 1980 hindered the Charismatic movement's efforts in Europe to facilitate ecumenical cooperation. However, a considerable number of people in the older churches continue to practice a charismatic form of Christianity, expressed in fellowship and prayer groups, Sunday services, and "renewal" conferences—to some extent inspired and encouraged by similar movements in other parts of the world. The older churches have responded to the growth of Pentecostalism with innovations that can be described as "Charismatic," where a place is given to gifts of the Spirit. This is even more noticeable in the majority world, where historic Protestant churches have become minority groups with small congregations compared to the pentecostal and Charismatic mega-churches. The result has been to adapt to the changing "pentecostalization" taking place. In Latin America, the vast majority of Protestants, termed "evangélicos" (evangelicals), are pentecostal, and those who are not are forced to come to terms with the changes. The most prominent healing evangelist in India in recent years was D. G. S. Dhinakaran (1935–2008), a member of the Church of South India and a bank clerk who began full-time ministry in 1962, public evangelism in 1970, and a regular television program in 1980. His massive healing meetings drew crowds in the hundreds of thousands, and his Jesus Calls Ministry shows many parallels to the organizations of Oral Roberts— including Karunya University with some 7,000 students and a prayer tower near Coimbatore, Tamil Nadu. The university began as a self-financing Karunya Institute of Technology in 1986. Apart from his evangelistic, educational, and healing activities, Dhinakaran also established Seesha, a social welfare organization whose stated objective is "to educate underprivileged children and improve the life and health of people in rural areas." The Jesus Calls Ministry continues under Dhinakaran's son Paul Dhinakaran.[14]

In 1967 the Catholic Church entered the Charismatic renewal for the first time in its modern history. Catholic Charismatics worldwide, but especially in countries like the Philippines, India, Brazil, and many parts of Africa, now number well over 120 million, and there are as many Catholic Charismatics in the world today as there are classical pentecostals. Several factors account for this remarkable phenomenon, but the preparatory work was laid by the momentous changes instituted by the Second Vatican Council, 1962–65, where Pope John XXIII had prayed that the Council might be a "new Pentecost" for the church. Catholic Charismatics see themselves as the fulfillment of that prayer. Encouragement from successive popes has fostered steady growth and formal organization within the Catholic Church. The Catholic Charismatic Renewal (CCR) began at Duquesne University in Pittsburgh, Pennsylvania. Two lay theology faculty members there had studied David Wilkerson's book *The Cross and the Switchblade;* they received Spirit baptism and at a retreat passed it on to about thirty students, who then formed the first CCR prayer group. The CCR spread from there to the University of Notre Dame and Michigan State University, and grew rapidly to include 300,000 people by 1976, spreading internationally into Latin America, Europe, and Asia. Various CCR communities became centers of the renewal. An annual conference was held at Notre Dame, increasing in size every year and peaking at 30,000 in 1974. From 1973 Cardinal Léon-Joseph Suenens (1904–96), primate of Belgium and one of the four moderators of the Second Vatican Council, was acknowledged leader of Catholic Charismatics worldwide and advisor to the pope on Charismatic issues. In the early 1970s, theological publications by Catholic scholars placing the movement firmly within Catholic tradition were important to the movement. These included works by the Benedictine Kilian McDonnell, Edward O'Connor, and the more popular writings of lay Catholics Kevin and Dorothy Ranaghan. Kevin Ranaghan was executive director of the CCR's National Service Committee from its inception in 1970 until his retirement in 1985. The formal structures given to the CCR provided an effective leadership, communication between the different communities and prayer groups, and literature to guide participants in the renewal. As a result the movement was able to expand rapidly in North America and to other parts of the world.[15]

The first continental European Charismatic Leaders' Conference was held in 1972, with sixteen countries represented, and was held every two years until 1988. A "Pentecost over Europe" celebration was held at Strasbourg in 1982 with 20,000 participants mainly from France, West Germany, and Switzerland. It was the apex of the movement in Europe. The CCR in France spread rapidly from 1972 to 1975, and there were more Catholic Charismatics in France (about half a million) than anywhere else in Europe. In 1975 Pope Paul VI addressed a weekend Congress of 10,000 Catholic Charismatics in Rome, in which he encouraged the "spiritual renewal," and Cardinal Suenens conducted the first Charismatic mass at St. Peter's Square. In March 1992, while urging the need for "fidelity to the Church and her Magisterium" and "the deepening of your Catholic identity," Pope John Paul II gave an address to the International Catholic Charismatic Renewal Office, now the International Catholic Charismatic Renewal Services, based in Rome:

> The emergence of the Renewal following the Second Vatican Council was a particular gift of the Holy Spirit to the Church....At this moment in the Church's history, the Charismatic Renewal can play a significant role in promoting the much-needed defense [*sic*] of Christian life in societies where secularism and materialism have weakened many people's ability to respond to the Spirit and to discern God's loving call. Your contribution to the re-evangelization of society will be made in the first place by personal witness to the indwelling Spirit and by showing forth His presence through works of holiness and solidarity.... I pray that your work will contribute to the growth of the Church, in fidelity to the Lord's will and to the mission which she has received. I commend all of you to the loving intercession of Mary, Mother of the Church.... To all of you I cordially impart my Apostolic Blessing.[16]

This statement was made by the pope in the same year that he condemned Latin American pentecostals, but these and similar pronouncements by the various pontiffs encouraged the growth of the CCR. By 2010 there were over 120 million Catholic Charismatics in 220 countries, almost 10 percent of all Catholics. This remarkable growth, which has been especially noticeable in the majority world, has probably slowed down the exodus from the Catholic Church into pentecostal churches. One of the best-known examples from Africa was the controversial healing ministry in the 1970s of Archbishop of Zambia Emmanuel Milingo (b. 1930), who was removed to Rome in 1983 and excommunicated over his marriage in 2001 and ordination of married priests in 2006. There is also a thriving Charismatic movement among Catholics in Uganda, Ghana, and Nigeria.[17]

After a period of steady decline, Latin America has seen a rapid growth in the CCR in recent years, and large rallies usually held in football stadiums are attended by tens of thousands throughout the region. As far back as 1982, one estimate held that at least a fifth of Catholic churches in Colombia were Charismatic. The most prominent Latin American Catholic Charismatic is the Brazilian, Father Marcelo Rossi, a former aerobics instructor who preaches to thousands in open-air rallies using pentecostal methods of evangelism. One open-air event in São Paulo reportedly attracted 2.4 million people, and Rossi now holds regular masses in a converted warehouse that seats 10,000. In 2011 Rossi was in the process of building a mega-church in São Paulo holding 100,000 worshippers. The BBC reported on his amazing success in 1999 and *Time* did so in 2007. Rossi has become a best-selling author and has sold millions of CDs featuring him singing up-beat Charismatic songs; he hosts a daily radio show and a twice-weekly television program, and he runs a busy web portal. In a country where the proportion of Catholics dropped from 83 percent to 73 percent during the 1990s, while that of evangelicals (mostly pentecostals) rose from 8 percent to 16 percent, Rossi's success with this new approach is welcome to the Catholic hierarchy, and he was honored at the Vatican by Pope Benedict XVI in 2010.[18]

The CCR is especially strong in India (with perhaps 5 million members) and in the Philippines (at least 11 million). The CCR in India commenced in 1972 when two priests who had returned from the United States as Charismatics began prayer groups that spread from Mumbai to other parts of India. India has its own National Catholic Charismatic Renewal Services in Delhi that publishes a monthly magazine, *Charisindia*. The Divine Retreat Centre in Muringoor, Kerala, is one of the best-known centers of the CCR in India, founded in 1987 by Father Matthew Naikomparambil. Since 1990, week long healing and evangelism meetings draw between 10,000 and 20,000 people every week. Its claim to be the largest Catholic retreat center in the world is plausible, and the Centre is now headed by Father Augustine Vallooran and a team of priests. In the Philippines, the Catholic Charismatic movement of El Shaddai began in 1981 as a radio program and is led by layman Mariano ("Mike") Velarde (b.1939), called the Servant Leader and popularly known as "Brother Mike." It is the largest of all national CCR movements with at least 9 million members. This indigenous Filipino movement is characterized by large weekly, emotional Sunday services with half a million in attendance, and there is an emphasis on healing and prosperity. Its unorthodox ways—for Velarde's style and oratory can hardly be distinguished from those of American prosperity preachers—have brought some tension between it and the Catholic hierarchy in the Philippines.

But like Rossi in Brazil, Velarde has helped stem the tide of conversions from Catholicism to pentecostal churches in his country.[19]

Independent Neo-Pentecostalism

At about the same time as the start of the CCR, the Jesus People movement (JPM) arose in the American hippie counterculture, especially on the US West Coast. The JPM appealed to disenchanted hippies, almost all of them under thirty years of age, and was decidedly pentecostal in orientation. It was distinct from both classical Pentecostalism and the Charismatic movement because it operated in a very different milieu and was often in tension with established churches, including pentecostal ones. Although the JPM had largely dissipated by the end of the 1970s, new independent churches formed by some of its leaders were the vanguard of a fresh proliferation of American independent churches and mega-churches in the 1980s. The JPM began on the Pacific Coast in 1967 when thousands of former hippies became Christians through ministries in Christian coffeehouses and communes offering deliverance from drug addiction. Some of the best known of these were the Living Room founded by Ted Wise in San Francisco, the Ark started by Linda Meissner in Seattle, and His Place run by Arthur Blessitt in Los Angeles. Blessitt continues to make news traveling the world bearing a large wooden cross. Converts often lived in Christian communes in rural areas and kept aspects of their hippie subculture. By the early 1970s it was estimated that at least 300,000 young people were in the JPM. One of the leading centers of this movement was the Calvary Chapel in Costa Mesa, California, led by Chuck Smith, which in a few years had 25,000 mainly young people attending its Sunday services. This was but one of several churches that emerged at this time and have since become significant denominations across the nation. Another was the Vineyard Association, later headed by John Wimber, with early connections to Calvary Chapel.[20]

By the late 1970s the new "nondenominational" and independent Pentecostalism was emerging, emphasizing house groups and "radical" discipleship, and some groups were also known as "restoration" churches. The terms "pentecostal" and "Charismatic" began to be used interchangeably and the term "neopentecostal" was first applied to the "nondenominational" churches, later also referred to as "neocharismatic." The proliferation of such terms has only served to increase the confusion. The new networks of independent churches were soon the fastest growing churches in the English-speaking world. In the United States, the "Fort Lauderdale Five" of Charles Simpson (b. 1937), Derek Prince (1915–2003), Ern Baxter (1914–93), Bob Mumford (b. 1930), and Don Basham (1926–89) came together in 1970 to lead Christian Growth Ministries, known as the "shepherding" or "discipleship" movement because of its strong and controversial emphasis on submission to "shepherds" or church leaders. Large numbers of independent Charismatic pastors were associated with this group, which created a rift in the American Charismatic movement from which it never really recovered. In 1975 Pat Robertson publicly denounced the shepherding movement on CBN, followed by Demos Shakarian of FGBMFI and Charismatic healing evangelist Kathryn Kuhlman. Critics accused the Fort Lauderdale Five of heresy, of creating a hierarchical denomination, and of exploiting "disciples" who were totally dependent on their shepherds, to whom they had to submit every area of their lives, including the most intimate. But the shepherding movement had some 100,000 associated members in North America at its zenith, with a publishing arm called Integrity Communications and the highly influential *New Wine* magazine. Its leaders moved to Mobile, Alabama in 1978 and were in great demand as speakers both nationally and internationally. Prince left the association in 1983 and the remaining four disbanded in 1986. Only Simpson remained in Mobile to form the Fellowship of Covenant Ministers and Conferences in 1987 and continued to lead an association of churches.[21]

A parallel British "restoration" movement arose in the late 1950s. Some of its first leaders were Brethren who had been expelled because of their pentecostal experiences and, like the American Latter Rain movement, taught a "restoration" of the "five-fold ministry" of apostles, prophets, evangelists, pastors, and teachers. Known at first as the "house church movement" and later as "New Churches," the restoration movement became the fastest-growing church group in the country; by 1982 it may have had as many as 100,000 house groups. Major new church networks emerged, such as New Frontiers, Covenant Ministries International, Salt and Light Ministries, Pioneers, Cornerstone Ministries, and Ichthus Christian Fellowship. New Frontiers is now the largest of these networks, nurtured during the 1990s by the annual Stoneleigh Bible Weeks near Coventry. Together with the Vineyard Association, which started in Britain in 1987, these networks have effectively become denominations. By 2000, the New Churches collectively were the most numerous of the pentecostal and Charismatic groups in Britain.

In the 1980s, Fuller Theological Seminary's Peter Wagner, following what he termed the "First Wave" of classical Pentecostalism and the "Second Wave" of the Charismatic movement, identified the "Third Wave" of a new renewal with the central figure of John Wimber (1934–97), who taught the popular "Signs and Wonders" course with Wagner at Fuller and whose Vineyard Christian Fellowship in Anaheim, California, spearheaded a new emphasis on renewal in the established, mainly evangelical churches throughout the English-speaking world. But as a term to cover global events, "Third Wave" is inappropriate and misleading. Even in the North American context, it overlooks the JPM and the much earlier Latter Rain movement. Wimber joined the Vineyard Church in Anaheim, California, in 1982, but the congregation emerged in 1977 during the JPM era. Most Charismatics did not stress the "initial evidence" doctrine of tongues, but they still promoted a crisis experience subsequent to baptism or conversion. The new movement moved away from the idea of a "second blessing" experience and toward Spirit baptism occurring at conversion, with an emphasis on the gifts of the Spirit in evangelism and as a normal part of Christian life—a concept that many evangelicals found more acceptable. A network of over 550 Vineyard churches in the United States and 1,500 worldwide had emerged by 2011. One of the Vineyard churches, since 1998 known as the Toronto Airport Christian Fellowship, became a center of pilgrimage for a revival movement known as the "Toronto blessing" from 1994 onward. Wimber's influence on the Charismatic renewal in Britain was enormous. His laid-back style of promoting "power evangelism" was widely accepted by older churches, especially evangelical Anglican ones. The churches of Holy Trinity, Brompton (HTB, under Sandy Millar) and St. Andrew's, Chorleywood (Bishop David Pytches) became centers of the new renewal in the mid-1980s. The rapidly expanding and interdenominational Alpha evangelism program at HTB commenced in 1990 under Millar's associate and successor Nicky Gumbel and has opened up many non-Charismatic churches to the area of spiritual gifts. By 2011, more than 7,000 British churches of all varieties were running Alpha courses, and 33,500 courses are offered in 163 countries worldwide.[22]

The most direct impact of the fall of Communism has been in former Soviet and Soviet bloc countries, where the repressive policies of government toward pentecostals have been taken over by religious agencies. Some of the new churches emerging since the collapse of Communism have succeeded in attracting large crowds to their services and number their membership in the thousands. One of the reasons for the relative success of these new charismatic groups is their openness to the forces of globalization. They look "modern" in sharp contrast with the tendency toward self-isolation and puritanical dress codes that still characterize many of the older Eastern European pentecostal groups after many years of repression. For younger people growing up in a secular society, older churches look strangely irrelevant. As the Latvian scholar Valdis Teraudkalns observed:

> Most Classical Pentecostals still live and worship in the context of painful memories of being ridiculed and persecuted. It has left a lasting impact on the ways in which people tend to act. Marginalization by force, in some cases, has turned into the process of marginalizing by choice.... However, there are positive signs of change.[23]

Although there has been more freedom for pentecostals in Central and Eastern Europe since the disintegration of Communism, there have also been challenges. Pentecostal expansion has met with stiff opposition. The role of resistance to Pentecostalism that characterized the Communist era has been taken up by both the newly emerging secular governments and especially by the dominant Orthodox Christianity. The latter has struggled to reestablish its hegemony in newly emerging secular democracies—and in some cases, like that of the post-Communist Russian Orthodox Church, it has been quite effective. The Forum 18 news service in Oslo, Norway, regularly documents the religious persecution of pentecostals and other minority religious groups in the former Soviet bloc under harsh Religion Laws. The worst cases are in the Central Asian states of Uzbekistan, Tajikistan, and Kazakhstan, where pentecostals and other religious groups are harassed by police and leaders are imprisoned. Several European governments like those of Serbia, Macedonia, and Belarus refuse to legalize pentecostal and other "non-traditional" churches. Here and in Russia itself, new churches have insurmountable difficulties getting planning permission to erect buildings. Some new pentecostal churches like the New Life Church, which operates throughout the former Soviet Union, have had services raided by police in Kazakhstan and Belarus. Recently, the government of Belarus has called "neo-Protestant sects" a threat to national security and has expelled any "foreign" workers, usually from other Eastern European nations.[24]

The flip side is that new pentecostal and charismatic groups with support from the West have entered former Communist countries with aggressive evangelistic techniques provoking opposition from Orthodox churches and national governments. The institutionalizing of those pentecostal denominations that had been forced to share their identity with evangelicals and Baptists, and the creation and expansion of pentecostal theological colleges has resulted in a more inward-looking pentecostal movement in some former Communist countries. The pentecostal churches in these countries were in danger of becoming dependent on North American pentecostals for theological education, although there are also signs of resistance to any such dependency. The situation is still in a state of flux, and the next few years will determine the direction that pentecostal Christianity will take in Eastern Europe. Most of Pentecostalism there, however, is largely independent of missionaries, and with the dynamic growth that is occurring in the region, the future still looks promising for European Pentecostalism. It may be that renewal stimulated by pentecostal and charismatic forms of Christianity will help rescue the Church as a whole from pending oblivion in this so-called post-Christian continent.

The Word of Faith

Quite different from the movements traced above is the Word of Faith movement, which originated in the American Bible Belt. In some parts of the majority world, especially in Nigeria and Brazil, this has become Pentecostalism's most prominent and controversial expression. Classical pentecostals have mostly distanced themselves from this and openly criticized its emphasis. Somewhat ironically, Word of Faith teaching is in continuity with the pentecostal healing evangelists who promoted the concept of faith as an active force bringing inevitable healing, success, and prosperity in all areas of life—a message greatly attractive in post-Depression America. The emphasis of the Word of Faith movement is now one of the most widely influential in world Pentecostalism and often characteristic of new churches in Africa, Asia, and Latin America. This is also sometimes known as the "faith message" and by its detractors as the "prosperity gospel" and the "health and wealth gospel." Some critics have tried to link the Word of Faith teaching with Positive Thinking, dualistic materialism, and nineteenth-century New Thought, but these arguments remain unsubstantiated. It is probably more helpful to see this movement developing out of Pentecostalism's healing emphasis, and as recently pointed out, greatly influenced by the Latter Rain movement. Its roots are found in the teaching of Essek W. Kenyon (1867–1948) concerning "the positive confession of the Word of God" and a "law of faith" working by predetermined divine principles. Although often read by pentecostals, Kenyon was only loosely connected to them, being an independent Baptist pastor based in Los Angeles and later in Seattle. He also taught that sickness was "spiritual," the work of Satan, and against God's will for a Christian. He espoused a dichotomous contrast between the written word "Logos" and the spoken word "Rhema," and between natural "Sense Knowledge" faith and spiritual "Revelation Knowledge" faith. The popular development of the movement after Kenyon was stimulated by the teachings of such evangelists as Branham and Roberts, contemporary televangelists, and the Charismatic movement in North America.[25]

But the main promoter of Kenyon's ideas from the late 1960s onward was Kenneth E. Hagin (1917–2003) in Tulsa, Oklahoma. Widely regarded as "father of the Faith Movement," Hagin was an AG pastor from 1939 to 1949, moved to Tulsa in 1966, and started the Rhema Bible Training Centre there in 1974, where he taught his faith gospel of health, wealth, and success. More than 40,000 students had graduated from Rhema by 2011 and have propagated this Word of Faith message internationally, and many millions of Hagin's books, videos, and tapes have been sold. Hagin's ministry is now run by his son, Kenneth W. Hagin. The older Hagin had imbibed—and in some cases plagiarized—Kenyon's teachings, supported by selective Bible quotations, that every Christian believer should be physically healthy and materially prosperous. This teaching begins with a belief in guaranteed healing through the atoning work of Christ. Hagin wrote that it is not enough to believe what the Bible says; the Bible must also be confessed, and that what a person says (confesses) is what will happen. A person should therefore positively confess his faith in healing even when the "symptoms" remain. Hagin's impact was enormous and reached many parts of the developing world where it was selectively used by newly emerging preachers as the basis for their fast-growing urban churches and corresponding successful financial enterprises. Hagin's influence may have even extended as far as to the Catholic El Shaddai movement in the Philippines, the Living Faith World Outreach in Nigeria, and the Universal Church of the Kingdom of God in Brazil, all of which are prominent propagators of different forms of a health and wealth gospel. Among Hagin's disciples are Kenneth Copeland (b.1937) of Fort Worth, Texas, the African American preacher Frederick Price (b.1932) of Crenshaw Christian Center in Los Angeles and, among many others, Ray McCauley (b.1949) of Rhema Ministries, one of the most influential Charismatic ministers in South Africa. The best-known American proponents of the Word of Faith now are Kenneth and Gloria Copeland, whose even more radical version of the Word of Faith is carried around the world with their *Voice of Victory* television and radio ministry, founded in 1968.[26]

The Word of Faith teaching, however, although a less developed form, has been part of Pentecostalism since its beginnings. Healing evangelists, especially Oral Roberts and T. L. Osborne, but also earlier John G. Lake and Maria Woodworth-Etter, are often quoted by Hagin and his followers. Copeland developed Hagin's teaching with a greater emphasis on financial prosperity and formulated "laws of prosperity" to be observed by those seeking health and wealth. Poverty is seen as a curse to be overcome through faith. Through "faith-force," believers regain their rightful divine authority over their circumstances. Hagin convened a meeting in 1999 to warn his disciples (including Copeland who was present) of the excesses of teaching prosperity, and stated that financial prosperity is not a sign of God's blessing. He published these views in one of his last publications:

> During my more than sixty-five years of ministry, I have often dealt with the issue of prosperity for believers, insistently emphasizing a balanced, scriptural approach. I have observed many teachings and practices that have both helped and hindered the Body of Christ. I have seen some faith men of God stay the course, and move accurately with the truth of the Word and the Spirit,...many others become side-tracked by extremism, ultimately shipwrecking their ministries and hurting and disillusioning many people in the process.[27]

Despite these warnings by the comparatively moderate Hagin, the practices of the prosperity preachers, particularly their lavish lifestyles, leave many questions. Many of them have exorbitant salaries, live in enormous mansions, own private jets and airfields, and have fleets of luxurious cars. TBN founders Paul and Jan Crouch, whose network promotes prosperity preachers, own thirty homes, a ranch, and a private jet. The Copelands live in a luxurious, heavily secured lakeside mansion of 18,000 square feet on 1,500 acres of land outside Dallas, Texas. Their ministry owns nine airplanes, and the Copelands are linked to an array of for-profit companies involved in livestock, aviation, real-estate development, and gas and oil wells. Copeland and fellow prosperity preachers Joyce Meyer, Creflo Dollar, Eddie Long, and healing evangelist Benny Hinn came under Senate investigation in 2007 regarding their tax-exempt status. Hinn and Meyer cooperated and were cleared. Copeland defiantly refused to comply with Senate demands for financial disclosure, insisting that his empire complies with the law, and declaring a "holy war" on the leader of the investigation, Senator Charles Grassley.[28]

Some faith teachers, like the first pentecostals, reject the use of medicine as evidence of a weak faith. Access to modern communications and globalization has resulted in the popularizing of the Word of Faith throughout the world. Some American televangelists propagate this teaching in Africa, some making regular visits and broadcasting their own programs there, curiously enabling them to bolster their own support at home. Many pentecostal preachers have propounded a modified form of prosperity teaching to suit their own contexts, and leading exponents include Singaporean Kong Hee, Nigerian David Oyedepo, Ghanaians Nicholas Duncan-Williams and Mensa Otabil, Ulf Ekman of Sweden, Edir Macedo of Brazil, and Hector Gimenez of Argentina. In Hungary, since the fall of Communism in 1989, a prosperity-oriented Faith Church led by Sàndor Nèmeth grew to some 5,000 members in Budapest in less than twenty years and opened branches in other Hungarian cities totaling some 40,000 members. But it would be a mistake to assume that prosperity is the only emphasis of all these preachers.

Many pentecostals, however, have rejected Word of Faith as inconsistent with a balanced view of healing in the Bible, including the AG, John Wimber, David Wilkerson, and Jimmy Swaggart. Among its most questionable features is the possibility that human faith is placed above the sovereignty and grace of God and becomes a condition for God's action. The strength of faith is measured by results; material and financial prosperity and health are sometimes seen as evidence of spirituality. Consequently, the positive and necessary role of suffering is often ignored. On the other hand, most pentecostals allege that the Bible is not silent on the question of material need and the enjoyment of God *and* God's gifts. For them, salvation means a restoration of wholeness to human life, in which people have communion with God and blessings from God that seem to include provision for human need. But this is nowhere portrayed in the Bible as an irreversible law of cause and effect, as most Word of Faith teachers allege. Yet one of the reasons for the emergence of Pentecostalism in the majority world was that many people there saw existing Christian missions as being exclusively concerned with the "not yet" and the salvation of the soul in the life hereafter; little was done for the pressing needs of the present life, the "here and now" challenges to be addressed by pentecostals. The emergence of the Word of Faith and its popularity in the developing world may well have something to do with this.[29]

9

Preachers and Entrepreneurs

The Fivefold Gospel of Yonggi Cho

The impressive growth of Pentecostalism in the majority world was partly attributable to its enterprising, entrepreneurial local preachers and leaders. The most remarkable growth of a single congregation took place under the ministry of David (earlier, Paul) Yonggi Cho (b. 1936) and his future mother-in-law Jashil Choi (1915–89). This has parallels to the Word of Faith movement discussed previously but with important contextual differences. In the aftermath of the devastating Korean War, Choi began a tent church in a slum area of Seoul in 1958 with five members and Cho as its pastor. In four years this congregation grew to 800 and in 1964 erected a building with seating for 2,000 in the Seodaemun district of Seoul. In 1969 Cho bought property on Yoido, an island on the Han River that is now the business and government center of Seoul. He dedicated a new 10,000-seat auditorium there in 1973, and the Full Gospel Central Church received international attention. The growth of Pentecostalism in Korea became virtually synonymous with the ministry of Cho. By 2000 the Korean Full Gospel (AG) churches had overtaken the Methodists as the second largest Protestant denomination with over a million members. The majority of these were in the Yoido congregation and its satellites, which had become Yoido Full Gospel Church (YFGC) in 1984. Cho became the second chairman of the World Assemblies of God Fellowship in 1992, and YFGC planted churches all over Korea, in Japan, and internationally. By 1993 YFGC reported 700,000 members under 700 pastors and was the largest Christian congregation in the world. When the Full Gospel Church joined the Korean National Council of Churches in 1999, the occasion was the first time any national Assemblies of God organization had entered an ecumenical council. The AG has divided into at least three warring factions, but the largest group consists of those churches associated with YFGC. Cho retired in 2008 and his position as senior pastor was taken by his long-time disciple Young Hoon Lee, who had an earned doctorate from Temple University, Philadelphia. The church began reorganizing, and after granting independence to its many satellite congregations, the number of members of YFGC dropped to less than a quarter of its previous size.[1]

For pentecostals in different parts of the world, the "freedom in the Spirit" allows them to formulate, often unconsciously, ideologies that have meaning for people in different life situations, and Cho's ministry is a leading example. Pentecostalism is inherently prone to contextualization: the vibrancy, enthusiasm, spontaneity, and spirituality for which pentecostals are so well known and their willingness to address problems of sickness, poverty, unemployment, loneliness, evil spirits, and sorcery has directly contributed to this growth. As we have seen, the idea of a self-supporting, self-governing, and self-propagating church has been an important feature of pentecostal missions. "Contextualization" assumes that Christianity is shaped by its particular context and must be so shaped to be meaningful. It relates the Christian message to all social contexts and cultures, especially those undergoing rapid change. Christianity in general and Pentecostalism in particular had taken on a distinctive form in Korea, quite different from that found in the West. Observers who have tried to emphasize the "American" nature of Pentecostalism throughout the world or the "Americanization" of Christianity in Korea and elsewhere often miss the fact that creative innovations and the selective transformation of foreign symbols are constantly occurring. Quite naturally, a synthesizing process takes place as new forms of Christianity like Pentecostalism interact with older religions like Korean shamanism and Buddhism.[2]

The prayer mountain movement in Korea began in the 1950s and set aside mountains as retreats where Christians gather to pray, both individually and collectively. There are hundreds of Christian prayer retreats all over South Korea, including the prayer mountain of YFGC near the border with North Korea. Mountains as places of spiritual retreat and pilgrimage have been a characteristic of Korean religions for centuries. Beliefs in the mountain as the place to which God descends are not only part of Korean tradition but are also ideas fully at home in the Old Testament. Buddhist temples are usually built on mountainsides, and Korean cemeteries are found on hills outside residential areas. The many mountains of Korea were believed to be places where good spirits lived and where both shamans and ordinary pilgrims would receive power from the particular spirit on each mountain. The prayer mountain movement may be said to be a culturally relevant form of Christian practice that reflects the ancient spirituality of Korean people. Similarly, Korean people suffering from their accumulated grief or *han* seek healing and "blessings" from shamans to alleviate their deep pain, such as in the years following the Korean War or during the International Monetary Fund crisis in Asia in 1997–98, where South Korea was the country most affected by the economic meltdown. A prominent part of Cho's message that Korean people readily accepted proclaimed that God brings "blessings" and healings.[3]

Some scholars suggest that Korean pentecostals in general and YFGC in particular have succeeded because they have combined Christianity with shamanism. Korean Pentecostalism should be interpreted from the categories of a shamanistic culture rather than from historical and theological categories imposed from outside. This idea of a link between Korean Pentecostalism and shamanism has been assumed and perpetuated by Westerners. As Harvey Cox contends, "primal spirituality [is] now surfacing in Korea...[and] underlies the original biblical faith as well," the main reason for the growth of Pentecostalism in Korea and in other countries of the world. However, the "link" with shamanism should be assessed in a quite different way. It is more appropriate to consider Cho's Pentecostalism as a contextual form of Korean Christianity *interacting with* shamanism, for Korean pentecostals justify their practices of healing and doctrine of blessings by referring to the Bible as their prime source. Cho's reaction to shamanism and his teachings on healing and "threefold blessings" are better viewed within the context of his contact with international Pentecostalism, and must be assessed not only within the internal cultural and religious context of Korea, but also in light of the external influence of globalization. Western scholars may not have reflected enough on the enormous difference between interacting with shamanism (as Korean pentecostals obviously do) and *becoming* shamanistic. The latter is an untenable position for pentecostals; Cho himself clearly rejects traditional shamanism and says that shamans "serve demons."[4]

Consideration must be given to whether Cho's message has adapted to and transformed its cultural and religious environment. Clearly, Cho himself has wanted to be seen in these terms, although he does not use the word "contextual":

Being a Korean and having been saved out of the Buddhist religion, I have been able to appreciate the distinctive position of

Christians who come from the Third World.... We evangelical Korean Christians have developed our own traditions. This is very important because it makes it possible for us to be Christian without being less Korean. In the past, missionaries not only brought their religion but also their culture to the countries they evangelized. So it became apparent that the new converts lost much of their natural heritage. I believe that this produced an unnecessary hindrance to the acceptance of the gospel of Jesus Christ.[5]

Nevertheless, Cho does not advocate uncritical use of Korean cultural principles. This is especially apparent in his "revolutionary" use of women leaders. Despite the "male-oriented" Korean culture, Cho took these steps because "God showed me." The success of Cho's Pentecostalism should be seen as a response to the influence of the worldview of shamanism that permeates and underlies Korean society. Both Korean Pentecostalism and older Korean religions acknowledge and respond to the world of spirits, as Korean pentecostal scholars have pointed out. Shamanism provides a fertile ground into which the "full gospel" is more easily planted. If pentecostal pastors like Cho sometimes appear to be functioning as "shamans," it is because they respond to needs arising from a shamanistic world; but, like pentecostals all over the world, they emphatically deny any mixture with traditional religions. Similarly, the dominant conservative Protestant Christianity, with its strict moral law, finds fertile ground in peoples whose cultures are heavily influenced by Confucianism—as is clearly the case in Korean and Chinese societies. Cho often refers to the Confucian background of Korea in a favorable light, and usually points out that Confucianism is not a religion but an ethical system observed by Koreans.[6]

Cho's many writings and sermons demonstrate, first, that his "contextual theology" is born in Korean suffering, and second, that Cho has advocated a "pentecostal theology" that is standard classical pentecostal theology worldwide, influenced by healing evangelists like Oral Roberts and years of working with North American Pentecostals. Cho is uncompromising and polemical with regard to the religious background of Korea: his former experience as a "devout Buddhist" could not help him solve his problems, he considered it foreign to the compassion of Christ, and he had known only what he calls "well-organized and sterile Buddhist philosophies and rituals," which were "theoretically very profound," but which he refers to as "heathenism" and "doctrines of devils." Zen Buddhism in particular is singled out for critical treatment, and Cho compares and contrasts it with Holy Spirit "Fourth-Dimensional Christianity." But at the same time, Cho's concept of the "fourth dimension" is linked to his familiarity with Eastern religions with their own miraculous powers. He refers to the "evil spirit world" in this "fourth dimension" that is "under the power and authority of almighty God." Although these ideas have brought serious criticism from evangelical polemicists, Cho carefully maintains the distinction between the Asian religious world and the Christian revelation. But his experience of this Asian religious spirituality and its element of the miraculous has brought him to the understanding of the "fourth dimension," where visions and dreams are the language and "incubation" or "pregnancy" is the process through which believers receive their requests from God. This "incubation" in the "fourth dimension," he declares, is also the way that miracles happen in other religions. This particular teaching can only be understood by reference to the Asian pluralistic religious background in which Koreans are immersed.[7]

While Korean pentecostal scholars appreciate the importance of the ancient religious system to Pentecostalism, they also point out its dangers. The 1950s, when Cho was converted from Buddhism to Christianity and the Full Gospel Central Church was founded in the slums of Seoul, was a traumatic time. That trauma was a very significant part of Cho's message and the foundation of the theology he developed. He refers to the sufferings created by the Japanese occupation and the Korean War, and his own personal poverty and gradual healing from tuberculosis. This was a time when many were "struggling for existence," when he identified himself with the hundreds of refugees on the streets and became "one of the hopeless" himself. In the aftermath of the Korean War, when people lost families and businesses, had mental breakdowns, and became "completely possessed by the devil," his ministry began in a poverty-stricken area where people were not interested in a message about heaven and hell in their daily struggle for survival. His teaching on healing was closely related to this rampant poverty and sickness. His teaching on blessings and prosperity was his "theological counteraction" to the *han* (accumulated grief) caused by the ravages of the Korean War. For Cho, the message of Christ and the power of the Holy Spirit gave hope to a suffering and destitute community.[8]

His views on poverty are clear, again determined by his context:

Poverty is a curse from Satan. God desires that all His people prosper and be healthy as their soul prospers (3 John 1:2). Yet much of the world has not really seen poverty as I have seen it. Especially in the Third World, people live their lives in despair, struggling to survive for one more day. I am from the Third World. I know first-hand what it is not to have anything to eat.[9]

Elsewhere he writes that it is because of his "oppressed background" that he has been able "to understand the plight of many oppressed people who have no hope for a future." Cho's views on poverty and prosperity come out of his own Korean context. But Cho is also influenced by North American Pentecostalism and is arguably the most influential minister in the AG during the twentieth century. He was trained in the denomination's Bible school in Seoul, where he received his own experience of "baptism of the Spirit." Even though he may be regarded in many ways as a theological innovator (one of the reasons his books have been so popular), his theology is unmistakably classical pentecostal. He stresses the importance of being "filled with the Holy Spirit" and speaking in tongues. Cho sees this as an experience subsequent to and distinct from regeneration or conversion, and distinguishes between speaking in tongues as a "sign" and as a "gift." Like many pentecostals, for him, speaking or praying in tongues is very important. Cho distinguishes between being "filled with" and having "fellowship with" the Spirit, between speaking in tongues and being filled with the Spirit, as the latter results in people having an "overflowing blessing" to share with others. The fellowship with the Holy Spirit for every believer is an important emphasis, and perhaps one of the many theological innovations that tends to give Cho's theology a pneumatological rather than Christological center. The Holy Spirit is the "Senior Partner" in his ministry, and Cho says that intimacy or communion with the Holy Spirit is "the greatest experience" of his life. Cho's understanding of evangelism is also pentecostal, motivated by and completely dependent upon the enabling of the Spirit. His preaching is based on the goodness of God, the redemption of Christ, and biblical "principles of success," so that meeting the personal needs of people is his priority above theology, history, and politics.[10]

Cho's teaching on sickness and emphasis on healing is also pentecostal; physical healing is seen as part of Christ's redemption; sickness is "from the devil" and a "curse"; and all people can be healed. There can be little doubt that healing was probably the strongest feature of his appeal. However, Cho's emphasis on healing did not emerge only from pentecostal sources, for it was already prominent in the revival movements within

Korean Presbyterianism, the dominant Protestant group. The healing Presbyterian preacher Kim Ik Du was particularly effective in drawing large crowds to his mass services in the 1920s and 1930s, where there were claims of 10,000 healed from all sorts of illness and delivered from demons. Cho and other popular Korean preachers from the 1960s onward continued in this tradition. Like most pentecostal preachers, Cho makes extensive use of personal experience or "testimony" to illustrate his theology. This is particularly noticeable on the subject of healing, as Cho often refers to his own sicknesses and healing, and gives testimonies of people healed during his ministry to them. Cho makes much of the experience of being "born again" and all his books have a strong soteriological and Christocentric tone. This holistic view of salvation is one of the reasons the pentecostal message has spread rapidly among people in need. Cho even espouses premillennial eschatology complete with end-time apocalyptic predictions about the union of Europe, the revival of Israel, and anti-Communist rhetoric. In all these emphases, Cho is probably influenced by the ideology of the AG.[11]

Another innovation in Cho's teaching is the addition of "threefold blessings" to the fourfold gospel of Jesus the Savior, Healer, Baptizer with the Holy Spirit, and Soon Coming King, making it a "fivefold" gospel. A passage Cho quotes often, a favorite with American "prosperity preachers," is 3 John 2: "Beloved, I pray that in all respects you may prosper and be in good health, just as your soul prospers." Cho's message of threefold blessings emerged in the midst of poverty and destitution after the Korean War, and this was to become the foundation of all his preaching and ministry thereafter. The way to receive the threefold blessings is to believe that God is a "good God" and that salvation includes forgiveness of sins, health, and prosperity, intended to bring "overflowing blessings" to those outsiders in contact with believers. The "threefold blessings" doctrine is the most emphasized in all Cho's writings. The official brochure of YFGC states that the "fivefold message of the Gospel" includes (1) renewal, or "salvation," expressed in classical pentecostal terms; (2) the fullness of the Spirit; (3) healing, one of the main emphases of Cho's ministry; (4) blessing, Cho's addition to the "fourfold" gospel, which is declared to be "an abundant life of blessing which would be enough to share with others"; and (5) the Second Coming of Christ. The "threefold blessings of salvation" are further explained to include "soul prosperity," "prosperity in all things," and "a healthy life," based on 3 John 2. Although this is a clear promise of health and prosperity for believers, Cho writes that happiness does not come from "mere material gain," but from "solutions to our deep, inner problems," and he condemns those who think that happiness comes from power and wealth.[12]

Cho's theology is also Christocentric, focusing on Jesus Christ and his redemptive work as Savior from sin, sickness, demon possession, poverty, and trouble of every kind. For Cho, "prosperity" cannot be an end in itself, for God blesses his people only so that they may meet the needs of the poor and the needy. Keeping up with the modernization of Korea that occurred from the 1980s onward, Cho adapted to the changing context and also attracted the emerging middle class with his message of overcoming success in all circumstances, including business ventures. Yet Cho condemns modern Western culture with its rapid pace, pleasure-loving activities, and entertainment-centered churches. These things, he declares, hinder people and churches from having "the full blessings of the Lord," because people need time for prayer ("waiting upon the Lord"), worship, and the preaching of God's Word, the emphases of Cho's services. He says that many "traditional churches" in the West have "forgotten the vitality of Christianity and have become dead and sterile." Pentecostalism has been a world-denying movement that saw the churches of the day as dry, formal, and lifeless, needing to be restored by experiencing the power of God. Some passages in Cho's writings are very hard to swallow, such as his teaching that in the kingdom of God there is no poverty.[13]

Those who censure Korean pentecostals for their alleged "shamanism" often fail to see that the practices thought to parallel ancient religions are also found in the biblical record. These pentecostals define their healing and deliverance practices by reference to the Bible rather than to shamanism and see their activities as creative adaptations to the local context. At the same time, pentecostals might need a greater appreciation for the diversity of their cultural and religious past. Demonizing this past does not explain the present attraction of Pentecostalism for peoples deeply influenced by their ancient religions and cultures, even though such a demonization might help in the religious competition that is a feature of pluralist societies. Many pentecostals have found both cultural and biblical alternatives to and adaptations from the practices of their ancient religions and seek to provide answers to the needs inherent in their own context. It is the ability to make these adaptations that has transformed world Christianity in the last century. Healing was the major attraction of Pentecostalism in various parts of the world; and miracles, exorcisms, and "power encounters" became standard pentecostal practices. But these practices did not occur in a vacuum—in most of the world they were conditioned by a context of poverty, marginalization, and despair. These were reasons for the appeal of teachings relating to healing and prosperity in the global South, but there were obviously corresponding dangers.

The 1990s were the decade of the "cell church" in Pentecostalism worldwide, as a direct result of Cho's pioneering work in the 1970s, and that of Lawrence Kwang in Singapore and the writings of Ralph Neighbour Jr. in the 1980s. The "cell church" strategy with its emphasis on the home cell group as the focus of pastoral care, discipleship, and evangelism is now widely used in pentecostal churches. Cho was one of the first pentecostals to use the cell system to provide care and leadership for what was the world's largest congregation, making use of thousands of women to lead small groups of church members in relation to both the local community and the church leadership structure. This method is particularly effective in maintaining cohesion in mega-churches.[14]

Cho has been criticized as being unconcerned with social change and structures of oppression, but his church has extensive social care programs and has been involved in national relief and economic aid for North Korea. This has not received sufficient attention with the controversies about Cho; as Young-gi Hong points out, "Cho's social ministry does not draw proper recognition compared to its contribution." Although Minjung theology, a form of Korean liberation theology, has espoused the concerns of the poor and oppressed, it is pentecostal churches like YFGC to which the poor and oppressed have flocked for relief. Ig-Jin Kim has pointed out that the social ethics of Korean Pentecostalism's "fivefold gospel" is characterized by its transformative nature, so as to transform society. This transformation and participation in the wider society takes many forms, including "relief activities, the saving of souls, the establishing of facilities for social welfare, and the shaping of public opinion through mass media." The social activities of the Yoido church are extensive and obvious to any casual observer. During my visit to the church in 2002, a cyclone had hit the eastern coast of South Korea causing widespread devastation. Some of the church service that Sunday morning was taken up with Cho describing the relief efforts that were initiated by the church and for which blankets, food, and other relief had been provided by church members.[15]

As far back as 1982, the church instituted a "Sharing Campaign," which manages the ongoing distribution of members' offerings in cash and kind to support an orphanage, a home for senior citizens, slum relief, and provincial churches, low-income households, and a leprosarium, among other ventures. The Elim Welfare Town was begun in 1986 for destitute children and the elderly poor. The church has become well known for the free heart disease operations it finances for needy children in other Asian countries as well as in Korea, both North and South, and over 4,000 children had received surgery under this scheme by 2007. The Full Gospel Medical Center was founded in 2003 and, with more than a thousand voluntary medical personnel among its members, YFGC is carrying out a systematic medical service for the city of Seoul. The church also runs paper recycling, clothing relief, and disaster relief programs. Since 1991, the "Bread of Grace Sharing Campaign" has provided relief for those suffering from hunger, disease, and war all over the world, in Bangladesh, Mongolia, Vietnam, Cambodia, Mozambique, Kenya, Ethiopia, and Somalia, and has sent medical supplies to Guatemala and Chile. In 2008 a Heart Centre in Pyongyang, North Korea was built by the church. A charity established by the church in 1999 called "Good People World Family," has extensive projects internationally, providing food for needy children in North Korea and China, a hospital, a college for asylum seekers, free ophthalmic clinics including cataract operations, food and medical services for the poor in Seoul's inner city, and an urban ecological educational park on the banks of the river Han. In addition, various relief, educational, and medical projects are supported by this charity in the Philippines, Indonesia, Vietnam, Sri Lanka, Bangladesh, Afghanistan, and among refugees suffering from the conflict in the Middle East. Cho entered the mass media industry with "Invitation to Happiness," the first Christian television program in Korea, and the first and only Christian daily newspaper, the *Kookmin Daily News*, in 1998. This paper offers a Christian perspective on all aspects of Korean society and is a leading supporter of Christian outreach by charitable activities. The church now uses satellite and Internet broadcasts for its services and messages. Upon his formal retirement in 2008 as senior pastor of YFGC, Cho's emphasis shifted significantly from an involvement of his church in charitable acts to a commitment of himself and his personal resources to an ongoing social ministry. Cho's ministry among the poor, the opportunities he has given to women leaders, and the social activities of YFGC demonstrate the potential within Pentecostalism to be a force for social transformation.[16]

Charismatic Churches in Africa

In the 1970s, independent pentecostal churches began to emerge all over Africa, but especially in Nigeria and Ghana, where they permeate every facet of society and are strikingly obvious to every visitor. Many of these vigorous churches were influenced by the Charismatic renewal in the North, the Word of Faith movement, and by established classical pentecostal churches in Africa like the Assemblies of God. Largely independent of foreign churches, many of these new churches arose in the context of interdenominational evangelical campus and school Christian organizations, from which young charismatic leaders emerged with significant followings. Most notably commencing in the Scripture Union and the Christian Union in universities and colleges, these groups later became "fellowships" that grew into full-blown denominations often led by former lecturers and teachers. At first they were termed "nondenominational," but as they expanded they developed denominational structures, "episcopized" prominent leaders, and became international churches. They initially tended to appeal to a younger, more educated, and consequently more Westernized clientele, including young professionals and middle-class urbanites. In leadership structures, theology, and liturgy, these new organizations differ quite markedly from the older churches, including pentecostal ones. Their services are usually emotional and enthusiastic, featuring electronic musical instruments. They publish their own literature, have a prominent media focus, and run their own Bible training centers for preachers (both men and women) to further propagate their message. Many of these churches encourage the planting of new, independent congregations, and make use of schoolrooms, cinemas, community halls, and hotel conference rooms for their meetings. Church leaders travel across the continent and beyond, and some produce glossy booklets and broadcast radio and television programs. They are often linked to wider international networks of independent Charismatic preachers but are by no means dominated by North Americans.[7]

The new movement has its own momentum in Africa, where hundreds of preachers propagate a gospel of success in impoverished cities. The promotion of the Word of Faith message in Africa has resulted in the rapid growth of a form of Christianity that has appealed especially to the new urbanized generation of Africans. The new Charismatic churches throughout Africa often focus on success and prosperity but share an emphasis on the power of the Spirit with older pentecostals, including many African independent churches. Like classical pentecostals, they teach a personal conversion experience (being "born again"); they advocate long periods of individual and communal prayer, including fasting and prayer retreats, prayer for healing and for individualized problems like unemployment and poverty, deliverance from demons and "the occult" (this term often means traditional beliefs and witchcraft); and they support the use of spiritual gifts like speaking in tongues and prophecy. To a lesser or greater degree, these features characterize all these churches, which are also found throughout Asia, Latin America, and the Caribbean. In Africa they are essentially a local initiative, churches instituted by Africans for Africans and almost entirely self-governing, self-propagating, and self-supporting. They seldom have organizational links with any foreign church or denomination, even when they are part of an international network. They try to address the problems faced by Africans, particularly by offering a radical reorientation toward modern, industrial, global society. This new expression of Pentecostalism echoes the popular method of tent evangelism pioneered by North Americans in the 1940s and 1950s and continued with considerable effect by popular South African evangelists Nicholas Bhengu and Richard Ngidi, and later by Nigerian Benson Idahosa and German evangelist Reinhard Bonnke. Bonnke has had the greatest impact on these African churches with his Christ for All Nations mass evangelism meetings (given the unfortunate misnomer "crusades"). With crowds of hundreds of thousands in daily attendance, Nigeria has seen the most of Bonnke and his American successor Daniel Kolenda, who now runs most of the mass meetings. Nigeria, the most populous nation in Africa, has one of the most remarkable pentecostal success stories in the world in recent times. Bonnke is reported to have preached to 6 million Nigerians in Lagos on his return to the country in 2000 after a ten-year ban by a Muslim-dominated Nigerian government for preaching to over a million people in a Muslim stronghold. Kalu observes that the "competing fundamentalisms" and demonization of Islam by Nigerian pentecostals has caused great harm and hindered conflict resolution in this troubled country.[18]

But in southern Nigeria and Ghana, new pentecostal churches, some of which have international profiles, abound in almost every neighborhood. One of the first and most influential new churches in Africa was the Church of God Mission International of Benson Idahosa (1938–98), founded in 1972. The church had its headquarters in Benin City, where a "Miracle Center" seating over 10,000 was erected in 1975. Thousands flocked there every week. Idahosa, who became one of the best-known preachers in Africa, briefly attended the Christ for the Nations Institute in 1971, an independent pentecostal college in Dallas, Texas. His stay there was short-lived, however, and he returned to Nigeria after three months with an increased "burden" for his people. He began the first of many mass evangelistic campaigns for which he was well known and worked closely with Bonnke during the latter's first mass meetings in Nigeria. Idahosa received considerable financial support from well-known independent pentecostal preachers in the United States, including his mentor, Gordon Lindsay, the healing evangelist T. L. Osborne, and soon-to-be-jailed televangelist Jim Bakker. Idahosa's church ran the All Nations for Christ Bible Institute, the most popular and influential Bible school in West Africa at the time, from which hundreds of preachers went out into different parts of the region, often to plant new churches. Idahosa became "bishop" in 1981 and later "archbishop," titles now used by scores of new church leaders, most without theological qualifications. Idahosa had informal ties with other new churches throughout Africa—especially in Ghana, where he held his first campaign in 1978. As seen in an earlier chapter, after Idahosa's death in 1998, his wife Margaret Idahosa, who had shared ministry and leadership with her husband since the church began, took his place as head and bishop of the Church of God Mission— later its archbishop. At the time, the church had 300,000 members.[19]

One of the Nigerian movements, Deeper Life Bible Church, with branches all over Africa and on other continents, had over half a million members in Nigeria only ten years after its founding in 1982 and had become the leading new Nigerian pentecostal denomination. Unlike many of its contemporaries, this is a church with a strict "holiness" rather than a "prosperity" emphasis. William Folorunso Kumuyi (b.1941) was a former education lecturer at the University of Lagos and an Anglican who became a pentecostal in the Apostolic Faith Church. In 1973 he began a weekly interdenominational Bible study group, Deeper Christian Life Ministry, that spread to other parts of Nigeria. The Apostolic Faith expelled him in 1975—possibly for preaching without ordination—and Kumuyi began holding retreats at Easter and Christmas, emphasizing healing and miracles and living a holy life. His followers distributed thousands of free tracts, evangelized, and established Bible study groups all over southwestern Nigeria. The first Sunday service held by Deeper Life was in Lagos in 1982, and the following year Kumuyi sent some of his leading pastors to Yonggi Cho's church in Seoul, after which a system of "house fellowships" based on the Korean model was instituted. There were 15,000 such fellowships by the end of 1983. Deeper Life emphasizes personal holiness evidenced by rejection of the "world" and the keeping of a strict ethical code—probably evidence of its strong Apostolic Faith roots. The church prides itself in being a wholly African church totally independent of Western links, and here it differs from those churches that regularly promote Western televangelists.[20]

The most prominent Nigerian pentecostal church in the twenty-first century is the Redeemed Christian Church of God (RCCG) led by Enock A. Adeboye (b. 1942), who is a respected leader in Nigerian Christianity and also a former university lecturer with a PhD in mathematics. Founded by Josiah O. Akindayomi (1909–80), the RCCG was an ethnic Yoruba church that had seceded from the Aladura movement Cherubim and Seraphim in 1958. When Akindayomi died in 1980, Adeboye was his designated successor. Adeboye transformed the small Yoruba denomination into a new, multiethnic church that by 2011 was the largest in Nigeria, with meetings in the "Redemption Camp" headquarters that draw more than half a million people every month. The church has spread worldwide wherever Nigerians have migrated and has established large networks of congregations in North America and Britain. In London, the church has some of the largest congregations in the country, including Jesus House in North London. Another prominent Nigerian denomination was started in 1981 by David Oyedepo, a trained architect. Since 2000 this denomination has erected a 50,000 seat auditorium called Faith Tabernacle that is one of the largest church buildings in the world, in an impressive complex of modern buildings at the 300 acre "Canaan Land." The church has also founded Covenant University and an elite private secondary school on the same premises. Oyedepo, later called Presiding Bishop of Living Faith World Outreach Center, is thought to be Nigeria's richest preacher, with more than 300 congregations in Nigeria commonly called "Winner's Chapels" and more than 400 pastors in forty African nations in 2011.[21]

Other prominent Nigerian examples among many include the Mountain of Fire and Miracles Ministries founded in 1994 by Daniel Kolawole Olukoya, a medical scientist with a PhD from a British university; Christ Embassy of Chris Oyakhilome; the Household of God of Chris Okotie, three-time unsuccessful Nigerian presidential candidate; and the controversial Synagogue Church of All Nations of Temitope B. Joshua. Joshua had Zambia's president Frederick Chiluba as his special guest in November 2000, is a personal friend of Ghanaian president Atta Mills, and is widely recognized for his healing powers in other parts of Africa—but in Nigeria his practices are regarded with some suspicion. In 1986 the Pentecostal Fellowship of Nigeria (PFN) was formed, an ecumenical association incorporating all the various "born again" movements and one of the most influential ecumenical organizations in Nigeria. In 1995, Adeboye was president of the PFN, considered the most powerful voice in the national Christian Association of Nigeria of which it is a part. In 1991, more than 700 churches were registered as members of PFN in Lagos State alone. The PFN sees one of its main tasks as uniting Christians against the perceived danger of the "Islamization" of Nigeria.[22]

Idahosa's 1978 evangelistic meetings in Accra resulted in the subsequent formation of the first independent Charismatic churches in Ghana. Bishop Nicholas Duncan-Williams, formerly a member of the Church of Pentecost, is leader of the earliest one, Christian Action Faith Ministries, founded in 1980. Trained at Idahosa's Bible Institute, Duncan-Williams heads an association called the Council of Charismatic Ministers. Fraternization between the new churches and the Rawlings government in Ghana led to a new church-state alliance, particularly as Duncan-Williams became virtually national chaplain to the regime. The largest Ghanaian Charismatic church is the International Central Gospel Church founded in 1984 by former Anglican Mensa Otabil, probably the Ghanaian Charismatic leader who is best known outside Ghana. Otabil also heads an umbrella organization called Charismatic Ministries Network and in 2000 opened a Christian university, Central University College. Otabil became well known for his brand of black consciousness and preaching that takes him to different parts of Africa. Other leading churches in Ghana include one that took a stand against the Rawlings government, the Lighthouse Chapel International of Dag Heward-Mills (a former medical doctor), the Holy Fire Ministries of Bishop Ofori Twumasi, the Royal House Chapel (formerly International Bible Worship Centre) of Sam Korankye-Ankrah, Victory Bible Church of Nii Tackie-Yarboi, and Fountain Gate Chapel (formerly Broken Yoke Foundation) of Eastwood Anaba. The last is an organization active in the remote and largely rural northeast region of Ghana. The new churches in Ghana also make extensive use of home groups to effectively manage pastoral care.[23]

These Charismatic churches have spread to several other West African countries, including Liberia and Côte d'Ivoire. Bethel World Outreach, founded in 1986 in Monrovia, is another example of the "prosperity" type of church popular in African cities, and in Abidjan a large church organization led by Dion Robert, Église Protestante Baptiste Oeuvres et Mission Internationales, claimed over 70,000 members in 1995 and is based on a well-structured home group system. In May 2011 the church was attacked by the new Côte d'Ivoire government because of its perceived support of the previous Gbagbo regime.[24]

During the 1980s, rapidly growing new Charismatic groups began to emerge in East Africa, where they were sometimes seen as a threat by older churches from whom they often gained members. Some of these new churches were directly affected by Nigerians and Ghanaians, as Idahosa, Oyedepo, Duncan-Williams, and Otabil have traveled extensively in Africa. One of the fastest growing churches in Kenya is the Winners Chapel in Nairobi, which dedicated a building in 1998 for its 3,500-member congregation after only one year of existence. The media advertising hype for the dedication service in Nairobi gushed, "Winners Chapel, Nairobi was built entirely debt free. No loans of bank borrowing and certainly no begging trips to the West!" Winners Chapel in Nairobi was founded by Dayo Olutayo, who was sent from Oyedepo's church in Nigeria. Olutayo had arrived in Kenya in 1995 and in 2011 another Nigerian, David Adeoye had become the senior pastor. By this time the denomination had expanded rapidly, with some seventy branches throughout Kenya.[25]

Uganda, dominated by Catholic and Anglican missions over the past century, has been fertile ground for new churches since its emergence from repressive dictatorships in the late 1980s. Paul Gifford speaks of "homegrown pentecostal churches...mushrooming in luxuriant fashion" in Uganda. Three of the largest in Kampala are the Watoto Church (formerly Kampala Pentecostal Church), an English-language church founded by a white Zimbabwean, Gary Skinner in 1983, with 20,000 members; Namirembe Christian Fellowship founded by Simeon Kayiwa, a preacher known for his healing and miracle ministry; and the Christian Life Church founded by Jackson Senyonga. The new churches in East Africa follow the emphasis of the East African Revival of a personal experience of God through being "born again," to which they add the pentecostal emphasis on the power of the Spirit manifested in healing, speaking in tongues, prophecy, and deliverance from demons, manifestations that the East African Revival later discouraged. It was this that brought tension with the inheritors of the Revival legacy, the Anglicans, and added to the impetus behind the new churches. In Malawi, young preachers in Blantyre in the 1970s propagated a "born again" message in their revival meetings that at first did not always result in the formation of new churches, but by the 1980s the pattern elsewhere in Africa was emerging and the revival meetings had developed into "ministries" and "fellowships," and inevitably some were further institutionalized into new churches. One of the largest of these was the Living Water Church founded by Stanley Ndovie in 1985. As elsewhere, these Malawian movements focused on young people in schools, colleges, and universities. President Frederick Chiluba (1943–2011), a "born again" Christian with a pentecostal experience, declared Zambia a "Christian nation" two months after his landslide election victory in 1991. He appointed "born again" Christians to government posts, and regularly promoted pentecostal evangelistic campaigns and conventions, where he is sometimes featured as a preacher. His vice-president Godfrey Miyanda attended a pentecostal church, the Jesus Worship Center led by Ernest Chelelwa. Pentecostal churches are now in abundance in Zambia and the charismatic movement has split some "mainline" churches. A leading preacher in the 1990s who since entered political and diplomatic service, Nevers Mumba, founded Victory Faith Ministries in 1985 and is another product of Christ for the Nations Institute in Dallas.[26]

One of the largest denominations in Zimbabwe is the Zimbabwe Assemblies of God Africa (popularly called Zaoga, pronounced "za-oh-ja"), a church with roots in South African Pentecostalism. Zaoga was born in urban areas of Zimbabwe and is led by Archbishop Ezekiel Guti (b.1923). In 1959, Guti and a group of young African pastors were expelled from the Apostolic Faith Mission of South Africa (AFM) after a disagreement with white missionaries. The group joined the South African Assemblies of God of Nicholas Bhengu but separated in 1967 to form the Assemblies of God, Africa (later Zaoga). Guti went to Christ for the Nations Institute in 1971 just as Idahosa had done, and he too received financial and other resources from the United States. But Guti resists any attempts to identify his church with the "religious right" in the United States or to be controlled by "neo-colonial" interests. In a very pertinent development in 1986, leaders of twelve of the largest pentecostal churches in Zimbabwe, including Guti, wrote a "blistering rebuttal" to a right-wing attack on the Zimbabwean state by a North American Charismatic preacher. Since 1986, Zaoga has also begun churches in Britain, Zimbabwean missionaries went to South Africa to plant churches there in 1989, and the church also has branches in seventeen other African countries called "Forward in Faith." Zaoga is a fully fledged denomination with complex administrative structures headed by Guti. By 2011 it claimed to have over 2 million members, which if true (and the figure is much disputed) makes it the largest denomination in Zimbabwe after the Roman Catholics. Guti's leadership style and expensive overseas trips were contentious issues, as were the lifestyles of some of his more powerful pastors; also, the links between Zaoga and the Mugabe government have been contentious. The denomination has experienced various splits, one of the earliest led by Guti's co-founder, Abel Sande. There are several other large pentecostal churches with branches throughout Zimbabwe, such as the Family of God founded by Andrew Wutawunashe and the Glad Tidings Fellowship of Richmond Chiudza.[27]

One of the largest single Christian congregations in South Africa is the Grace Bible Church led by Mosa Sono in Soweto, with over 10,000 members in 2010. This church has planted new congregations in some major urban areas, including a poverty-stricken informal settlement area. Sono, born in Soweto in 1961, grew up in the Dutch Reformed Church and attended the AFM Bible college in Soshanguve before leaving to attend white charismatic leader Ray McCauley's Rhema Bible Training Centre near Johannesburg. He formed Grace Bible Church in 1984; in 1996 he became vice-president of the International Federation of Christian Churches, the formerly white-dominated and largest association of charismatic churches in Southern Africa, whose honorary president is McCauley. Sono is now executive chairman of this organization. McCauley's original inspiration and training came from Kenneth Hagin, but in spite of this association, Sono is more cautious and has repeatedly sought to distance himself from prosperity teaching and Western, white domination, his stance having had a positive influence on McCauley.[28]

In the closing years of South African apartheid, I researched the participation of pentecostals and members of African independent churches in political affairs. The African National Congress, a party with socialist leanings, would have won a free election there at the time of this survey in 1990–91, and Nelson Mandela was the most popular political leader—the 1994 elections would bear this out. It was mistakenly thought that pentecostals were "apolitical" or even "anti-political," but this was not true even among white pentecostals in South Africa, who were often among the most politically conservative, sometimes overtly supporting white supremacy organizations. The political awareness among African pentecostals did not differ perceptibly from that of the overall population: 43 percent of pentecostals would have voted for Nelson Mandela and the ANC in 1991, compared to 47 percent of the survey respondents. There was no clearly discernible pattern linking one or another church with a particular political stance. Some pentecostals were concerned at the seeming lack of political awareness in their church, and especially among their pastors.

One member felt that Christians should involve themselves in political affairs so that a just government could be established based on the laws of God. Most believed that Christians alone had the answers to bring peace and security to the land, and the ANC was the best government to bring this about. If they stuck to the principles of the 1912 Freedom Charter then the country would be in safe hands. Pentecostals felt that by allowing Christians to participate in political activity, the church was thereby able to exert its influence on the world.

A number of pentecostals are involved formally in South African politics. One of the most prominent is Kenneth Meshoe (b. 1954), who has been a member of the South African Parliament since the elections of 1994 and is president of the African Christian Democratic Party. This party polled enough votes in the 1999 elections to gain seven members in the proportionate representation parliament. Meshoe also pastors the Hope of Glory Tabernacle and was an evangelist in Bonnke's Christ for All Nations (CfAN) organization for ten years. The director general of the Office of the President under former president Thabo Mbeki, Frank Chikane (b. 1951), is an AFM pastor who became vice-president of the AFM and later president of the AFM International. Chikane remains a person of considerable influence in South Africa and is well placed to speak on behalf of South Africa's large Christian constituency. Since the fall of Mbeki in 2008, his strong influence with the ruling ANC hierarchy has declined, but he continues personal contact with church leaders and politicians across the board. He has the unique distinction of having been general secretary of the South African Council of Churches during apartheid's final years, the only pentecostal to have occupied that position.[29]

Asamoah-Gyadu thinks that one of the basic differences between the older African churches and the new ones lies in the "the democratisation of charisma"—that in the older "spiritual" churches "members are the clients of the prophets who may be the custodians of powers to overcome the ills of life," but in the new churches "each believer is empowered through the baptism of the Holy Spirit to overcome them." This might be somewhat idealistic, for in the spiritual churches, too, provision is made for any person to become a prophet and therefore to be a custodian of spiritual power. Some of the new churches certainly do move in the direction of single, dominant leaders who are custodians of power—the difference is disappearing with the passing of time. Methods employed by the new churches to propagate their faith are very similar to those used by other pentecostals, but a particular feature of African churches is an emphasis on deliverance from a whole host of demonic forces, most of which are identified with traditional deities and "ancestral curses." Access to modern communications has resulted in the popularization of independent pentecostal "televangelists" from the West, several of whom make regular visits to Africa and broadcast their own television programs there. The strategies employed by these new churches are subject to criticism and leave many ethical questions, but have promoted a form of Christianity that has appealed especially to urban African youth. [30]

The phenomenon of growing pentecostal churches indicates that there are unresolved questions facing the church, such as the role of "success" and "prosperity" in God's economy; enjoying God's gifts, including healing and material provision; and the holistic dimension of "salvation now." Many African pentecostals see financial success and prosperity as evidence of the blessing of God and the reward for faith in difficult financial circumstances. However, this "prosperity" is also seen as the means for advancing the work of God and for the ability to give generously to the needy. The "here-and-now" problems being addressed by these churches are problems that still challenge the church as a whole. [31]

One Nigerian preacher in the United States put it like this:

We live in rather difficult times; dreams are constantly being dashed against the rocks of adversity. People desperately need to know that things will get better.... We preach that there is hope for tomorrow beyond yesterday's failure.... We preach that miracles still happen! God still fixes shattered lives. Often, the only thing that prevents a suicide from taking place is one word of hope or comfort. This message of hope transcends race, culture, class and creed. Everybody needs hope. A church that preaches a message that gives people hope, encouragement and healing will never lack for attendance. [32]

The remarkable global growth of Pentecostalism in the midst of incredible economic, political, and natural adversity in Africa, and the corresponding decline in membership among older churches means that there might be something that pentecostals are doing from which other Christians can learn. What is happening in Africa is happening throughout the majority world, with new pentecostal mega-churches springing up wherever large cities and relative religious freedom are to be found.

Charismatic Churches in India

Pentecostalism is now found all over India. Its controversial growth in North India's Hindu heartlands in the latter part of the twentieth century has come about largely through the work of South Indians, some of whom have attracted Western funding but not control. Scores of graduates from South Indian pentecostal theological colleges are sent out annually to plant churches in North India. Not all independent churches are pentecostal and founded by South Indians. One of the most prominent ones, simply called the Assemblies, was founded by Bakht Singh (1903–2000), a Sikh from Punjab whose impact was greatest in Tamilnadu and Andhra Pradesh, where he established his headquarters. Bhakt Singh was clearly not pentecostal but was a prominent evangelical leader who for six decades engaged in aggressive evangelism, prayer for healing and deliverance, and church planting. There are several recent examples of Indian evangelicals causing concern for Hindu extremists as the rate of conversion rises. Some Indian websites try to expose these organizations, one questioning the "efficacy of the pernicious and enormously well-funded missions to proselytise the marginalised sections of Indians"—referring to the propensity of these new churches to convert so-called Tribals and Dalits. The Believers' Church, founded by K. P. Johannan in 1993 and now with episcopal governance, started fifteen years earlier as a pentecostal missionary society called Gospel for Asia. This organization has expanded rapidly and runs Bible Colleges across India training preachers to plant churches.[33]

In Udaipur, Rajasthan, the Filadelfia Fellowship Church of India (FFCI) runs the Filadelfia Bible College, with some 120 students and staff with PhDs in theology from British universities. FFCI was founded by Thomas Mathews (1944–2005) in Kerala, where his parents, who were of Syrian Christian background, had become members of the IPC. It is now the largest pentecostal church in Rajasthan. After a dramatic rescue from drowning, Mathews attended a four-month course at Shalom Bible School in Kottayam, where he met a pioneering IPC missionary to Rajasthan, K. V. Philip (c.1935–79), who impressed on Mathews the needs of this state considered backward and hostile to Christianity. In 1963, at the age of nineteen, he left Kerala to be an independent missionary in Rajasthan, confronting an unfamiliar culture and language. Although there had been pentecostals in this state before the 1960s and K. E. Abraham had preached there in 1944, South Indians advanced the growth of Pentecostalism significantly. After K. V. Philip, Mathews was the second South Indian pentecostal missionary to settle there permanently. Both Philip and Mathews had attended the IPC's Shalom Bible School and worked together initially, at first holding meetings in Banaswara. Philip, who arrived in 1960, moved to Jodhpur and founded an IPC congregation. Mathews married Mary, a student of K. E. Abraham, in Kerala in 1966 and they established an independent congregation in Udaipur called the Rajasthan Pentecostal Church. In 1977 they started a press to print Bible studies and devotional books in Hindi, and a regular magazine called *Cross & Crown*. By this time there were several outlying village congregations associated with the Udaipur church, and in 1979 Mathews founded the Native Missionary Movement. The Filadelfia Bible College started in Songadh, Gujarat, in 1981, moving to Udaipur the following year and into a new, much larger property in 1985; this structure now also houses a secondary school and (following the purchase of an adjacent property) a primary school. All these projects were financed on a shoestring budget "by faith" with the help of Indian believers and Indians who had migrated to the West. Mathews himself completed a PhD in English literature at Mohanlal Sukhadia University, Udaipur, writing a thesis on John Milton. By 2000, FFCI had about 750 congregations in ten states of India, the great majority of members being Tribals (especially Bhils). Although Thomas Mathews died prematurely five years later, the denomination was well organized and continued to grow. By 2011 there were an estimated 1,400 congregations with over 300,000 members in sixteen Indian states as well as Bhutan and Nepal. Various community projects including orphanages, schools, medical clinics, and vocational training facilities were established in places where FFCI operated. In November 2009, I attended FFCI's annual Navapur Convention in rural Maharashtra, one of the largest gatherings of Christians in North India, where some 30,000 local people, pastors, and college students had assembled for a week of preaching, prayer, and worship. About forty college graduates were commissioned there, most to establish new congregations throughout North India.[34]

I have attempted to steer a path through a maze of enterprising personalities and events that have transformed the shape of contemporary Christianity. Most countries of the world have been affected profoundly by this explosion of Charismatic Christianity. The only exceptions are in those mainly Islamic countries with religious monopolies where religion and state exist in alliance, and in the few remaining vestiges of atheistic Communism—but even here, China is en route to having the most evangelical and pentecostal Christians in the world and may already have them. The patterns established by the new churches in Africa, Asia, and Latin America have become paradigmatic of Pentecostalism in the twenty-first century. Charismatic Christianity today is full of religious entrepreneurs who, like their predecessors in early Pentecostalism, are on a mission to take their message to as many people as possible. They declare a call from God and have an uncanny ability to communicate with and in some cases, manipulate crowds of people. These preachers are stage actors par excellence. Their message of hope and faith attracts the crowds who give of their substance and enable the enterprise to succeed; in countries like Nigeria, Charismatic leaders are among the wealthiest people in the nation. The successive "waves" of revivalist movements where new "moves" and revelations of the Spirit are promoted and where new charismatic preachers and religious entrepreneurs emerge are seemingly unstoppable.

Conclusions

The Growth of Pentecostalism

The global South has seen a remarkable expansion of pentecostal forms of Christianity in the last century, an expansion that has altered global religious demographics considerably. In Latin America, Africa, and Asia, many large urban mega-churches have arisen, and much of the rapid growth in Chinese Christianity has come among those who have a pentecostal inclination. The internationalizing of the Charismatic movement in the 1960s and 1970s began to erode the isolation of indigenous independent churches in the global South, but these changes had already been brewing for decades. Rapid improvements in communications and travel brought the outside world closer to hitherto isolated communities. With new nation-states created out of former colonies came resistance to foreign cultural symbols, including Western hegemony in ecclesiastical affairs.

Nowhere was this more apparent than in China after 1949, but the entire majority world was affected. As we have seen, China developed its own forms of Christianity without recourse to the outside world. Although we may describe much of this as affected by Pentecostalism, applying this nomenclature to Chinese indigenous churches indiscriminately is as inappropriate as it is in the cases of Spirit churches in sub-Saharan Africa. India, with its closer ties to the West, has more claim on the title "pentecostal" for many of its independent churches, but even this must be qualified. Latin America, with more than a century of independence, had its own momentum; and there Pentecostalism took a different turn, although not unaffected by what was happening in the North. Nevertheless, large denominations that eschewed contact with the United States emerged there from the mid-1950s onward, sometimes referred to as the second phase of Pentecostalism in Latin America, following the first denominations founded by foreigners. The Philippines, with its centuries of majority Catholicism, presented a somewhat similar situation, and indigenous leaders emerged to form new movements making a considerable impact on the religious scene. At the same time, the massive Catholic Charismatic Renewal in Brazil, the Philippines, and India helped stem the flow of Catholics into pentecostal churches.

Independent pentecostal churches have proliferated worldwide. Those formed in the first half of the twentieth century and birthed in indigenous revival movements were the thin end of the wedge. They expanded rapidly and formed their own traditions, remaining isolated from mainstream Christianity for decades. For the most part, classical Pentecostalism distanced itself from them. Western pentecostal missionaries saw them as a threat or nuisance at best, or as heretics at worst—especially in the case of more heterodox movements like the True Jesus Church and the Zion Christian Church. Their hostility was passed on to the national churches that emerged from their work, and that hostility was reciprocated. Increasingly, complex and multifarious networks of new independent churches have mushroomed in recent years, making them possibly the largest grouping within Pentecostalism as a whole. The recent history of Pentecostalism is littered with "revival" movements causing schisms that have become its defining feature.

Facts and figures on the growth of any global religious movement are notoriously difficult to come by, yet statistics on the growth of Pentecostalism are exultingly quoted, especially by classical pentecostals. The most frequently quoted ones are those of Barrett and Johnson, who estimated that Pentecostalism had some 614 million adherents in 2010, a quarter of the world's Christian population, which they projected would rise to almost 800 million by 2025. This figure was placed at only 67 million in 1970, and this enormous increase has coincided with Europe's secularization zenith. North America started earlier and made steady progress in the course of the twentieth century, but classical Pentecostalism there, while influential, is not as significant as is sometimes claimed. A survey conducted by the Pew Forum on Religion and Public Life in 2007 on religious affiliation in the United States found that pentecostals (including black pentecostals) were 4 percent of the total population. This constituted part of the 26 percent classified as "Evangelical Protestant Churches," compared to 18 percent called "Mainline Protestant Churches," and 24 percent Catholic. Of course, this 4 percent only refers to classical pentecostal denominations. The largest older Protestant denominations, the various Baptists and Methodists, had 17 percent and 6 percent, respectively. With

16 percent of US Americans now declaring themselves unaffiliated to any religious faith and with Catholic numbers growing, the United States is on the verge of losing its Protestant majority.[1]

The other northern continent is very different. Europe retains significant remnants of state churches: Catholic, Orthodox, Protestant, and Anglican. Although pentecostals have made modest increases in Europe, they remain a very small minority—less than 2 percent of the overall population in all European countries except Portugal, where Pentecostalism was influenced by the vibrant Brazilian variety. They are more significant as a proportion of the European churchgoing population. We do not know how many people transfer into pentecostal churches from older churches or have dual allegiance, as is the case in Latin America and in Europe. David Martin takes issue with the common secularization theories in explaining the "exceptionalism" of Europe and suggests that Pentecostalism is less likely to succeed in the developed world because it "represents the mobilization of a minority of people at the varied margins of that world, whereas in the developing world it represents the mobilization of large masses." He thinks that Pentecostalism flourishes in the United States because of its well-established Protestant pluralism and voluntarism, and that in Europe, Pentecostalism does not do as well where there is a strong state church—unless there is more religious plurality with a significant minority of free churches, as is the case in Romania and Ukraine, where the numbers of classical pentecostals are greater than in any other European nation.[2]

In fact, the dramatic growth in what are now termed "Renewalists" is best explained by reference to the three majority world continents. There are indeed many reasons for the emergence and growth of Pentecostalism in the majority world, and any attempt on my part to enumerate these runs the risk of reductionism. But I will try to highlight some of the major ones. Pentecostalism is an "ends of the earth" form of Christian mission with a transnational orientation based on personal enterprise, the ubiquitous voluntarism of its membership, and the constant multiplication of multi-centered, variegated organizations whose primary purpose is to evangelize and spread their influence worldwide. These constant efforts to expand and proselytize are underpinned by a firm belief in the Bible as an independent source of authority, one that resonates with local customs and relates better to a spiritual and holistic worldview—and by theological convictions based on a common experience of the Spirit who empowers believers' mission to the world. The personal conversion of individuals is the goal of these efforts. To their credit, pentecostal missionaries, themselves

largely untrained and uneducated, practiced "indigenous church" principles. They quickly found and trained thousands of local leaders, who took
the "full gospel" much further than the foreign missionaries had done.
This swift transfer to local leadership was unprecedented in the history of
Christianity, and pentecostal churches became indigenous and "three-self"
(self-governing, self-supporting, and self-propagating) before the older
missions had even begun the process.

The histories recounted here demonstrate that contemporary
Pentecostalism is the product of a long process of development with precedents going back to a much earlier time. Its history was in continuity
with the revivalist movements out of which it emerged. Its mission was
to liberate very ordinary people from colonial and ecclesiastical hegemony
and (at least originally) to free women from male patriarchy. It encouraged free enterprise in a global religious market. The revival movements
challenged Western hegemony and created a multitude of new indigenous churches—a type of Christianity in local idiom that was a cultural
protest movement, but was also bound to include emphases on power
to overcome an evil spirit world and manifestations of the miraculous.
Pentecostalism addressed allegations of both the foreignness and the
irrelevance of Christianity in pluralistic societies. With its emphasis on
the priesthood of all true believers, it broke down barriers of race, gender,
and class, and challenged the exclusive preserves of ordained male, foreign clergy. Of course, this development included multiple schisms that,
while increasing division, also proliferated local leadership and encouraged religious competition.

What is often not appreciated is the extent to which Pentecostalism
takes on distinctive forms in different contexts. One of the main reasons for the growth of Pentecostalism has been its ability to adapt itself
to different cultures and societies and give contextualized expressions to
Christianity. These are expressed in its energetic and energizing worship
and liturgies, in its music and dance, in its prayer with the free use of the
emotions, and in its communities of concerned and committed believers. Pentecostals are becoming more socially aware and active in efforts to
relieve poverty and disease. Of all Christian expressions, Pentecostalism
has an ability to transpose itself into local cultures and religions effortlessly because of its primary emphases on the experience of the Spirit and
the spiritual calling of leaders who do not have to be formally educated in
church dogma. This often leads to schism, but also assists multiplication.
In particular, the ministry of healing and the claims of the miraculous

have assisted Pentecostalism in its appeal to a world where supernatural events are taken for granted.

Some of the features of Pentecostalism that have made it attractive have been discussed here. Pentecostalism developed its own characteristics and identities in different parts of the world without losing its transnational connections. The widespread use of mass media, the setting up of new networks that often incorporate the word "international" in their titles, frequent conferences with international speakers that reinforce transnationalism, and the growth of churches that provide total environments for members—these are all features of this multidimensional Pentecostalism, which promotes this global meta-culture constantly. The opening up of what was formerly a closed world after the fall of the Iron Curtain and the post-1980 reforms in China rapidly accelerated the expansion of this transnational movement. Although sociopolitical and historical factors undoubtedly had a role in the spread of pentecostal Christianity, religious and ideological factors were probably more significant. The ability of Pentecostalism to adapt to and fulfill people's religious aspirations continues to be its strength. A belief in a divine encounter and the involvement or breaking through of the sacred into the mundane, including healing from sickness, deliverance from hostile evil forces, and perhaps above all, a heady and spontaneous spirituality that refuses to separate "spiritual" from "physical" or "sacred" from "secular" are all important factors in Pentecostalism's growth. It has been able to tap into ancient religious traditions with one eye on the changing world of modernity. This combination of the old with the new has enabled it to attract people who relate to both these worlds. With its offer of the power of the Spirit to all regardless of education, language, race, class, or gender, Pentecostalism has been a movement on a mission to subvert convention. Unlike older forms of Christian mission, its methods were not so dependent on Western specialists and trained clergy and the transmission of Western forms of Christian liturgy and leadership. In fact, Pentecostalism in its earliest forms broke down the dichotomy between clergy and laity that was the legacy of older churches. The author of *The Secular City*, Harvey Cox, in his 1995 book *Fire from Heaven*, reversed his well-known position on secularization and wrote of Pentecostalism as a manifestation of the "unanticipated reappearance of primal spirituality in our time" that would reshape religion in the twenty-first century.[3]

A book of this nature can only look at some of the many aspects of Pentecostalism worldwide. There are several important themes that I have not fully explored, such as the most recent forms of independent noncon-formity, the function of mega-churches, and the mass market, including the use of media, technologies, and networking. Research must still be done on areas that have only been hinted at here: the power of free asso-ciation and personal and local agency, the role and nature of the church in Pentecostalism, its leadership patterns, its structural and anti-struc-tural permutations, church authority, governance, and the ways in which leadership patterns change over time. Pentecostals and environmental concerns, the changes affecting established institutions and structures, Pentecostalism as liberation and an option for the poor, pentecostals involved in various types of social and public engagement—all these areas deserve more attention than I have given them. Much work has already been done in the area of the migration of pentecostals from the South to the North in recent years, and I have touched only briefly on this sub-ject. The extent to which globalization and migration in the late twentieth century have affected Pentecostalism is something that requires a much more careful analysis. The shapes of the new Pentecostalisms that have emerged as a result of the globalization process, how they differ from the older networks of denominational Pentecostalism, and what the features of this global shift of center to the South means for Pentecostalism have yet to be precisely described. There is a certain tension between the global and the local in Pentecostalism, and often the local character overshadows globalizing forces that might seek uniformity. Another area that needs further investigation is the extent to which Pentecostalism has perme-ated and affected the beliefs, values, and practices of other Christians. Only when these investigations have taken place will we be better able to understand those external forces that forge the religious identities of people in our contemporary societies and the increasingly important role of Pentecostalism in this pluralistic world. Many questions will remain unanswered, and indeed, some questions will not have answers.

Present Prospects

It can no longer be said without qualification that there are now over 600 million "Pentecostals" worldwide. When considering what diverse and mutually independent movements are included in the statistics, any attempt at definition will fall short of precision, and Pentecostalism can probably never be defined adequately. Only about a quarter of this figure consists of classical pentecostals, those with direct or indirect historical links to the Azusa Street revival in Los Angeles. But some 150 million classical pentecostals worldwide after only a century is still impressive. If we add the many independent churches with pentecostal orientation, plus the Charismatic churches and renewal movements within older churches, then we have a clearer picture of its magnitude. It is no accident that the southward shift in Christianity's center of gravity over the twentieth century has coincided with the emergence and expansion of Pentecostalism. Over three-quarters of pentecostal adherents live in the majority world. Worldwide the number of Christians has doubled in forty years, from 1.1 billion in 1970 to 2.2 billion in 2010. In Africa, it was estimated that Christians exceeded Muslims for the first time in 1985, and Christians are now almost the majority—a phenomenon so epoch-making that Lamin Sanneh describes it as "a continental shift of historic proportions." There are now over four times as many Christians in Africa as there were in 1970 and almost the same is true in Asia, while the Christian population of Latin America over this period has almost doubled. Of course, some of this has to do with differentials in population growth; but it remains true that much of the global growth of Christianity has occurred through conversion in the global South, where the influence of Pentecostalism is strongest. In contrast, the Christian population of Europe during the same period has increased only by about a quarter, and that of North America by about a third. The decrease in the percentage of world Christianity in the global North is likely to continue. But even if the statistics are wildly speculative, the fact that this movement had only a handful of adherents at the beginning of the twentieth century makes its growth an astounding development. Although this growth has reversed in some more developed countries like South Korea and among Anglos in the United States, there is no sign that the rate worldwide has slowed down, and in places like sub-Saharan Africa, China, Central America, and India it may still be increasing. But even in the former countries, many pentecostals haven't left the faith altogether but have simply transferred to other Christian groups.[4]

A 2006 Pew Forum report (admittedly focused on urban populations) estimated that classical pentecostals formed 20 percent of the population in Guatemala, 15 percent in Brazil (the largest population of pentecostals in any country), and 9 percent in Chile. Impressive also are the figures in the African countries of Kenya (33 percent), Nigeria (18 percent), and South Africa (10 percent). With Charismatics and independent churches added in, the figures increase considerably and what they have termed

"Renewalists" approximate half the national populations in Guatemala (60 percent), Brazil (49 percent), Kenya (56 percent), and the Philippines (44 percent). In these countries Pentecostalism in all its various forms is not only a significant proportion of Christianity but also a sizable chunk of the entire population with enormous sociopolitical clout. Its adherents are often on the cutting edge of the encounter with people of other faiths, albeit sometimes confrontationally so. These confrontations play out in places like Nigeria and India where other religions form majorities, and this conflict, which has already claimed many lives, is in danger of escalating. Because of its tendency to proselytize, Pentecostalism also finds itself in conflict with other Christians in their traditional strongholds, such as with the Orthodox in Eastern Europe, Catholics in Latin America and the Philippines, and the (Coptic) Orthodox in Ethiopia and Eritrea.[5]

Proponents of the secularization thesis have to reckon with the fact that the future of global Christianity is affected by this seismic change in its character. In his latest work on secularization, David Martin makes the point that secularization is a process that is neither inevitable nor undisputed and is subject to differentiation within different social spheres. This social differentiation, where religious and other cultural monopolies are broken, is determined by historical contexts and actually promotes religious competition and plurality in certain societies while favoring secularization in others. The historical factors producing social differentiation must be taken into account, because these push secularization in different directions. For these reasons, secularization varies enormously in different social groups. Martin considers that the grand meta-narrative of secularization might be "an ideological and philosophical imposition *on* history rather than an inference *from* history." The growth of Pentecostalism in Latin America is an example of the effects of social differentiation, where the dominant Catholic Church was no longer seen as the binding glue of society, especially among the poorer classes. Its monopoly was broken and consequently, Latin American societies became more pluralistic. The same is true of Buddhism in Korea and China, Hinduism among India's oppressed classes, and Orthodoxy in Ukraine. As one consequence, Pentecostalism has thrived.[6]

The rise of the Charismatic movement in the Western world certainly made pentecostal ideas and practices more acceptable to traditional forms of Christianity. But this might also be seen as one result of the privatization of religion beginning in the 1960s, when the established churches no longer held monopoly and authority over all things sacred. It could be argued that Charismatic Christianity provided a panacea for the spiritual deficit in organized religion and in Western society as a whole. Or, as Harvey Cox has put it, not only were people disillusioned with traditional religions in the 1960s, but also disappointed by "the bright promises of science and progress." Cox remarks that the "kernel of truth" in the "overblown claims" of the "death of God" theologians was that "the abstract deity of Western theologies and philosophical systems had come to the end of its run." For Cox, the dramatic growth of Pentecostalism seemed to confirm rather than contradict what he had written about the "death of God" in *The Secular City* three decades earlier, but it had provided an unanticipated and unwanted solution.[7]

After the 1980s, the "Pentecostalization" of older churches outside the Western world, especially in Africa and Asia, accelerated as these churches adjusted to the rapid growth of new pentecostal churches in their midst. They began to adopt their methods, particularly appealing to the young and urbanized. Simultaneously, the new form of Pentecostalism exhibited a fierce independence that eschewed denominations and preferred associations in loose "fellowships." This gave rise to the pentecostal mega-churches that operate in cities like Lagos, Rio de Janeiro, Seoul, and Singapore, but also in unexpected European places like Kyiv (a Ukrainian church with a Nigerian leader), Budapest, and Uppsala. Each of these European cases is the largest congregation in its respective country; and in London the largest congregation is a predominantly Nigerian one. The mega-churches form networks of similar churches across the world, and these transnational associations are not only North-South, but also South-South and East-South. In most cases, these transnational churches in the North have been unable to break free from their ethnic minority character.[8]

It is neither wise nor possible to predict the future of Pentecostalism, but a sense of where Pentecostalism has been in the past century will give an inkling of where it might go in the present one. Contemporary Pentecostalism is very much the result of the process of globalization, and "health and wealth" advocates are as much at home in Lagos and Rio as they are in Tulsa or Fort Worth. In many cases, the only ones who get rich in poverty-ravaged countries are the preachers. The mass media, beginning with the use of periodicals and newsletters, followed by a ready acceptance of new technologies—first radio and then television and Internet—tourism and pilgrimages to mega-churches, ubiquitous voluntarism, and an international economy, combined to create conditions conducive to the spread of a globally friendly religion like Pentecostalism. This manifested itself in many different ways. Some of the networks have begun to take on the appearance of new denominations. Some have passed to a second generation of leadership whose organizational ideas were quite different from those of the founders. Some of the new churches leave much to be desired—especially those with wealthy leaders whose questionable and exploitative practices continue to be debated in public forums.

The adaptability of Pentecostalism to a culture is more easily achieved in those parts of the world where a spiritual universe exists and healing and the supernatural are regarded as "normal" experiences. Pentecostalism also grows where a pluralistic religious environment is the norm. This makes pentecostal forms of Christianity more amenable to the United States than to Germany or France. But, of course, the principle of social differentiation means that there will always be groups for whom Pentecostalism is an attractive religious option, even in those countries where voluntarism, pluralism, and freedom of association are limited. China watchers and Chinese scholars themselves observe that the burgeoning new Christian movements there have many pentecostal features, so that China may soon eclipse Brazil as the country with the most pentecostals, but pentecostals of a very different kind who may not use the name "pentecostal" at all. The Christian world has become more interconnected than ever before; and increasingly pentecostals are having conversations with other Christians that are bringing them out of their largely self-imposed isolation. Whether this will result in more unity or more division and diversity is anyone's guess. It is certain that the continuous change and transformation in world Christianity will continue. But Pentecostalism in the majority world, as Philip Jenkins has observed about Christianity in the global South, does not represent a global religion with roots in the North, but a new type of Christianity altogether.[9]

Social scientific generalizations about the growth and future of religion are just that. We cannot avoid theological factors. The emphasis on a personal, heart-felt experience of God through the Spirit is offered to all people without preconditions, enabling them to be "powerful" and assertive in societies where they have been marginalized. They are offered solutions to their felt needs in all their varieties. This will continue to draw people in the majority world to pentecostal churches. When yours is an all-encompassing, omnipotent, and personal God who enters into a personal relationship with individual believers, everything becomes a matter for potential prayer. The "born-again" experience focusing on a radical break with the past attracts young people disenchanted with the ways of their parents. Pentecostalism's incessant evangelism, offering healing and deliverance, draws large crowds and its organized system of following up contacts means that more "unchurched" people are reached with this message and joined to pentecostal communities. Its cultural flexibility in its experiential and participatory liturgy, offering a place-to-feel-at-home, a measure of religious continuity with the past spirit world, and (at least to some observers) the appearance of an egalitarian community meeting the "felt needs" of ordinary people—all combine to provide an overarching explanation for the appeal of Pentecostalism and the transformation of Christianity in the majority world.[10]

Notes

INTRODUCTION

1. Hugh McLeod, "The Crisis of Christianity in the West: Entering a Post-Christian Era?" in Hugh McLeod (ed.), *The Cambridge History of Christianity: World Christianity c. 1914–c.2000* (Cambridge: Cambridge University Press, 2006): 323–47; Hugh McLeod, *The Religious Crisis of the 60s* (Oxford: Oxford University Press, 2010); Callum G. Brown, *The Death of Christian Britain* (London: Routledge, 2001). In this book, the nouns "Pentecostalism" and "Evangelicalism" will be capitalized while "pentecostal" and "evangelical" will be used as both nouns and adjectives.
2. Charles H. Gabriel, "Pentecostal Power," *Redemption Hymnal: With Tunes* (London: Assemblies of God Publishing House, 1955): no. 244; Todd M. Johnson, David B. Barrett, & Peter F. Crossing, "Christianity 2010: A View from the New Atlas of Global Christianity," *International Bulletin of Missionary Research* 34:1 (2010): 29–36, 36.
3. Lamin Sanneh, *Disciples of All Nations: Pillars of World Christianity* (New York: Oxford University Press, 2008): 275; Philip Jenkins, *The Next Christendom: The Coming of Global Christianity* (New York: Oxford University Press, 2007): 8–9; Robert Wuthnow, *Boundless Faith: The Global Outreach of American Churches* (Berkeley: University of California Press, 2010): 34–47.
4. Vinson Synan, *The Holiness-Pentecostal Tradition: Charismatic Movements in the Twentieth Century* (Grand Rapids: Eerdmans, 1997).
5. Johnson, Barrett, & Crossing, "Christianity 2010," 36.
6. Allan Anderson, "Varieties, Definitions and Taxonomies," in Allan Anderson, Michael Bergunder, André Droogers, & Cornelis van der Laan (eds.), *Studying Global Pentecostalism: Theories and Methods* (Berkeley: University of California Press, 2010): 13–29; Douglas Jacobsen, *Thinking in the Spirit: Theologies of the Early Pentecostal Movement* (Bloomington: Indiana University Press, 2003): 11–12.

7. Robert Mapes Anderson, *Vision of the Disinherited: The Making of American Pentecostalism* (Peabody, MA: Hendrickson, 1979).

CHAPTER 1

1. John Wolffe, *The Expansion of Evangelicalism: The Age of Wilberforce, More, Chalmers and Finney* (Downer's Grove, IL: IVP, 2007): 80–82; C. Gordon Strachan, *The Pentecostal Theology of Edward Irving* (London: Darton, Longman & Todd, 1973).

2. Gary B. McGee, *Miracles, Missions, and American Pentecostalism* (Maryknoll, NY: Orbis, 2010): 3–98; Marshall is quoted in McGee, *Miracles, Missions,* 8.

3. McGee, *Miracles, Missions,* 7–8, 24–25; David W. Bebbington, *The Dominance of Evangelicalism: The Age of Spurgeon and Moody* (Downer's Grove, IL: IVP, 2005): 107–8.

4. Allan Anderson, *Spreading Fires: The Missionary Nature of Early Pentecostalism* (London: SCM, 2007): 39, 40–42.

5. William K. Kay, *Pentecostalism* (London: SCM, 2009): 59; J. Edwin Orr, *Evangelical Awakenings in Southern Asia* (Minneapolis, MN: Bethany Fellowship, 1970): vii.

6. Minnie F. Abrams, *The Baptism of the Holy Ghost and Fire* (Kedgaon: Pandita Ramabai Mukti Mission, 1906): v.

7. *TF* 1:1 (January 1881): 1, 3–5; Jennifer A. Miskov, *Life on Wings: The Forgotten Life and Theology of Carrie Judd Montgomery (1858–1946)*, PhD thesis (University of Birmingham, 2011); Kimberley Ervin Alexander, *Pentecostal Healing: Models in Theology and Practice* (Blandford Forum, Dorset: Deo Publishing, 2006): 24–27, 151–60.

8. Anderson, *Spreading Fires,* 31–35.

9. David Martin, *On Secularization: Towards a Revised General Theory* (Aldershot, Hants: Ashgate, 2005): 144.

10. Stanley H. Frodsham, *"With Signs Following": The Story of the Latter-Day Pentecostal Revival* (Springfield, MO: Gospel Publishing House, 1926): 234; Anderson, *Spreading Fires,* 18–26; Morton Kelsey, *Tongue Speaking: The History and Meaning of Charismatic Experience* (New York: Crossroad, 1981): 52–59, 65–68.

11. G. H. Lang, *The History and Diaries of an Indian Christian* (London: Thinne, 1939): 193, 201–3. Later Lang wrote a booklet in opposition to the Pentecostal movement: G. H. Lang, *The Earlier Years of the Modern Tongues Movement* (Enfield, Middlesex: Metcalfe Collier, c.1946).

12. "Account of the Half Yearly Examination of the Male Seminary, July 6th & 7th 1826." Box 101, 2/0, 198/52–116. CMS Archives, University of Birmingham; Lang, *History and Diaries,* 16–21, 28, 30.

13. Quoted in Lang, *History and Diaries,* 32; emphases in original.

14. Lang, *Histories and Diaries,* 33, 91–92, 116, 147.

15. Wilbert Shenk, "Rufus Anderson and Henry Venn: A Special Relationship?" *International Bulletin of Missionary Research* 5:4 (October 1981): 161–72; Orr, *Southern Asia,* 58–59; Lang, *History and Diaries,* 140–41.

16. Lang, *History and Diaries,* 140–41.

17. Lang, *History and Diaries*, 186.
18. Quoted in Lang, *History and Diaries*, 143–45.
19. Lang, *History and Diaries*, 145–46.
20. Lang, *History and Diaries*, 154–55, 197–99.
21. Quoted in Lang, *History and Diaries*, 158–59.
22. From *The Bombay Guardian*, quoted in Lang, *History and Diaries*, 164.
23. Lang, *History and Diaries*, 163–65, 169–70, 177.
24. Quoted in Lang, *History and Diaries*, 178–79.
25. Lang, *History and Diaries*, 216–20; Orr, *Southern Asia*, 61–63; Edith L. Blumhofer, "Consuming Fire: Pandita Ramabai and the Early Pentecostal Impulse," in Roger E. Hedlund, Sebastian Kim, & Rajkumar Boaz Johnson (eds.), *Indian and Christian: The Life and Legacy of Pandita Ramabai* (Chennai: MIIS/CMS/ISPCK, 2011): 138.
26. *Conf* 1:1 (April 1908): 17; 1:2 (May 1908): 13; Barratt, *When the Fire Fell*, 1; Anderson, *Spreading Fires*, 85.
27. Adhav, *Pandita Ramabai*, 147. A fuller account of Ramabai's revival and its connections with Pentecostalism is given in Anderson, *Spreading Fires*, 77–103; see also Blumhofer, "Consuming Fire," 127–54; Allan Anderson, "'The Present World-Wide Revival... Brought Up in India': Pandita Ramabai and the Origins of Pentecostalism," in Roger E. Hedlund, Sebastian Kim, & Rajkumar Boaz Johnson (eds.), *Indian and Christian: The Life and Legacy of Pandita Ramabai* (Chennai: MIIS/CMS/ISPCK, 2011): 307–25; Gary F. McGee, "Minnie F. Abrams: Another Context, Another Founder," in James R. Goff & Grant Wacker (eds.), *Portraits of a Generation: Early Pentecostal Leaders* (Fayetteville: University of Arkansas Press, 2002): 87–104; Edith L. Blumhofer, "'From India's Coral Strand': Pandita Ramabai and U.S. Support for Foreign Missions," in Daniel H. Bays & Grant Wacker (eds.), *The Foreign Missionary Enterprise at Home: Explorations in North American Cultural History* (Tuscaloosa: University of Alabama Press, 2003): 152–70; *BM* 126 (1 February 1913): 1; *Mukti Prayer-Bell* (September 1907): 21–22; Meera Kosambi (ed. & trans.), *Pandita Ramabai Through Her Own Words: Selected Works* (New Delhi: Oxford University Press, 2000): 9–12, 181–244; Mary L. B. Fuller, *The Triumph of an Indian Widow: The Life of Pandita Ramabai* (New York: Christian Alliance, 1927): 30–35; Jessie H. Mair, *Bungalows in Heaven: The Story of Pandita Ramabai* (Kedgaon, India: Pandita Ramabai Mukti Mission, 2003): 87–88; Shamsundar Manohar Adhav, *Pandita Ramabai* (Madras: Christian Literature Society, 1979): 201–202.
28. Rajas K. Dongre & Josephine F. Patterson, *Pandita Ramabai: A Life of Faith and Prayer* (Madras: Christian Literature Society, 1963): 18, 24, 72–73; Fuller, *Triumph of an Indian Widow*, 41; Blumhofer, "From India's Coral Strand," 164.
29. Blumhofer, "From India's Coral Strand," 167; Adhav, *Pandita Ramabai*, 216; Helen Dyer, *Revival in India 1905–1906* (Akola: Alliance Publications, 1987): 29–30.
30. *LRE* 1:10 (July 1910): 8, 11; McGee, "Minnie F. Abrams," 93; Dongre & Patterson, *Pandita Ramabai*, 78; Kosambi, *Pandita Ramabai*, 320; Dyer, *Revival*

in India, 45; Padmini Sengupta, *Pandita Ramabai Saraswati: Her Life and Work* (London: Asia Publishing House, 1970): 287–88.

31. *WW* 28:4 (April 1906): 16; 28:5 (May 1906): 145; *Trust* 9:8 (October 1910): 12–13; Dyer, *Revival in India,* 40, 68; Adhav, *Pandita Ramabai,* 232.

32. *AF* 1:3 (November 1906): 1; cf. McGee, "Minnie F. Abrams," 97; Orr, *Southern Asia,* 118–27, 129, 135–43.

33. *The India Alliance* 6:4 (September 1906): 30.

34. *AF* 1:7 (April 1907): 2; later reprinted in *TF* 28:1 (January 1908): 14–16; Gary B. McGee, "'Latter Rain' Falling in the East: Early-Twentieth-Century Pentecostalism in India and the Debate over Speaking in Tongues," *Church History* 68:3 (1999): 648–65; Gary B. McGee, "The Calcutta Revival of 1907 and the Reformulation of Charles F. Parham's 'Bible Evidence' Doctrine," *Asian Journal of Pentecostal Studies* 6:1 (2003): 123–43; Abrams, *The Baptism,* 36.

35. Abrams, *The Baptism,* 41–42; *AF* 9 (June–September 1907): 1, 4; cf. *WW* 33:8 (August 1911): 247.

36. *Mukti Prayer-Bell* (September 1907): 17–21; *WW* 32:4 (April 1910): 138–41; Frodsham, *With Signs Following,* 131–34.

37. *AF* 1:12 (January 1908): 1; *Mukti Prayer-Bell* (September 1907): 3, 4, 6, 8; *Bombay Guardian and Banner of Asia* (7 November 1905): 9; *Trust* 9:8 (October 1910): 16; *Conf* 5:6 (June 1912): 142; Mair, *Bungalows in Heaven,* 76.

38. Barratt, *When the Fire Fell,* 167; *Conf* 1:6 (September 1908): 14, 16; *UR* 1:1 (June 1909): 6; *WW* 31:8 (August 1909): 169; *BM* 68 (15 August 1910): 2; 77 (1 January 1911): 4; *TF* 29:12 (December 1909): 288; *Pent* 2:4 (March 1910): 4; *LRE* 1:9 (June 1909): 10–13; 1:10 (July 1909): 6–13; 1:12 (September 1909): 3–9; 2:6 (March 1910): 13–18; 2:7 (April 1910): 12–15; 2:11 (August 1910): 6–12; Dongre & Patterson, *Pandita Ramabai,* 27–28; Kosambi, *Pandita Ramabai,* 12–13.

39. Bartleman, *Azusa Street,* 19, 90; McGee, "'Latter Rain' Falling," 650.

40. Abrams, *The Baptism; Pent* 2:11–12 (November–December 1910): 9; *LRE* 3:7 (April 1911): 19; *BM* 126 (1 February 1913): 1; Frodsham, *With Signs Following,* 175; Anderson, *Spreading Fires,* 90.

41. Quoted in Lian Xi, *Redeemed by Fire: The Rise of Popular Christianity in Modern China* (New Haven, CT: Yale University Press, 2010): 105.

42. Lian Xi, *Redeemed by Fire,* 28–31; Geraldine Taylor, *Pastor Hsi: A Struggle for Chinese Christianity* (Singapore: Overseas Missionary Fellowship, 1900, 1949, 1997): 164–65, 191; Daniel H. Bays, *A New History of Christianity in China* (Chichester, UK: Wiley-Blackwell, 2012): 82.

43. *LRE* 11:5 (February 1919): 20; *BM* 7 (1 February 1908): 1; *WW* 33:1 (January 1911): 27; Park, "Korean Pentecost," 192; Blair & Hunt, *Korean Pentecost,* 71, 75; Koo Dong Yun, "Pentecostalism from Below: *Minjung* Liberation and Asian Pentecostal Theology," in Veli-Matti Kärkkäinen (ed.), *The Spirit in the World: Emerging Pentecostal Theologies in Global Contexts* (Grand Rapids, MI:

Eerdmans, 2009): 89–114: 104; Sean C. Kim, "Reenchanted: Divine Healing in Korean Protestantism," in Candy Gunther Brown (ed.), *Global Pentecostal and Charismatic Healing* (Oxford: Oxford University Press, 2011): 274.

44. William Nesbitt Brewster, *A Modern Pentecost in South China* (Shanghai: Methodist Publishing House, 1909): 47; Xi, *Redeemed by Fire*, 87–89; Daniel H. Bays, "Christian Revival in China, 1900–1937," in Edith L. Blumhofer & Randall Balmer (eds.), *Modern Christian Revivals* (Urbana: University of Illinois Press, 1993):162–65; W. W. Simpson, "Contending for the Faith" (unpublished type-script, 1953): pp. 2–4; *Trust* 8:12 (February 1910): 2; *UR* 1:3 (August 1909): 5; *TF* 29:8 (August 1909): 181.

45. Sanneh, *Disciples of All Nations*, 193–204; Anderson, *Spreading Fires*, 162–65.

CHAPTER 2

1. Jean Comaroff, *Body of Power, Spirit of Resistance: The Culture and History of a South African People* (Chicago: University of Chicago Press, 1985): 165–68, 175–76, 191.

2. Adrian Hastings, *The Church in Africa 1450–1930* (Oxford: Clarendon, 1994): 530–31; Harold W. Turner, *Religious Innovation in Africa* (Boston: G. K. Hall, 1979): 19; M. L. Daneel, *Quest for Belonging* (Gweru, Zimbabwe: Mambo Press, 1987): 78.

3. Simon S. Maimela, "Salvation in African Traditional Religions," *Missionalia* 13: 2 (1985): 63–77, 71; M. L. Daneel, *Old and New in Southern Shona Inde-pendent Churches*, Vol. 2 (The Hague: Mouton, 1974); John S. Pobee & Gabriel Ositelu II, *African Initiatives in Christianity: The Growth, Gifts and Diversi-ties of Indigenous African Churches—A Challenge to the Ecumenical Movement* (Geneva: World Council of Churches, 1998): 34, 40–42.

4. Hastings, *Church in Africa*, 512, 530; Daneel, *Quest for Belonging*, 99, 101; Comaroff, *Body of Power*, 169, 186 ; David B. Barrett, *Schism and Renewal in Africa: An Analysis of Six Thousand Contemporary Religious Movements* (Nairobi: Oxford University Press, 1968): 95–96.

5. Bays, *New History*, 79, 106; Simpson, "Contending for the Faith," 21.

6. Hastings, *Church in Africa*, 527, 532–33; Barrett, *Schism and Renewal*, 101.

7. Barrett, *Schism and Renewal*, 83; Anderson, *Spreading Fires*, 57–65.

8. F. B. Welbourn & B. A. Ogot, *A Place to Feel at Home* (London: Oxford University Press, 1966); Hastings, *Church in Africa*, 529; Comaroff, *Body of Power*, 172.

9. Walter J. Hollenweger, *Pentecostalism: Origins and Developments Worldwide* (Pea-body, MA: Hendrickson, 1997): 18–24; Douglas J. Nelson, *For Such a Time as This: The Story of William J. Seymour and the Azusa Street Revival*, PhD thesis, (University of Birmingham, UK, 1981); Faupel, *The Everlasting Gospel*; Frank Bartleman, *Azusa Street*, (S. Plainfield, NJ: Bridge Publishing, 1925, 1980): 54.

10. Hollenweger, *Pentecostalism*, 18–19; Harvey Cox, *Fire from Heaven: The Rise of Pentecostal Spirituality and the Reshaping of Religion in the Twenty-first Century*

(London: Cassell, 1996): 46–48; Bartleman, *Azusa Street,* 63; Cecil M. Robeck Jr., *The Azusa Street Mission and Revival: The Birth of the Global Pentecostal Movement* (Nashville, TN: Thomas Nelson, 2006); Augustus Cerillo Jr., "Interpretive Approaches to the History of American Pentecostal Origins," *Pneuma* 19 (Spring 1997): 29–52; Joe Creech, "Visions of Glory: The Place of the Azusa Street Revival in Pentecostal History," *Church History* 65:3 (September 1996): 405–24, 406.

11. *AF* 1 (September1906): 1; 3 (November 1906): 2; Anderson, *Spreading Fires,* 57–65.

12. McGee, "Latter Rain Falling," 649–51, 653–59, 664; Anderson, *Spreading Fires,* 77–101; *TF* 25:11 (November 1905): 251–53; for Sisson, see *TF* 26:3 (March 1906): 57–60; *Live Coals* 3:48 (18 October 1905): 1; 4:21 (23 May 1906): 1; *Holiness Advocate* 6:3 (15 May 1906): 8; *WW* 32:5 (May 1910): 138–40; Bartleman, *Azusa Street,* 35; *AF* 3 (November 1906): 1.

13. Allan H. Anderson, *An Introduction to Pentecostalism: Global Charismatic Christianity* (Cambridge University Press, 2004): 45–57.

14. Reed, David A. *"In Jesus' Name": The History and Beliefs of Oneness Pentecostalism* (Blandford Forum, UK: Deo Publishing, 2008); Talmadge Leon French, *Early Oneness Pentecostalism, Garfield Thomas Haywood, and the Interracial Pentecostal Assemblies of the World (1906–1931),* PhD thesis (University of Birmingham, 2011).

15. *Enrichment Journal* (Fall 1999): http://enrichmentjournal.ag.org/199904/076_hogan.cfm, accessed 19 November 2011.

16. C. W. Conn, "Church of God (Cleveland, TN)," *NIDPCM,* 530–35; H. D. Hunter, "Church of God of Prophecy," *NIDPCM,* 539–42.

17. H. V. Synan, "International Pentecostal Holiness Church," *NIDPCM,* 798–801.

18. David Bundy, "Thomas Ball Barratt: From Methodist to Pentecostal," *JEPTA* 13 (1994): 19–40; David Bundy, "Historical and Theological Analysis of the Pentecostal Church in Norway," *JEPTA* 20 (2000): 66–92.

19. D. D. Bundy, "Pethrus, Lewi," *NIDPCM,* 986–87; Joseph R. Colletti, "Lewi Pethrus: His Influence upon Scandinavian-American Pentecostalism," *Pneuma* 5:2 (1983): 18–29; Connie Ho Yan Au, *Grassroots Unity in the Charismatic Renewal* (Eugene, OR: Wipf & Stock, 2011): 78–79.

20. For Boddy, see *AF* 6 (February–March 1907): 1; Walter J. Hollenweger, *The Pentecostals* (London: SCM, 1972): 184–85; Hollenweger, *Pentecostalism,* 343–45; Cornelis van der Laan, "The Proceedings of the Leaders' Meetings (1908–1911) and of the International Pentecostal Council (1912–1914)," *Pneuma* 10:1 (1988): 36–49.

21. Malcolm R. Hathaway, "The Elim Pentecostal Church: Origins, Development and Distinctives," Keith Warrington (ed.), *Pentecostal Perspectives* (Carlisle, UK: Paternoster, 1998): 1–39.

22. William K. Kay, *Pentecostals in Britain* (Carlisle, UK: Paternoster, 2000): 74; William K. Kay, "Assemblies of God: Distinctive Continuity and Distinctive Change," in Keith Warrington (ed.), *Pentecostal Perspectives* (Carlisle, UK: Paternoster, 1999): 40–63.

23. Everett A. Wilson, *Strategy of the Spirit: J. Philip Hogan and the Growth of the Assemblies of God Worldwide 1960–1990* (Carlisle, UK: Paternoster, 1997): 3, 15, 179; http://ag.org/top/; http://worldagfellowship.orgwww.churchofgod.org/index.php/pages/history; www.foursquare.org/, accessed 19 November 2011.

CHAPTER 3

1. *LRE* 2:3 (December 1909): 9.
2. Daneel, *Quest for Belonging*, 92.
3. Anderson, *Spreading Fires,* 288; Gary B. McGee, "Pentecostals and Their Various Strategies for Global Mission," in Murray A. Dempster, Byron D. Klaus, & Douglas Petersen (eds.), *Called and Empowered: Global Mission in Pentecostal Perspective* (Peabody: Hendrickson, 1991): 212.
4. *LRE* 2:11 (August 1910): 15.
5. *AF* 7 (April 1907): 1; 9 (June–September 1907): 1; *LRE* 6:3 (December 1913): 23; *WW* 29:6 (June 1907): 184; Robeck, *Azusa Street,* 250–2; Thompson & Gordon, *Alfred Garr,* 81–9; *DPCM,* 248.
6. *WW* 32 (January 1910): 30; *BM* 1 (1 October 1907): 2, 4; 9 (1 March 1908): 2; 11 (1 April 1908): 1, 2; *AF* 10 (September 1907): 2; 12 (January 1908): 1; 13 (May 1908): 4.
7. *BM* 17 (1 July 1908): 1; 18 (15 July 1908): 1; 41 (1 July 1909): 2.
8. *TF* 29:1 (January 1909): 9–10; *AF* 13 (May 1908): 3.
9. *TF* 29:5 (May 1909): 100–101, 115; 29:7 (July 1909): 158; *Pentecostal Truths* 2:3 (March 1909): 4 (trans. Connie Au).
10. Law, *Pentecostal Mission Work,* 2; *Conf* 5:5 (May 1912): 113; *BM* 129 (15 March 1913): 3; *LRE* 11:8 (May 1919): 11; 12:12 (September 1920): 20; *Pentecostal Truths* 2:13 (January 1909): 2 (trans. Connie Au); *AF* 11 (January 1908): 1; 13 (May 1908): 3; Robeck, *Azusa Street,* 246; Thompson & Gordon, *Alfred Garr,* 70, 90–95; Shanghai periodical quoted in Bays, "Protestant Missionary Establishment," 54.
11. *Conf* 2:7 (July 1909): 147; *BM* 129 (15 March 1913): 3; *WE* 122 (8 January 1916): 12; Thompson & Gordon, *Alfred Garr,* 106–72; Aimee Semple McPherson, *This Is That: Personal Experiences, Sermons and Writings* (Los Angeles: Echo Park Evangelistic Association, 1923): 63–68.
12. *Conf* 1:7 (October 1908): 7–8; 2:1 (January 1909): 13–15; 2:8 (August 1909): 174–75, 183; 2:11 (November 1909): 253; 4:3 (March 1911): 67; 5:5 (May 1912): 111. The PMU training is described in detail in Anderson, *Spreading Fires,* 263–65.
13. A full account of these activities is given in Anderson, *Spreading Fires,* 123–30; *Pentecostal Truths* 3:10 (November 1910): 4; *Conf* 3:8 (August 1910): 199–200; 3:11 (November 1910): 272; 3:12 (December 1910): 293; 4:1 (January 1911): 20; 4:3 (March 1911): 69; 6:4 (April 1913): 83; *BM* 75 (1 December 1910): 4; 108 (15 April 1912): 1; *UR* 2:1 (August 1910): 6; "Combined Minutes," 1920, 66.

14. *Conf* 2:4 (April 1909): 86–87; *BM* 64 (15 June 1910): 3; *FF* 38 (May 1916): 8–9; PMU Minutes, 2 December 1910, 88; Letters (Donald Gee Centre, Mattersey, England): A. Williams to T. H. Mundell, 13 January 1911, F. Trevitt to T. H. Mundell, 14 January 1911; A. Kok to T. H. Mundell, 14 September 1913; Letter, F. Trevitt to T. H. Mundell, 13 October 1913; PMU Minutes, 4 September 1913; H. French Ridley to C. Polhill, 22 November 1915; W. Glassby (Bedford) to T. H. Mundell (postcard): n.d.; T. H. Mundell to Maggie Trevitt, 16 May 1916; Maggie Trevitt, Yunnan-fu to T. H. Mundell, 13 July 1916.

15. *FF* 38 (May 1916): 8–9.

16. Paul L. King, *Genuine Gold: The Cautiously Charismatic Story of the Early Christian and Missionary Alliance* (Tulsa, OK: Word & Spirit Press, 2006): 151–78; *AF* 13 (May 1908): 4; *BM* 9 (1 March 1908): 2; *Conf* 1:5 (August 1908): 22–23.

17. *Christian & Missionary Alliance* 30:3 (18 April 1908): 38–39; Simpson, "Contending for the Faith," 2–11; W. W. Simpson, "Notes from Kansu," *The Alliance Weekly* 39:22 (1 March 1913): 345–46; Simpson, "Contending for the Faith," 15–16; *Conf* 6:1 (January 1913): 4–5; *TF* 33:3 (March 1913): 52–56.

18. *FF* 9 (January 1913): 7.

19. Simpson, "Contending for the Faith," 18–19; Letters (Donald Gee Centre, Mattersey, England): W. W. Simpson to T. H. Mundell, 5 February 1914, 18 May 1914; *LRE* 8:4 (January 1916): 8.

20. Anderson, *Spreading Fires*, 135; Frodsham, *With Signs Following*, 139–43; Simpson, "Contending for the Faith," 20–24, 90; Xi, *Redeemed by Fire*, 98–99.

21. Letters (Donald Gee Centre, Mattersey, England): W. W. Simpson to C. Polhill, 12 August 1914, D. E. Hoste to Cecil Polhill, 4 January 1915, enclosing copy of circular letter from Simpson; *CE* 53 (8 August 1914): 4; *FF* 29 (July 1915): 9.

22. *WE* 179 (3 March 1917): 14; *TF* 39:6 (June 1919): 143; *LRE* 12:10 (July 1920): 15; *WW* 42:3 (March 1920): 28; 42:4 (April 1920): 29; 42:5 (May 1920): 30; "Minutes of the General Council of the Assemblies of God," 4–11 September 1918, 28; Simpson, "Contending for the Faith," 45–48, 57, 61, 87, 113.

23. Simpson, "Contending for the Faith," 94.

24. For details on Berg's work in India, see Anderson, *Spreading Fires*, 95–97; Bergunder, *The South Indian Pentecostal Movement*, 25; Robert F. Cook, *A Quarter Century of Divine Leading in India* (Chengannur, S. India: The Church of God in India, 1939): 2–6, , 19–23, 45–46.

25. *Trust* 12:8 (October 1913): 11; *WWit* 9:9 (September 1913): 4; 12:5 (May 1915): 6; *WE* 93 (5 June 1915): 4; 216 (24 November 1917): 12; "Combined Minutes," 1920, 67; "Constitution and By-Laws," 1927, 114; Cook, *Quarter Century*, 25, 51; Bergunder, *The South Indian Pentecostal Movement*, 27–34, 263–64.

26. Cook, *Quarter Century*, 57.

27. J. H. Ingram, *Around the World with the Gospel Light* (Cleveland, TN: Church of God Publishing House, 1938): 85–93; Cook, *Quarter Century*, 60–62, inserted page, "Extent of the Work"; *Conf* 6:1 (January 1913): 20; *BM* 125 (15 January

1913): 3; 135 (15 June 1913): 2; 138 (15 August 1913): 2; 145 (1 December 1913): 1; *WW* 36:6 (June 1914): 187; 36:10 (October 1914): 316; 36:11 (November 1914): 349–50; 42:1 (January 1920): 14, 20; 42:6 (June 1920): 13; *CE* 56 (29 August 1914): 4; *WWit* 12:5 (May 1915): 6; Bergunder, "Constructing Indian Pentecostalism," 192; Bergunder, *The South Indian Pentecostal Movement,* 27–34.

28. Gordon MacKay Haliburton, *The Prophet Harris: A Study of an African Prophet and His Mass Movement in the Ivory Coast and the Gold Coast 1913–1915* (London: Longman, 1971): 28–35.

29. *AF* 11 (January 1908): 2; Robeck, *Azusa Street,* 269–70.

30. *AF* 13 (May 1908): 1; *Conf* 2:4 (April 1909): 92; 6:2 (February 1913): 39; 6:9 (September1913): 184; 7:2 (February 1914): 36; *UR* 1:3 (August 1909): 7; 2:3 (August1910): 6; *LRE* 2:11 (August 1910): 21; 3:10 (July 1911): 17; 3:11 (August1911): 17; 5:3 (December 1912): 12; 6:2 (November 1913): 2; 8:11 (August 1916): 18–21; *BM* 67 (1 August 1910): 4; 69 (1 September 1910): 2; 75 (1 December 1910): 3, 4; 79 (1 February 1911): 4; 81 (1 March 1911): 4; 104 (15 February 1912): 2; 106 (15 March 1912): 1, 3; 130 (1 April 1913): 4; *Trust* 10:1 (March 1911): 19; 10:2 (April 1911): 15–16; 11:8 (October 1912): 19; *CE* 55 (22 August 1914): 4; Robeck, *Azusa Street,* 271–72.

31. *AF* 5 (January 1907): 3, 4; 6 (February–March 1907): 3; *Pent* 1:1 (August 1908): 2; *LRE* 13:2 (November 1920): 20–23; Robeck, *Azusa Street,* 274–80; Kemp Pendleton Burpeau, *God's Showman: A Historical Study of John G. Lake and South African/ American Pentecostalism* (Oslo: Refleks Publishing, 2004): 44–45; William F. P. Burton, *When God Makes a Pastor* (London: Victory Press, 1934): 30–31.

32. *Leaves of Healing* 15:25 (8 October 1904): 853–54; 18:11 (30 December 1905): 314–20; *BM* 29 (1 January 1909): 4; *WW* 32:7 (July 1910): 213; *TF* 30:9 (September 1910): 195; Gerhardus C. Oosthuizen, *The Birth of Christian Zionism in South Africa* (KwaDlangezwa, South Africa: University of Zululand, 1987): 30; Burton, *When God Makes,* 31; B. G. M. Sundkler, *Zulu Zion and Some Swazi Zionists* (London: Oxford, 1976): 51.

33. *Pent* 1:1 (August 1908): 7; 1:2 (September 1908): 2; 1:7 (June 1909): 2; *WW* 30:11 (November 1908): 344–5; *Conf* 2:2 (February 1909): 28; *UR* 1:7 (February 1910): 7; *BM* 115 (1 August 1912): 1.

34. *Pent* 1:5 (January–February 1909): 4; 1:10 (September 1909): 4; *Conf* 2:3 (March 1909): 74; *BM* 38 (15 May 1909): 4; 39 (1 June 1909): 4; 47 (1 October 1909): 2; *UR* 1:1 (June 1909): 3; 1:5 (October–November1909): 1; 1:7 (February 1910): 7; 2:3 (November 1910): 1–2, 6–8; 2:4 (January 1911): 6; *WW* 32:4 (April 1910): 121; *Advocate* 1:8 (21 June 1917): 10; 4:49 (7 April 1921): 10; *PE* 656 (17 July 1926): 3; Sundkler, *Zulu Zion,* 55–6, n54; Burpeau, *God's Showman,* 120–25.

35. *UR* 1:7 (February 1910): 7; 2:5 (May 1911): 6; *BM* 62 (15 May 1910): 4; 82 (15 March 1911): 1; Anderson, *Spreading Fires,* 167–81; Allan Anderson, *Zion and Pentecost: The Spirituality and Experience of Pentecostal and Zionist/Apostolic*

Churches in South Africa (Pretoria: University of South Africa Press, 2000): 85–114.

36. David Maxwell "The Soul of the Luba: W. F. Burton, "Missionary Ethnography and Belgian Colonial Science," *History and Anthropology* 19:4 (2008): 325–51, 328; Letter (Donald Gee Centre, Mattersey, England): Alma Doering (St. Croix, Switzerland) to T. H. Mundell, 11 February 1914; *WE* 140 (20 May 1916): 11; 199 (21 July 1917): 12; Burton, *God Working*, 18–19; Womersley & Garrard, *Into Africa*, 29, 51, 56, 110, 115–16; Moorhead, *Missionary Pioneering*, 20, 24, 45–46, 74, 103–4.

37. Moorhead, *Missionary Pioneering*, 72, 108–9, 114, 163, 215–16; Frodsham, *With Signs Following*, 154; Maxwell, "The Soul of the Luba," 336; Womersley & Garrard, *Into Africa*, 66–67; Burton, *God Working*, 108; Burton in *Redemption Tidings* 1:4 (January 1925): 12; Corry in Burton, *When God Changes a Village*, vi.

38. Burton, *God Working*, 106; Moorhead, *Missionary Pioneering*, 207; Womersley, *Wm F. Burton*, 77, 113.

39. Maxwell, "The Soul of the Luba," 331–33; David Maxwell, "Photography and the Religious Encounter: Ambiguity and Aesthetics in Missionary Representations of the Luba of South East Belgian Congo," *Comparative Studies in Society and History* 53:1 (2011): 38–74.

40. Brian Stanley, *The World Missionary Conference, Edinburgh 1910* (Grand Rapids, MI: Eerdmans, 2009): 1, 3.

41. Stanley, *World Missionary Conference*, 12; Brian Stanley, "Twentieth Century World Christianity: A Perspective from the History of Missions," in Donald M. Lewis (ed.), *Christianity Reborn: The Global Expansion of Evangelicalism in the Twentieth Century* (Grand Rapids, MI: Eerdmans, 2004): 52–83, 77.

42. Stanley, *World Missionary Conference*, 17.

43. *BM* 69 (1 September 1910): 1; *LRE* 2:6 (March 1910): 12; 2:11 (August 1910): 6.

44. *FF* 9 (January 1913): 3.

45. *LRE* 12:6 (March 1920): 15; *WW* 21:1 (May 1899): 18.

46. Sanneh, *Disciples of All Nations*, 218–34.

47. Roland Allen, *Missionary Methods: St Paul's or Ours?* (Grand Rapids, MI: Eerdmans, 1962): 149.

48. *PE* 374–5 (8 January 1921): 6–7; 376–77 (22 January 1921): 6, 11; 378–79 (5 February 1921): 6–7; Anderson, *Spreading Fires*, 90.

49. Melvin L. Hodges, *The Indigenous Church* (Springfield, MO: Gospel Publishing House, 1953): 10–12, 22.

50. Hodges, *Indigenous Church*, 14.

51. Hodges, *Indigenous Church*, 9.

52. Allen, *Missionary Methods*, 142–43.

53. William F. P. Burton, *When God Changes a Village* (London: Victory Press, 1933): 127–28.

CHAPTER 4

1. *TF* 6:12 (December 1886): 270–73.

2. Jacob Baynham, "Hong Kong Missionary Uses Intensive Prayer to Help Heroin Addicts," *San Francisco Chronicle* (14 December 2007): www.sfgate.com/cgi-bin/article.cgi?f=/c/a/2007/12/14/MNIKT2BIA.DTL&feed=rss.news, accessed 8 September 2011; Donald E. Miller & Tetsunao Yamamori, *Global Pentecostalism: The New Face of Christian Social Engagement* (Berkeley: University of California Press, 2007): 99–105; www.irismin.org/about/history, accessed 28 August 2011.

3. *WW* 22:11 (November 1900): 337; letter, J. A. Dowie to A. A. Boddy, 12 June 1903, reproduced in *Conf* 6:2 (February 1913): 38.

4. *AF* 12 (January 1908): 3; Constitution quoted in Larry Martin (ed.), *Doctrines and Disciplines of the Azusa Street Mission of Los Angeles California* (Joplin, MO: Christian Life Books, 2000).

5. Estrelda Alexander, *The Women of Azusa* Street (Cleveland, TN: Pilgrim Press, 2005): 39–46, 59–70; Sutton, *Aimee Semple McPherson*, 204–209.

6. Edith L. Blumhofer, *Aimee Semple McPherson: Everybody's Sister* (Grand Rapids, MI: Eerdmans, 1993); Matthew Avery Sutton, *Aimee Semple McPherson and the Resurrection of Christian America* (Cambridge, MA: Harvard, 2007).

7. Grant Wacker, "Are the Golden Oldies Still Worth Playing? Reflections on History Writing among Early Pentecostals," *Pneuma* 8:2 (1986): 81–100: 95; Anderson, *Spreading Fires*, 88–89, 135, 202.

8. *AF* 1:3 (November 1906): 4.

9. *Conf* 2:1 (January 1909): 22; *Pent* 1:5 (January–February 1909): 5; *BM* 29 (1 January 1909): 1; 32 (15 February 1909): 1; 33 (1 March 1909): 2; *WW* 31:8 (August 1909): 168; *TF* 29:6 (June 1909): 125; *UR* 1:6 (January 1910): 6; 1:7 (February 1910): 6; Anderson, *Spreading Fires*, 152–53; Alexander, *Women of Azusa* Street, 71–79; Barbara Cavaness, "Spiritual Chain Reactions: Women Used of God," *Assemblies of God Heritage* 25:4 (2005–06): 24–29.

10. *WW* 32:10 (October 1910): 315; 39:16 (May 1917): 254; *UR* 1:10 (May 1910): 7; 1:11 (June 1910): 8; 2:2 (September–October 1910): 7; *LRE* 5:2 (November 1912): 11; 5:5 (February 1913): 11; 5:7 (April 1913): 15; 5:12 (September 1913): 16; 11:9 (June 1919): 11; 11:12 (September 1919): 14–19; 12:1 (October 1919): 7–8; *WWit* 8:8 (October 1912): 4; 9:2 (February 1913): 2; *CE* 72 (26 December 1914): 4; *WE* 191 (26 May 1917): 12; *TF* 38:4 (April 1918): 90; *NIDPCM*, 1153; *AG Heritage* 4:4 (Winter 1984–85): 1–8.

11. *LRE* 12:3 (December 1919): 12–13; *Trust* 17:2 (April 1918): 9; 19:2 (April 1920): 2; Wacker, *Heaven Below*, 158.

12. Diana Chapman, *Searching the Source of the River: Forgotten Women of the British Pentecostal Revival 1907–1914* (London: Push Publishing, 2007): 14–23, 114–31.

13. *LRE* 6:3 (December 1913): 4; *BM* 134 (1 June 1913): 3.

14. Letters, E. Cook to T. H. Mundell, 6 February 1915; W. J. Boyd to T. H. Mundell, 26 August 1916 (Donald Gee Centre, Mattersey, England); *BM* 80 (15 February 1911): 2.

15. *Mukti Prayer-Bell* (September 1907): 3, 4, 6, 8, 10; Kosambi, *Pandita Ramabai*, 12, 18, 23–24; c.f. McGee, "Latter Rain," 660–61; McGee, "Calcutta Revival," 131–32; Robert, *Occupy Until I Come*, 263.

16. *Mukti Prayer-Bell* (September 1907): 10–12; Kosambi, *Pandita Ramabai*, 26.

17. *Mukti Prayer-Bell* (September 1907): 10–11, 13; *PE* 543 (29 April 1922): 7–8; cf. Edith L. Blumhofer, "Consuming Fire: Pandita Ramabai and the Early Pentecostal Impulse," in Roger E. Hedlund, Sebastian Kim, & Rajkumar Boaz Johnson (eds.), *Indian and Christian: The Life and Legacy of Pandita Ramabai* (Chennai: MIIS/CMS/ISPCK, 2011): 127–54, 147–48.

18. *PE* 543 (19 April 1924): 9. First Abrams quote in *TF* 31:1 (January 1911): 5; second Abrams quote in *LRE* 2:11 (August 1910): 10; third Abrams quote at *WW* 33:7 (July 1911): 218.

19. *WW* 26:3 (March 1904): 84; 32:4 (April 1910): 122.

20. *Trust* 17:7 (September 1918): 11; *LRE* 5:4 (January 1913): 11; Powar quoted in *LRE* 5:6 (March 1913): 24; *NIDPCM*, 844–45.

21. Ying Fuk Tsang, " From a Film Star to a Prophetess: The Legend of Mui Yee," *Christian and Missionary Alliance Monthly* 44 (August 2003); 45 (September 2003), www.cmacuhk.org.hk/version3/mag/mag_monews_45/mag_monews_shadow_45a.htm, original in Chinese, accessed 17 April 2010; Paul Farrelly, "Mount Zion and Typhoon Morakot: A New Religion's Response to a Natural Disaster," www.religion.info/pdf/2010_04_Farrelly.pdf, accessed 3 September 2011; Tan Jin Huat, "Pentecostals and Charismatics in Malaysia and Singapore," in Allan H. Anderson & Edmond Tang (eds.), *Asian and Pentecostal: The Charismatic Face of Christianity in Asia* (Oxford: Regnum, 2011): 238–58.

22. Choi Jashil, *Hallelujah Lady* (Seoul: Seoul Logos, 2009): 10, 175–79; Julie C. Ma, "Korean Spirituality: A Case Study of Jashil Choi," in Wonsuk Ma & Robert P. Menzies (eds.), *The Spirit and Spirituality: Essays in Honour of Russell P. Spittler* (London: T&T Clark, 2004): 298–313; cf. Julie C. Ma, "Asian Women and Pentecostal Ministry," in Allan H. Anderson & Edmond Tang (eds.), *Asian and Pentecostal: The Charismatic Face of Christianity in Asia* (Oxford: Regnum, 2011): 109–24; Yeol Soo Eim, "The Amazing Ministry of Dr Seen SookAhn," www.pctii.org/cyberj/cyberj6/eim.html, accessed 6 September 2011; Ma, "Asian Women," 138–39; I visited Daejeong and met Dr. Ahn in 2008.

23. Martin West, *Bishops and Prophets in a Black City* (Cape Town: David Philip, 1975): 65; Sundkler, *Zulu Zion*, 79–82; Anderson, *Zion and Pentecost*, 72–74.

24. West, *Bishops and Prophets*, 66; Sundkler, *Zulu Zion*, 82; Peter Körner, "The St. John's Apostolic Faith Mission and Politics: The Political Dimension of an Apolitical Independent Church," in Gordon Mitchell & Eve Mullen (eds.), *Religion and the Political Imagination in a Changing South Africa* (Münster, Germany: Waxmann, 2002): 133–50; Christina Landman, "Christinah Nku and

St John's: A Hundred Years Later," *Studia Historiae Ecclesiasticae* 32:3 (2006): 1–32.

25. Paul Gifford, *Christianity, Politics and Public Life in Kenya* (London: Hurst, 2009): 116–18, 163–64; Kalu, *African Pentecostalism*, 150–www.idahosa.com/ Bishop_Margaret.html; http://archbishopmargaretbensonidahosa.com/ archbishop-margaret-idahosa; www.jiam.org/about_us/bishop_profile.aspx; http://allafrica.com/stories/201108220771.html, accessed 6 September 2011.

26. Bernice Martin, "The Pentecostal Gender Paradox: A Cautionary Tale for the Sociology of Religion," Richard K. Fenn (ed.), *The Blackwell Companion to Sociology of Religion* (Oxford: Blackwell, 2003): 52–66; quote at 54.

27. *Conf* 7:11 (November 1914): 208–209, 212–14.

28. *WWit* 10:1 (January 1914): 2; "Minutes of the General Council" (2–12 April 1914): 7; Wacker, *Heaven Below*, 165–68; Edith L. Blumhofer, *Restoring the Faith: The Assemblies of God, Pentecostalism, and American Culture* (Urbana: University of Illinois Press, 1993): 174.

29. Cheryl Bridges Johns, "Pentecostal Spirituality and the Conscientization of Women," in Harold D. Hunter & P. D. Hocken (eds.), *All Together in One Place: Theological Papers from the Brighton Conference on World Evangelization* (Sheffield, UK: Sheffield Academic Press, 1993): 53–65, 165.

30. Brusco, "Gender and Power," 83–84; Anthea D. Butler, *Women in the Church of God in Christ: Making a Sanctified World* (Chapel Hill: University of North Carolina Press, 2007).

31. Elizabeth E. Brusco, *The Reformation of Machismo: Evangelical Conversion and Gender in Colombia* (Austin: University of Texas Press, 1995): 86–87; Brusco, "Gender and Power," 76; Miller & Yamamori, *Global Pentecostalism*, 208; Deidre Helen Crumbley, *Spirit, Structure, and Flesh: Gendered Experiences in African Instituted Churches among the Yoruba of Nigeria* (Madison: University of Wisconsin Press, 2008); R. Andrew Chesnut,, *Born Again in Brazil: The Pentecostal Boom and the Pathogens of Poverty* (New Brunswick, NY: Rutgers University Press, 1997): 32.

32. Brusco, *Reformation of Machismo*, 78, 79–80, 100–102, 106, 114; quote at 5.

33. Brusco, *Reformation of Machismo*, 6; Martin, "Pentecostal Gender Paradox," 54; Kristina Helgesson, *"Walking in the Spirit": The Complexity of Belonging in Two Pentecostal Churches in Durban, South Africa*, PhD thesis (Uppsala University, 2006): 169–201; Mark J. Cartledge, "Family Socialisation, Godly Love and Pentecostal Spirituality," *Research in the Social Scientific Study of Religion* 23 (2012), 1–27.

34. Brusco, "Gender and Power," 81; Lesley Gill, "'Like a Veil to Cover Them': Women and the Pentecostal Movement in La Paz," *American Ethnologist* 17:4 (1990): 708–21.

35. Jonathan Friedmann, "Liberating Domesticity: Women and the Home in Orthodox Judaism and Latin American Pentecostalism," *Journal of Religion & Society* 10 (2008): 1–55; David Martin, *Forbidden Revolutions: Pentecostalism in Latin America*

and Catholicism in Eastern Europe (London: SPCK, 1996): 52; Anne Motley Hallum, "Taking Stock and Building Bridges: Feminism, Women's Movements, and Pentecostalism in Latin America," *Latin American Research Review* 38: 1 (2003): 169–86; Brusco, *Reformation of Machismo*, 137; Cecília Loreto Mariz & María das Dores Campos Machado, "Pentecostalism and Women in Brazil," in Edward L. Cleary & Hannah W. Stewart-Gambino (eds.), *Power, Politics, and Pentecostals in Latin America* (Boulder, CO: Westview, 1997): 41–54, 44.

CHAPTER 5

1. Frodsham, *With Signs Following*, 207; Hollenweger, *The Pentecostals*, xvi, 321–22.
2. Philip Jenkins, *The New Faces of Christianity: Believing the Bible in the Global South* (New York: Oxford University Press, 2006).
3. Hastings, *Church in Africa*, 527, 529; Barrett, *Schism and Renewal*, 117, 120–21.
4. Lamin Sanneh, *Whose Religion Is Christianity: The Gospel beyond the West* (Grand Rapids, MI: Eerdmans, 2003): 10–11; Kenneth J. Archer, *A Pentecostal Hermeneutic for the Twenty-First Century: Spirit, Scripture and Community* (Cleveland, TN: CPT Press, 2009): 69; Carlos Mesters, "The Use of the Bible in Christian Communities of the Common People," in N. K. Gottwald and R. A. Horsley (eds.), *The Bible and Liberation* (New York: Orbis, 1993): 7; Elizabeth Brusco, "Gender and Power," in Allan H. Anderson, Michael Bergunder, André Droogers, & Cornelis van der Laan (eds.), *Studying Global Pentecostalism: Theories and Methods* (Berkeley, CA: University of California Press, 2010): 82–83.
5. *AF* 1:9 (June–September 1907): 2; 1:10 (September 1907): 2; *Advocate* 3:9 (26 June 1919): 6; Andrew Davies, "What Does It Mean to Read the Bible as a Pentecostal?" *JPT* 18:2 (2009): 219; Steven J. Land, *Pentecostal Spirituality: A Passion for the Kingdom* (Sheffield, UK: Sheffield Academic Press, 1993): 29, 39; Taylor quote in *Advocate* 4:10 (8 July 1920): 9; Kerr quote in *WE* 175 (3 February 1917): 4–5.
6. Davies, "What Does It Mean," 221; Archer, *Pentecostal Hermeneutic*, 168.
7. Sanneh, *Disciples of All Nations*, 25–29; Severino Croatto, *Biblical Hermeneutics* (New York: Orbis, 1987): 1; Davies, "What Does It Mean," 224.
8. Mesters, "The Use of the Bible," 14; Croatto, *Biblical Hermeneutics*, 6; Archer, *Pentecostal Hermeneutic*, 96.
9. Mesters, "The Use of the Bible," 9; John McKay, "When the Veil Is Taken Away: The Impact of Prophetic Experience on Biblical Interpretation," *Journal of Pentecostal Theology* 5 (1994): 38.
10. M. L. Daneel, *Old and New in Southern Shona Independent Churches*, Vol. III (Gweru, Zimbabwe: Mambo Press, 1988): 117–18.
11. *WW* 21: 5 (September 1899): 145; 25:8 (August 1903): 245; Post quote in *LRE* 5:7 (April 1913): 15; *WWit* 10:3 (March 1914): 3; letter, E. Cook to T. H. Mundell, 8 August 1914 (Donald Gee Centre, Mattersey, England); Cook, *Quarter Century*, 50.
12. *FF* (May 1917): 4–7.

13. Letter, T. H. Mundell to the Leighs, 18 September 1918 (Donald Gee Centre, Mattersey, England)

14. *LRE* 10:9 (June 1918): 16.

15. *LRE* 3:6 (March 1911): 14; *TF* 5:10 (October 1885): 222; *NIDPCM*, 372–73; Anderson, *Spreading Fires*, 260–61.

16. *LRE* 2:9 (June 1910): 23; *NIDPCM*, 375; Anderson, *Spreading Fires*, 262, 273.

17. *Conf* 2:1 (January 1909): 14; 2:6 (June 1909): 129; Moorhead, *Missionary Pioneering*, 215–16; Womersley & Garrard, *Into Africa*, 66–67; Anderson, *Spreading Fires*, 264–65.

18. *LRE* 5:4 (January 1913): 22; *WWit* 12:5 (May 1915): 5.

19. Henry I. Lederle, "Pentecostals and Ecumenical Theological Education," *Ministerial Formation* 80 (January 1998): 46; Byron D. Klaus & Loren O. Triplett, "National Leadership in Pentecostal Missions," in Murray A. Dempster, Byron D. Klaus, & Douglas Petersen (eds.), *Called and Empowered: Global Mission in Pentecostal Perspective* (Peabody: Hendrickson, 1991): 227–29; Benjamin Sun, "Assemblies of God Theological Education in Asia Pacific: A Reflection," *Asian Journal of Pentecostal Studies* 3:2 (July 2000): 230; Cox, *Fire from Heaven*, 303.

20. Hwa Yung, "Critical Issues Facing Theological Education in Asia," *Transformation* (October–December 1995): 1; Allan Anderson, "The 'Fury and Wonder'? Pentecostal-Charismatic Spirituality in Theological Education," *Pneuma* 23:2 (2001): 287–302.

21. Christian Lalive d'Epinay, "The Training of Pastors and Theological Education: The Case of Chile," *International Review of Missions* 56: 222 (April 1967): 185, 191; Juan Sepúlveda, "The Challenge for Theological Education from a Pentecostal Standpoint," *Ministerial Formation* 87 (October 1999): 29–30.

22. www.pentvars.edu.gh/; accessed 30 August 2011; Interview with Chinese house church leader, May 2011.

23. Andrew F. Walls, "Of Ivory Towers and Ashrams: Some Reflections on Theological Scholarship in Africa," *Journal of African Christian Thought* 3:1 (June 2000): 1–3.

24. Willem A. Saayman, "Some Reflections on the Development of the Pentecostal Mission Model in South Africa," *Missionalia* 21:1 (April 1993): 40–56, 43.

25. Land, *Pentecostal Spirituality*, 22; Daniel E. Albrecht, *Rites in the Spirit: A Ritual Approach to Pentecostal/Charismatic Spirituality* (Sheffield, UK: Sheffield Academic Press, 1999): 22; Cox, *Fire from Heaven*, 101.

26. Mark J. Cartledge, *Testimony in the Spirit: Rescripting Ordinary Pentecostal Theology* (Farnham, UK: Ashgate, 2010): 29.

27. J. Kwabena Asamoah-Gyadu, "Reversing Christian Mission: African Pentecostal Pastor Establishes 'God's Embassy' in the Ukraine" (unpublished paper, May 2004), 4.

28. Martin West, *Bishops and Prophets*, 196–99

29. Paul Gifford, *African Christianity: Its Public Role* (London: Hurst, 1998): 197–205; Jason Mandryk, *Operation World*, 7th ed. (Colorado Springs: Biblica, 2010): 683;

Eddie Villanueva, "A Consuming Passion," in Cityland Foundation, *This Is My Story: 31 Lives, Stories, Miracles* (Manila: OMF Literature, 2004): 224–33; http://pewforum.org/Christian/Evangelical-Protestant-Churches/Historical-Overview-of-Pentecostalism-in-Philippines.aspx, accessed 11 September 2011.

30. Joel Robbins, "Anthropology of Religion," in Allan H. Anderson, Michael Bergunder, André Droogers, & Cornelis van der Laan (eds.), *Studying Global Pentecostalism: Theories and Methods* (Berkeley: University of California Press, 2010): 156–78, 172; Kalu, *African Pentecostalism*, 194, 199; Miller & Yamamori, *Global Pentecostalism*, 211.

31. Vinson Synan, *The Century of the Holy Spirit: 100 Years of Pentecostal and Charismatic Renewal* (Nashville, TN: Thomas Nelson, 2001); www.persecution.net/eritrea.htm; www.christiantoday.com/article/eritrean.officials.imprison.35.members.of.underground.church/16749.htm; www.amnesty.org.uk/actions_details.asp?ActionID=10; www.unhcr.org/refworld/country,,USDOS,,ERI,,4cf2d09ec,0.html, c.f. Michael Kagan, "Refugee Credibility Assessment and the 'Religious Imposter' Problem: A Case Study of Eritrean Pentecostal Claims in Egypt," *Vanderbilt Journal of Transnational Law* 43:5 (November 2010): 1179–233; author's interviews with pentecostal asylum seekers from Eritrea during the period 2008–11.

32. *NIDPCM*, 9, Kalu, *African Pentecostalism*, 225, 240–46.

CHAPTER 6

1. *LRE* 4:1 (October1911): 23.

2. Donald W. Dayton, *Theological Roots of Pentecostalism* (Metuchen, NJ: Scarecrow Press, 1987), 19–28.

3. *BM* 110 (15 May 1912): 1; circular letter, W. W. Simpson to missionaries in China, undated, likely 1914 (Donald Gee Centre, Mattersey, England).

4. *Conf* 2:2 (February1909): 28.

5. Candy Gunther Brown, "Introduction: Pentecostalism and the Globalization of Illness and Healing," in Candy Gunther Brown (ed.), *Global Pentecostal and Charismatic Healing* (New York: Oxford, 2011): 3, 8, 14.

6. *WW* 24:7 (July 1902): 210; Alexander, *Pentecostal Healing*, 16–23, 58–63; Heather D. Curtis, "The Global Character of Nineteenth-Century Divine Healing" in Candy Gunther Brown (ed.), *Global Pentecostal and Charismatic Healing* (New York: Oxford, 2011): 29–45; David Edwin Harrell Jr., *All Things Are Possible: The Healing and Charismatic Revivals in Modern America* (Bloomington: Indiana University Press, 1975): 13; Faupel, *Everlasting Gospel*, 121, 123, 127, 132–35; Anderson, *Spreading Fires*, 37–39.

7. *TF* 1:1 (January 1881): 1, 3–5; Alexander, *Pentecostal Healing*, 24–27, 151–60; Jennifer Ann Miskov, *Life on Wings: The Forgotten Life and Theology of Carrie Judd Montgomery (1858–1946)*, PhD thesis (University of Birmingham, 2011).

8. In Frodsham, *With Signs Following*, 142.

9. Matthew Marostica, "Learning from the Master: Carlos Annacondia and the Standardization of Pentecostal Practices in and beyond Argentina," in Candy Gunther Brown (ed.), *Global Pentecostal and Charismatic Healing* (New York: Oxford, 2011): 207–27.

10. Harrell, *All Things Are Possible,* 20–21; 27–52, 79–80, 150–72, 194–208; *NIDPCM,* 440–41, 713, 950–51, 1024–25.

11. *BM* 91 (1 August1911): 1; Gary B. McGee, "'Power from on High': A Historical Perspective on the Radical Strategy in Missions," in Wonsuk Ma & Robert P. Menzies (eds.): *Pentecostalism in Context* (Sheffield: Sheffield Academic Press, 1997): 317, 324, 329; McGee, "Pentecostals and Their Various Strategies," 215; Moorhead, *Missionary Pioneering,* 76–79; David Edwin Harrell Jr. "Foreword," in C. Douglas Weaver, *The Healer-Prophet: William Marrion Branham, A Study of the Prophetic in American Pentecostalism* (Macon, GA: Mercer University Press, 2000): 3.

12. Moorhead, *Missionary Pioneering,* 39–40; *Pentecost* 1:7 (June 1909): 2; *Conf* 2:2 (February 1909): 29.

13. *FF* 3 (January 1912): 5; *BM* 84 (15 April 1911): 2; letter, Maggie Trevitt to T. H. Mundell, 9 October 1915 (Donald Gee Centre, Mattersey, England).

14. Moorhead, *Missionary Pioneering,* 12, 15.

15. Allan H. Anderson, *Zion and Pentecost: The Spirituality and Experience of Pentecostal and Zionist/Apostolic Churches in South Africa* (Pretoria: University of South Africa Press, 2000): 120–26.

16. John Sung, *The Diaries of John Sung,* Stephen L. Sheng (trans.) (Brighton, MI: Stephen L. Sheng, 1995): 1–19, 40, 43, 51, 56, 88, 91, 93; Lian Xi, *Redeemed by Fire: The Rise of Popular Christianity in Modern China* (New Haven, CT: Yale University Press, 2010): 137–41.

17. Sung, *Diaries,* 24, 26–27, 29, 32, 56, 64, 67, 118–19, 183, 223–26, 231; Xi, *Redeemed by Fire,* 146–47; William E. Shubert, "I Remember John Sung," in Timothy Tow (ed.), *The Asian Awakening* (Singapore: Christian Life Publishers, 1988): 178; Leslie T. Lyall, *John Sung* (Singapore: Armour Publishing, 2004): 236–45.

18. *IRM* 93:370–1 (July/October 2004); "The Healing Mission of the Church," in *"You Are the Light of the World": Statements on Mission by the World Council of Churches 1980–2005* (Geneva: World Council of Churches Publications, 2005): 141–42, 145–46.

19. Samuel Kobia, "Opening Remarks," draft CWME paper, Athens, Greece, 10 May 2005, 1; "A Statement by Pentecostal and Charismatic Participants in the Conference on World Mission and Evangelism," Athens, Greece, 9–16 May 2005.

20. Allan Anderson, "Pentecostals, Healing and Ecumenism," *IRM* 93:370–71 (July/October 2004): 489.

21. Wonsuk Ma, "'When the Poor Are Fired Up': The Role of Pneumatology in Pentecostal Mission," draft CWME paper, Athens, Greece, 10 May 2005, 1–2.

22. World Council of Churches, "The Healing Mission of the Church," 149–50, 159–60; Allan Anderson, "Pentecostal Approaches to Faith and Healing," *IRM* 91:363 (2002): 523–34.
23. *AF* 1 (September 1906): 1; Anderson, *Spreading Fires*, 46–68.
24. Anderson, *Spreading Fires*, 53–54, 57–65.
25. *AF* 6 (February–March 1907): 1 (a reference to Acts 1:8); Faupel, *Everlasting Gospel*, 212–16; Robeck, "Pentecostal Origins," 176–77; T. B. Barratt, *In the Days of the Latter Rain* (London: Simpkin, Marshall, Hamilton, Kent & Co, 1909): 144.
26. Acts 1:8; 2:4, New International Version; Flower quoted in McGee, "Pentecostals and Their Various Strategies," 206; Polhill in *Conf* 2:1 (January 1909): 15; 2:6 (June 1909): 129; 3:8 (August 1910): 198; Boddy in *Conf* 3:8 (August 1910): 199.
27. *LRE* 3:8 (May 1911): 8; *WW* 33:8 (August 1911): 244.
28. Polhill in *FF* 12 (July 1913): 3; Willis Collins Hoover & Mario G. Hoover (trans.), *History of the Pentecostal Revival in Chile* (Santiago, Chile: Imprenta Eben-Ezer, 1930, 2000): 124.
29. Faupel, *Everlasting Gospel*, 99, 104–5, 110–12.
30. Paul Alexander, *Peace to War: Shifting Allegiances in the Assemblies of God* (Telford, PA: Cascadia, 2009); Anderson, *Spreading Fires*, 223–28; www.pcpj.org/, accessed 20 October 2011.
31. Norton in *BM* 97 (1 November 1911): 1; Simpson in *Pentecostal Truths* 34 (April 1912): 4.
32. *BM* 94 (15 September 1911): 1; Brian Stanley, *The Bible and the Flag: Protestant Missions and British Imperialism in the Nineteenth and Twentieth Centuries* (Leicester, UK: Apollos, 1990), 76.
33. Währisch-Oblau, Claudia, "God Can Make Us Healthy Through and Through: On Prayers for the Sick and Healing Experiences in Christian Churches in China and African Immigrant Congregations in Germany," *IRM* 90:356/357 (2001): 87–102, 94, 99.

CHAPTER 7

1. *BM* 59 (1 April 1910): 4; *WE* 144 (17 June 1916): 8.
2. Supplement to *Conf* 2:6 (June 1909): 12; *LRE* 3:7 (April 1911): 19; Frodsham, *With Signs Following*, 175; Anderson, *Spreading Fires*, 20–21.
3. Hoover, *History*, 9, 18–20, 29–32, 36, 68–73; *WW* 32:3 (March 1910): 94; 32:5 (May 1910): 156–57; *UR* 1:6 (January 1910): 5; 1:10 (May 1910): 5; *TF* 30:6 (June 1910): 26–27; *Trust* 9:8 (October 1910): 18; *LRE* 3:7 (April 1911): 20; *DPCM*, 770–71.
4. Hoover, *History*, 74–100, 240–47; *Trust* 9:8 (October 1910): 19; *UR* 2:5 (May 1911): 5; *LRE* 3:10 (July 1911): 21–24; 6:9 (June 1914): 19; 13:4 (January 1921): 2–5; *BM* 97 (1 November 1911): 4; *TF* 32:2 (February 1912): 48; Frodsham, *With Signs Following*, 185–86.
5. www.imepch.cl/actualidad/reportajes/939-datos-biograficos-del-reverendo-manuel-umana-salinas.html, accessed 25 May 2011.

6. Edward L. Cleary & Juan Sepúlveda, "Chilean Pentecostalism: Coming of Age," in Edward L. Cleary & Hannah W. Stewart-Gambino (eds.), *Power, Politics, and Pentecostals in Latin America* (Boulder, CO: Westview, 1997): 97–121, 114.

7. Paul Freston, *Evangelicals and Politics in Asia, Africa and Latin America* (Cambridge: Cambridge University Press, 2001): 215–21; Cleary & Sepúlveda, "Chilean Pentecostalism," 103.

8. Paul Freston, *Evangelicals and Politics in Asia, Africa and Latin America* (Cambridge: Cambridge University Press, 2001): 226, 266–80; Mandryk, *Operation World*, 210, 393; Cleary & Sepúlveda, "Chilean Pentecostalism," 112. *NID-PCM*, 55–57; http://pewforum.org/Christian/Evangelical-Protestant-Churches/ Historical-Overview-of-Pentecostalism-in-Chile.aspx, accessed 11 September 2011; www.state.gov/g/drl/rls/irf/2008/108518.htm, accessed 25 May 2011.

9. Hollenweger, *The Pentecostals*, 85–92; Mandryk, *Operation World*, 163.

10. Vingren in *LRE* 8:4 (January 1916): 14; *WWit* 9:10 (October 1913): 2; 10:3 (March 1914): 4; *LRE* 8:4 (January 1916): 14–16; 12:3 (December 1919): 11; *WE* 213 (3 November 1917): 13; Hollenweger, *The Pentecostals*, 75–79.

11. Hollenweger, *The Pentecostals*, 75, 78; Chesnut, *Born Again*, 26–27, 30; Cox, *Fire*, 163–67; Phillip Berryman, *Religion in the Megacity: Catholic and Protestant Portraits from Latin America* (Maryknoll, NY: Orbis, 1996): 17.

12. Freston, *Evangelicals and Politics*, 9; Mandryk, *Operation World*, 163; Cox, *Fire from Heaven*, 163–67; www.blackpast.org/?q=gah/da-silva-benedita-1942, accessed 21 November 2011; www.minhamarina.org.br/home/home.php, accessed 2 October 2011; interview with Brazilian pentecostal leader, 21 September 2011, Quito, Ecuador.

13. John Paul II, "Opening Address," in Alfred T. Hennelly (ed.), *Santo Domingo and Beyond: Documents and Commentaries from the Historic Meeting of the Latin American Bishops Conference* (Maryknoll, NJ: Orbis Books, 1993): 48; Bryan Froehle, "Pentecostals and Evangelicals in Venezuela: Consolidating Gains, Moving in New Directions," in Edward L. Cleary & Hannah W. Stewart-Gambino (eds.), *Power, Politics, and Pentecostals in Latin America* (Boulder, CO: Westview, 1997): 213–14; cf. Jean-Pierre Bastian, "Pentecostalism, Market Logic and Religious Transnationalisation in Costa Rica," in André Corten & Ruth Marshall-Fratani (eds.), *Between Babel and Pentecost: Transnational Pentecostalism in Africa and Latin America* (Bloomington: Indiana University Press, 2001): 167; Edward L. Cleary, "Introduction: Pentecostals, Prominence, and Politics," in Edward L. Cleary & Hannah W. Stewart-Gambino (eds.), *Power, Politics, and Pentecostals in Latin America* (Boulder, CO: Westview, 1997): 10; Edward L. Cleary, "Movement of Latin American Catholic Charismatics to the United States," unpublished paper, May 2010; Chesnut, *Born Again*, 174.

14. Sanneh, *Disciples of All Nations*, 187–90; Kalu, *African Pentecostalism*, 38–39.

15. Anderson, *Spreading Fires*, 159–61; Sanneh, *Disciples of All Nations*, 193–210; Allan H. Anderson, *African Reformation: African Initiated Christianity in the 20th Century* (Trenton, NJ: Africa World Press, 2001): 69–76.

16. E. Kingsley Larbi, *Pentecostalism: The Eddies of Ghanaian Christianity* (Accra, Ghana: Centre for Pentecostal and Charismatic Studies, 2001): 63–68; Anderson, *African Reformation*, 76–78.

17. Larbi, *Pentecostalism*, 104–37.

18. Yaw Bredwa-Mensah, "The Church of Pentecost in Retrospect," in Opoku Onyinah (ed.), *50 Years of the Church of Pentecost* (Accra: Church of Pentecost, 2004): 8, 21–26, 30–45; McKeown quoted in Opoku Onyinah, "The Man James McKeown," in Opoku Onyinah (ed.), *50 Years of the Church of Pentecost* (Accra: Church of Pentecost, 2004): 71, 86.

19. Larbi, *Pentecostalism*, 175–294; Onyinah, *50 Years*, 168; http://thecophq.org/ accessed 10 April 2011; information from COP Chairman, Dr. Opoku Onyinah, personal conversation, 27 May 2011.

20. Harold W. Turner, *History of an African Independent Church (1) The Church of the Lord (Aladura)* (Oxford: Clarendon Press, 1967): 6, 11–12.

21. Turner, *History*, 22–25, 32; J. D. Y. Peel, *Aladura: A Religious Movement among the Yoruba* (Oxford: Oxford University Press, 1968), 91; Anderson, *African Reformation*, 82–88; Sanneh, *Disciples of All Nations*, 190–91.

22. I witnessed this myself at the ZCC Easter 1992 conference. Anderson, *Zion and Pentecost*, 56–76; Anderson, *Spreading Fires*, 173–81.

23. C. Hanekom, *Krisis en Kultus* (Pretoria: Academica, 1975): 39–40; E. K. Lukhaimane, *The Zion Christian Church of Ignatius (Engenas) Lekganyane, 1924 to 1948: An African Experiment with Christianity*, MA thesis (University of the North, Pietersburg, 1980): 9, 14–18, 20.

24. Lukhaimane, *Zion Christian Church*, 41, 62, 65–67, 72–76; *World* quoted in Hanekom, *Krisis en Kultus*, 44; "South African Population Census 2001, by gender, religion recode (derived): population." www.statssa.gov.za/census01/html, accessed 13 July 2011.

25. Anderson, *Zion and Pentecost*, 166–72.

26. *BM* 52 (15 December 1909): 4; *UR* 1:10 (May 1910): 6; 2:2 (September–October 1910): 3; 2:4 (January 1911): 6, 8; 2:5 (May 1911): 6; *Conf* 4:12 (December 1911): 284; *WE* 124 (22 January 1916): 13; Anderson, *African Reformation*, 97, 153–60.

27. *WWit* 9:1 (January 1913): 2; 9:11 (November 1913): 4; 9:12 (December 1913): 1; 10:4 (April 1914): 4; 12:5 (May 1915): 7; *BM* 144 (15 November 1913): 1; *CE* 70 (12 December 1914): 4; *WE* 91 (22 May 1915): 4; G. P. V. Somaratna, *Origins of the Pentecostal Mission in Sri Lanka* (Mirihana-Nugegoda: Margaya Fellowship of Sri Lanka, 1996): 12–23, 27–32, 41, 45–47; Bergunder, *South Indian Pentecostal*, 31–32, 41–44; Paul C. Martin "A Brief History of the Ceylon Pentecostal Church," in Roger E. Hedlund (ed.), *Christianity Is Indian: The Emergence of an Indigenous Community* (Delhi: ISPCK, 2000): 437–44; Anderson, *Spreading Fires*, 102.

28. Sara Abraham, "Indian Pentecostal Church of God and Its Indigenous Nature," in Roger E. Hedlund (ed.), *Christianity Is Indian: The Emergence of an Indigenous Community* (Delhi: ISPCK, 2000): 457; Bergunder, *South Indian Pentecostal*,

27–34, 50–57; Roger Hedlund, "Indigenous Pentecostalism in India," in Allan H. Anderson & Edmond Tang (eds.), *Asian and Pentecostal: The Charismatic Face of Christianity in Asia* (Oxford: Regnum, 2011): 183–207; Paulson Pullikottil, "Ramankutty Paul: A Dalit Contribution to Pentecostalism," in Allan H. Anderson & Edmond Tang (eds.), *Asian and Pentecostal: The Charismatic Face of Christianity in Asia* (Oxford: Regnum, 2011): 208–18.

29. *The Hongkong Government Gazette*, 22 May, 1886, 449; *AF* 13 (May 1908): 1–2; "Registrar General's Report for the Year 1892," Hong Kong, 1 June 1893, 257; *BM* 39 (1 June 1909): 3; *Conf* 2:12 (December 1909): 282–83; *LRE* 2:3 (December 1909): 22–23; *Pentecostal Truths* 37 (November 1914): 4; S. H. Sung, "History of Pentecostal Mission, Hong Kong & Kowloon," in *Pentecostal Mission, Hong Kong & Kowloon 75 Anniversary 1907–1982*, 8; Daniel Woods, "Failure and Success in the Ministry of T. J. McIntosh, the First Pentecostal Missionary to China," *Cyberjournal for Pentecostal Charismatic Research* 12, 15 April 2003, www.pctii. org/cyberj/cyberj12/woods.html.

30. *Conf* 2:12 (December 1909): 283.

31. *UR* (September 1909): 30; *Pentecostal Truths* 2:4 (April 1909): 1; 37 (November 1914): 1.

32. *Conf* 2:7 (July 1909): 147; 2:11 (November 1909): 259; 2:12 (December 1909): 283–84; *BM* 38 (15 May 1909): 2; 52 (15 December 1909): 2; 53 (1 January 1910): 2; *UR* (September 1909): 30; (February 1910): 54; *LRE* 2:3 (December 1909): 22–23; *Pentecostal Truths* 2:4 (April 1909): 4; Letters of Cora Fritsch, 23 January 1909, 27 January 1909, 5 February 1909, 31 March 1909 (personal collection).

33. *UR* 1:7 (February 1910): 54; (April 1910): 5; (June 1910): 5; (August 1910): 5; *Conf* 3:4 (April 1910): 91; *BM* 59 (1 April 1910): 4; 63 (1 June 1910): 1; 69 (1 September 1910): 4; 73 (1 November 1910): 4; Joseph H. King, *Yet Speaketh: Memoirs of the Late Bishop Joseph H. King* (Franklin Springs, GA: Pentecostal Holiness Church, 1949): 164–65.

34. *Pentecostal Truths* 3:10 (November 1910): 1 (trans. Connie Ho Yan Au).

35. *WWit* 9:11 (20 November 1913): 4; *Pentecostal Truths* 37 (November 1914): 1; 38 (March 1915): 1; 39 (April 1917): 1, 4; personal communication, Connie Ho Yan Au.

36. Hong Kong Legislative Council report, 18 July 1921, 84–85; letter, S. H. Sung to author, 22 July 2005; Sung, "History of Pentecostal Mission," 8–9; www. pentecostal-mission.org/, accessed 21 July 2011.

37. David Aikman, *Jesus in Beijing* (Oxford: Monarch, 2006): 21; Mandryk, *Operation World*, 215–16; Bays, "Christian Revival in China," 162; David A. Reed, "Missionary Resources for an Independent Church—Case Study of the True Jesus Church," Paper presented at the 40th Annual Meeting of the Society for Pentecostal Studies, March 2011.

38. *Bridge* 41: 8; 62: 5, 9–12; 63: 3, 5–7, 9–11, 14; Xi, *Redeemed by Fire*, 42–63, 183–84, 200–202; Bays, "Christian Revival," 170; Deng Zhaoming, "Indigenous Chinese

Pentecostal Denominations," in Allan H. Anderson & Edmond Tang (eds.), *Asian and Pentecostal: The Charismatic Face of Christianity in Asia* (Oxford: Regnum, 2011): 369–93.

39. *TF* 37:6 (June 1917): 127; *LRE* 11:3 (December 1917): 16; Bays, "Protestant Missionary Establishment," 58; Frodsham, *With Signs Following*, 147; Deng, "Indigenous Chinese Pentecostal Denominations," 452–64; Xi, *Redeemed by Fire*, 64–84, 185, 200.

40. Xi, *Redeemed by Fire*, 95–108, 185–86; Bays, "Christian Revival in China," 173–74.

41. Xi, *Redeemed by Fire*, 202, 204–207; Bays, "Christian Revival in China," 174–75; Aikman, *Jesus in Beijing*, 20–31, 66; Sanneh, *Disciples of All Nations*, 264.

42. Anderson, *Spreading Fires*, 65–68.

CHAPTER 8

1. It is now generally accepted that the term "Charismatic movement" in its original usage referred to the practice of spiritual gifts and the experience of Spirit baptism in sections of the mainline churches in the Western world after 1960.

2. Anderson, *Spreading Fires*, 29–31, 90–95, 201–204; Hollenweger, *Pentecostalism*, 334–49; Kay, *Pentecostalism*, 168–75; Stephen Hayes, *Black Charismatic Anglicans: The Iviyo loFakazi bakaKristu and its Relations with other Renewal Movements* (Pretoria: University of South Africa, 1990); *NIDPCM*, 477–519.

3. Hollenweger, *The Pentecostals*, 6–7; *NIDPCM*, 1024–25.

4. Michael J. McClymond, "Prosperity Already and Not Yet: An Eschatological Interpretation of the Health-and-Wealth Emphasis in the North American Pentecostal-Charismatic Movement," in Peter Althouse & Robby Waddell (eds.), *Perspectives in Pentecostal Eschatologies: World without End* (Eugene, OR: Pickwick, 2010): 297–303; *NIDPCM*, 830–33.

5. *NIDPCM*, 653–54.

6. David du Plessis, *A Man Called Mr. Pentecost* (Plainfield, NJ: Logos, 1977): 1–3; *NIDPCM*, 589–93.

7. *Los Angeles Times*, 20 April 1992, http://articles.latimes.com/1992–04–20/local/me-395_1_van-nuys, accessed 4 August 2011.

8. Dennis Bennett, *Nine O'Clock in the Morning* (Plainfield, NJ: Bridge Publishing, 1970); *NIDPCM*, 477–519; Synan, *Holiness-Pentecostal*, 226–33; David Wilkerson, *The Cross and the Switchblade* (New York: Random House, 1963); John L. Sherrill, *They Speak with Other Tongues* (New York: McGraw-Hill, 1964).

9. Wuthnow, *Boundless Faith*, 83; http://mediamatters.org/mmtv/200508220006; www.salon.com/news/haiti/index.html?story=/news/2010/01/13/haiti_robertson, accessed 12 September 2011.

10. Jim Bakker, *I Wwas Wrong* (Nashville, TN: Thomas Nelson, 1996): 535; Synan, *Holiness-Pentecostal*, 289–90; *NIDPCM*, 352–55, 1111; Wuthnow, *Boundless Faith*,

138; www.jsm.org/index.php; http://jimbakkershow.com/about-us/about-jim/, accessed 28 August 2011.

11. Mandryk, *Operation World*, 862; Anderson, *Introduction to Pentecostalism*, 253–58; Anderson et al., *Studying Global Pentecostalism*.

12. Connie Ho Yan Au, *Grassroots Unity in the Charismatic Renewal: Ecumenism in the Fountain Trust International Conferences* (Eugene, OR: Wipf & Stock, 2010): 19–56; Nigel Scotland, *Charismatics and the New Millennium* (London: Hodder & Stoughton, 1995): 1–17; Kay, *Pentecostalism*, 175–92.

13. Hayes, *Black Charismatic Anglicans*; Josiah R. Mlahagwa, "Contending for the Faith: Spiritual Revival and the Fellowship Church in Tanzania," in Thomas Spear & Isaria N. Kimambo (eds.), *East African Expressions of Christianity* (Oxford: James Currey, 1999): 296–306; Gifford, *African Christianity*, 95–96, 154, 227–8, 330; *NIDPCM*, 230–31, 450–51.

14. Brusco, *Reformation of Machismo*, 28–29; Michael Bergunder, "'Ministry of Compassion': D. G. S. Dhinakaran—Christian Healer-Prophet from Tamil Nadu," in Roger E. Hedlund (ed.), *Christianity Is Indian: The Emergence of an Indigenous Community* (Mylapore & Delhi: MIIS/ISPCK, 2000): 160–61; "Evangelist Dhinakaran Dead," *The Hindu*, 21 February 2008, www.hindu.com/2008/02/21/stories/2008022159540800.htm.

15. Kevin Ranaghan & Dorothy Ranaghan, *Catholic Pentecostals* (New York: Paulist Press, 1969); Kilian McDonnell, *Catholic Pentecostalism* (Pecos, NM: Dove Publications, 1970); Edward O'Connor, *The Pentecostal Movement in the Catholic Church* (Notre Dame, IN: Ave Maria Press, 1971).

16. http://catholiccharismatic.us/ccc/articles/John_Paul/John_Paul_001.html, accessed 7 August 2011.

17. Synan, *Holiness-Pentecostal*, 246–52; *NIDPCM*, 460–67; http://iccrs.org/en/index.php/ccr/, accessed 7 August 2011; http://press.catholica.va/news_services/bulletin/news/18881.php?index=18881&po_date=26.09.2006&lang=fr#Testo%20in%20lingua%20inglese, accessed 17 July 2012.

18. Brusco, *Reformation of Machismo*, 28; www.time.com/time/world/article/0,8599,1618439,00.html; www.padremarcelorossi.com.br/, accessed 7 August 2011; http://www.thedailybeast.com/newsweek/2011/10/02/brazil-s-superstar-preacher-marcelo-rossi.html, accessed 11 August 2011.

19. *NIDPCM*, 124, 206–207; www.missionofjesus.com/divine_centre/; www.drcm.org/, accessed 7 August 2011; Katharine L. Wiegele, *Investing in Miracles: El Shaddai and the Transformation of Popular Catholicism in the Philippines* (Honolulu, HI: University of Hawaii Press, 2005).

20. Richard Bustraan, *Upon Your Sons and Daughters: An Analysis of the Pentecostalism in the Jesus People Movement and Its Aftermath*, PhD thesis (University of Birmingham, 2011); Synan, *Holiness-Pentecostal*, 255–56; Anderson, *Introduction to Pentecostalism*, 144–55.

21. Synan, *Holiness-Pentecostal*, 260–66; *NIDPCM*, 484–88, 1060–62.

22. Richard Bustraan, "The Jesus People Movement and the Charismatic Movement: A Case for Inclusion," *PentecoStudies* 10:1 (2011): 29–49; Scotland, *Charismatics,* 202–28; Kay, *Pentecostalism,* 198–200; www.vineyardusa.org/site/about/vineyard-history, http://uk.alpha.org/, accessed 7 August 2011.

23. Valdis Teraudkalns, "Pentecostalism in the Baltics: Historical Retrospection," *Journal of the European Pentecostal Theological Association* 21 (2001): 91–108, 107.

24. *Forum 18* news reports: 3 November 2006; 17 May, 4 July, 14 August, 30 December 2007; 16 January, 31 March; 2 April, 30 May 2008. http://forum18.org accessed 30 May 2010.

25. McClymond, "Prosperity Already and Not Yet," 303–309; E. W. Kenyon, *The Wonderful Name of Jesus* (Seattle, WA: Kenyon's Gospel Publishing Society, 1927): 53–55; E. W. Kenyon, *The Hidden Man* (Seattle, WA: Kenyon's Gospel Publishing Society, 1955): 95–111; E. W. Kenyon, *Jesus the Healer* (Lynnwood, WA: Kenyon's Gospel Publishing Society, 1995): 15, 24, 31; Paul Gifford, *Christianity and Politics in Doe's Liberia* (Cambridge: Cambridge University Press, 1993): 147.

26. H. Terris Neumann, "Cultic Origins of the Word-Faith Theology within the Charismatic Movement," *Pneuma* 12:1 (1990): 32–55, 33–34; Allan Anderson, "The Prosperity Message in the Eschatology of Some New Charismatic Churches," *Missionalia* 15:2 (1987): 72–83, 74; www.rbtc.org/about-us, accessed 7 August 2011.

27. Kenneth E. Hagin, *The Midas Touch: A Balanced Approach to Biblical Prosperity* (Tulsa, OK: Faith Library, 2000): xiii.

28. Wuthnow, *Boundless Faith,* 138; www.cbsnews.com/stories/2008/01/29/cbsnews_investigates/main3767305.shtml, www.inplainsite.org/html/tele-evangelist_lifestyles.html#Tele-Copeland, accessed 5 April 2012.

29. Anderson, "Prosperity Message," 80–81; Andrew Perriman (ed.), *Faith, Health and Prosperity: A Report on "Word of Faith" and "Positive Confession" Theologies* (Carlisle, UK: Paternoster, 2003).

CHAPTER 9

1. Jeong Chong Hee, *The Formation and Development of Korean Pentecostalism from the Viewpoint of a Dynamic Contextual Theology,* ThD thesis (University of Birmingham, 2001): 161–195; Mandryk, *Operation World,* 510.

2. Hodges, *The Indigenous Church.*

3. Sunghoon Myung, *Spiritual Dimension of Church Growth as Applied in Yoido Full Gospel Church,* PhD thesis (Fuller Theological Seminary, 1990): 156.

4. Hollenweger, *Pentecostalism,* 100, n 2, 104; Cox, *Fire from Heaven,* 219–26; David Martin, *Pentecostalism: The World Their Parish* (Oxford: Blackwell, 2002): 161; Mark R. Mullins, *Christianity Made in Japan: A Study of Indigenous Movements* (Honolulu: University of Hawaii Press, 1998): 175–77; David Yonggi Cho, *How Can I Be Healed?* (Seoul: Seoul Logos Co., 1999): 98–100.

5. David Yonggi Cho, *More than Numbers* (Waco, TX: Word Books, 1984): 9.

6. Cho, *More than Numbers*, 43, 101, 144; David Yonggi Cho, with Harold Hostetler, *Successful Home Cell Groups* (Seoul: Seoul Logos Co., 1997): 23–29; Myung, "Spiritual Dimension," 235; Allan Anderson, "Pentecostalism in East Asia: Indigenous Oriental Christianity?" *Pneuma* 22:1 (Spring 2000): 115–32; David Martin, *Tongues of Fire: The Explosion of Protestantism in Latin America* (Oxford: Blackwell, 1990): 140–41.

7. David (Paul) Yonggi Cho, *The Fourth Dimension* (Seoul: Seoul Logos Co., 1979): 10–11, 46–49, 71, 173; Cho, *Successful Home Cell*, 149; David Yonggi Cho, *The Fourth Dimension*, Vol. 2 (South Plainfield, NJ: Bridge Publishing, 1983): 36, 76, 83–85.

8. Cho, *Fourth Dimension*, 9–10, 14, 110, 172; Cho, *Fourth Dimension 2*, xi–xviii, 20, 27; David Yonggi Cho, *Solving Life's Problems* (Seoul: Seoul Logos Co., 1980): 48, 73, 125, 132, 135; Cho, *Successful Home Cell*, 3; Cho, *More than Numbers*, 23–24, 97, 118; David Yonggi Cho, *Praying with Jesus* (Altamonte Springs, FL: Creation House, 1987): 91; David Yonggi Cho, *Salvation, Health and Prosperity: Our Three-fold Blessings in Christ* (Altamonte Springs, FL: Creation House, 1987): 11; David Yonggi Cho, *The Holy Spirit, My Senior Partner: Understanding the Holy Spirit and His Gifts* (Seoul: Seoul Logos Co., 1989): 8; Lee Young Hoon, *The Holy Spirit Movement in Korea: Its Historical and Doctrinal Development*, PhD thesis (Temple University, 1996): 19–21, 25–26, 179, 204–205, 212–13; Jeong, "Formation and Development," 17, 26–27, 30, 216, 225–27, 235, 246–56; Myung, "Spiritual Dimension," 111, 235–36.

9. Cho, *Fourth Dimension 2*, 137–138.

10. Cho, *More than Numbers*, 24; Cho, *Holy Spirit*, 8–9, 13, 21, 100–102, 111, 167–68; David Yonggi Cho, *How to Pray: Patterns of Prayer* (Seoul: Seoul Logos Co., 1997): 76–83; Cho, *Salvation*, 32, 49; Cho, *Successful Home Cell*, 119–20, 131, 149, 153–56; David (Paul) Yonggi Cho, *Great Businessmen* (Seoul: Seoul Logos Co., 1995): 69–75.

11. Paul Yonggi Cho, *Suffering... Why Me?* (South Plainfield, NJ: Bridge Publishing, 1986): 6, 13, 17, 33–41, 57–62, 89–93; Cho, *Salvation*, 115–56; Cho, *How Can I Be Healed?* 15–20; Cho, *Praying with Jesus*, 115–26; Cho, *Successful Home Cell*, 41–44; Paul Yonggi Cho, *Daniel: Insight on the Life and Dreams of the Prophet from Babylon* (Lake Mary, FL: Creation House, 1990); David Yonggi Cho, *Revelation: Visions of our Ultimate Victory in Christ* (Seoul: Seoul Logos Co., 1991).

12. Yoido Full Gospel Church, *Yoido Full Gospel Church* (Seoul, 1993): 1; Cho, *Solving Life's Problems*, 15–16, 47; Cho, *Salvation*, 11–12, 16–18, 49–50; Cho, *Praying with Jesus*, 26.

13. Cho, *Fourth Dimension*, 33–34, 91, 105–106; Cho, *Fourth Dimension 2*, 76–77, 153–54; Cho, *Praying with Jesus*, 50–51; Cho, *Salvation*, 68; Lee, "Holy Spirit," 214. For a fuller treatment of this subject, see Allan Anderson, "The Contribution of David Yonggi Cho to a Contextual Theology in Korea," *JPT* 12:1 (2003): 87–107.

14. David Yonggi Cho, *Successful Home Cell Groups* (Seoul: Seoul Logos Co., 1997); Ralph W. Neighbour Jr., *Where Do We Go from Here? A Guidebook for the Cell Group Church* (Houston, TX: Touch Publications, 1990).

15. Hong Young-gi, "Social Leadership and Church Growth," in Wonsuk Ma, William Menzies, & Hyeon-sung Bae (eds.), *David Yonggi Cho: A Close Look at his Theology and Ministry* (Baguio, Philippines: APTS & Goonpo, S Korea: Hansei University Press, 2004): 249; Ig-Jin Kim, *History and Theology of Korean Pentecostalism: Sunbogeum (Pure Gospel) Pentecostalism* (Zoetermeer, Netherlands: Uitgeverij Boekencentrum, 2003): 289; Allan Anderson, "A 'Time to Share Love': Global Pentecostalism and the Social Ministry of David Yonggi Cho," *JPT* 21 (2012): 152–67.

16. "The Social Service Activities of Yoido Full Gospel Church," in Yoido Full Gospel Church, *50th Anniversary of Yoido Full Gospel Church* (Seoul: YFGC, 2008); Hong, "Social Leadership," 241–44.

17. Matthews A. Ojo, *The End-Time Army: Charismatic Movements in Modern Nigeria* (Trenton, NJ: Africa World Press, 2006): 23–31; Richard Burgess, *Nigeria's Christian Revolution: The Civil War Revival and Its Pentecostal Progeny (1967–2006)* (Oxford: Regnum, 2008): 67–109; Kalu, *African Pentecostalism,* 90–94.

18. Anderson, *Zion and Pentecost,* 87–92; Kalu, *African Pentecostalism,* 240–41; www. charismamag.com/index.php/online-exclusives/1515–35th-anniversary/29036-milestones-in-the-movement, accessed 28 August 2011.

19. Ruthanne Garlock, *Fire in His Bones: The Story of Benson Idahosa* (South Plainfield, GA: Logos, 1981): 117.

20. Ojo, *End-Time Army,* 148–58.

21. Asonzeh Ukah, *A New Paradigm of Pentecostal Power: A Study of the Redeemed Christian Church of God in Nigeria* (Trenton, NJ: Africa World Press, 2008); Ruth Marshall-Fratani, "Mediating the Global and Local in Nigerian Pentecostalism," *Journal of Religion in Africa* 28:4 (1998): 298; www.davidoyedepoministries.org/domi-network/lfcww; I visited these churches in southwestern Nigeria in May 2001.

22. Burgess, *Nigeria's Christian Revolution,* 272–73, 278.

23. Mensa Otabil, *Beyond the Rivers of Ethiopia: A Biblical Revelation on God's Purpose for the Black Race* (Accra, 1992); J. Kwabena Asamoah-Gyadu, *African Charismatics: Current Developments within Independent Indigenous Pentecostalism in Ghana* (Leiden, Netherlands: Brill, 2005): 112–28, 153; Gerrie ter Haar, "Standing Up for Jesus: A Survey of New Developments in Christianity in Ghana," *Exchange* 23:3 (1994): 225–36; Gifford, *African Christianity,* 76–109.

24. Gifford, *Christianity and Politics,* 163; Leslie H. Brickman, *Rapid Cell Church Growth and Reproduction: Case Study of Eglise Protestante Baptiste Oeuvres et Mission Internationale, Abid January, Cote d'Ivoire,* DMin Dissertation (Regent University, 2001); http://neighbourgrams.blogspot.com/2011/05/cell-church-in-ivory-coast-in-grave.html, accessed 20 December 2011.

25. Charles Ouko, "The Triumph of Vision," *Sunday Nation*, Nairobi, 15 February 1998, www.winnersnairobi.org/, accessed 20 December 2011.

26. Richard van Dijk, "Young Born-Again Preachers in Post-Independence Malawi: The Significance of an Extraneous Identity," in Paul Gifford (ed.), *New Dimensions in African Christianity* (Nairobi: All Africa Conference of Churches, 1992): 55–65; Gifford, *African Christianity*, 157–68, 197–205, 220, 230, 233.

27. David Maxwell, "'Delivered from the Spirit of Poverty': Pentecostalism, Prosperity and Modernity in Zimbabwe," *Journal of Religion in Africa* 28:4 (1998): 351–52, 357, 366–68, 372; David Maxwell, *African Gifts of the Spirit: Pentecostalism and the Rise of a Zimbabwean Transnational Religious Movement* (Oxford: James Currey, 2006).

28. Anderson, "Prosperity Message," 74–75; Anderson, *Zion and Pentecost*, 76–78; Gifford, *African Christianity*, 236–37.

29. Allan Anderson, *Bazalwane: African Pentecostals in South Africa* (Pretoria: Unisa, 1992): 137–52; Anderson, *Zion and Pentecost*, 166–72.

30. Kwabena J. Asamoah-Gyadu, "The Church in the African State: The Pentecostal/ Charismatic Experience in Ghana," *Journal of African Christian Thought*, 1:2, 1998, 56; Asamoah-Gyadu, *African Charismatics*, 96; Birgit Meyer, "'Make a Complete Break with the Past': Memory and Post-Colonial Modernity in Ghanaian Pentecostalist Discourse," *Journal of Religion in Africa* 28:4 (1998): 323–24; Gifford, *African Christianity*, 97–109.

31. Anderson, *African Reformation: African Initiated Christianity in the Twentieth Century* (Trenton, NJ: Africa World Press, 2001): 175–86.

32. Paul Adefarasin, "The Kingdoms of This World," in C. Peter Wagner & Joseph Thompson (eds.), *Out of Africa* (Ventura, CA: Regal, 2004): 134–50, 144.

33. T. E. Koshy, *Brother Bakht Singh of India* (Secunderabad: OM Books, 2003): 57, 438–39, 521; www.tehelka.com/story_main.asp?filename=ts013004qaeda. asp&id=5; www.nicmission.org/; www.operationagape.com; accessed 13 July 2011.

34. Personal communication, Wessly Lukose, 14 July 2011; Mandryk, *Operation World*, 408; Jon Thollander, *He Saw a Man Named Mathews* (Udaipur: Cross & Crown, 2000); Wessly Lukose, A *Contextual Missiology of the Spirit: A Study of Pentecostalism in Rajasthan, India*, PhD thesis (University of Birmingham, 2009): 112–22.

CONCLUSIONS

1. Johnson, Barrett & Crossing, "Christianity 2010," 36; http://religions.pewforum. org/affiliations, accessed 9 April 2010.

2. Anderson, *Introduction to Pentecostalism*, 97; Martin, *Pentecostalism*, 67–70.

3. Cox, *Fire from Heaven*, 83.

4. Sanneh, *Disciples of All Nations*, 274–75; Johnson, Barrett & Crossing, "Christianity 2010," 36; Douglas Jacobsen, *The World's Christians: Who They Are, Where*

They Are, and How They Got There (Chichester, UK: Wiley-Blackwell, 2011): 373; Jenkins, *New Faces of Christianity,* 188.

5. http://pewforum.org/Christian/Evangelical-Protestant-Churches/ Spirit-and-Power.aspx, accessed 9 April 2010.

6. Martin, *On Secularization,* 19, 58–59; Jenkins, *The New Faces of Christianity,* 187–89.

7. Cox, *Fire from Heaven,* xvi, 83, 104.

8. Jenkins, *The Next Christendom,* 245–49.

9. Jenkins, *The Next Christendom,* 254.

10. Miller, *Global Pentecostalism,* 221.

Bibliography

PRIMARY LITERATURE

Church Missionary Society archives, University of Birmingham, England
"Combined Minutes of the General Council of the Assemblies of God," 1914–39, Flower Pentecostal Heritage Center, Springfield, Missouri
"Constitution and By-Laws of the General Council of the Assemblies of God," 1927–39, Flower Pentecostal Heritage Center, Springfield, Missouri
"Minutes of the General Council of the Assemblies of God," 1914–19, Flower Pentecostal Heritage Center, Springfield, Missouri
Pentecostal Missionary Union correspondence and minutes, Donald Gee Centre, Mattersey, England
Simpson, W. W., "Contending for the Faith," unpublished typescript, 1953 (courtesy of Cecil M. Robeck Jr.)
Simpson, W. W., Circular letter to missionaries, undated, c.1914, Donald Gee Centre, Mattersey, England

ARCHIVAL PERIODICALS & MAGAZINES

The Alliance Weekly (New York), earlier *The Christian and Missionary Alliance*, 1906–13
The Apostolic Faith (Los Angeles, California), 1906–08
Bombay Guardian and Banner of Asia (Bombay, India), 7 November 1905
The Bridegroom's Messenger (Atlanta, Georgia), 1909–16
Confidence (Sunderland, England), 1908–20
Flames of Fire (London, England), 1911–18
The India Alliance (Bombay, India), 1905–09
The Latter Rain Evangel (Chicago, Illinois), 1908–20
Leaves of Healing (Zion, Illinois), 1904–05

Live Coals (Mercer, Missouri, and Royston, Georgia), 1904–07

Mukti Prayer-Bell (Kedgaon, India), September 1907

The Pentecost (Indianapolis, Indiana, and Kansas City, Missouri), 1908–10

The Pentecostal Evangel (Springfield, Missouri), 1913–20, earlier *The Christian Evangel* (Plainfield, Indiana; Findlay, Ohio, and St. Louis, Missouri), 1913–15, 1918–19, and *The Weekly Evangel* (Springfield, Missouri), 1915–18

The Pentecostal Holiness Advocate (Falcon, North Carolina), 1917–20

Pentecostal Truths (Hong Kong, China), 1908–17

Triumphs of Faith (Buffalo, New York, and Oakland, California), 1881–1920

Trust (Rochester, New York), 1908–20

Word and Witness (Malvern, Arkansas) 1912–15

Word and Work (Framingham, Massachusetts), 1899–1920

The Upper Room (Los Angeles, California), 1909–11

SECONDARY LITERATURE

Abrams, Minnie F. *The Baptism of the Holy Ghost and Fire* (Kedgaon: Pandita Ramabai Mukti Mission, 1906)

Adefarasin, Paul, "The Kingdoms of This World," in C. Peter Wagner & Joseph Thompson (eds.), *Out of Africa* (Ventura, CA: Regal, 2004): 134–50

Adhav, Shamsundar Manohar, *Pandita Ramabai* (Madras: Christian Literature Society, 1979)

Aikman, David, *Jesus in Beijing* (Oxford: Monarch, 2006)

Albrecht, Daniel E. *Rites in the Spirit: A Ritual Approach to Pentecostal/Charismatic Spirituality* (Sheffield, UK: Sheffield Academic Press, 1999)

Alexander, Estrelda, *The Women of Azusa Street* (Cleveland, TN: Pilgrim Press, 2005)

Alexander, Kimberley Ervin, *Pentecostal Healing: Models in Theology and Practice* (Blandford Forum, Dorset: Deo Publishing, 2006)

Alexander, Paul, *Peace to War: Shifting Allegiances in the Assemblies of God* (Telford, PA: Cascadia, 2009)

Allen, Roland, *Missionary Methods: St. Paul's or Ours?* (Grand Rapids, MI: Eerdmans, 1962)

Althouse, Peter & Robby Waddell (eds.), *Perspectives in Pentecostal Eschatologies: World Without End* (Eugene, OR: Pickwick, 2010)

Anderson, Allan H. "The Prosperity Message in the Eschatology of Some New Charismatic Churches," *Missionalia* 15:2 (1987), 72–83

———, *Bazalwane: African Pentecostals in South Africa* (Pretoria: University of South Africa Press, 1992)

———, *Zion and Pentecost: The Spirituality and Experience of Pentecostal and Zionist/Apostolic Churches in South Africa* (Pretoria: University of South Africa Press, 2000)

———, "Pentecostalism in East Asia: Indigenous Oriental Christianity?" *Pneuma* 22:1 (2000), 115–32.

————, "The 'Fury and Wonder'? Pentecostal-Charismatic Spirituality in Theological Education," *Pneuma* 23:2 (2001), 287–302

————, *African Reformation: African Initiated Christianity in the 20th Century* (Trenton, NJ: Africa World Press, 2001)

————, "Pentecostal Approaches to Faith and Healing," *International Review of Mission* 91:363 (2002), 523–34

————, "The Contribution of David Yonggi Cho to a Contextual Theology in Korea," *Journal of Pentecostal Theology* 12:1 (2003), 87–107

————, *An Introduction to Pentecostalism: Global Charismatic Christianity* (Cambridge University Press, 2004)

————, "Pentecostals, Healing and Ecumenism," *International Review of Mission* 93:370–1 (2004), 486–96

————, *Spreading Fires: The Missionary Nature of Early Pentecostalism* (London: SCM & Maryknoll, NY: Orbis, 2007)

————, "'The Present World-Wide Revival . . . Brought Up in India': Pandita Ramabai and the Origins of Pentecostalism," in Roger E. Hedlund, Sebastian Kim, & Rajkumar Boaz Johnson (eds.), *Indian and Christian: The Life and Legacy of Pandita Ramabai* (Chennai: MIIS/CMS/ISPCK, 2011): 307–25

————, "A 'Time to Share Love': Global Pentecostalism and the Social Ministry of David Yonggi Cho," *Journal of Pentecostal Theology* 21 (2012), 152–67

Anderson, Allan H., Michael Bergunder, André Droogers, & Cornelis van der Laan (eds.), *Studying Global Pentecostalism: Theories and Methods* (Berkeley: University of California Press, 2010)

Anderson, Allan H. & Edmond Tang (eds.), *Asian and Pentecostal: The Charismatic Face of Christianity in Asia* (Oxford: Regnum, 2011)

Anderson, Robert Mapes, *Vision of the Disinherited: The Making of American Pentecostalism* (Peabody, MA: Hendrickson, 1979)

Archer, Kenneth J. *A Pentecostal Hermeneutic for the Twenty-First Century: Spirit, Scripture and Community* (Cleveland, TN: CPT Press, 2009)

Asamoah-Gyadu, J. Kwabena, "The Church in the African State: The Pentecostal/ Charismatic Experience in Ghana," *Journal of African Christian Thought,* 1:2 (1998), 51–57

————, "Reversing Christian Mission: African Pentecostal Pastor Establishes 'God's Embassy' in the Ukraine," unpublished paper, May 2004

————, *African Charismatics: Current Developments within Independent Indigenous Pentecostalism in Ghana* (Leiden, Netherlands: Brill, 2005)

Au, Connie Ho Yan, *Grassroots Unity in the Charismatic Renewal: Ecumenism in the Fountain Trust International Conferences* (Eugene, OR: Wipf & Stock, 2010)

Bakker, Jim, *I Was Wrong* (Nashville, TN: Thomas Nelson, 1996)

Barratt, T. B. *In the Days of the Latter Rain* (London: Simpkin, Marshall, Hamilton, Kent, 1909)

————, *When the Fire Fell and an Outline of my Life* (Oslo: Hansen and Sonner, 1927)

Barrett, David B. *Schism and Renewal in Africa: An Analysis of Six Thousand Contemporary Religious Movements* (Nairobi: Oxford University Press, 1968)

Bartleman, Frank, *Azusa Street* (S. Plainfield, NJ: Bridge Publishing, 1925, 1980)

Bastian, Jean-Pierre, "Pentecostalism, Market Logic and Religious Transnationalisation in Costa Rica," in André Corten & Ruth Marshall-Fratani (eds.), *Between Babel and Pentecost: Transnational Pentecostalism in Africa and Latin America* (Bloomington: Indiana University Press, 2001): 163–80

Baynham, Jacob, "Hong Kong Missionary Uses Intensive Prayer to Help Heroin Addicts," *San Francisco Chronicle* (14 December 2007), www.sfgate.com/cgi-bin/article.cgi?f=/c/a/2007/12/14/MNIKT2BIA.DTL&feed=rss.news, accessed 8 September 2011

Bays, Daniel H. "Christian Revival in China, 1900–1937," in Edith L. Blumhofer & Randall Balmer (eds.), *Modern Christian Revivals* (Urbana: University of Illinois Press, 1993): 162–65

———, *A New History of Christianity in China* (Chichester, UK: Wiley-Blackwell, 2012)

Bays, Daniel H. & Grant Wacker (eds.), *The Foreign Missionary Enterprise at Home: Explorations in North American Cultural History* (Tuscaloosa: University of Alabama Press, 2003)

Bebbington, David W. *The Dominance of Evangelicalism: The Age of Spurgeon and Moody* (Downer's Grove, IL: InterVarsity Press, 2005)

Bennett, Dennis, *Nine O'Clock in the Morning* (Plainfield, NJ: Bridge, 1970)

Bergunder, Michael, *The South Indian Pentecostal Movement in the Twentieth Century* (Grand Rapids, MI: Eerdmans, 2008)

Berryman, Phillip, *Religion in the Megacity: Catholic and Protestant Portraits from Latin America* (Maryknoll, NY: Orbis, 1996)

Blair, William N. & Bruce Hunt, *The Korean Pentecost and the Sufferings Which Followed* (Edinburgh: Banner of Truth Trust, 1977)

Bloch-Hoell, Nils, *The Pentecostal Movement* (Oslo: Universitetsforlaget, 1964)

Blumhofer, Edith L. *Aimee Semple McPherson: Everybody's Sister* (Grand Rapids, MI: Eerdmans, 1993)

———, *Restoring the Faith: The Assemblies of God, Pentecostalism, and American Culture* (Urbana: University of Illinois Press, 1993)

———, "'From India's Coral Strand': Pandita Ramabai and U.S. Support for Foreign Missions," in Daniel H. Bays & Grant Wacker (eds.), *The Foreign Missionary Enterprise at Home: Explorations in North American Cultural History* (Tuscaloosa: University of Alabama Press, 2003): 152–70

———, "Consuming Fire: Pandita Ramabai and the Early Pentecostal Impulse," in Roger E. Hedlund, Sebastian Kim, & Rajkumar Boaz Johnson (eds.), *Indian and Christian: The Life and Legacy of Pandita Ramabai* (Chennai: MIIS/CMS/ISPCK, 2011): 127–54

Blumhofer, Edith L. & Randall Balmer (eds.), *Modern Christian Revivals* (Urbana: University of Illinois Press, 1993)

Blumhofer, Edith L., Russell P. Spittler, & Grant A. Wacker (eds.), *Pentecostal Currents in American Protestantism* (Urbana: University of Illinois Press, 1999)

Bredwa-Mensah, Yaw, "The Church of Pentecost in Retrospect," in Opoku Onyinah (ed.), *The Church of Pentecost: 50 Years of Sustainable Growth* (Accra: Church of Pentecost, 2004): 8–45

Brewster, William Nesbitt, *A Modern Pentecost in South China* (Shanghai: Methodist Publishing House, 1909)

Brickman, Leslie H. *Rapid Cell Church Growth and Reproduction: Case Study of Eglise Protestante Baptiste Oeuvres et Mission Internationale, Abidjan, Cote d'Ivoire* (DMin Dissertation, Regent University, 2001)

Brown, Callum G., *The Death of Christian Britain* (London: Routledge, 2001).

Brown, Candy Gunther (ed.), *Global Pentecostal and Charismatic Healing* (New York: Oxford, 2011)

Brusco, Elizabeth E. *The Reformation of Machismo: Evangelical Conversion and Gender in Colombia* (Austin: University of Texas Press, 1995)

———, "Gender and Power," in Allan H. Anderson, Michael Bergunder, André Droogers, & Cornelis van der Laan (eds.), *Studying Global Pentecostalism: Theories and Methods* (Berkeley, CA: University of California Press, 2010): 74–92

Burgess, Richard, *Nigeria's Christian Revolution: The Civil War Revival and Its Pentecostal Progeny (1967–2006)* (Oxford: Regnum, 2008)

Burpeau, Kemp Pendleton, *God's Showman: A Historical Study of John G. Lake and South African/American Pentecostalism* (Oslo: Refleks, 2004)

Burton, William F. P. *God Working with Them* (London: Victory Press, 1932)

———, *When God Changes a Village* (London: Victory Press, 1933)

———, *When God Makes a Pastor* (London: Victory Press, 1934)

Bustraan, Richard, *Upon Your Sons and Daughters: An Analysis of the Pentecostalism in the Jesus People Movement and Its Aftermath* (PhD thesis, University of Birmingham, 2011)

Butler, Anthea D. *Women in the Church of God in Christ: Making a Sanctified World* (Chapel Hill: University of North Carolina Press, 2007)

Cartledge, Mark J. *Testimony in the Spirit: Rescripting Ordinary Pentecostal Theology* (Farnham, UK: Ashgate, 2010)

———, "Family Socialisation, Godly Love and Pentecostal Spirituality," *Research in the Social Scientific Study of Religion* 23 (2012), 1–27

Cavaness, Barbara, "Spiritual Chain Reactions: Women Used of God," *Assemblies of God Heritage*, 2008, 40–43

Cerillo, Augustus Jr., "Interpretive Approaches to the History of American Pentecostal Origins," *Pneuma* 19 (Spring 1997), 29–52

Chapman, Diana, *Searching the Source of the River: Forgotten Women of the British Pentecostal Revival 1907–1914* (London: Push, 2007)

Chesnut, R. Andrew, *Born Again in Brazil: The Pentecostal Boom and the Pathogens of Poverty* (New Brunswick, NJ: Rutgers University Press, 1997)

Cho, David (Paul) Yonggi, *The Fourth Dimension* (Seoul: Seoul Logos, 1979)

———, *Solving Life's Problems* (Seoul: Seoul Logos, 1980)

———, *The Fourth Dimension*, Vol. 2 (South Plainfield, NJ: Bridge, 1983)

———, *More than Numbers* (Waco, TX: Word Books, 1984)

———, *Suffering… Why Me?* (South Plainfield, NJ: Bridge, 1986)

———, *Praying with Jesus* (Altamonte Springs, FL: Creation House, 1987)

———, *Salvation, Health and Prosperity: Our Threefold Blessings in Christ* (Altamonte Springs, FL: Creation House, 1987)

———, *The Holy Spirit, My Senior Partner: Understanding the Holy Spirit and His Gifts* (Seoul: Seoul Logos, 1989)

———, *Daniel: Insight on the Life and Dreams of the Prophet from Babylon* (Lake Mary, FL: Creation House, 1990)

———, *Revelation: Visions of Our Ultimate Victory in Christ* (Seoul: Seoul Logos, 1991)

———, *Great Businessmen* (Seoul: Seoul Logos, 1995)

———, with Harold Hostetler, *Successful Home Cell Groups* (Seoul: Seoul Logos, 1997)

———, *How to Pray: Patterns of Prayer* (Seoul: Seoul Logos, 1997)

———, *How Can I Be Healed?* (Seoul: Seoul Logos, 1999)

Choi, Jashil, *Hallelujah Lady* (Seoul: Seoul Logos, 2009)

Cityland Foundation, *This Is My Story: 31 Lives, Stories, Miracles* (Manila: OMF Literature, 2004)

Cleary, Edward L. "Introduction: Pentecostals, Prominence, and Politics," in Edward L. Cleary & Hannah W. Stewart-Gambino (eds.), *Power, Politics, and Pentecostals in Latin America* (Boulder, CO: Westview, 1997): 1–24

———, "Movement of Latin American Catholic Charismatics to the United States," unpublished paper, May 2010

Cleary, Edward L. & Hannah W. Stewart-Gambino (eds.), *Power, Politics, and Pentecostals in Latin America* (Boulder, CO: Westview, 1997)

Cleary, Edward L. & Juan Sepúlveda, "Chilean Pentecostalism: Coming of Age," in Edward L. Cleary & Hannah W. Stewart-Gambino (eds.), *Power, Politics, and Pentecostals in Latin America* (Boulder, CO: Westview, 1997): 97–121

Colletti, Joseph R. "Lewi Pethrus: His Influence upon Scandinavian-American Pentecostalism," *Pneuma* 5:2 (1983), 18–29

Comaroff, Jean, *Body of Power, Spirit of Resistance: The Culture and History of a South African People* (Chicago: University of Chicago Press, 1985)

Cook, Robert F. *A Quarter Century of Divine Leading in India* (Chengannur, S. India: Church of God in India, 1939)

Corten, André & Ruth Marshall-Fratani (eds.), *Between Babel and Pentecost: Transnational Pentecostalism in Africa and Latin America* (Bloomington: Indiana University Press, 2001)

Cox, Harvey, *Fire from Heaven: The Rise of Pentecostal Spirituality and the Reshaping of Religion in the Twenty-first Century* (London: Cassell, 1996)

Creech, Joe, "Visions of Glory: The Place of the Azusa Street Revival in Pentecostal History," *Church History* 65:3 (September 1996), 405–24.

Croatto, Severino, *Biblical Hermeneutics* (Maryknoll, NY: Orbis, 1987)

Crumbley, Deidre Helen, *Spirit, Structure, and Flesh: Gendered Experiences in African Instituted Churches among the Yoruba of Nigeria* (Madison: University of Wisconsin Press, 2008)

Daneel, M. L. *Old and New in Southern Shona Independent Churches,* Vol. 2 (The Hague: Moulton, 1974)

———, *Quest for Belonging* (Gweru, Zimbabwe: Mambo Press, 1987)

———, *Old and New in Southern Shona Independent Churches,* Vol. 3 (Gweru, Zimbabwe: Mambo Press, 1988)

Davies, Andrew, "What Does It Mean to Read the Bible as a Pentecostal?" *Journal of Pentecostal Theology* 18:2 (2009), 216–29

Dayton, Donald W. *Theological Roots of Pentecostalism* (Metuchen, NJ: Scarecrow Press, 1987)

Dempster, Murray A., Byron D. Klaus, & Douglas Petersen (eds.), *Called and Empowered: Global Mission in Pentecostal Perspective* (Peabody, MA: Hendrickson, 1991)

Deng Zhaoming, "Indigenous Chinese Pentecostal Denominations," in Allan H. Anderson & Edmond Tang (eds.), *Asian and Pentecostal: The Charismatic Face of Christianity in Asia* (Oxford: Regnum, 2011): 369–93

Dongre, Rajas K. & Josephine F. Patterson, *Pandita Ramabai: A Life of Faith and Prayer* (Madras: Christian Literature Society, 1963)

Du Plessis, David, *A Man Called Mr. Pentecost* (Plainfield, NJ: Logos, 1977)

Dyer, Helen, *Revival in India 1905–1906* (Akola: Alliance Publications, 1987)

Eim, Yeol Soo, "The Amazing Ministry of Dr Seen SookAhn," *Cyberjournal for Pentecostal Charismatic Research* 6, August 1999, www.pctii.org/cyberj/cyberj6/eim.html

Farrelly, Paul, "Mount Zion and Typhoon Morakot: A New Religion's Response to a Natural Disaster," www.religion.info/pdf/2010_04_Farrelly.pdf, accessed 3 September 2011

Faupel, D. William, *The Everlasting Gospel: The Significance of Eschatology in the Development of Pentecostal Thought* (Sheffield, UK: Sheffield Academic Press, 1996)

Fenn, Richard K. (ed.), *The Blackwell Companion to Sociology of Religion* (Oxford: Blackwell, 2003)

French, Talmadge Leon, *Early Oneness Pentecostalism, Garfield Thomas Haywood, and the Interracial Pentecostal Assemblies of the World (1906–1931)* (PhD thesis, University of Birmingham, 2011)

Freston, Paul, *Evangelicals and Politics in Asia, Africa and Latin America* (Cambridge: Cambridge University Press, 2001)

Friedmann, Jonathan, "Liberating Domesticity: Women and the Home in Orthodox Judaism and Latin American Pentecostalism," *Journal of Religion & Society* 10 (2008), 1–55

Frodsham, Stanley H. *"With Signs Following": The Story of the Latter-Day Pentecostal Revival* (Springfield, MO: Gospel Publishing House, 1926)

Fuller, Mary L. B. *The Triumph of an Indian Widow: The Life of Pandita Ramabai* (New York: Christian Alliance, 1927)

Gabriel, Charles H. "Pentecostal Power," *Redemption Hymnal: With Tunes* (London: Assemblies of God Publishing House, 1955): no. 244

Garlock, Ruthanne, *Fire in His Bones: The Story of Benson Idahosa* (South Plainfield, NJ: Logos, 1981)

Gifford, Paul (ed.), *New Dimensions in African Christianity* (Nairobi: All Africa Conference of Churches, 1992)

———, *Christianity and Politics in Doe's Liberia* (Cambridge: Cambridge University Press, 1993)

———, *African Christianity: Its Public Role* (London: Hurst, 1998)

———, *Christianity, Politics and Public Life in Kenya* (London: Hurst, 2009)

Gill, Lesley, "'Like a Veil to Cover Them': Women and the Pentecostal Movement in La Paz," *American Ethnologist* 17:4 (1990), 708–21

Goff, James R. Jr. & Grant Wacker (eds.), *Portraits of a Generation: Early Pentecostal Leaders* (Fayetteville: University of Arkansas Press, 2002)

Gottwald, N. K. & R. A. Horsley (eds.), *The Bible and Liberation* (Maryknoll, NY: Orbis, 1993)

Hagin, Kenneth E. *The Midas Touch: A Balanced Approach to Biblical Prosperity* (Tulsa, OK: Faith Library, 2000)

Haliburton, Gordon MacKay, *The Prophet Harris: A Study of an African Prophet and His Mass Movement in the Ivory Coast and the Gold Coast 1913–1915* (London: Longman, 1971)

Hallum, Anne Motley, "Taking Stock and Building Bridges: Feminism, Women's Movements, and Pentecostalism in Latin America," *Latin American Research Review* 38: 1 (2003), 169–86

Hanekom, C. *Krisis en Kultus* (Pretoria: Academica, 1975)

Harrell, David Edwin Jr., *All Things Are Possible: The Healing and Charismatic Revivals in Modern America* (Bloomington: Indiana University Press, 1975)

———, "Foreword," in C. Douglas Weaver, *The Healer-Prophet: William Marrion Branham, A Study of the Prophetic in American Pentecostalism* (Macon, GA: Mercer University Press, 2000): 1–4

Hastings, Adrian, *The Church in Africa 1450–1930* (Oxford: Clarendon, 1994)

Hathaway, Malcolm R. "The Elim Pentecostal Church: Origins, Development and Distinctives," in Keith Warrington (ed.), *Pentecostal Perspectives* (Carlisle, UK: Paternoster, 1998): 1–39

Hayes, Stephen, *Black Charismatic Anglicans: The Iviyo loFakazi bakaKristu and Its Relations with Other Renewal Movements* (Pretoria: University of South Africa, 1990)

Hedlund, Roger E. (ed.), *Christianity Is Indian: The Emergence of an Indigenous Community* (Mylapore: MIIS/ISPCK, 2000)

————,"Indigenous Pentecostalism in India," in Allan H. Anderson & Edmond Tang (eds.), *Asian and Pentecostal: The Charismatic Face of Christianity in Asia* (Oxford: Regnum, 2011): 183–207

Hedlund, Roger E., Sebastian Kim, & Rajkumar Boaz Johnson (eds.), *Indian and Christian: The Life and Legacy of Pandita Ramabai* (Chennai: MIIS/CMS/ISPCK, 2011)

Helgesson, Kristina, *"Walking in the Spirit": The Complexity of Belonging in Two Pentecostal Churches in Durban, South Africa* (PhD thesis, Uppsala University, 2006)

Hennelly, Alfred T. (ed.), *Santo Domingo and Beyond: Documents and Commentaries from the Historic Meeting of the Latin American Bishops Conference* (Maryknoll, NY: Orbis, 1993)

Hodges, Melvin L., *The Indigenous Church* (Springfield, MO: Gospel Publishing House, 1953)

Hodgson, Janet, "Ntsikana—A Precursor of Independency?" *Missionalia* 12:1 (1984), 19–33

————, "A Study of the Xhosa Prophet Nxele," *Missionalia* 13:1 (1985), 11–36

Hollenweger, Walter J. *The Pentecostals* (London: SCM, 1972)

————, *Pentecostalism: Origins and Developments Worldwide* (Peabody, MA: Hendrickson, 1997)

Hong, Young-gi, "Social Leadership and Church Growth," in Wonsuk Ma, William Menzies, & Hyeon-sung Bae (eds.), *David Yonggi Cho: A Close Look at His Theology and Ministry* (Baguio, Philippines: APTS & Goonpo, S. Korea: Hansei University Press, 2004): 221–51

Hoover, Willis Collins & Mario G. Hoover (trans.), *History of the Pentecostal Revival in Chile* (Santiago, Chile: Imprenta Eben-Ezer, 1930, 2000)

Hunter, Harold D. & P. D. Hocken (eds.), *All Together in One Place: Theological Papers from the Brighton Conference on World Evangelization* (Sheffield, UK: Sheffield Academic Press, 1993)

Hwa Yung, "Critical Issues Facing Theological Education in Asia," *Transformation* (October–December 1995), 1–6

Ingram, J. H. *Around the World with the Gospel Light* (Cleveland, TN: Church of God Publishing House, 1938)

Jacobsen, Douglas, *Thinking in the Spirit: Theologies of the Early Pentecostal Movement* (Bloomington: Indiana University Press, 2003)

————, *The World's Christians: Who They Are, Where They Are, and How They Got There* (Chichester, UK: Wiley-Blackwell, 2011)

Jenkins, Philip, *The New Faces of Christianity: Believing the Bible in the Global South* (New York: Oxford University Press, 2006)

————, *The Next Christendom: The Coming of Global Christianity* (New York: Oxford University Press, 2007)

Jeong, Chong Hee, *The Formation and Development of Korean Pentecostalism from the Viewpoint of a Dynamic Contextual Theology* (ThD thesis, University of Birmingham, 2001)

John Paul II, "Opening Address," in Alfred T. Hennelly (ed.), *Santo Domingo and Beyond: Documents and Commentaries from the Historic Meeting of the Latin American Bishops Conference* (Maryknoll, NY: Orbis, 1993): 41–60

Johnson, Todd M., David B. Barrett, & Peter F. Crossing, "Christianity 2010: A View from the New Atlas of Global Christianity," *International Bulletin of Missionary Research* 34:1(2010), 29–36

———, "Christianity 2012: The 200th Anniversary of American Foreign Missions," *International Bulletin of Missionary Research* 36:1 (2012), 28–29

Kagan, Michael, "Refugee Credibility Assessment and the 'Religious Imposter' Problem: A Case Study of Eritrean Pentecostal Claims in Egypt," *Vanderbilt Journal of Transnational Law* 43:5 (November 2010), 1179–233

Kärkkäinen, Veli-Matti (ed.), *The Spirit in the World: Emerging Pentecostal Theologies in Global Contexts* (Grand Rapids, MI: Eerdmans, 2009)

Kalu, Ogbu, *African Pentecostalism: An Introduction* (New York: Oxford University Press, 2008)

Kay, William K. "Assemblies of God: Distinctive Continuity and Distinctive Change," in Keith Warrington (ed.), *Pentecostal Perspectives* (Carlisle, UK: Paternoster, 1999): 40–63

———, *Pentecostals in Britain* (Carlisle, UK: Paternoster, 2000)

———, *Pentecostalism* (London: SCM, 2009)

Kelsey, Morton, *Tongue Speaking: The History and Meaning of Charismatic Experience* (New York: Crossroad, 1981)

Kenyon, E.W. *The Wonderful Name of Jesus* (Seattle, WA: Kenyon's Gospel Publishing Society, 1927)

———, *The Hidden Man* (Seattle, WA: Kenyon's Gospel Publishing Society, 1955)

———, *Jesus the Healer* (Lynnwood, WA: Kenyon's Gospel Publishing Society, 1995)

Kim, Ig-jin, *History and Theology of Korean Pentecostalism: Sunbogeum (Pure Gospel) Pentecostalism* (Zoetermeer, Netherlands: Uitgeverij Boekencentrum, 2003)

Kim, Sean C. "Reenchanted: Divine Healing in Korean Protestantism," in Candy Gunther Brown (ed.), *Global Pentecostal and Charismatic Healing* (Oxford: Oxford University Press, 2011): 267–85

King, Joseph H. *Yet Speaketh: Memoirs of the Late Bishop Joseph H. King* (Franklin Springs, GA: Pentecostal Holiness Church, 1949)

King, Paul L. *Genuine Gold: The Cautiously Charismatic Story of the Early Christian and Missionary Alliance* (Tulsa, OK: Word & Spirit Press, 2006)

Kobia, Samuel, "Opening Remarks," draft Commission for World Mission and Evangelism paper, Athens, Greece, 10 May 2005

Körner, Peter, "The St. John's Apostolic Faith Mission and Politics: The Political Dimension of an Apolitical Independent Church," in Gordon Mitchell & Eve Mullen (eds.), *Religion and the Political Imagination in a Changing South Africa* (Münster, Germany: Waxmann, 2002): 133–50

Kosambi, Meera (ed. & trans.), *Pandita Ramabai Through Her Own Words: Selected Works* (New Delhi: Oxford University Press, 2000)

Koshy, T. E. *Brother Bakht Singh of India* (Secunderabad: OM Books, 2003)

Lalive d'Épinay, Christian, "The Training of Pastors and Theological Education: The Case of Chile," *International Review of Missions* 56: 222 (April 1967), 185–91

Land, Steven J. *Pentecostal Spirituality: A Passion for the Kingdom* (Sheffield, UK: Sheffield Academic Press, 1993)

Landman, Christina, "Christinah Nku and St John's: A Hundred Years Later," *Studia Historiae Ecclesiasticae* 32:3 (2006), 1–32

Lang, G. H. *The History and Diaries of an Indian Christian* (London: Thinne, 1939)

———, *The Earlier Years of the Modern Tongues Movement* (Enfield, Middlesex: Metcalfe Collier, c.1946)

Larbi, E. Kingsley, *Pentecostalism: The Eddies of Ghanaian Christianity* (Accra, Ghana: Centre for Pentecostal and Charismatic Studies, 2001)

Law, E. May, *Pentecostal Mission Work in South China: An Appeal for Missions* (Falcon, NC: Falcon, 1915)

Lederle, Henry I. "Pentecostals and Ecumenical Theological Education," *Ministerial Formation* 80 (January 1998), 46.

Lee, Young Hoon, *The Holy Spirit Movement in Korea: Its Historical and Doctrinal Development* (PhD thesis, Temple University, 1996)

Lewis, Donald M. (ed.), *Christianity Reborn: The Global Expansion of Evangelicalism in the Twentieth Century* (Grand Rapids, MI: Eerdmans, 2004)

Lukhaimane, E. K. *The Zion Christian Church of Ignatius (Engenas) Lekganyane, 1924 to 1948: An African Experiment with Christianity* (MA thesis, University of the North, Pietersburg, 1980)

Lukose, Wessly, *A Contextual Missiology of the Spirit: A Study of Pentecostalism in Rajasthan, India,* (PhD thesis, University of Birmingham, 2009)

Lyall, Leslie T. *John Sung* (Singapore: Armour, 2004)

Ma, Julie C. "Korean Spirituality: A Case Study of Jashil Choi," in Wonsuk Ma & Robert P. Menzies (eds.), *The Spirit and Spirituality: Essays in Honour of Russell P. Spittler* (London: T&T Clark, 2004): 298–313

——— "Asian Women and Pentecostal Ministry," in Allan H. Anderson & Edmond Tang (eds.), *Asian and Pentecostal: The Charismatic Face of Christianity in Asia* (Oxford: Regnum, 2011): 109–24

Ma, Wonsuk & Robert P. Menzies (eds.), *Pentecostalism in Context* (Sheffield, UK: Sheffield Academic Press, 1997)

———, & Robert P. Menzies (eds.), *The Spirit and Spirituality: Essays in Honour of Russell P. Spittler* (London: T&T Clark, 2004)

———, William Menzies, & Hyeon-sung Bae (eds.), *David Yonggi Cho: A Close Look at His Theology and Ministry* (Baguio, Philippines: APTS, 2004)

———, "'When the Poor Are Fired Up': The Role of Pneumatology in Pentecostal Mission," draft Commision for World Mission and Evangelism paper, Athens, Greece, 10 May 2005

Maimela, Simon S. "Salvation in African Traditional Religions," *Missionalia* 13: 2 (1985), 63–77

Mair, Jessie H. *Bungalows in Heaven: The Story of Pandita Ramabai* (Kedgaon, India: Pandita Ramabai Mukti Mission, 2003)

Mandryk, Jason, *Operation World*, 7th ed. (Colorado Springs: Biblica, 2010)

Mariz, Cecília Loreto & María das Dores Campos Machado, "Pentecostalism and Women in Brazil," in Edward L. Cleary & Hannah W. Stewart-Gambino (eds.), *Power, Politics, and Pentecostals in Latin America* (Boulder, CO: Westview, 1997): 41–54

Marshall-Fratani, Ruth, "Mediating the Global and Local in Nigerian Pentecostalism," *Journal of Religion in Africa* 28:4 (1998), 278–315

Martin, Bernice, "The Pentecostal Gender Paradox: A Cautionary Tale for the Sociology of Religion," Richard K. Fenn (ed.), *The Blackwell Companion to Sociology of Religion* (Oxford: Blackwell, 2003): 52–66

Martin, David, *Tongues of Fire: The Explosion of Protestantism in Latin America* (Oxford: Blackwell, 1990)

———, *Forbidden Revolutions: Pentecostalism in Latin America and Catholicism in Eastern Europe* (London: SPCK, 1996)

———, *Pentecostalism: The World Their Parish* (Oxford: Blackwell, 2002)

———, *On Secularization: Towards a Revised General Theory* (Aldershot, Hants: Ashgate, 2005)

Martin, Larry (ed.), *Doctrines and Disciplines of the Azusa Street Mission of Los Angeles California* (Joplin, MO: Christian Life Books, 2000)

Martin, Paul C. "A Brief History of the Ceylon Pentecostal Church," in Roger E. Hedlund (ed.), *Christianity Is Indian: The Emergence of an Indigenous Community* (Delhi: ISPCK, 2000): 437–44

Maxwell, David, "'Delivered from the Spirit of Poverty': Pentecostalism, Prosperity and Modernity in Zimbabwe," *Journal of Religion in Africa* 28:4 (1998), 351–72

———, *African Gifts of the Spirit: Pentecostalism and the Rise of a Zimbabwean Transnational Religious Movement* (Oxford: James Currey, 2006)

———, "The Soul of the Luba: W. F. P. Burton, Missionary Ethnography and Belgian Colonial Science," *History and Anthropology* 19:4 (2008), 325–51

———, "Photography and the Religious Encounter: Ambiguity and Aesthetics in Missionary Representations of the Luba of South East Belgian Congo," *Comparative Studies in Society and History* 53:1 (2011), 38–74

McClymond, Michael J. "Prosperity Already and Not Yet: An Eschatological Interpretation of the Health-and-Wealth Emphasis in the North American Pentecostal-Charismatic Movement," in Peter Althouse & Robby Waddell (eds.), *Perspectives in Pentecostal Eschatologies: World without End* (Eugene, OR: Pickwick, 2010): 293–312.

McDonnell, Kilian, *Catholic Pentecostalism* (Pecos, NM: Dove, 1970)

McGee, Gary B. "Pentecostals and Their Various Strategies for Global Mission," in Murray A. Dempster, Byron D. Klaus, & Douglas Petersen (eds.), *Called and Empowered: Global Mission in Pentecostal Perspective* (Peabody, MA: Hendrickson, 1991): 203–24

———, "'Power from on High': A Historical Perspective on the Radical Strategy in Missions," in Wonsuk Ma & Robert P. Menzies (eds.), *Pentecostalism in Context* (Sheffield: Sheffield Academic Press, 1997): 317–36

———, "'Latter Rain' Falling in the East: Early-Twentieth-Century Pentecostalism in India and the Debate over Speaking in Tongues," *Church History* 68:3 (1999), 648–65

———, "Minnie F. Abrams: Another Context, Another Founder," in James R. Goff & Grant Wacker (eds.), *Portraits of a Generation: Early Pentecostal Leaders* (Fayetteville: University of Arkansas Press, 2002): 87–104

———, "The Calcutta Revival of 1907 and the Reformulation of Charles F. Parham's 'Bible Evidence' Doctrine," *Asian Journal of Pentecostal Studies* 6:1 (2003), 123–43

———, *Miracles, Missions, and American Pentecostalism* (Maryknoll, NY: Orbis, 2010)

McKay, John, "When the Veil Is Taken Away: The Impact of Prophetic Experience on Biblical Interpretation," *Journal of Pentecostal Theology* 5 (1994), 38

McLeod, Hugh, "The Crisis of Christianity in the West: Entering a Post-Christian Era?" in Hugh McLeod (ed.), *The Cambridge History of Christianity: World Christianity c. 1914–c. 2000* (Cambridge: Cambridge University Press, 2006): 323–47

———, *The Religious Crisis of the 1960s* (Oxford: Oxford University Press, 2010)

McPherson, Aimee Semple, *This Is That: Personal Experiences, Sermons and Writings* (Los Angeles: Echo Park Evangelistic Association, 1923)

Mesters, Carlos, "The Use of the Bible in Christian Communities of the Common People," in N. K. Gottwald and R. A. Horsley (eds.), *The Bible and Liberation* (Maryknoll, NY: Orbis, 1993)

Meyer, Birgit, "'Make a Complete Break with the Past': Memory and Post-Colonial Modernity in Ghanaian Pentecostalist Discourse," *Journal of Religion in Africa* 28:4 (1998), 316–49

Miller, Donald E. & Tetsunao Yamamori, *Global Pentecostalism: The New Face of Christian Social Engagement* (Berkeley: University of California Press, 2007)

Miskov, Jennifer Ann, *Life on Wings: The Forgotten Life and Theology of Carrie Judd Montgomery (1858–1946)* (PhD thesis, University of Birmingham, 2011)

Mitchell, Gordon & Eve Mullen (eds.), *Religion and the Political Imagination in a Changing South Africa* (Münster, Germany: Waxmann, 2002)

Moorhead, Max W. (ed.), *Missionary Pioneering in Congo Forests: A Narrative of the Labours of William F. P. Burton and His Companions in the Native Villages of Luba-land* (Preston, UK: R. Seed, 1922)

Mullins, Mark R. *Christianity Made in Japan: A Study of Indigenous Movements* (Honolulu: University of Hawaii Press, 1998)

Myung, Sunghoon, *Spiritual Dimension of Church Growth as Applied in Yoido Full Gospel Church* (PhD thesis, Fuller Theological Seminary, 1990)

Neighbour, Ralph W. Jr., *Where Do We Go from Here? A Guidebook for the Cell Group Church* (Houston, TX: Touch Publications, 1990)

Nelson, Douglas J. *For Such a Time as This: The Story of William J. Seymour and the Azusa Street Revival* (PhD thesis, University of Birmingham, UK, 1981)

O'Connor, Edward, *The Pentecostal Movement in the Catholic Church* (Notre Dame, IN: Ave Maria Press, 1971)

Ojo, Matthews A. *The End-Time Army: Charismatic Movements in Modern Nigeria* (Trenton, NJ: Africa World Press, 2006)

Onyinah, Opoku, "The Man James McKeown," in Opoku Onyinah (ed.), *The Church of Pentecost: 50 Years of Sustainable Growth* (Accra: Church of Pentecost, 2004): 56–104

——— (ed.), *The Church of Pentecost: 50 Years of Sustainable Growth* (Accra: Church of Pentecost, 2004)

Oosthuizen, Gerhardus C. *The Birth of Christian Zionism in South Africa* (KwaDlangezwa, South Africa: University of Zululand, 1987)

Orr, J. Edwin, *Evangelical Awakenings in Southern Asia* (Minneapolis, MN: Bethany Fellowship, 1970)

Otabil, Mensa, *Beyond the Rivers of Ethiopia: A Biblical Revelation on God's Purpose for the Black Race* (Accra: Altar International, 1992)

Peel, J. D. Y. *Aladura: A Religious Movement among the Yoruba* (Oxford: Oxford University Press, 1968)

Peires, J. B. *The Dead Will Arise: Nongqawuse and the Great Xhosa Cattle-Killing Movement of 1856–7* (Johannesburg: Ravan Press, 1989)

Perriman, Andrew (ed.), *Faith, Health and Prosperity: A Report on "Word of Faith" and "Positive Confession" Theologies* (Carlisle, UK: Paternoster, 2003)

Pobee, John S. & Gabriel Ositelu II, *African Initiatives in Christianity: The Growth, Gifts and Diversities of Indigenous African Churches—A Challenge to the Ecumenical Movement* (Geneva: World Council of Churches, 1998)

Pullikottil, Paulson, "Ramankutty Paul: A Dalit Contribution to Pentecostalism," in Allan H. Anderson & Edmond Tang (eds.), *Asian and Pentecostal: The Charismatic Face of Christianity in Asia* (Oxford: Regnum, 2011): 208–18.

Ranaghan, Kevin & Dorothy Ranaghan, *Catholic Pentecostals* (New York: Paulist Press, 1969)

Reed, David A. *"In Jesus' Name": The History and Beliefs of Oneness Pentecostalism* (Blandford Forum, UK: Deo Publishing, 2008)

———, "Missionary Resources for an Independent Church—Case Study of the True Jesus Church," Paper presented at the 40th Annual Meeting of the Society for Pentecostal Studies, March 2011

Robeck, Cecil M. Jr. *The Azusa Street Mission and Revival: The Birth of the Global Pentecostal Movement* (Nashville, Tennessee: Nelson, 2006)

Robert, Dana, *Occupy Until I Come: A. T. Pierson and the Evangelization of the World* (Grand Rapids, MI: Eerdmans, 2003)

Saayman, Willem A. "Some Reflections on the Development of the Pentecostal Mission Model in South Africa," *Missionalia* 21:1 (April 1993), 40–56

Sanneh, Lamin, *Whose Religion Is Christianity: The Gospel beyond the West* (Grand Rapids, MI: Eerdmans, 2003)

———, *Disciples of All Nations: Pillars of World Christianity* (New York: Oxford University Press, 2008)

Scotland, Nigel, *Charismatics and the New Millennium* (London: Hodder & Stoughton, 1995)

Sengupta, Padmini, *Pandita Ramabai Saraswati: Her Life and Work* (London: Asia Publishing House, 1970)

Sepúlveda, Juan, "The Challenge for Theological Education from a Pentecostal Standpoint," *Ministerial Formation* 87 (October 1999), 29–30

Shenk, Wilbert, "Rufus Anderson and Henry Venn: A Special Relationship?" *International Bulletin of Missionary Research,* 5:4 (October 1981), 161–72.

Sherrill, John L. *They Speak with Other Tongues* (New York: McGraw-Hill, 1964)

Shubert, William E. "I Remember John Sung," in Timothy Tow (ed.), *The Asian Awakening* (Singapore: Christian Life Publishers, 1988): 137–83

Somaratna, G.P.V. *Origins of the Pentecostal Mission in Sri Lanka* (Mirihana-Nugegoda: Margaya Fellowship of Sri Lanka, 1996)

Spear, Thomas & Isaria N. Kimambo (eds.), *East African Expressions of Christianity* (Oxford: James Currey, 1999)

Stanley, Brian, *The Bible and the Flag: Protestant Missions and British Imperialism in the Nineteenth and Twentieth Centuries* (Leicester, UK: Apollos, 1990)

———, "Twentieth Century World Christianity: A Perspective from the History of Missions," in Donald M. Lewis (ed.), *Christianity Reborn: The Global Expansion of Evangelicalism in the Twentieth Century* (Grand Rapids, MI: Eerdmans, 2004): 52–83

———, *The World Missionary Conference, Edinburgh 1910* (Grand Rapids, MI: Eerdmans, 2009)

Strachan, C. Gordon, *The Pentecostal Theology of Edward Irving* (London: Darton, Longman & Todd, 1973)

Sun, Benjamin, "Assemblies of God Theological Education in Asia Pacific: A Reflection," *Asian Journal of Pentecostal Studies* 3:2 (July 2000), 230

Sundkler, B. G. M. *Zulu Zion and Some Swazi Zionists* (London: Oxford University Press, 1976)

Sung, John, *The Diaries of John Sung,* Stephen L. Sheng (trans.) (Brighton, MI: Stephen L. Sheng, 1995)

Sung, S. H. "History of Pentecostal Mission, Hong Kong & Kowloon," in S.H. Sung (ed.), *Pentecostal Mission, Hong Kong & Kowloon 75 Anniversary 1907–1982* (Hong Kong: Pentecostal Mission, 1982): 8–10

Sutton, Matthew Avery, *Aimee Semple McPherson and the Resurrection of Christian America* (Cambridge, MA: Harvard, 2007)

Synan, Vinson, *The Holiness-Pentecostal Tradition: Charismatic Movements in the Twentieth Century* (Grand Rapids, MI: Eerdmans, 1997)

———, *The Century of the Holy Spirit: 100 Years of Pentecostal and Charismatic Renewal* (Nashville, TN: Thomas Nelson, 2001)

Tan, Jin Huat, "Pentecostals and Charismatics in Malaysia and Singapore," in Allan H. Anderson & Edmond Tang (eds.), *Asian and Pentecostal: The Charismatic Face of Christianity in Asia* (Oxford: Regnum, 2011): 238–58

Taylor, Geraldine, *Pastor Hsi: A Struggle for Chinese Christianity* (Singapore: Overseas Missionary Fellowship, 1900, 1949, 1997)

Teraudkalns, Valdis, "Pentecostalism in the Baltics: Historical Retrospection," *Journal of the European Pentecostal Theological Association* 21 (2001), 91–108

Ter Haar, Gerrie, "Standing Up for Jesus: A Survey of New Developments in Christianity in Ghana," *Exchange* 23:3 (1994), 225–36

Thollander, Jon, *He Saw a Man Named Mathews* (Udaipur: Cross & Crown, 2000)

Thompson, Steve & Adam Gordon, *A 20th Century Apostle: The Life of Alfred Garr* (Wilkesboro, NC: MorningStar Publications, 2003)

Tow, Timothy (ed.), *The Asian Awakening* (Singapore: Christian Life, 1988)

Tsang, Ying Fuk, "From a Film Star to a Prophetess: The Legend of Mui Yee," *Christian and Missionary Alliance Monthly* 44 (August 2003); 45 (September 2003), www.cmacuhk.org.hk/version3/mag/mag_monews_45/mag_monews_shadow_45a.htm, original in Chinese, accessed 17 April 2010

Turner, Harold W. *History of an African Independent Church (1) The Church of the Lord (Aladura)* (Oxford: Clarendon Press, 1967)

———, *Religious Innovation in Africa* (Boston, MA: G. K. Hall, 1979)

Ukah, Asonzeh, *A New Paradigm of Pentecostal Power: A Study of the Redeemed Christian Church of God in Nigeria* (Trenton, NJ: Africa World Press, 2008)

Van der Laan, Cornelis, "The Proceedings of the Leaders' Meetings (1908–1911) and of the International Pentecostal Council (1912–1914)," *Pneuma* 10:1 (1988), 36–49

Villanueva, Eddie, "A Consuming Passion," in Cityland Foundation, *This Is My Story: 31 Lives, Stories, Miracles* (Manila: OMF Literature, 2004): 224–33

Wacker, Grant, "Are the Golden Oldies Still Worth Playing? Reflections on History Writing among Early Pentecostals," *Pneuma* 8:2 (1986), 81–100

———, *Heaven Below: Early Pentecostals and American Culture* (Cambridge, MA: Harvard University Press, 2001)

Wagner, C. Peter & Joseph Thompson (eds.), *Out of Africa* (Ventura, CA: Regal, 2004)

Währisch-Oblau, Claudia, "God Can Make Us Healthy Through and Through: On Prayers for the Sick and Healing Experiences in Christian Churches in China and African Immigrant Congregations in Germany," *International Review of Mission* 90:356/357 (2001), 87–102

Walls, Andrew F. "Of Ivory Towers and Ashrams: Some Reflections on theological Scholarship in Africa," *Journal of African Christian Thought* 3:1 (June 2000), 1–3.

Warrington, Keith (ed.), *Pentecostal Perspectives* (Carlisle, UK: Paternoster, 1998)

Weaver, C. Douglas, *The Healer-Prophet: William Marrion Branham, a Study of the Prophetic in American Pentecostalism* (Macon, GA: Mercer University Press, 2000)

Welbourn, F. B. & B. A. Ogot, *A Place to Feel at Home* (London: Oxford University Press, 1966)

West, Martin, *Bishops and Prophets in a Black City* (Cape Town: David Philip, 1975)

Wiegele, Katharine L. *Investing in Miracles: El Shaddai and the Transformation of Popular Catholicism in the Philippines* (Honolulu, HI: University of Hawaii Press, 2005)

Wilkerson, David, *The Cross and the Switchblade* (New York: Random House, 1963)

Wilson, Everett A. *Strategy of the Spirit: J. Philip Hogan and the Growth of the Assemblies of God Worldwide 1960–1990* (Carlisle, UK: Paternoster, 1997)

Wolffe, John, *The Expansion of Evangelicalism: The Age of Wilberforce, More, Chalmers and Finney* (Downer's Grove, IL: InterVarsity Press, 2007)

Womersley, David & David Garrard (eds.), *Into Africa: The Thrilling Story of William Burton and Central African Missions* (Nottingham, UK: New Life Publishing, 2005)

Woods, Daniel, "Failure and Success in the Ministry of T. J. McIntosh, the First Pentecostal Missionary to China," *Cyberjournal for Pentecostal Charismatic Research* 12, April 2003, www.pctii.org/cyberj/cyberj12/woods.html

World Council of Churches, *"You Are the Light of the World": Statements on Mission by the World Council of Churches 1980–2005* (Geneva: World Council of Churches Publications, 2005)

Wuthnow, Robert, *Boundless Faith: The Global Outreach of American Churches* (Berkeley: University of California Press, 2010)

Xi, Lian, *Redeemed by Fire: The Rise of Popular Christianity in Modern China* (New Haven, CT: Yale University Press, 2010)

Yoido Full Gospel Church, *Yoido Full Gospel Church* (Seoul: Yoido Full Gospel Church, 1993)

———, *50th Anniversary of Yoido Full Gospel Church* (Seoul: Yoido Full Gospel Church, 2008)

Yong, Amos, *The Spirit Poured Out on All Flesh: Pentecostalism and the Possibility of Global Theology* (Grand Rapids, MI: Baker Academic, 2005)

Yrigoyen, Charles Jr. *The Global Impact of the Wesleyan Traditions and Their Related Movements* (Lanham, MD: Scarecrow, 2000)

Yun, Koo Dong, "Pentecostalism from Below: Minjung Liberation and Asian Pentecostal Theology," in Veli-Matti Kärkkäinen (ed.), *The Spirit in the World: Emerging Pentecostal Theologies in Global Contexts* (Grand Rapids, MI: Eerdmans, 2009): 89–114

Index